CHICAGO'S
BEST RESTAURANTS

SHERMAN KAPLAN

Bonus Books, Inc., Chicago

05   04   03   02   01   5   4   3   2   1

ISBN: 1-56625-156-7

Library of Congress Control Number: 00-108941

Bonus Books, Inc.
160 East Illinois Street
Chicago, IL 60611

Printed in the United States of America

CONTENTS

INTRODUCTION TO THE NINTH EDITION

CHICAGO'S BEST RESTAURANTS

The first edition of *Chicago's Best Restaurants*, under the title *Best Restaurants Chicago*, was published in 1977. Looking back through its pages, I am struck by the fact that less than a dozen restaurants included then are still with us in this latest collection of reviews.

Restaurants have changed over the years, and I suppose my opinions and tastes have similarly evolved. In the course of that evolution, I have tried to utilize my K/RATING as a more or less useful guide to better dining, and a quick way to convey my understanding of a restaurant and its mission.

The K/RATING is a 20-point scale. The best restaurants are 20/20. Nothing in this book has a KR less than 15/20. I have made some changes over the years to the numerical assignments of each aspect of criticism, with food receiving the highest emphasis, followed by service, decor and value. This edition expands a bit more on the concept of decor, by assigning the category Ambiance/Decor. In making my evaluation, I am concerned not only with how a restaurant looks, or how it is decorated, but with the impression and tone its atmosphere and decoration can create for a diner. So, I have taken such intrusions as noise in the dining room, or the separation of smoking and nonsmoking sections into my calculations. Ambiance/Decor is meant to suggest a much broader range of inquiry than has the singular designation Decor in previous reviews.

Value continues to speak for itself and, fortunately, I think an overwhelming number of restaurants deliver good value for dollars spent. In that regard, restaurants are designated with one to three dollar signs as an indication of cost:

$ = under $20 a person
$$ = $20–$40   a person
$$$ = $40–???   a person

Tax, drinks and tip are added to these figures. As for tipping, the best advice I can offer is to be generous when service is exceptional, and less so when service is lacking. But, be fair before deciding that service is not what you would want it to be. And, when critical of service, or any other aspect of a restaurant's operation, call it to the attention of the management. I am confident that the restaurants you find here will respond positively to any problems that might arise. Incidentally, before being too critical, try to understand the problem from the perspective of server or management. It is not the server's fault if a dish is poorly prepared, and it may not be his or her fault that service is slow. Sometimes, a kitchen simply cannot keep up with the demand on a given evening, such as one in which the restaurant is packed, and the kitchen is short an employee. Tips, by the way, should begin at 15% for most restaurants, and 20% or more for fine dining restaurants.

All things change, especially the popularity of restaurants. I make no claim that this, or previous editions of this book include every single great restaurant in and around Chicago. But, *Chicago's Best Restaurants* continues to be the only Chicago restaurant guide that represents the opinions of one consistent viewpoint. There are no surveys, no opinions other than mine, for which I take full responsibility and blame or credit. Speaking of credit, I wish to thank the management of WBBM NEWS-RADIO 780 and *North Shore Magazine* for graciously allowing me to include reviews that first appeared on broadcasts or in print. Should you ever wish to make a suggestion or comment about these restaurants, or one of your favorites that is not included, you may email me at shermank@enteract.com

Dining is a social, not a solitary experience, even if restaurant criticism is a singular endeavor. There are people who have been with me over the years, friends who have been part of my dining experience. It is time to credit their good cheer and patience. Thanks to Maria Battaglia, Paula and Vince Comerci, Peter and Kate McGovern, Randy Newman and Bob Parr, Joe and Dotty Zoller, Peter and Sharon Eisendrath, Jody and Alan Jacobs, Marge and Bob Howard, Marsha and Steven Price, Lee and Kathy Greenberg, Steve and Bette Feinerman, Henry and Lucille Krasnow, Richard and Deanne Mincer, the late Edward Robert Brooks, Jerry Buster and Ned Hammel. I thank my daughter Shawna and her husband Barry Sabransky, and my son Joshua, for bringing pleasure to our table. And, as from the very beginning, I dedicate this book to my wife, Eileen, who shares not just my meals, but my life.

Sherman Kaplan
2000

ADOBO GRILL
KR 19/20
Decor 4/4   Hospitality 5/5   Food   9/10   Value 1/1

- **Mexican**
- **Chicago/Near North**
- **$$**

1610 North Wells Street
Chicago
(312) 266-7999
Troubleshooter: George Ortiz
(manager)

Hours: Mon–Thurs 5:30–10:30 pm, Fri–Sat 5:30–11:30 pm, Sun 11 am–9:30 pm
Credit Cards: All majors
Reservations: Recommended
Handicapped: Accessible, but there are a couple of steps at entrance, tight for wheelchairs
Smoking and nonsmoking sections: Smoking tables
Parking: Valet $7

The red flock walls and bawdy house look of Chicago's venerable That Steak Joint are gone, replaced by the new and chic Mexican-influenced Adobo Grill. The idea being conveyed is that Mexican cookery is much, much more than what is found in neighborhood storefronts, much more than tacos, enchiladas and burritos. Adobo Grill carries it out rather well with a complex, though not too lengthy menu. There are some unique attractions such as *guacamole* that is made at tableside. The whole avocado is set in a lava rock pestle, mashed into a paste and seasoned. If anything, this version is a bit spicier than other versions routinely served in Mexican restaurants.

There's lots more to chew on than *guacamole* and taco chips. Among other appetizers, or *antojitos*, as they are called, is a delicious codfish and plantain stuffed pastry, or *empanada*. This is the Mexican version of the egg roll or pierogi, in this case given a palate of seasonings and ingredients including chopped green olives, capers and *epazote*, an herb with a pungent taste akin to coriander.

Other selections include classic tortilla soup with a swirl of sour cream to enrich the broth, roasted jalapeño peppers stuffed with creamy chihuahua cheese and grilled baby octopus with roasted pumpkin seeds and salsa. This is another clear winner from a kitchen that seems to have a restrained hand on seasonings and flavor balances.

The Adobo Grill menu lists traditional platters, which include *chiles rellenos*, grilled flank steak and stewed chicken in typical Mexican village recipes. Lamb can be particularly delicious with a side of pinto beans and salsa. Another version brings a whole rack with a red molé and roasted sweet potatoes flavored with poblano peppers. As for seafood, whole red snapper is served in a blanket of chopped tomatoes, olives and capers in the classic Veracruzana style. Trout comes fresh from the steamer wrapped in a corn husk with an array of side vegetables including rice, squash, chopped carrots and the fresh guacamole.

Grilled breast of duck is another regular menu attraction, plated along with a duck leg Mexican-style confit. Other poultry includes roasted chicken breast with molé, rice and black beans flavored with epazote. Cornish hen rests in an almond-based molé plated with fried plantains as part of its presentation.

Desserts include a roundup of Mexican specialties, often with the restaurant's own stamp.

AKAI HANA
KR 17.5/20
Decor 4/4   Hospitality   4/5   Food 8.5/1   Value 1/1

- **Japanese**
- **Wilmette**
- **$$**

3217 West Lake Avenue
Wilmette
(847) 251-0384
Troubleshooter: Noboru Nakamura (manager)

Hours: Lunch Mon–Sun 11:30 am–2 pm, Dinner Mon–Thurs 5–9:45 pm, Fri–Sat until 9:45 pm, Sun 4:30–8:45 pm
Credit Cards: All majors except Transmedia
Reservations: Taken for 6 or more
Handicapped: Accessible
Smoking and nonsmoking sections: 100% nonsmoking
Parking: In lot

For health conscious and calorie conscious diners, Japanese restaurants offer some wonderful opportunities. The cuisine is naturally lean and offers a wide choice of seafood, albeit some raw, and portion sizes which satisfy, without over-filling.

These thoughts come to mind about Akahi Hana: The restaurant is brightly lit, an anomaly in a world of noisy, often dark and overcrowded dining spots. Blond wood moldings and rice paper ceiling lanterns help frame the atmosphere. Diners may sit at the sushi bar and watch what is being prepared, or at conventional tables, where it is easier for larger groups to gather for conversation.

Sushi and Sashimi are offered in à la carte or combination portions. A combination platter brings tuna, octopus, and other choices for finger nibbling. Appetizers will be familiar to those who enjoy Japanese dining. *Gomae,* cold spinach in a sesame sauce is typically sweet, a characteristic which carries over into many dishes of the region. Tempura shrimp and vegetables are lightly battered, with no discernible trace of oiliness. Fried or steamed dumplings filled with meat are tantalizing little morsels, the Japanese version of ravioli or pierogis. There are some grilled teriyaki choices in appetizer or entree size as well as several more deep-fried seafoods such as oysters.

To the Japanese, the preparation and consumption of *soba*, or buckwheat noodles is an art form. At Akai Hana, soba noodles are served on a distinctive platter with a light dipping sauce and a small mound of green wasabi mustard. Negotiating soba with chopsticks is a lot more difficult than twirling spaghetti on a fork, but the effort is worth the while.

From among entrees, sukiyaki is comfort food of the best kind during cold weather. Teriyaki beef or chicken is somewhat too sweet for my taste, but that is a property of their preparation. Broiled tuna is dotted with sesame seeds; its flavor is only mildly sweet. The most interesting may be a combination platter, handsomely displayed in a lacquer enamel box that holds a few rolls of California maki, teriyaki chicken, marinated cucumber with thin slivers of crabmeat and a couple pieces of sushi.

AMBRIA
KR 19.5/20
Decor 4/4   Hospitality 5/5   Food 9.5/10   Value 1/1

- **French**
- **Chicago/Mid-North**
- **$$$**

2300 North Lincoln Park West
Chicago
(773) 472-5959
Troubleshooter: Gabino Sotelino (owner/managing partner)

Hours: Mon–Thurs 6:30–9:30 pm, Fri–Sat 6–10:30 pm
Credit Cards: All majors
Reservations: Required
Handicapped: Accessible
Smoking and nonsmoking sections: Smoking in bar only, no smoking in dining room
Parking: Valet $6
Dress: Jacket and tie required for gentlemen

At a time when many new restaurants look like circuses or worse, it's refreshing to return to a real restaurant like Ambria. Dark wood walls and mirrors, café lamps on white robed tables, tuxedoed servers and low lighting help make this one of the city's more romantic dining destinations.

Among first course selections, risotto with a topping of braised rabbit in a clear au jus is magnificent. The flavors are almost peppery in their exuberance, a dish that practically calls out to be richly consumed. Similarly, a trio of seared scallops rests on a solid platform of formed gnocchi with chanterelles and a sweet vanilla sauce. Here, too, the dining is exceptional. The same can be said for snails, fricassees with mushrooms and small flageolets beans that add more texture than flavor. But, the essence of the snails is the true measure of quality here. Even a composed salad of greens, sprouts and asparagus is special, with a rare white balsamic vinaigrette dressing.

The best test of a fine restaurant kitchen is in the treatment of soups. Clear game consommé brings a golden glow to the table and a deceptively deep flavor. A fine chop of herbs sits at the bottom of the bowl, while small dumplings float on the surface. In a word, this, too, is excellence.

Among entrees, snapper is crusted with crushed pumpkin seed. It gives a nutty texture and taste. Pureed acorn squash and a creamy lobster sauce complete the plating. In another selection, roasted squab sits in a dark truffle sauce atop a trio of grains, quinoa, barley and cracked wheat. Here, too, there is a contrast of flavors and texture that works beautifully. Yet another game platter, sautéed breast of mallard, is sliced thin and fanned across its plate. Twin mounds of red onion confit are at either side. Slices of poached pear offer their fruited goodness, while the entire creation rests in a verdant sauce of green pepper corns. Other selections include grilled sirloin in a Rioja wine sauce with vegetables and soufflé potatoes while another choice offers roasted rack of lamb with couscous and a rosemary sauce to compliment the meat.

Desserts are presented from an elegant three tiered pastry cart, baroque in their conception and execution. A selection of soufflés can be ordered earlier to allow for baking time.

ANDIES
KR 15/20

Decor 2.5/4   Hospitality 4/5   Food 7.5/10   Value 1/1

- **Lebanese**
- **Chicago Far North**
- **$**

5235 North Clark Street
Chicago
(773) 784-8616
Troubleshooter: Andy
Famarous (owner)
Other Location
1467 West Montrose, Chicago;
(773) 348-0654; Party Facilities:
Private party facilities plus
catering

Hours: Sun–Thurs 10 am–
midnight, Fri–Sat until 1 am
Credit Cards: Diners, Discover,
MC, Visa
Parking: On street or nearby lot
Handicapped: Accessible
Bar: Service bar with wine and
beer
**Smoking and nonsmoking
sections:** Both available
Party Facilities: None available

In what is still called Andersonville, and where the Swedish Cultural Museum is located, strollers find not just a sense of Scandinavia, but more than a little touch of the Middle East. As population patterns change, so do businesses. Thus, diners will find Andies. Though it looks like any other small storefront Middle Eastern restaurant, there is a different approach to the foods served here.

For one thing, the seasonings are pronounced, and in many cases, quite imaginative. For example, spinach and barley soup is that and more. The broth is touched with mint, which adds the kind of freshness one would not associate with such an otherwise heavy broth. Even lentil soup gets a little kick from a complexity of cinnamon and peppers, perhaps even vinegar reminiscent of a seasoning with Tabasco sauce.

There is more to the menu than soups. Order a combination platter and get a generous taste of a quartet of appetizers. *Humus*, the traditional Middle Eastern spread of ground chickpeas, lemon and olive oil is somewhat sharper in taste than others. However, the *baba ganoush*, that puree of smoked and roasted eggplant is milder than one might expect. The dark smokey flavor is absent, and the eggplant, instead of being pureed, is cut into a pulpy chop. *Falafel*, available in appetizer- or dinner-sized portions, seems to have been seasoned with fresh herbs, which add their own unusual contribution to the otherwise mild flavors of these deep-fried chickpea balls.

Easily one of the best selections, also available in appetizer or dinner portions is *dolma*, stuffed grape leaves. Many versions are filled with lightly seasoned rice or ground meat. Dolma is given a more exotic cast with a taste that suggests aromatic flavors such as those from cardamom and cinnamon.

The menu is sprinkled with more substantial offerings such as chicken, lamb or beef shishkebab, all in very generous portions. The shishkebab comes bedded on dilled rice pilaf. Other entrees include several Greek dishes, such as delicious, though somewhat oily, spinach pie, as well as a dozen or so other vegetarian entrees.

Andies is that very rare restaurant which offers a cuisine readily available in and around Chicago, but with a different sort of spin that makes it a bit audacious.

ANGELINA
KR 16.5/20
Decor 3/4   Hospitality 5/5   Food 7.5/10   Value 1/1

- **Italian**
- **Chicago/North**
- **$$**

3561 North Broadway
Chicago
(773) 935-5933
Troubleshooters: Cal Fortis
(owner) Zachary Pass (manager)
David Rosenthal (chef)

Hours: Sun–Thurs 5:30–10:30 pm, Fri–Sat 11:30 pm
Credit Cards: All majors
Reservations: Suggested, especially Fri and Sat nights
Handicapped: Accessible
Smoking and nonsmoking sections: Both available
Parking: Valet Fri–Sat, other evenings street parking is tight

Angelina may be showing its age, but it is easy to understand why it has been a popular Italian restaurant in its mid-North neighborhood over the past 12 years. The restaurant is meant to look old with its earth tone walls and antiqued rococo chandeliers.

The menu is rather small, but portions are large. Though not indicated on the menu, pastas can be ordered in half servings, which is not only economical, but allows diners to taste more than one dish if that is to their liking.

Beginning with the *antipasti*, tender rounds of calamari are bathed in a red sauce that leaves just a bit of pepper bite. It's the kind of sauce that tastes so good when soaked up in a piece of bread. Other antipasti include asparagus salad with shaved Parmesan and an unusual whip of goat cheese with roasted peppers and thin crusts of garlic buttered Italian bread.

À la carte salads can follow, or you can move right on to a pasta. There are a dozen, including one or two daily specials not on the printed menu. They are as simple as your choice of noodle with a light fresh tomato sauce to an elaborate linguine with *prosciutto*, spinach, garlic and oregano with fresh tomatoes. Spicy *arrabiatta* sauce with rigatoni or your choice of pasta has the proper light pepper bite. A special of the evening married mushrooms and white wine in a sauce that tasted as if it might have had some sweet Marsala splashed in.

As for entrees, the house version of Chicken Vesuvio deviates from standard issue around Chicago by substituting house mashed potatoes with ricotta cheese and garlic for the usual side of roasted potato wedges. We could taste neither the ricotta nor the garlic. The large split chicken was deliciously juicy, perfumed with rosemary and oregano. The house named *Pollo Angelina* was smothered in sliced button mushrooms in a rosemary and wine sauce with a side of fresh broccoli.

Other entrees include a daily fish selection, veal, Italian-style meatloaf and roasted sausage in a sauce that brings together balsamic vinegar, pine nuts and raisins. Desserts include some traditional Italian selections. Service is informal, and correctly so for this type of restaurant. There is valet parking on Friday and Saturday nights; other nights can be a hassle.

ANN SATHER
KR 20/20
Decor 4/4   Hospitality 5/5   Food 10/10   Value 1/1

- **Swedish American**
- **Chicago/Mid-North**
- **$**

929 West Belmont, Chicago
(773) 348-2378
Troubleshooter: Tom Tunney (owner)

Other Locations
5207 North Clark Street, Chicago; (773) 271-6677; Hours: Daily 7 am–10 pm; Private party facilities for 20–100
2665 North Clark Street, Chicago; (773) 327-9522; Hours: Daily 7 am–5 pm
1329 East 57th Street; (773) 947-9323; Hours: Daily 7 am–10 pm

Hours: Daily 7 am–11 pm
Credit Cards: Amex, Diners, MC, Visa
Reservations: Taken except for Sat and Sun mornings
Handicapped: Accessible
Bar: Full service
Parking: Private lot, street parking is tight
Dress: Casual
Party Facilities: Private party facilities for 20–220

You would be hard pressed to find a more homey kind of restaurant than Ann Sather. The original restaurant remains at its famous Belmont

Street location, while three newer locations offer virtually the same thing in service and value.

No matter what time of day or night, every meal begins with a bowl of cinnamon buns and a variety of breads brought to each table. The cinnamon rolls alone might be reason enough to come here.

Breakfast is served all day, highlighted by Swedish pancakes. Sausages and egg dishes, including a variety of three-egg omelettes are always featured.

Getting into the dinner menu, choices run the gamut from salads and sandwiches, to full course meals. One good introduction to the Swedish-style cooking is to order the Swedish Sampler. The platter includes delicious roasted duck with a traditional lingonberry glaze, Swedish meatballs in gravy, potato sausage (which blends veal, pork and potatoes), dumplings, sauerkraut and brown baked beans.

Other selections regularly include pan-fried pork chops or chicken livers, veal steak and old fashioned chicken croquettes served with candied sweet potatoes and creamed peas. Seafood choices are equally ample and include of fried perch, catfish, or broiled trout. All dinners include two side vegetables, soup or juice and dessert.

ARUN'S
KR 19.5/20

Decor 4/4   Hospitality 5/5   Food 10/10   Value .5/1

• **Thai**	**Hours:** Tues–Sat 5–10 pm, Sun 5–9 pm
• **Chicago/Far North**	**Credit Cards:** All majors
• **$$$**	**Reservations:** Required
4156 North Kedzie Avenue	**Smoking and nonsmoking sections:** No smoking
Chicago	**Parking:** Ample street space available
(773) 539-1909	**Dress:** Casual neat, but jackets and ties are not out of place
Troubleshooter: Arun Sampanthavivat (chef/owner)	

It is not often that diners have the opportunity to enjoy dinner in an art museum. But, that is precisely what an evening at Arun's is like. The walls are hung with works of Thai culture, each graphic illustrating a story.

In this sort of setting, it is obligatory that the dining match in taste, what the eye sees. Chef/owner Arun Sampanthavivat is a self-trained culinary artist. He knows his obligation well, and practices it virtually without fault.

For diners more accustomed to Thai restaurants in small storefronts, where dinner for two might cost little more than $20, Arun's presents a case of sticker shock. In other words (and this holds true for any great cuisine or work of art), value is measured by the sensibility involved in its preparation, not the cost of its ingredients.

With that said, pampering of guests is a primary goal at Arun's. Service is accomplished by a team of people, any of whom might bring a course, or clear one away. A tasting dinner brings at least five different appetizers and three main course selections, plus dessert and tea or coffee. Any dietary restrictions are accommodated, as are other special requests.

A first course gave us a preview of the plating artistry to be displayed throughout dinner. At the center of its platter stood a small basket, intricately carved from a large carrot, even to the extent of engravings in geometric pattern around its base. Inside, small bits of turnip or radish had been carved into tiny flowers. Meanwhile, a collection of finger foods was arranged around this beautiful centerpiece. One was a flower shaped edible basket, golden colored and filled with sweet corn, bits of shitake mushrooms, chicken and shrimp. Next to it was a smooth rice dumpling, its ever so glassy texture contrasted with a filling of ground crab meat and shrimp with jicama. A complex sweet and sour vinaigrette was set in a small bowl at the side of the plate, with a tiny spoon to dollop the liquid onto the dumpling for a bit of extra flavor. Another glossy noodle served as wrapping, much like a spring roll for carefully placed bits of vegetable arranged as much for eye appeal as for taste.

A second platter might be laden with steamed crabmeat plus shrimp, shitakes and chicken filling a noodle wrapping. The platter is painted with red stripes of sweet sauce and little kisses of hot mustard. Among other first course choices is a mild pancake, endowed with shitakes and scallions, with soy and sesame seed vinaigrette on the side or spicy chicken and roasted cashew nuts bound together with shallots, fresh pungent ginger, lime juice and hot chili peppers.

Chef Arun prepares his version of *pad Thai* with similar ingredients as at other Thai restaurants, but he keeps seasonings in check, perhaps to emphasize texture. By contrast, a Thai curry can bring some peppery spice to the table. Thai curries are distinctively colored to identify intensity of seasonings. Green curry is the hottest, red somewhat less so. Just as certain ingredients such as garlic, olive oil and onions, are standard in French and Italian cookery, one can be sure that basil, coriander, a fish sauce called *nam pla* and lime will be standard ingredients in much of what comes from Thai kitchens. Some curries will be thickened by coconut milk, some not. In all cases, however, flavors will be complexities of sweet, hot and sour.

To bring things to their proper conclusion any of several custards will bring smiles and satisfaction. Among them are sweet coconut custard, another smoother one with mung beans, a third called tri-colored custard for its layers of white, pink and green set atop a cube of rice, and finally *babin*, or what Arun calls "crazy" custard, though it tastes sane enough.

ASPEN GRILLE
KR 19/20
Decor 4/4   Hospitality 5/5   Food 9/10   Value 1/1

- **American**
- **Lincolnwood**
- **$$**

250 Marriott Drive (across from the Marriott Resort complex)
Lincolnshire
(847) 634-0700
Troubleshooter: Manager on duty

Hours: Sun–Thurs 11 am–9 pm, Fri 11 am–10 pm, Sat 11 am–11 pm
Credit Cards: All majors
Reservations: Suggested
Handicapped: Accessible
Smoking and nonsmoking sections: The dining room is non-smoking, smoking is allowed in the lounge where seating is available
Parking: Free in large lot

Aspen Grille's menu showcases some tremendously imaginative variations on the basic concept of putting flame to steaks, chops, fish and poultry. Under the menu category listed as "Grille" there is Aspen Country which the menu describes as "Roasted chicken, chicken sausage and shrimp in a white wine garlic sauce with roasted peppers, redskin potatoes and fresh string beans." As good as that sounds, it tastes even better. For one thing the sauce is deep flavored and abiding in the way it lingers on the palate. Each of the components remains separate in taste, yet somehow manages to contribute a certain flair or essence to everything else.

Among other Grille choices are three more chicken variations, including a skillet roasted version with proscuitto, spinach, goat cheese and red wine sauce. A trio offers portions of grilled skirtsteak, lamb chops and garlic roasted chicken with wild mushroom red sauce, while among other choices, ten ounces of sirloin comes stuffed with roasted Anaheim pepper, a collection of cheeses and vegetables. Then, all of this is wrapped in bacon and grilled. That one may be pushing the envelope!

But, for all the simplicity of a chargrilled filet mignon, the outcome is hardly prosaic. I think the deep plumy red wine sauce, almost reduced to a syrup gets the credit, though the rare meat is tender and flavorful on its own. Among seafood selections, choices run the gamut from trout with rock shrimp and vegetables in brown butter sauce to grilled salmon in mustard dill sauce to something as direct as "peel your own" shrimp that have already been peeled for you to make it just that much easier to gobble down those little morsels.

There are a dozen or so appetizers; on the list of pizzas from their wood-fired oven, Ruthy's Run, with its collection of vegetables and a smoky flavored mozzarella is great with a pint of beer; one pizza is enough to share among a party of four. Salads are dinner size; a dozen or so sandwiches are a handful, while pasta selections are similarly over-portioned. Threads of angel hair noodles in a tomato sauce with mushrooms, asparagus and chive is delicious enough, but slices of grilled salmon are added to the bounty. As for desserts, let your own taste be the guide.

ATHENA
KR 19/20
Decor 4/4   Hospitality 5/5   Food 9/10   Value 1/1

- **Greek**
- **Chicago/Near West**
- **$$**

212 South Halsted Street
Chicago
(312) 655-0000
Troubleshooters: George
Tsouklas, Nick Tsouklas (owners)

Hours: Sun–Thurs 11 am–midnight, Fri–Sat 11–1 am
Credit Cards: Amex, Visa, MC, Diners
Reservations: Recommended
Handicapped: Accessible
Smoking and nonsmoking sections: Both available
Parking: Complimentary valet

In warm weather months, restaurants with outdoor patios or rooftops in Greektown are ideal for dining, drinking, and enjoying the view of Chicago's glorious skyline. Athena has a patio to enjoy the view; while indoors the restaurant assumes the nearly ubiquitous Greektown personality of a *taberna* with its whitewashed walls, light colored wood trim and accents to pick up the blue and white national colors of Greece.

One of the things that struck me about Athena the first time I visited, was the excellence of the foods. Then, I learned that its chef has worked right next door at Roditys, (q.v.) which happens to be just about my favorite Greektown restaurant. So, with that connection, the good food and great service are a natural.

Athena offers all of the traditional favorites of Greek dining. But, along with the *saganaki, dolmades,* sausage meatballs and all the rest are a few surprises. One of them is delicious roasted red peppers stuffed with feta cheese. The platter is garnished with a sprig of fresh dill, the balance of flavors is wonderfully fresh.

Like other restaurants along the Greektown strip, fresh fish is always a menu highlight, while combinations platters allow diners to taste many of the traditional entrees at a virtual bargain price. I did find *pastitsio*, baked macaroni casserole with meat a bit dry around the edges. But, there were no such problems with some companion selections including the lasagna-like *moussaka*, mild tasting leg of lamb and the delicately seasoned stuffed grape leaves called *dolmades*.

Among other winning entree selections *shrimp Athena* is a bounty of large prawns in a savory tomato sauce with a topping of feta cheese. If you love garlic, try the companion shrimp *skordati* with intensely flavored garlic sauce. Pan-fried salt cod also comes with that garlic sauce, while mild Norwegian salmon is simply broiled and served with a light lemon sauce.

A collection of kebabs, pork, beef, chicken, shrimp and swordfish brings two large skewers bedded on rice and ringed by fresh vegetables and roasted potatoes. An order of lamb chops, five to the serving, look so good they practically demand you pick them up to get every last morsel from the bone.

Desserts include all the traditional super sweets.

ATLANTIQUE
KR 19/20
Decor 3.5/4   Hospitality 4.5/5   Food 10/10   Value 1/1

• **French Seafood** • **Chicago North** • **$$** 5151 North Clark Street Chicago (773) 275-9191 **Troubleshooter:** Jack Jones (chef/owner)	**Hours:** Mon–Thurs 5:30–10:30 pm, Fri–Sat 5:30–11 pm, Sun 5–9:30 pm **Credit Cards:** Amex, MC, Visa, Diners **Reservations:** Suggested **Handicapped:** Accessible **Smoking and nonsmoking sections:** Both available **Parking:** Valet $6 Thurs–Sat, spaces behind the building for Mon–Wed

People who know Daniel J's and Jack's (q.v.) will love Atlantique. It is the newest of Chef Jack Jones's restaurant enterprises. At Atlantique, Jones gets to be flashier than he does at his two other eateries. For instance, he has paired *foie gras* on brioche with a mango and carrot emulsion that can be ordered alone, or with a suggested sauternes. Among other first course choices is tuna tartare, in a mounded upright cylinder with crisp crackers on the side. Small rounds of vidalia onion slaw with a bit of dressing complete the plating. In another presentation, two crab cakes are stacked Napoleon-style between thin crispy potato chips. Tarragon hollandaise is a flavor accent, though the crab cakes have their own spiced seasonings.

Diners can choose from a trio of second course à la carte salads. One brings chunks of Yukon Gold potatoes with slivers of braised fennel and vidalia onions. But, the real star here are the twin lobster claws, delicious, sweet and succulent.

Entrees continue to demonstrate Chef Jones's adept talents. Scallops have been seared in one recipe, still hot and juicy inside. They are plated with a lobster- and mushroom-infused polenta, which is itself coupled with a basil lobster sauce that seems to have been derived from a light fish stock. In another entree clean white halibut is baked and then served in a casserole with a variety of seasonal vegetables, some littleneck clams tucked in their shells and a simple seafood au jus.

The menu is studded with other tempting standouts ranging from tuna with strands of seaweed, oriental rice and a ginger, wasabi mustard and lemongrass sauce, to traditional bouillabaisse whose perfume can be sensed throughout the dining room. For diners who would prefer something other than seafood, loin of roasted venison is being set out with a duckling confit, all the while bedecked with mushroom and shallot ragout and port wine cherry sauce. Beef tenderloin is treated to truffle oil–infused mashed potatoes along with a stylized bordelaise sauce which draws upon caramelized mangos in a cognac demi glace. If that's not enough of a choice, there is also roasted breast of squab plated with foie gras, peaches and sherry sauce glaze.

Desserts include such temptations as banana bread pudding, chocolate ganache and other goodies.

ATWOOD CAFÉ
KR 18/20
Decor 4/4   Hospitality 5/5   Food 8/10   Value 1/1

- **American**
- **Chicago Loop**
- **$$**

1 West Washington (at State)
Chicago
(312) 368-1900
Troubleshooter: Manager on duty

Hours: Breakfast Mon–Fri 7–10 am, Sat 8–10:30 am, Brunch Sun 8 am–3 pm, Lunch Mon–Sat 11:30 am–3 pm, Dinner daily 5:30–10 pm, Tea Service daily 3–5 pm, bar menu nightly 3–10 pm
Credit Cards: All majors
Reservations: Suggested
Handicapped: Accessible
Smoking and nonsmoking sections: No smoking except at bar
Parking: Valet

The Atwood Café is an absolutely beautiful creation with soaring ceilings, magnificent art deco accents and huge picture windows which give diners a view of everything going on outside. The restaurant was built in the newly restored Reliance Building, off the lobby of the Hotel Burnham.

With all those trimmings, one might expect the dining to be overwhelmed. It isn't. Things are fine on the culinary side, though a menu with perhaps a few more selections would be welcome. As it is, Chef Heather Terhune is doing a fine job with a basic American eclectic selection. Among them is a house specialty, the pot pie with a different filling each evening; be careful, it might be sold out.

Among first course starters roasted duck is pulled into shreds and stuffed into half-moon–shaped quesadillas with Mexican white cheese, while a tangy salsa and sour cream are the garnish. Baked goat cheese is served with sun-dried tomatoes and *crostini* toast, while smoked salmon is stacked in slices atop corn and scallion cakes which the menu calls waffles, along with a creamy mascarpone cheese.

Several salads are listed as separate courses, some such as sesame crusted Ahi Tuna, are adequate as a pre-theater dinner entree, perhaps along with a bowl of soup. That tuna, by the way, is sweet and fresh, set in an Oriental array with mixed greens, shredded wonton noodles and wasabi horseradish.

Among entrees, grilled salmon comes atop a charred tomato sauce. Potato salad with shredded fennel adds a welcome accompaniment to the plate. For meat-eaters, a large pork chop is glazed with maple syrup and plated with mashed potatoes and a *ragout* of shredded cabbage and apple slices in perfect concert with the chop. Roasted chicken is plated with garlic-infused mashed potatoes in an Atwood Café version of comfort food. And, there are a couple of pastas. Fettucine is combined with cayenne seasoned shrimp, basil, garlic and a tomato concasse, while *orchiette*, tiny ear-shaped pasta, is set out with sharp flavored rapini, smoked sausage for some depth and white beans with roasted tomatoes for the sauce.

Service seems well attuned to those who have a time consideration, though diners who wish to linger are not hurried on their way.

AUBRIOT
KR 19/20

Decor 4/4   Hospitality 5/5   Food 9/10   Value 1/1

- **French**
- **Chicago/North**
- **$$$**

1962 North Halsted
Chicago
(773) 281-4211

Hours: Tues–Thurs 5:30–9:30 pm, Fri–Sat 5:30–10 pm, Sun 5:30–9 pm, closed Mon
Credit Cards: All majors
Reservations: Recommended
Handicapped: Accessible
Smoking and nonsmoking sections: No smoking
Parking: Valet $6

When Chef Eric Aubriot left the stoves of Carlos's in Highland Park to open his own restaurant in Chicago he brought more than just another French restaurant to the neighborhood. The young chef is working not so much to reinvent French cuisine as he is to present his interpretations in forthright, and sometimes imaginative ways. Diners who remember his work from Carlos's will see some familiar choices on the menu. His risotto appetizer, studded with plump green peas, slices of celery root and a bit of fresh rosemary is tasty as ever, accented with a parmesan cheese *tuile* which pokes up from the mound of steaming risotto.

Dining begins with a small complimentary *amusé*, recently a wedge of rare tuna sitting atop small potato cubes. The platter was dotted with a basil emulsion, more for color than taste. In addition to the risotto appetizer, other selections include a pair of sautéed shrimp plated with a course chop of tomato and a very lightly scented lemon vinaigrette. For something complex there is a *fricassee*, a nicer way to say "stew," of frog legs and veal kidneys in a cream sauce. On the other hand, a portobello mushroom terrine brings slices of the mushroom and its vegetable bindings; the flavor is ephemeral, there for a moment before fading.

Entrees reflect the chef's dedication to contemporary French cookery. But, there are some surprises. For instance, loin of lamb suggests medallions, or slices. Instead, the lamb is ground into a course forcemeat and bound together with seasonings in a patty suggestive of something North African, or more specifically, Moroccan. Other selections play out on more traditional French themes. Slices of duck breast are fanned out with a medley of baby vegetables in a sauce whose flavor is derived from a mushroom and veal stock reduction. The kitchen attempts nothing drastic or cutting edge with its grilled beef tenderloin, plated with a reduction of red wine and meat juices and sides of mashed potatoes and caramelized onions.

Fish might include monkfish with the complexities of bacon and a cardamom veal stock with carrots, potatoes and fried leeks. For simpler dining, fettucine has been plated with flavorful mushrooms and tomatoes in a light parmesan broth.

Dessert choices are abundant, though if you want a hot soufflé or warm chocolate cake with a liquid center in the manner of an Italian *budino*, they should be ordered early in the evening to allow for preparation time. Wines are a little on the pricey side. Service is excellent. The restaurant is handsomely decorated with vintage 19th Century French posters and warm lighting to show off the wood trim that makes Aubriot look like something more than just another bistro.

THE BABALUCI
KR 16.5/20
Decor 3/4   Hospitality 5/5   Food 7.5/10   Value 1/1

- **Italian**
- **Chicago/Near Northwest**
- **$$**

2152 North Damen Avenue
Chicago
(773) 486-5300
Troubleshooter: Frank Amanti

Hours: Sun 4–10 pm, Mon–Thurs 11 am–11 pm, Fri 11 am–midnight, Sat 4 pm–midnight
Credit Cards: Amex, Diners, MC, Visa
Reservations: Taken weekends only for parties of 8 or more
Handicapped: Accessible
Bar: Full service
Smoking and nonsmoking sections: Both available
Parking: Valet or street, plus lot across the street
Party Facilities: Private party space for 40–60 people on 2nd floor with piano

You won't find snails on the menu at The Babaluci, which may seem somewhat odd since the restaurant's name means "snails" in a Sicilian dialect. Owner Frank Amanti confides that his yuppie customers want no part of them.

But, they evidently are satisfied with something about The Babaluci, which if not packed, is usually bustling and noisy. This is a friendly sort of a place, with no visual clues other than its menu to suggest it is an Italian restaurant. The decor is neo-contemporary storefront, a bit of modern op-art ceiling decoration, and otherwise more or less the atmosphere of a coffee house.

But, the cooking is Italian, though not necessarily old style spaghetti, meatballs and red sauce. You could order it that way, but why not try something a little different? Tri colored rotini with a quartet of romano, pecorino, gorgonzola and parmesan cheeses is delightfully rich. Baked mostaciolli, served à la carte or as a side dish with some of the meat or fish entrees, is as close as the restaurant gets to a straight ahead marinara sauce.

Though traditional grilled Italian sausage served with polenta may be among the evening specials on the blackboard listings, other entrees can be somewhat more adventurous. Consider thin and wispy angel hair pasta with delicious grilled calamari, and a spiced marinara. Among other selections is pasta putanesca, the so-called "harlot's sauce," dubbed that because it was said to be quick and easy fixings for ladies of the night. Putanesca brings together olives, capers, anchovies, and the unusual addition of eggplant in The Babaluci version. Among other selections veal and chicken come together in picatta style laced with pine nuts and capers as tradition demands.

From among appetizers, the thin crusted pizza can be ordered with a variety of toppings; forget California style-affectations. A huge stuffed artichoke awash with a breadcrumb filling makes for tasty snacking while diners await other courses. What makes The Babaluci interesting is how the kitchen manages to balance the traditional or expected style of mainstream Italian cookery with the more unusual, without going so far as to be cutting edge.

Desserts include a couple of chocolate concoctions, cheesecake and other *dolci*. The restaurant's version of *tiramisu* is served more like pudding than cake. Service is as friendly as one might expect from a restaurant whose management knows that its bread and butter is the customer's satisfaction with theirs.

BANDO
KR 16/20
Decor 3/4   Hospitality 4/5   Food 7/10   Value 2/2

- **Korean**
- **Chicago/Far North**
- **$$**

2200 West Lawrence Avenue
Chicago
(773) 728-7400
Troubleshooter: Manager on duty

Hours: Daily 11 am–10:30 pm
Credit Cards: Amex, MC, Visa
Handicapped: Accessible
Bar: Full service, good selection of Oriental beers
Reservations: Taken
Parking: Street parking is usually ample

Bando is unlike any Korean restaurant I have ever visited. It certainly looks like no other Korean restaurant in Chicago. The decor includes an indoor waterfall and crystal chandeliers. Like some other Korean restaurants, diners are seated at large tables, each of which has a central gas fired grill for those dinners that require some tableside presentation.

The restaurant seems well supported by Chicago's Korean-American population, always a good sign for authenticity. For an appetizer, you should not miss what the menu describes simply as "pan-fried mixed vegetables." Actually, this is a plate dwarfing pancake about the size of a 12 inch pizza. Various cooked vegetables are arranged attractively somewhat like spokes around a center hub. The batter is studded with pieces of clam, which lends a slight, but not unpleasant, fishy undertaste. This can be easily disguised with a little sesame soy and ginger sauce, liberally studded with garlic and pepper.

Among other appetizer choices, pan-fried dumplings, known in most Oriental restaurants as pot stickers, are tasty little morsels akin to fried ravioli. Other appetizers run the gamut from sashimi to fried fish and oysters and a couple of different styles of tempura.

Some kind of substantial soup should always be ordered in traditional Korean dining. Yellow corvina, a Pacific fish cut up into chunks, is served in a hot pepper fish stock with nuggets of other seafood, including a large oyster. This dish is a good example of the traditional approach which might not appeal to American tastes.

Elsewhere on the menu, the Bando version of *dak bokuhm*, which the restaurant calls *dak-yah-chae-bolkum*, is widely different from the fried chicken pieces in a spicy sweet hot glaze as served in other Korean restaurants. This seemed more like steamed chicken and vegetables in a clear sauce that was without much flavor or character. Even *Bee-bim-bop*, a casserole of rice, assorted vegetables and a fried egg all tossed together is somehow different, largely because of what I suspect is a sweet bean-based sauce used to bind the ingredients together.

An attempt is made at friendly service, though language can be a barrier.

BANK LANE BISTRO
KR 18/20
Decor 4/4   Hospitality 5/5   Food 8/10   Value 1/1

- **Eclectic Bistro**
- **Lake Forest**
- **$$$**

670 Bank Lane
Lake Forest
(847) 234-8802
Troubleshooter: Todd Neely
(general manager)

Hours: Lunch Tues–Fri 11:30 am–2 pm, Dinner Tues–Thurs 5:30–9 pm, Fri–Sat 5:30–10 pm, closed Sun and Mon
Credit Cards: All majors
Reservations: Suggested
Handicapped: Accessible via elevator
Smoking and nonsmoking sections: No smoking
Parking: On street and Market Square

There's something about a restaurant on the second floor of a building that reminds me of England. Think of the image, a raw and stormy night, a horseman gallops up to an inn, dismounts, climbs a flight of stairs and warms himself by the fire as he gulps a mug of ale and contemplates a haunch of beef. At Bank Lane Bistro, it's more likely people drive up in a Lexus or a BMW than on horseback, but the imagery remains similar.

Chef de Cuisine Marijke Neely has created a menu which changes from time to time, while keeping some core elements. Onion soup is the traditional baked-in-the-crock variety, this one not as sweet as others, but still with a good bite.

Speaking of onions, they are at the heart of a wonderful caramelized onion tart appetizer. It is set on mesclun, the tart's crust brown and flaky. The heart of the tart is its creamy texture and sweet onion taste. Incidentally, the portion is large enough so that a party of four or six can each enjoy a taste and move on to other appetizers.

Among them is classic Country Paté set out with sharp pommery mustard, tiny cornichons and toast. Escargots also get the classic treatment in browned butter with garlic and lemon.

Salads are à la carte. The house bistro salad is wrapped in thinly sliced cucumber sheets. It makes for not just a handsome, but a completely edible presentation.

The rest of the menu is, by and large, good solid bistro fare including steak and fries, *coq au vin* and similarly popular comestibles. The *coq au vin* comes to the table looking and smelling like a good, hearty chicken stew. There are tiny pearl onions, cut up carrots and other vegetables, pieces of smoked bacon and of course, potatoes and a cut-up roasted chicken.

Whitefish is less complicated than the *coq au vin*, a simple broil

BANK LANE BISTRO

Marijke Neely

Marijke Neely, Chef de Cuisine
Marco Hernandez, Sous Chef

Soups

Onion Soup Gratin	5.25
Soup Du Jour	3.75/5.00

Salads

Spinach Salad *with Warm Bacon and Egg Vinaigrette*	5.25
Bistro Salad *with Champagne Vinaigrette*	4.95

Appetizers

Neapolitan Pizza *Proscuitto, Mushrooms, Artichoke Hearts & Olive Pesto*	8.95
Garlic Chicken Pizza *with Scallions & Sesame*	9.75
Pizza Margherite *with Roma Tomatoes & Basil*	8.95
Provençal Pizza *Arugula, Tomatoes, Olives & Lemon*	8.95
Seared Duck Breast Salad *with Goat Cheese, Walnuts &* *Raspberry Vinaigrette*	13.95
Baked Brie *with Orange Glaze and Granny Smith Apples*	9.95
Country Pâté *with Cornichons, Pommery Mustard & Toast Points*	9.50
Escargots *with Garlic, Lemon and Brown Butter*	9.75
Steamed Prince Edward Island Mussels *with White Wine and Butter*	9.95

Entrees

Pan Roasted Chilean Sea Bass *with Ratatouille & Redskin Potatoes*	19.95
Pork Tenderloin *with Pommery Potatoes & Haricots Verts*	19.50
Salad Niçoise *with Seared Tuna, Haricots Verts and* *New Potatoes*	13.50
Broiled Lake Superior Whitefish *with Lemon Remoulade*	17.95
Pasta du Jour *Sautéed with Chicken, Tomatoes, Fresh Mozzarella & Basil*	15.95
Chicken Breast *en Papiotte* *with Julienne Vegetables, White Wine & Fresh Herbs*	16.50
Steak Frites *with Maitre d'Hotel Butter*	20.50
Wood Oven Roasted Rack of Lamb *with Mashed Potatoes, Mustard & Balsamic Glazes*	27.50
Filet Mignon *with Vermont Cheddar &Chive Mashed Potatoes*	26.75
Oven Roasted Coq au Vin	16.50

670 Bank Lane Lake Forest (847) 234 - 8802
A Gratuity of 18% will be added to the bill for tables of six or more

served with a course of cooked vegetables; the sauce is lemon remoulade, with its creamy mayonnaise base. Among other recent entree
selections, pork tenderloin is set with pommery mustard flavored potatoes and delicate French green beans.

A pasta de jour is simple and direct. For instance, penne could be
sautéed with nothing more complicated than pieces of roasted chicken,
some tomatoes, basil and a generous grating of mozzarella cheese. Like
so much else on the Bank Lane Bistro menu, this sort of preparation
proves that good eating need not be complicated.

To be sure, there are some ambitious entrees. Rack of lamb comes
hot from the wood-fired oven, roasted to a sheen, set on a bed of
mashed potatoes glazed with mustard and balsamic vinegar. These are so
good, you will want to pick up each bone and glean off all the meat you
can. Another version of lamb brings the shank with a portion of root vegetables, not quite a stew, but one of those rich and hearty meals that is
so very satisfying on a wintry night.

Desserts can be as simple as mixed berries, to a more elaborate fruit
tarte or *crème brûlée* with a sharper caramelized burnt sugar crust.

BARBA YIANNI
KR 18/20

Decor 4/4   Hospitality 5/5   Food 8/10   Value 1/1

- **Greek**
- **Chicago/Far North**
- **$$**

4761 North Lincoln Avenue
Chicago
(773) 878-6400
Troubleshooter: Ziad Ihmoud
(owner)

Hours: Daily 11 am–midnight
Credit Cards: All Majors
Reservations: Recommended
Handicapped: Accessible
**Smoking and nonsmoking
sections:** Both available
Parking: On street, can be tight

There's really nothing left of the North Greektown neighborhood at the
intersections of Lawrence, Western and Lincoln. It's changed, in the way
neighborhoods have of evolving. But, there is at least one Greek restau-
rant nearby, on that little strip known as Lincoln Square. The restaurant
is Barba Yianni, as charming and as inviting as any of the Greek restau-
rants that were once so prevalent.

The look is that of a courtyard taberna. The menu is large, typical of
Greek restaurants as we have come to know them in Chicago. Cooking is
well up to par, and then some. If all you know of Greek food is *gyros,* you
will find that ubiquitous street snack, but also a wide selection of other tastes.

Try an appetizer platter, hot or cold for an instant sample. The cold plate brings generous portions of roasted eggplant puree, the fish roe spread called *taramasalata*, its garlic cousin, *skordelia*, as well as a tart yogurt flavored with fresh dill and chopped cucumbers called *tzatziki*. Ask for an order of that, and you're already talking like a Greek.

Among hot appetizers a selection of meatballs, fried or broiled squid, grilled quail and sautéed sweetbreads are among several choices. They can be ordered individually, or as part of a combo platter for two or four people. Add a Greek salad topped with cubes of feta cheese, tomato wedges and thick slices of cucumber for a delicious palate-refreshing taste before you order an entree.

There are literally several dozen selections, including chef's specials that rotate daily. Fish include salmon, seabass and red snapper, and if it is not fresh, it certainly will not be served. Lamb is a major part of the Greek diet. Order this delicious meat in any of several fashions ranging from simple chops, broiled and plated with roasted potatoes or rice. Roasted and grilled chicken and a wide variety of shishkebabs and *souvlaki*, or grilled pork round out the major meat choices.

From among other selections, half a dozen good sized shrimp are grilled, and given a final sauté with a mild tomato sauce and melted feta cheese, then bedded on plumped rice. It's a delicious approach to shrimp. Barba Yianni offers several pasta choices, or *makaronada*; if that word suggests macaroni, you have the idea. But, Greek macaroni dishes are distinctly different from Italian, with softer flavors. A house specialty brings strips of sautéed chicken breast on macaroni in a sauce with a light tomato flavor touched by garlic, basil and oregano.

Desserts include all the usual Hellenic sweets. Wines are by the glass, carafe or bottle. Service is informative and friendly.

BARRINGTON COUNTRY BISTRO
KR 18.5/20
Decor 4/4   Hospitality 5/5   Food 8.5/10   Value 1/1

- **Country French**
- **Barrington**
- **$$**

700 West Northwest Highway
Barrington
(847) 842-1300
Troubleshooters: Jean-Pierre
and Denise LeRoux (owners)

Hours: Lunch Mon–Fri 11:30 am–2 pm, Sat until 2:30 pm, Dinner Sun–Thurs 5–8:30 pm, Fri–Sat 5–9:30 pm
Credit Cards: Amex, MC, Visa
Reservations: Suggested
Handicapped: Accessible
Smoking and nonsmoking sections: Smoking in bar only
Parking: Ample free parking in lot

Barrington Country Bistro is not actually in the country, but it is in Barrington and it is a bistro. You have to go inside the restaurant to get that country feel, thanks to its furnishings, café curtains and lamps and the handsome wall murals which evoke a sense of golden flecked fields ripe with burnished stalks of grain.

There are some established assumptions about bistro menus which Barrington Country Bistro follows. So, the French onion soup comes baked-in-the-crock, with an abundant layer of melted cheese oozing its savory richness over a fat crouton of French bread that has soaked up as much liquid as it can absorb. The soup flavor is more wine-like or even nutty than sweet.

Among other standards of this good bistro kitchen, is a traditional take on baked snails with garlic and butter sauce, though there is a bit of a lemon butter embellishment. *Mussels marinière* suggest Mediterranean coastal inspirations, while a typical order of steak and fries is right out of a Parisian bistro kitchen.

Among other traditional entrees, *coq au vin* is one of the tastiest approaches to chicken stew that exists. A sturdy red wine is the finishing touch, perhaps along with some Cognac, plus an array of carrots, onions, mushrooms and other fresh vegetables, plus potatoes and salt pork lardons.

The hearty French country cooking continues with several other temptations. Cornish game hen is set in a sauce informed by lemons and oregano with herbed barley as the accompaniment. A ¾ pound roasted pork chop is just that, with its natural *au jus*. Braised lamb shanks in rosemary *au jus* come with delicate white beans, while osso bucco is a succulent choice, a bit of a stretch from the French countryside, but why quibble.

In fact, there are a couple of Italian pasta choices including broad ribbons of fettucine with chunks of chicken, tomatoes, slices of sweet roasted peppers, and porcini mushrooms in a reduced sauce of mushroom juices and fresh rosemary. Seafood gets some attention with linguine, shrimp and other soft or shellfish in a tomato herb sauce. Fresh fish usually includes tilapia in a tomato and caper butter sauce or salmon given an Asian influence thanks to its ginger and soy sauce and stir fried vegetable accompaniment.

Service is very helpful, the wine list appropriate and surroundings conducive to dinner for two, or a larger gathering. When so many bistros are almost cloned, this one offers some welcome variation on the theme.

BEN PAO
KR 19.5/20
Decor 4/4   Hospitality 5/5   Food 9.5/10   Value 1/1

- **Chinese**
- **Chicago/Near North**
- **$$**

52 West Illinois Street
Chicago
(312) 222-1888
Troubleshooters: John Buchanan (managing partner), Ed Culleney (general manager)

Hours: Lunch Mon–Fri 11:30 am–2 pm, Dinner Mon–Thurs 5–10 pm, Fri–Sat 5–11 pm, Sun 5–9 pm
Credit Cards: All majors
Reservations: Accepted
Handicapped: Accessible
Bar: Full bar, somewhat pricey wine list
Smoking and nonsmoking sections: Both available
Parking: Valet for lunch and dinner

There are times when the Chinese restaurant in your neighborhood just will not do. You want something a bit dressier, more elaborate, something with more finesse. How about if you could have all of that, at prices comparable to the neighborhood?

You'll find it at Ben Pao. The entryway is flanked by two grand shimmering columns of cascading water. The bar is over to one side, and behind is the spacious dining room, its decor clean, neat, without embellishment.

As for the menu, you won't find egg rolls, but you will discover delicious steamed dumplings, or pot stickers, which are steamed and then seared to give the wrappings a slightly firmer texture. Fillings are delicious; the mushroom stuffing is almost sensuous, though even chicken or vegetable fillings are hard to beat. Other appetizers include delicious chopped chicken in lettuce. The idea is to take a chilled lettuce cup, fill it with a small mound of lightly spiced chicken, add a sauce if you like, then wrap it all together into a hand held pouch. Other starters include pulled pork with puffy steamed dumplings, chicken satay, ribs with Chinese five spice and wonderfully aromatic hot and sour soup with a complexity of flavors and ingredients.

When a designation indicates "spicy," take the menu at its word; there are no seasoning punches pulled here. One of the very nicest entrees tasted recently was steamed walleye pike. This meaty, clean flavored fish came in a mild sauce of mushrooms, bamboo shoots and a lightly seasoned broth. Fish can also be had in an alternative spicy style.

The fish could be balanced with an order of fiery Szechuan noodles, which are just as peppery as described. This dish, or any of the other noodle selections, also works well as an appetizer to be shared. There are plenty of vegetarian choices. One of the best is Hong Kong Spicy Eggplant, which is spicy, and immensely palatable. From among poultry selections, Tony's Amazing Chicken is honestly described. A peppery broth adds bite, while steamed spinach brings a differing taste and texture to the preparation. Balance is respected at Ben Pao, as it should be in Chinese dining.

BERGHOFF
KR 16/20
Decor 4/4   Hospitality 3.5/5   Food 7.5/10   Value 1/1

- **German**
- **Chicago Loop**
- **$$**

17 West Adams
Chicago
(312) 427-3170
Troubleshooter: Herman
Berghoff (owner)

Hours: Mon–Thurs 11 am–9:30 pm, Fri–Sat until 10 pm, closed Sun and holidays
Credit Cards: Amex, MC, Visa
Reservations: Taken for 5 or more at lunch, 2 to 4 at dinner
Handicapped: Accessible
Bar: Full service, features house label Berghoff Beer, plus five or six more on tap and in bottles, call liquors, small wine list, some by the glass

Berghoff is a Chicago landmark restaurant, frequented by lawyers, judges, shoppers, tourists, and just plain hungry people. It is not a place to linger. There is a sociable bustle about the place. Waiters are from the old school of service: black trousers, white shirts and aprons are the attire. Their service is efficient without familiarity, perhaps until you become a regular.

Though daily specials are changed, there is a core of lunches and dinners which remain constant. These are the German specialties, *sauerbraten*, German pot roast, *kassler ribchen* and the like. All are rib sticking kinds of foods.

But, newer items including grilled shrimp and other grilled seafood, even a stir-fry of chicken and vegetables, make an appearance as an obeisance, perhaps to modern dining times and tastes. But, if that's what it takes to stay in business since 1898, they must be doing it right.

BETISE
KR 18/20
Decor 4/4   Hospitality 5/5   Food 8/10   Value 1/1

- **French**
- **Wilmette**
- **$$**

1515 Sheridan Road (Plaza del Lago Shopping Center) Wilmette
(847) 853-1711
Troubleshooter: Manager on duty

Hours: Lunch Mon–Sat 11:30 am–2 pm, Brunch Sun 11 am–2 pm, Dinner Sun–Thurs 5:30–9 pm, Fri–Sat until 10 pm
Credit Cards: All majors
Reservations: Suggested on weekend
Handicapped: Accessible
Smoking and nonsmoking sections: Smoking in designated seating area (no cigars or pipes)
Parking: Ample in Plaza de Lago lot

Time moves on, but over the years, it has not brought a lot of change to Betise. The restaurant retains its comfortable, pristine setting and the whimsy that its name French name insinuates. The cobbled a brick floor, window and all treatments coupled with the overall conviviality set as welcoming scene as ever.

This is unquestionably a regional French menu with most of the bells and whistles, yet one that respect contemporary dining sensibilities. Consider a first course selection of grilled calamari, given a sense of fusion with its plating around a central mound of Japanese soba noodles and a vinaigrette sauce with the clean taste of lemon. It's a fresh approach to the now commonly found calamari, whose flavor remains touched by grilling as its basic underpinning.

Among other appetizers, eggplant stuffed with a coarse chop of summer vegetables and goat cheese is a particularly refreshing plate, set in a pool of warm tomato *coulis.* Or, consider grilled scallops, in this case the centerpiece over wilted raddichio, snips of fresh basil and a sprinkling of capers, which seem to have been washed of most of their brine.

Sweetbreads are not seen as often as they used to be in these cholesterol conscious times, but they show up on the menu as a first course choice along with the chef's take on potato salad and arugula-infused olive oil. Somewhat more simple in approach are mussels in a basic white wine and garlic liquid fresh from the steamer. Or, among other basics, classic French onion soup comes with a hearty layer of melted gruyere and crouton baked in the crock. The broth is more wine like than sweet, perhaps a touch too intense.

Entrees carry out the French country theme of the restaurant with choices ranging from simple roasted chicken or steak and fries to grilled lamb and salmon. The salmon has been plated recently with fennel and artichoke shavings in a white wine–based sauce, but nothing too intense to interfere with the identifiable taste of the fish. Nightly specials have added brook trout in an almond crust to the seafood agenda. That special list might also bring a variation of venison served as a rack rather than as a chop or medallions, as is more often the case. For those less inclined to meat or seafood, skewered grilled vegetables are plated over couscous with a tomato *coulis* adding some more flavor. Other entree selections include chicken breast stuffed with and accompanied by ratatouille.

Those with a sweet tooth will find satisfaction from the dessert card which includes a wonderful apple *galette* and a deliciously, almost bittersweet caramel sauce, with a scoop of vanilla ice cream as an added enhancement. A somewhat more modest selection of angel food cake with mango sorbet and fresh berries provides another approach to satisfaction.

BICE
KR 18.5/20
Decor 4/4   Hospitality 5/5   Food 8.5/10   Value 1/1

- **Italian**
- **Chicago/Near North and Suburbs**
- **$$$**

158 East Ontario Street
Chicago
(312) 664-1474
Troubleshooter: Graziano Ferrari (general manager)
Other Location
2124 Northbrook Court, Northbrook; 847-272-9003; Hours: Lunch 11:30 am–2:30 pm, Dinner Mon–Thurs 5–10 pm, Fri–Sat 5–10:30 pm, Brunch Sun 11:30 am–2:30 pm; Credit Cards: All majors; Smoking and nonsmoking sections: Smoking only at bar or patio; Handicapped: Accessible; Parking: In lot; Troubleshooter: Graziano Ferrari (general manager)

Hours: Summer (May–September) Lunch Daily 11:30 am–4:30 pm, Dinner 4:30 pm–midnight, Winter (October–April) Lunch Daily 11:30 am–4 pm, Dinner 4:30 pm–10:30 pm (During March Bice opens for Sunday dinner at 5 pm)
Credit Cards: All majors
Smoking and nonsmoking sections: Both available in dining rooms, cigars permitted at bar
Parking: Valet
Handicapped: Not accessible

Bice is probably as close as we can come in Chicago to dinner in Milan. When it first opened Bice was much the trend setter. While other restaurants feature *carpaccio, risotto* or *panna cotta*, Bice does this and more in a manner which suggests something other than being in Chicago, a few steps from Michigan Avenue.

Bice is style and substance with the look of clean, crisp architecture and servers in white dinner jackets, their accents identifiably Italian. Beginning with antipasti choices can be simple, such as slices of mozzarella cheese on bright red tomatoes with basil. Or, they can be more elaborate in the way a thin slice of eggplant is rolled around a filling of goat cheese, a fine mince of spinach and the bite of sun-dried tomatoes, grilled to allow these flavors to marry.

In addition to classic beef *carpaccio* with shavings of parmesan cheese, Bice presents tastings of tuna or salmon *carpaccio*. The latter has a more intense flavor and is plated with croutons infused with mascarpone cheese. The tuna is meatier with a clean, fresh flavor.

Moving on to a pasta brings almost two dozen choices from the extensive menu. Risotto is prepared fresh, the plump grains of arborio rice so chewy they leave a gummy residue on the teeth. Among other selections, ravioli might be stuffed with a fine grind of veal or duck, perhaps plated on an intensely flavored mushroom sauce, glazed with truffle oil. The fresh, kitchen-made quality of the pastas is evident in an order of *tagliolini.* These are thin ribbons much like linguine, given a surprisingly perfunctory red sauce and a good selection of shell- and soft-fish in the manner of a *frutti de mare.*

Complex as the various flavors can be, they are never so forceful as to be assertive. There is a fine balance at work, a sense of refinement. Consider *osso bucco* among recent specials. The meat had an intense, but not too powerful flavor, well matched to a fine topping of *gremolada,* a classic mince of lemon peel, parsley and garlic. A trio of pureed potatoes garnished the platter, the best of the three enhanced with pesto for a fresh basil flavoring.

From a lengthy selection of desserts, the Bice version of *crème brûlee* is hard to top, while the eggless sweet custard called *panna cotta* is almost ephemeral.

BIG BOWL
KR 18.5/20
Decor 4/4   Hospitality 5/5   Food 8.5/10   Value 1/1

- **Asian Eclectic**
- **Chicago and Suburbs**
- **$**

159½ West Erie Street
Chicago
(312) 787-8297
Troubleshooter: Kevin Brown
(managing partner)
Other Locations
6 East Cedar Street, Chicago;
312-640-8888
60 East Ohio Street, Chicago;
312-951-1888
215 Parkway Drive, Lincolnshire;
847-808-8880
1950 East Higgins Road,
Schaumburg; 847-517-8881

Hours: Mon–Thurs 11:30
am–10 pm, Fri–Sat 11:30 am–
11 pm, Sun 5–9 pm
Credit Cards: All majors
Reservations: Not accepted
**Smoking and nonsmoking
sections:** No smoking in dining
area
Parking: Valet available

Big Bowl takes dining on a Pan-Asian whirl. Portions are generous, so an order of pot stickers and a bowl of soup should satisfy most anyone's appetite. Diners can order à la carte or choose from a list of combinations. For example, the Golden Combo offers generous portions of a crunchy Shanghai spring roll, potstickers filled with ground chicken and a pile of crisp fried and stuffed wonton noodles. Though this is in the budget dining category, the quality of food and ingredients suggests first class. The pot stickers, for example, have definite flavors to differentiate them depending on their fillings. Creativity and imagination marks virtually all facets of the menu. Vietnamese noodle soup, *pho*, is as tasty as any you might find in Chicago's Argyle/Broadway Vietnamese neighborhood. *Pad Thai* mimics that at traditional Thai restaurants, while Eight Vegetable Stir-Fry is akin to what vistors find in Chinatown. The restaurant has a semi-self-serve bar where diners may pick ingredients for a stir-fry, including meats and seafoods, plus vegetables and sauces, then have it cooked to order.

BIN 36
KR 17/20
Decor 3/4   Hospitality 4/5   Food 9/10   Value 1/1

- **American**
- **Chicago/Near North**
- **$$**

339 North Dearborn
Chicago
(312) 755-9463
Troubleshooter: David
Schneider (managing
partner/general manager)

Hours: Coffee Bar 7 am–5 pm,
Lunch Daily 11:30 am–2 pm,
Dinner Daily 5–11 pm
Credit Cards: Amex, Diners
Discover, MC, Visa
Reservations: Taken in main
dining room
Handicapped: Accessible
**Smoking and nonsmoking
sections:** Smoking in Tavern
section only
Parking: Valet

You need not know about or even care about wine to enjoy dining at Bin 36, a wine emporium and restaurant just across from House of Blues.

You get an instant education and suggestions from servers who will go through the routine of wines served in flights, by the glass or, of course, by bottle. Even if you don't care about wine, the dining, in most cases, is good enough to stand on its own.

Bin 36 serves an eclectic American bistro menu. Each course is listed with recommended wines, though you may pick whatever you like, or nothing at all. Begin with smoked salmon for an appetizer, which the menu correctly suggests can be accompanied by a Champagne. The salmon is set cone-shaped around a center of perhaps a little too much *crème fraiche* and a crisp fried potato cake for texture balance.

Other first course selections include steamed mussels with cilantro among its seasonings, lusciously decadent foie gras with cinnamon cranberry chutney, or luscious scallops, thicker than a hockey puck with a skillet-seared crust, tiny green peas and pearl onions.

À la carte soups and salads follow. The house Caesar salad has a buttermilk ranch dressing, not really tart at all and the same olive bread that shows up in the bread basket makes for some fine dried croutons in the salad.

The list of entrees ranges from strict vegan cannelloni with a red pepper sauce to grilled lamb, steaks, veal and pork. Amish chicken gets rotisserie treatment, slathered with seasonings that make this more than an ordinary roasted chicken. Whipped potatoes are bedded underneath, while parsnip spears are part of the garnish.

As for seafood, grouper has recently been served with light truffle infused gnocchi while grilled tuna has been among selections served on an Evening's Chef's Selection menu. Anything on the degustation, by the way, can be ordered à la carte, though be warned that the portion will be only tasting-size.

Servers take considerable time to explain all the wine and dining options and to make suggestions. However, there were some mistakes made on timing and correct delivery. And the support serving staff needs to be a little more attentive to detail.

The main dining room is large and open. There is also a smaller section, bar and a wine and gift shop.

BISTRO 110
KR 19/20
Decor 4/4   Hospitality 5/5   Food 9/10   Value 1/1

- **French**
- **Chicago**
- **$$**

110 East Pearson
Chicago
(312) 266-3110
Troubleshooter: Matt Weber
(general manager)

Hours: Mon–Thurs 11:30 am–11 pm, Fri–Sat until midnight, Sun until 10 pm
Credit Cards: All majors
Reservations: Suggested
Handicapped: Accessible
Bar: Full service, extensive list of French and American wines, many by the glass
Smoking and nonsmoking sections: Both available
Parking: Valet after 5 pm

There's no mistaking that Bistro 110 is 110% French. You can't miss the giant red neon Eiffel Tower, tilted to one side like a jaunty Frenchman's beret. This is the same Bistro 110 that puts a whole head of roasted garlic on your table along with the bread and butter. It's a signature, like the Eiffel Tower out front, as much a part of the restaurant as its noisy, bustling atmosphere.

The restaurant's wood-burning oven turns out orders of chicken, fish, and side vegetables, as well as the heads of garlic. Other house specialties include several kinds of pastas, sandwiches, and desserts. Our waiter claimed the wood-burning oven generated heat as high as 900 degrees. Maybe so, but I just wanted dinner, not my car painted and baked.

Entrees include some classic bistro food including, but not limited to traditional steak and fries, *cassoulet* loaded with chunks of duck and lamb, and slices of fatty sausage, and of course the white beans which are at the heart of the recipe. More than a whiff of fennel and garlic add to the complexity of seasonings, all of which is enriched with some *creme fraiche*.

~Dinner Specials ~
~ Appetizers ~

Assiette de Fromages et Fruits Frais
A selection of French cheeses made from goat, cow and sheep's milk with seasonal fruits and baguette. 11.95
Suggested wine: 1997 Cabernet Sauvignon, Kenwood, Sonoma, CA 9.50

Assortiment de Charcutailles à la Française
Chef's selection of country pate, sausage and French meats served with Cornichons, mustard and petite salade. 9.95
Suggested Wine: 1998 Syrah, Echelon, San Luis Obispo, CA 9.25

Tartare D'Asperges et de Melon aux Herbs
Asparagus and melon tartare with fresh herbs. 8.95

Poëllée de Calamars á la Persillade
Sautéed Calamari with parsley and garlic butter 9.95
Suggessted Wine: 1998 Pinot Blanc, Léon Beyer, Alsace 7.25

Carpaccio de St Jacques à la Purée de Haricots Blanc à L'Huile de Truffes
Scallop carpaccio with white bean purée and truffle oil. 10.95
Suggested Wine: Chardonnay, Cambria, Santa Maria, CA 10.00

~ Entreés ~

Entrecôte de Veau Grillée À Lembeurée de Choux. Jus Aux Echalottes et Citrons Rotis
Grilled Veal Ribeye with savoy cabbage. Roasted shallots, lemons and veal jus 29.95
Suggested Wine: 1996 Pinot Noir, Lorane Valley, Oregon 8.25

Poelée de Halibut avec Epinard et Sauce a L'Orange
Sauteed Alaskan halibut over spinach with boiled potatoes and Sauce a l'orange. 18.95
Suggested Wine: 1998 Pinot Gris 'Réserve', Trimbach, Alsace 9.75

~ Wood Oven Specialties ~

Wood Roasted Maine Sea Scallops
Nestled on a timbale of spinach and saffron Basmati rice, drizzled with infused olive oil of red pepper and caviar. 21.95

Filet of Salmon
Wood roasted North Atlantic salmon served with roasted market vegetables. 17.95

Steak Au Poivre
14 oz. New York strip steak crusted with peppercorns in a light Cognac cream sauce; garlic potato cake L'ami Louis. 25.95

Roasted Vegetables, Bistro 110 Style
A selection of seasonal vegetables roasted whole in our oak-fired oven. 14.95 Appetizer portion 9.95

Oven-Roasted Half Chicken
Bistro 110's specialty, prepared with rosemary and thyme; accompanied by roasted vegetables. 15.95

Poisson Rôti du Jour
Wood roasted whole fish seasoned with rosemary and thyme. Market Price.

Appetizers range from roasted mushrooms and French onion soup baked in a crock, to oven-roasted calamari with the flavor of basil-infused olive oil, plus roasted potatoes and tomatoes. The delicious basket of fries is large enough to keep the whole table nibbling away.

The restaurant features an enclosed sidewalk café setting which gives those lucky enough to get a table there in the winter, some wonderful views outside.

BISTROT MARGOT
KR 18/20
Decor 4/4   Hospitality 4.5/5   Food 8.5/10   Value 1/1

* **French Bistro**
* **Chicago/Near North**
* **$$**

1437 North Wells Street
Chicago
(312) 587-3660
Troubleshooter: Joe Doppes
(owner)

Hours: Sun–Mon 5–9 pm, Tues–Thurs 5–10 pm, Fri–Sat 5–11 pm
Credit Cards: Amex, Visa, Diners
Reservations: Recommend
Handicapped: Accessible
Smoking and nonsmoking sections: Smoking only at bar
Parking: Valet $6

Bistrot Margot recaptures the kind of place Toulouse LaTrec might sit at and sketch on a tablecloth. Instead of LaTrec's art, the walls are hung with photographs of the owner's young daughter, Margot, which adds a playfully sweet touch.

The menu is neo-classical French from the onion soup baked in a crock to the bouillabaisse and profiteroles. Starters include not only the onion soup, as sweet and darkly delicious as this broth can be, but mussels in white wine with herbs, snails in garlic butter, even a crab cake inspired by Chicago master chef, Jean Banchet. Among nightly specials, cream of wild mushroom soup is so delicious you might wish you had gills to breath it in.

À la carte salads include such standbys as Caesar or a house mix of spinach and warm bacon dressing. Endive with chopped walnuts is the best of the lot, touched with blue cheese and apple slices. These are natural flavor combinations in a lovely setting.

Entrees run from delicate whitefish roasted with tomatoes, fennel, onions and herbs, touched with a lemon zest confit for accent, to hearty rack of lamb with dijon mustard and bread crumbs forming a light crust. Evening specials add to the choices. Venison has been paired with roasted quail stuffed with herbed breadcrumbs. Twin venison loins are as tender as prime beef. A demiglace-based pepper sauce and sliced chanterelles bring things together. Bouillabaisse with monkfish, snapper,

APPETIZERS

LES CHAMPIGNONS SAUVAGES GRILLES...............................**$5.95**
Portobello Mushroom with Blue Cheese, Rosemary and Garlic

MOULES MARINIERES **$5.50**
Mussels simmered in White Wine with Fresh Herbs

ESCARGOTS EN COCOTTE **$6.95**
Snails Simmered in Garlic Butter

PATE MAISON (MOUSSE ET CAMPAGNE) **$5.95**
Country Style Pate and Chicken Liver Mousse

GALETTE DE CRABE, JEAN BANCHET....................................**$6.95**
Crab Cake served with a Velvety Mustard Sauce

PIZZA TAYLOR STREET BISTRO **$7.95**
Shrimp, Spinach and Goat's Cheese

SOUPE A L'OIGNON LYONNAISE **$3.50**
French Onion Soup Garnished with French Bread and Gruyere Cheese

RISOTTO DU CHEF ....**MARKET**
Special Arborio Rice Selection of the Day.   **PRICE**

LES ENTREES

SAUMON GRILLE' DUCHESS **$15.95**
Atlantic Salmon, Sweet Onions and Béarnaise Sauce, Duchess Potatoes

POULET ROTI, JUS NATUREL. **$12.95**
Roasted Chicken with Garlic, Lemon, and Herbs, with Pommes Frites

CAPPELLINI ET CREVETTES SAUTÉES AU BEURRE.......................**$14.50**
Angel Hair Pasta with Shrimp, Sun-Dried Tomatoes and Saffron Butter

ENTRECOTE AU POIVRE..**$15.95**
A Pan Roasted N.Y. Strip with Black Peppercorns, served with Frites

CARRE D' AGNEAU ROTI ET PERSILLE **$19.95**
Rack of Lamb basted with Dijon Mustard and Garlic Bread Crumbs

COTE DE PORC, SAUCE MOUTARDE....................................**$16.95**
Grilled Center Cut Pork Chops with Mustard Sauce and Potato Gratin

TILAPIA AUX NOIX **$16.95**
Roasted Tilapia with Asparagus,Walnuts, Balsamic-Brown Butter Sauce

POITRINE DE CANARD ET CUISSE CONFITE...........................**$14.95**
Roasted Duck Breast and Leg Confit, Citrus Sauce and Wild Rice

MEDAILLONS DE VEAU, SAUCE CHAMPIGNONS **$19.95**
Veal Loin Sautéed, Wild Mushroom Sauce

STEAK FRITES **$14.50**
Sirloin Butt Steak laced with Garlic Butter and Pommes Frites

scallops and shellfish is flavored with lemon in a broth that is somewhat softer tasting than others found in Chicago French restaurants. It's not a bad soup, just different.

Elsewhere among seafood choices, a large cut of pink salmon is set with onions and plump duchess potatoes. Béarnaise sauce makes a tasty appearance, and in moderation, compliments the taste of the salmon. The wine list is good, maybe a tad pricey.

BISTRO ULTRA
KR 18/20
Decor 4/4   Hospitality 4.5/5   Food 8.5/10   Value 1/1

- **Eclectic**
- **Chicago/Mid-North**
- **$$**

2239 North Clybourn
Chicago
(773) 529-3300
Troubleshooter: Juan Huraddo
(owner)

Hours: Daily 5 pm–midnight
Credit Cards: All majors
Reservations: Recommended
Handicapped: Accessible
Smoking and nonsmoking sections: Both available
Parking: On street

Bistro Ultra is inexpensive enough for casual dining, yet stylish enough to make the evening seem like something special. Decor accents include large maroon swag drapes to soften the bare brick walls, a handsome long bar that looks old enough to have some history, and a collection of framed prints, many of them authentic antiques, others handsome copies.

The menu is a mix of some traditional bistro entrees plus an eclectic selection which leans toward Mediterranean and American. Begin with a mushroom paté. The taste is freshened by sprigs of basil and a touch of tomato and onion. Other selections range from the chef's take on liver paté, with truffle oil, bay scallops simply sautéed in butter with garlic and a finish of diced tomatoes, a classic style of snails in a dome pastry puff and simply braised mussels in white wine, with a little cream enrichment, plus garlic and shallots.

That's not a bad list, but save room for a taste of soup. Classic French onion is a daily occurrence. A recent *soup du jour* brought a mushroom-infused broth to the table, creamy in texture, but without any cream. A trio of salads are, like other courses, à la carte. The Bistro Ultra house salad brings shreds of roasted tomato topped with a generous slab of goat cheese on mixed field greens. Anyone who likes goat cheese salads will love this one.

The goat cheese reappeared in a nightly pasta special, changing a tomato based sauce into a creamy blend that richly coated each strand of linguine. This one will be much too rich for some tastes, as it was for mine. From a selection of other entrees, *Pompeian shrimp*, sautéed in olive oil with spinach and a side of polenta, is simple but satisfying. Like so much else on the menu, the approach is direct, without flamboyance or contrivance. Other entrees include a couple of seafood choices, salmon or whitefish. Each is plated with appropriate accompaniment. In the case of the whitefish, capers and herbs bring flavor to a fish which is sautéed in a light bread crumb coating, then bedded on white rice.

Duck is roasted in a cranberry sauce baste and plated on wild rice. Beefsteak and fries is prepared in true bistro fashion, while pork tenderloin gets a heady dose of plum and port wine sauce. Chicken cordon blue and rack of lamb in its own juices bring a touch of more elegant fare.

Desserts vary from day to day, reflecting their freshness. The wine list is small, but appropriate, and like everything else reasonably priced.

BISTROT ZINC
KR 18/20
Decor 4/4   Hospitality 4.5/5   Food 8.5/10   Value 1/1

- **French Bistro**
- **Chicago/Mid-North (Original location)**
- **$$**

3443 North Southport
Chicago
(773) 281-3443
Troubleshooters: Carl Segal, Casey Eslick (co-owners)

Other Location

KR 18.5/20, Decor 4/4 Hospitality 5/5 Food 8.5/10 Value 1/1
1131 North State Street, Chicago; 312-337-1131; Troubleshooter: Carl Segal, Casey Eslick (co-owners); Hours: Lunch 11:30 am–2:30 pm, Brunch Sun starts at 10 am, Dinner Mon–Thurs 5–10 pm Fri–Sat 5–11 pm, Sun 5–9 pm (Note: a new bar menu is available 3–5 pm daily that includes pates, escargot (in garlic butter), French onion soup, and a cheese and sausage plate.); Credit Cards: Amex, Diners, MC, Visa; Handicapped: Accessible; Smoking and nonsmoking sections: Separate smoking and nonsmoking seating, smoking at bar; Parking: Valet available evenings starting at 5 pm, $7

Hours: Closed Mon, Bistro Tues–Thurs 5:30–10 pm, Fri 5:30–11 pm, Sun 5–9 pm Café Lunch Tues–Fri 11:30 am–3 pm, Dinner Tues–Thurs 5–10 pm, Fri 5–11 pm, Sat 11 am–11 pm, Sun 11 am–9 pm
Credit Cards: Amex, Diners MC, Visa
Reservations: Taken for parties of 2 or more
Parking: Valet $7
Handicapped: Accessible
Smoking and nonsmoking sections: Separate smoking and nonsmoking seating, smoking in Café, no smoking in Bistro

Bistro Zinc, one of Chicago's better French bistros has cloned itself into a second location, and though the name and menus are the same, the newer version has a decidedly different character than its namesake on North Southport. Maybe it's the neighborhood which makes the difference. The State Street Bistrot Zinc does not have the bakery and carry-out counter which characterizes the one on North Southport. But, there is the zinc-topped bar, the dark wood trim, turn of Century poster art, tile floors and tin ceiling.

Bistro dining is no longer a novelty in Chicago, so diners have a right to expect something special when there are so many restaurants from which to choose. Bistro Zinc is among the upper tier of its kind. There are classic choices, ubiquitous French onion soup, steamed mussels, steak and fries. Roasted chicken dubbed *Poulet Grand-Mere* is more sophisticated than the name suggests. Smoked bacon is the key, adding a savory sweetness to the chicken which is cooked with roasted garlic, potatoes and mushrooms among ingredients in its roasting pan. A mound of thin and crisp potato strings is the sort to give anyone a big case of the munchies.

From among other selections, grilled salmon is a rather simple affair garnished with French green beans; it really needs nothing more. Skate-fish is snow white and flaky. In this case, it is given a pan-sauté in butter and finished with artichokes, plus a red onion and green bean stylized salad. Speaking of salad, several are dinner size. In one, spinach and tomatoes are plated with a small onion tart, while in another, curled frisee lettuce is the bedding for chunks of crumbled roquefort cheese, walnuts, apple slices and bacon.

Several crepes are served regularly as is a classic *croque monsieur*, the French version of a ham sandwich, though this is nothing like what one will find in Mom's Diner, unless Mom happens to be named Nanette or Marie. Daily specials change regularly, while desserts include the requisite chocolate choices, tartes and *crème Brûlée*, plus fresh berries and ice creams.

Blackbird
KR 16.75/20
Decor 3/4   Hospitality 5/5   Food 8/10   Value .75/1

- **Eclectic**
- **Chicago/Near West**
- **$$**

619 West Randolph
Chicago
(312) 715-0708
Troubleshooter: Donnie Madia

Hours: Lunch Mon–Fri 11:30 am–2 pm, Dinner Mon–Thurs 5:30–10:30 pm, Fri–Sat 5:30–11:30 pm
Credit Cards: All majors
Reservations: Recommended
Handicapped: Accessible
Smoking and nonsmoking sections: Smoking at bar
Parking: Valet $6

I love the decor of Blackbird, clean, minimalist and, like the cuisine, without unnecessary embellishment. But, this is a dining room where conversation at a normal level is almost impossible. I don't want to make too much of this, other than to suggest that if a quiet evening out is more to your taste, this is not your kind of restaurant.

Otherwise, it's a genuine dining find, even if prices on some selections are a little out of line. There is no fault with the imaginative and creative cooking. Scallops are garnished with an orange and lobster-infused *aoili*, while sliced skirt steak tops a salad of arugula, cherry tomatoes and maytag blue cheese with a calamata olive dressing. Ahi tuna tartare is a splendid example of simplicity with a lime and ginger vinaigrette to embellish a collection of crisp French green beans and other vegetables.

Among entree choices, the selection runs the gamut of imaginative platings and ingredients. Sturgeon, an excellent firm fleshed fish is given a Mediterranean setting of couscous plus homemade yogurt with cucumbers all finished in a carrot and ginger sauce. Halibut is another mild and firm fleshed fish, in this case plated with a stylized reduction of mushrooms with a course buckwheat crepe.

Among other entrees, beef tenderloin is almost classic American-style with an intense red wine reduction sauce and creamed horseradish. Venison gets an appropriately stronger pairing with trumpet mushrooms cooked down into a red wine sauce with currants and a bit of thyme. Gleanings of Swiss chard and potatoes complete the platter. A vegetarian stew with mushrooms and assorted vegetables is pooled around a mild tasting bean cake which forms an island in the center of the plate. Flavors lean toward the bland on this one. Grilled Amish chicken billed as a *pot au feu* is not all that interesting, even with an embellishment of forest mushrooms, peas and slivers of roasted potatoes. This recipe simply lacks the deep flavored enriched qualities of a true *pot au feu*.

There's nothing lacking about desserts. Service seems genuinely caring.

BLACKHAWK LODGE
KR 19/20
Decor 4/4   Hospitality 5/5   Food 9/10   Value 1/1

- **American**
- **Chicago/Near North**
- **$$**

41 East Superior Street
Chicago
(312) 280-4080
Troubleshooter: Manager on
duty

Hours: Lunch Mon–Sat 11:30
am–3 pm, Dinner Sun–Thurs
5–10 pm, Fri–Sat 5–11 pm, Blue
Grass Brunch Sun 11:30 am–
3 pm features live entertainment
Credit Cards: All majors
Reservations: Accepted
Handicapped: Accessible
**Smoking and nonsmoking
sections:** Both available
Parking: Valet available nightly,
validated parking at Huron Place
(South of Superior on Wabash) at
all times

Blackhawk Lodge has the right balance with an appearance that suggests rustic, but not primitive. The look is one of bleached wood flooring, light-colored paneling, heavy field stone fireplaces and the like.

Diners are greeted with a welcoming basket of buttermilk biscuits, sourdough rolls and corn muffins, made even better with a raspberry red pepper jam or lemon honey.

Among appetizers on the seasonally changing menu, warm hazelnut-dusted goat cheese was served in soufflé fashion, while grits and cheddar cheese were baked with tasso ham sausage and wild mushrooms for something more formidable. On the seafood side of things, diners could savor crab cakes fried up on the griddle, served with lemon and chive mayonnaise and jicama matchsticks in cole slaw dressing.

From among a dozen or so entree selections, the American genesis of the Blackhawk Lodge theme shines through. Roast turkey comes with mashed potatoes and sage cream. You'll find the house version of barbecue baby back ribs no matter what the season. Among seafood selections, salmon is crusted with mushrooms, roasted in a wood-fired oven, and plated in a port wine reduction. From a short list of daily specials, mahi mahi had been grilled as was the delicious array of root vegetables and mushrooms. It's an interesting pairing of a deep water Pacific Ocean fish with overtones of the American Heartland. Another special brings beef tenderloin, butterflied and beautifully rare with a potato pancake. The meat is encrusted in cracked peppercorns, a classic combination of flavorings.

One of the poultry preparations is half a chicken breast is grilled over oak, and plated with whipped yams flavored with maple syrup; grilled vegetables tend to give some balance to the flavors. Fried chicken is also on the menu of a dozen or more entrees selections, with whipped potatoes and a mixed vegetable slaw. Other entrees worth more than passing attention are trout crusted with crushed pecans and served over a sweet corn sauce, while braised lamb shank is paired with Yukon gold mashed potatoes and root vegetables flavored with the lamb's natural pan juices.

For dessert, selections might include fruit cobbler, several kinds of rich ice cream, bread pudding and others from the heartland larder.

BLUE SAPPHIRE
KR 19/20
Decor 3.5/4   Hospitality 5/5   Food 9.5/10   Value 1/1

• **Thai**

• **Evanston**

• **$**

1709 Benson Avenue
Evanston
(847) 475-9374
Troubleshooter: Mike Hempal
(owner)

Hours: Mon–Thurs 11 am–9:30 pm, Fri–Sat 11 am–10:30 pm, Sun 4–9:30 pm
Credit Cards: All majors
Reservations: Accepted
Handicapped: Accessible
Smoking and nonsmoking sections: No smoking
Parking: City garage one block South on Benson, otherwise tight street parking

Thai restaurants in and around Chicago range from plain storefronts to the exotic and museum-like Arun's (q.v.). Blue Sapphire falls well above the middle ground, while still in the bargain dining category.

Start with a swarm of tasty appetizers including delicate spring rolls with a julienne of fresh vegetables wrapped inside rice paper noodle topped with a sweet plum sauce. Because no one flavor stands out over another, there is almost a contemplative enjoyment, if you allow yourself to find it.

Contrast two appetizer dumplings, steamed *shumai* and pan-fried pot stickers. The attention to detail should not be ignored to fully enjoy what Blue Sapphire has to offer. The *shumai* have a soft, doughy character with a smooth filling that includes ground shrimp. The pot stickers are crisp, kind of like a Polish *pierogi*, though clearly of Oriental origin. For a different experience, taste *tod mun*, deep-fried fish patties best enjoyed with a sweet and sour peanut sauce.

I think Thai soups should never be ignored. Blue Sapphire serves nearly a dozen ranging from the Thai version of chicken soup with a coconut milk stock to the complex *tom yom*, with the sweet an sour underpinnings of lime juice, sliced vegetables, mushrooms and a bouquet of spices.

Pud Thai is somewhat understated in its sweetness, and from my standpoint, that's a plus. Instead, there is a balance of sweet and tart in the mix of eggs, ground peanuts and seasonings which hold tofu, bean sprouts and transparent rice noodles together in a singular taste experience.

Thailand, like other parts of Southeast Asia, is influenced by nearby India, especially with its adaptation of curries. Most are made from a coconut milk base, which may be delicious, but is probably not acceptable for people who watch cholesterol and dietary fats. Instead, try *gang pa*, a red curry with bamboo shoots, eggplant, peas and an abundance of fresh basil. *Gang pa* demonstrates that not all curries need be super hot.

Among other selections on the extensive menu is a not to be missed gem simply called *curry noodles*. In this case, wide *chow fun* noodles are topped with a wonderfully flavorful peanut and chicken sauce. Broccoli flowerets add some color and texture balance. Among desserts, Thai custard with a mild coconut base is a little too dry. Service is friendly, the restaurant handsome in an understated manner.

BLUEPOINT OYSTER BAR
KR 17.5/20
Decor 4/4   Hospitality 3.5/5   Food 9/10   Value 1/1

- **American Seafood**
- **Chicago/Near West**
- **$$**

741 West Randolph Street
Chicago
(312) 207-1222
Troubleshooter: Kelly Kircher
(manager)

Hours: Lunch Mon–Fri 11 am–2 pm, Dinner Mon–Thurs 5–10 pm, Fri–Sat 5p–11p, Sun 4:30–9:30 pm
Credit Cards: All majors
Reservations: Recommended
Handicapped: Accessible
Smoking and nonsmoking sections: Both available
Parking: Valet $6

Where Barney's Market Club stood for decades, now stands Bluepoint Oyster Bar. There are no echoes of "Yes Sir, Senator!," but there is a 1940s-style deco restaurant with a bar that looks as if it had been there for years, not the couple of months the restaurant has been open.

Things are quite good, if not quite ship-shape in all departments. Service needs a little prodding now and then, and this is on a slow night. In the same vein, table bussing could be a little more thorough.

The menu is extensive, easy to navigate and as tempting as any fish house in the city. Oysters from the raw bar are à la carte and include well known species and a couple not so familiar. They go down the gullet like grease through a goose, eased along with a bit of cocktail sauce. But, even stark naked, they are great.

From the raw bar, it's an easy jump to a hot soup, either New England clam chowder or Chicago seafood gumbo which suggests perhaps, a broth of alewives, carp and zebra mussels. It is, in reality, much the New Orleans gumbo style, a fragrant blend of seasonings, sausage and vegetables along with its collection of seafood.

Entrees include a good selection of the daily catch ranging from North Atlantic salmon to Arctic char among a dozen or so species. They can be had cooked as you ask or in more elaborate presentations under a separate listing dubbed "Prime Seafood." Items designated with two stars are chef recommendations. One of them, seared jerk Florida grouper is plated with a pineapple relish. The jerk seasoning is authentic enough, but is better applied to chicken or pork than mild flavored grouper. Among other selections, escolar, a meaty firm fleshed fish has a delicious buttery taste when left unembellished. Arctic char, with its salmon-like underpinnings, works rather well with horseradish mashed potatoes, though a pool of raspberry and thyme vinaigrette sauce is an out-of-character intrusion.

Other choices are tempting and similarly elaborate. They include mahi mahi with a mushroom crust, risotto and chive beurre blanc, and grilled swordfish with an appropriate onion caper relish as its sauce. The variety continues with fried selections, ranging from fish and chips to tempura to Ipswich clams. For non-fish diners, there are a couple of steaks, roasted chicken and pasta. Desserts include key lime pie, a Wonka cake which promises to live up to its implied chocolate fantasy and streusel apple pie with a baked cheddar cheese and caramel crust.

BOB CHINN'S CRAB HOUSE
KR 17/20
Decor 3.5/4   Hospitality 4.5/5   Food 8/10   Value 1/1

- **American Seafood**
- **Wheeling**
- **$$**

393 South Milwaukee Avenue
Wheeling
(847) 520-3633
Troubleshooters: Bob Chinn
and Marilyn Chinn Le Tourneau
(owners), Frank D'Angelo
(manager)

Hours: Lunch Mon–Fri 11:30
am–2:30 pm, Sat noon–3 pm,
Dinner Mon–Thurs 4:30–10:30
pm, Fri–Sat 4:30–11:30 pm,
Sun 3–10 pm
Credit Cards: All majors
Reservations: Accepted for
parties of 5 or more will cut the
wait time in half
Handicapped: Accessible
Bar: Full service with handsome
lounge, antique long bar, and
whirling tropical fans, excellent
wine and beer selection plus
mixed drinks
Parking: Free lot

Bob Chinn's Crab House is somewhat the landmark in the American restaurant industry. Excluding fast food chains, no other restaurant in the United States serves so many people each day. Twenty-five hundred dinners could be typical on a given day.

With that kind of volume it would seem diners would have an inordinate wait for tables. And, that used to be the case. But, a renovation in the mid-1980s, including a major expansion, sped things up remarkabley. People may still feel as if they are moved in and out like so many widgets on a conveyor belt, but once in the hands of a waitress, things become much more cordial.

Soups are delicious. The seafood gumbo is the kind that sneaks up on you. Your first spoonful fills the mouth with comets of flavor. Then, when you think things are about to subside, a rush of pepper seasoning takes hold. This one is a real winner.

Entrees will change regularly, as will prices depending upon market conditions. Bob Chinn's really knows how to serve traditional lobster. After you are outfitted with a bib to catch all the juices, your waitress will bring out a large wooden platter with the lobster butterflied, and most of the shell cracking done. Then, the rest is up to you. Savor each delicious bite; saving the best for last, crack into the claws and remove them from the shell for the kind of dining that makes lobster the supreme treat it can be.

For soft-fish lovers, Pacific onaga is often on the menu, fished off the waters around Hawaii. Tuna is always a good choice. The large cut of tuna steak comes fresh from the grill, with hashmarks. The fish might be topped with a crackercrumb-based seasoning mix that leaves just a bit of saltiness, and perhaps the flavor of Worstershire on the tongue. Florida swordfish, Alaskan halibut, soft-shell crabs as well as crabs of almost any variety you might want, are featured when in season. Since this restaurant does such a huge volume, turnover virtually insures freshness.

Desserts include several chocolate goodies, cheesecake, ice cream and key lime pie which is too sweet.

THE BOULEVARD CAFÉ
KR 18/20

Decor 3.5/4   Hospitality 5/5   Food 8.5/10   Value 1/1

- **American**
- **Chicago/Northwest**
- **$**

3137 West Logan Boulevard
Chicago
(773) 384-8600
Troubleshooter: John Glynn

Hours: Weeknights 5–10 pm
5p–11p, Fri–Sat 5–11 pm,
Brunch Sun 10 am–2:30 pm,
Dinner 5–10
Credit Cards: All majors
Reservations: Recommended
Handicapped: Accessible
**Smoking and nonsmoking
sections:** Both available
Parking: In free lot around the
corner on Milwaukee Avenue

Chicago's Logan Square is in revival, big time. Part of that revival is The Boulevard Café, with an eclectic American menu that is about as funky as the art deco decor.

For starters, a Middle Eastern platter brings a generous bounty of *humus,* *baba gahnouj* and *tabouleh* with pita wedges and tomato slices. Baked goat cheese is perhaps a bit more elegant, while Everything on a Stick is a skewer of chunked chicken, beef and whole shrimp served with a separate sauce for each. Among other starters, The Boulevard Café version of French onion soup is topped with not one, but two cheeses, Swiss and parmesan. Entrees are served with a choice of soup or salad.

If you remember Mom's meatloaf, you will recognize some similar flavors, though chances are Mom did not make her meatloaf with ground turkey. I was concerned that this would be way too dry, but that was hardly the case at all. The meat was seasoned well, and plated with creamy delicious mashed potatoes. Roasted garlic infused the gravy; this was really too good to be turkey, but I'm willing to suspend my disbelief. Among other patriotic American selections is chicken pot pie, though the crust is probably more French pastry than diner road food.

The menu goes south of the border for its inspired version of mushroom enchiladas. In this case, wild field mushrooms, the dark, chewy sort are the filling for large corn tortillas. A sweet but spicy ancho chili sauce is an attention grabber, that surprisingly works well with the mushrooms. Spanish rice and black beans in ranchero sauce complete the platter.

Among other entrees, the selection includes grilled salmon bedded on couscous with arugula and dried tomatoes in white wine and garlic tomato sauce as part of its embellishment. Chicken breast, in another entree, is stuffed with roasted red peppers and chopped asparagus, in a mushroom sauce with garlic mashed potatoes. A couple of steaks and a pork chop, as well as a trio of pastas round out the dinner selections. There are also some sandwiches and dinner-size salads. In warm weather, the sidewalk café is the place to enjoy the neighborhood.

BRASSERIE JO
KR 19.5/20
Decor 4/4   Hospitality 5/5   Food 9.5/10   Value 1/1

- **French Bistro**
- **Chicago Near North**
- **$$**

59 West Hubbard
Chicago
(312) 595-0800
Troubleshooter: Tim Holmes (general manager), Jean Joho (chef/owner)

Hours: Lunch Mon–Fri 11:30 am–4 pm, Dinner Sun–Thurs 5–10 pm, Fri–Sat 5–11 pm
Credit Cards: All majors
Reservations: Accepted
Handicapped: Accessible
Parking: Valet available

Put a world-class chef into a brasserie and the result should be a world-class brasserie. That's what is happening at Chef Jean Joho's Brasserie Jo. The restaurant is almost cavernous with a high ceiling, marble and wood accents and a mosaic tile floor all bound together with a sense of *art deco*. The look is decidedly cosmopolitan, made busy by an eclectic menu and crowd to match. A powerful TV executive might be at one table, while over at another you could find the mayor.

Whatever the table talk, it inevitably must get around to the food, which on its brasserie level, is as exciting and challenging as Joho's work at the more formal Everest.

Because the tradition of the brasserie implies beer, a glass of the house draft lager is a good way to start, though any of several other French brands would do as well. You can pace your meal as you choose, taking only one course or several.

Try an onion tart and you will come to understand how the simple onion can be raised to near lofty culinary heights. Somewhat more elaborate is the terrine of ratatouille. The onion soup, with its topping of creamy melted gruyere is classic. Smoked salmon, another appetizer choice, is a perfect balance of flavor with wispy potato crisps and horse-radish cream offering taste and texture accents.

Entrees include one standard brought over by Chef Joho from the Everest menu. The Famous Shrimp Bag is actually a phyllo dough filled with roasted rock shrimp in a cream sauce. Joho also features some specialties from his native Alsace, including a plate of *charcuterie*, a selection of French delicatessen meats, best when accompanied by large draughts of beer or that peculiarly spicy Alsatian wine, Gewurztraminer.

Not everything need be so meaty. Vegetable *pot au feu* brings a collection of hearty root vegetables simmered in a flavorful court-bouillon, while the standard *croque monsieur* is given a vegetarian flip with vegetables in place of meat. Like any bistro or brasserie, Brasserie Jo serves steak and fries, the potatoes mounded over a cut of beef topped with herbed butter. *Coq au vin* brings a cut-up chicken that has been roasted with a delicious wine sauce flavored by pearl onions and bits of bacon, mushrooms and herbs, perfect for a cool evening's dining. Another chicken, this time roasted and plated with potatoes dauphin is similarly tempting, especially with those wonderful deep-fried potato puffs.

Desserts range from fruit sorbet to bread pudding and more elaborate concoctions. The restaurant's full service bar features an excellent wine list. Domestic and imported French beers are highlighted, including the restaurant's signature Alsatian style draft *hop-La* beer.

BRASSERIE T
KR 18/20
Decor 4/4   Hospitality 4/5   Food 9/10   Value 1/1

- **American Bistro**
- **Northfield**
- **$$**

305 South Happ Road
Northfield
(847) 446-0444
Troubleshooters: Rick Tramanto, Gale Gand, or manager on duty

Hours: Mon–Thurs 11:30 am–10 pm, Fri–Sat until 1 am, Sun 4:30–10 pm
Credit Cards: Amex, Discover, MC, Visa
Reservations: Recommended
Handicapped: Accessible
Smoking and nonsmoking sections: Both available
Parking: Ample free lot parking

While Rick Tramanto and his wife Gail Gand may be spending more time these days at their ultra chic restaurant Tru (q.v.), their bistro in the North Shore suburb of Northfield ticks merrily along. Where Tru is expensive, formal, elaborate, Brasserie T is a restaurant where meat loaf and pizza, albeit designer pizzas, are found on the same menu. The front is given over to a large bar, not exactly cozy, but a pleasant gathering place as you wait for a table in the main dining room. At the far end is an open kitchen, and a dramatic wood-burning oven where pizzas are baked and meats are grilled or roasted. The room reminds me of a modern version of a medieval refectory, the sort of place where Francois Villon might burst in on a cold Paris night, huddle with friends and break out with his latest poem or song.

Today the music is largely the crackling of wood burning in the stone-faced oven. This is a lively dining room with slate and marble floors. Overhead glass and copper trimmed chandeliers spill out the light.

This is more an American than a French brasserie, though the menu is geographically eclectic. There is a Gallic-style platter of *charcuterie* among appetizers, a collection of cured meats, pates, cornichon pickles and stone ground mustard. *Escargots* are snails with a French and, in this case, a garlic accent. As the menu puts it . . . "lots of garlic."

Baked goat cheese with a tomato and basil sauce, classic crock-baked French onion soup and tuna tartare are among other appetizers. The latter is a course grind atop arugula greens with a mild flavor and texture that spreads easily on a slice of bread.

Pizzas from the wood-burning oven are easily shared among a party of two to four people. From a handful of toppings, the caramelized onion is my favorite, with slices of grilled eggplant and sliced tomatoes, warm and juicy.

A salad and sandwich combine to make a light supper. If you want a good old American ham and cheese sandwich, eat elsewhere. The brasserie version is the French *croque monsieur*, four cheeses and ham on *brioche*, sort of a stylized patty melt, in a manner of speaking.

No American brasserie worth its salt and pepper could ignore pastas. At Brasserie T they range from gnocchi in a delicious stew-like melange of mushrooms, leek, tomatoes and asiago cheese, to fusilli, the little corkscrews with slices of chicken and asparagus in a belly busting Alfredo-based tomato sauce, to simple angel hair in tomato, basil and garlic sauce.

Elsewhere, the restaurant's version of good old American meat loaf is 100% veal, plated with a garnish of mushrooms, roasted garlic mashed potatoes and sauteed spinach plus a ladle or two of tomato sauce. Despite its wrappings, it still tastes like good old American meat loaf.

Other entrees include a lavishly abundant *osso buco, cassoulet*, the French bean stew that brings together duck confit, lamb, bacon and sausages, a grilled pork chop fresh out of the wood-burning oven and other fashions of poultry, lamb and beef. Seafood varies daily, though salmon from the wood grill is regularly available.

Though I usually pass dessert, I confess that my will power crumbles in the face of Gand's mud pie, a chocolate revel that would tempt a stylite.

BRUNA'S
KR 16.75/20
Decor 3.5/4   Hospitality 5/5   Food 7.5/10   Value .75/1

- **Italian**
- **Chicago/South**
- **$**

2424 South Oakley
Chicago
(773) 254-5550
Troubleshooter: Luciano
Silvestri

Hours: Sun–Thurs 11:30 am–
10 pm, Fri–Sat 11:30 am–11 pm
Credit Cards: All majors
Reservations: Recommended
Handicapped: Accessible, but
there are a couple of steps up to
the front door
**Smoking and nonsmoking
sections:** Small smoking section
Parking: Street parking can be
tight on weekends

Bruna's rests in the heart of the old Italian neighborhood. Just take a look around and you cannot miss it. I get this feeling every time I visit any of the South Oakley area restaurants. It's like a time warp or a movie set. But, there is no mistaking the fact that it is all real, just as Bruna's is real. Walking inside the restaurant there is a wave of nostalgia that suggests a past when dining was more family-oriented, when trattoria was a word hardly heard outside of Italy.

Bruna's is not a trendy trattoria. It is a family-style Italian restaurant which looks as it always has. There is no sacrifice of tradition here, and no effort to keep up with dining fashion or trends. For my money, the house specialty is anything with Bruna's deep rich and delicious bolognese sauce. This is a classic Italian sauce with its tinge of nutmeg sweetness, underneath the full flavors of cooked-down tomatoes, seasonings and a course grind of meats.

Among other entrees and pastas, the usual suspects abound, lasagna, spaghetti carbonara, *penne puttanesca* to name just three. Linguine *frutti di mare* is piled high with mixed seafood and a tomato sauce. Among meats, chicken vesuvio is the traditional treatment, meaty, full flavored, robust. Shrimp is also given the vesuvio treatment, though I do not think it works as well. Shrimp fra diavola is better. Several other chicken choices are listed as are steaks, and of course an abundance of veal. There is a wine list, a bit overpriced considering surroundings and the rest of the menu.

BUKARA
KR 16/20
Decor 4/4   Hospitality 3/5   Food 8/10   Value 1/1

- **Northwestern Indian**
- **Chicago/Near North**
- **$$**

2 East Ontario Street
Chicago
(312) 943-0188
Troubleshooter: Ravi Sahni
(manager)

Hours: Lunch Mon–Fri 11:30 am–2:15 pm, Sat–Sun noon–2:45 pm (Luncheon buffet), Dinner Sun–Thurs 5:30–9:45 pm, Fri–Sat 5:30–10:30 pm
Credit Cards: All majors
Reservations: Recommended
Handicapped: Accessible
Parking: Validated at 10 East Ontario Place ($3.75)

Bukara serves what its owners call "Indian North West Frontier Cuisine." Unlike other Indian restaurants, Bukara will freely serve beef, though a section of the menu also caters to vegetarian tastes. Diners sit at wood tables in large, almost oversized chairs. The whitewashed walls and planked floors are decorated with Bukhara carpets, their intricate designs repeated in endless repetition. Much of what is served, even a special salad, originates in tandoors, those large clay urns heated with charcoal coals that are clearly visible in the glassed enclosed kitchen. Any of the Vegetarian offerings are fine for appetizers. Try *dal Bukara*, a dish of lentil beans in subtle seasonings that leave just a hint of sweetness on the palate. Contrast the *dal* with *aloo bharvan*, an Indian version of stuffed baked potato. They are filled with a mix of cashew nuts, mild green chili peppers, raisins, cumin, and a traditional Indian blend of dried ground spices called *garum masala*, used in Indian cooking much the way a French chef would use a bouquet garni.

In addition to your opening course, order a basket of mixed breads. The breads become important, since diners are expected to eat with their hands, using the bread as scoops. You can have utensils on request, but, since Bukara gives each diner a large bib to protect clothing, using your hands becomes no trouble at all.

The several tandoor-roasted entrees have flavors unlike those I know from other Indian restaurants, even though entree names may have some similarities. For example, *barah kabab* has no resemblance to traditional kebab cooking, except that meat is in indivdual chunks. In this case, the meat is lamb, coated with a thick paste of seasonings and spices, and roasted to perfection in the tandoor. This is the kind of meat you want to nibble on right down to the very bones. Or try *murgh malai kabab*, which uses boned chicken that has been marinated in ginger and coriander, with a liberal addition of garlic. The flavors marry deliciously. Also a chicken entree, the house named *tandoori murgh bukhara* has an entirely different, more simple flavor that emphasizes the natual goodness of the chicken itself.

BUONA FORTUNA CAFÉ
KR 18/20
Decor 4/4   Hospitality 5/5   Food 8/10   Value 1/1

- **Italian**
- **Chicago/Near Northwest**
- **$$**

1540 North Milwaukee Avenue
Chicago
(773) 278-7797
Troubleshooter: Mario Szpark
(manager)

Hours: Mon–Thurs 5–10 pm, Fri–Sat 5–11:30 pm, closed Sun
Credit Cards: All majors except Discover
Reservations: Accepted
Handicapped: Accessible
Bar: Wine list is exclusively Italian, with heavier emphasis on reds
Smoking and nonsmoking sections: Both available
Parking: Valet or street when available

Buona Fortuna is an unpretentious neighborhood restaurant and it is worth leaving your neighborhood to visit it. The food is imaginative, without contrivance. Something as basic as *carpaccio*, paper-thin slices of filet mignon, are served traditionally with a drizzle of olive oil, a course grating of parmesan cheese, plus lemons, mushrooms and capers. Bruschetta, at three slices to the order is a bit overpriced, but tasty enough with its topping of crushed tomato, basil and oil. Traditional polenta with a side of sautéed mushrooms, fried or grilled calamari in balsamic vinegar, asparagus and eggs with lemons and olive oil round out the first course selections.

One could take an à la carte salad at this point, before moving on to pastas or entrees. Pasta courses are substantial enough to enjoy as an entree. The restaurant was willing to accommodate some of our special requests without difficulty.

One of the tastiest dishes may be pasta with anchovy sauce. In this recipe, the anchovies are evidently cut into small pieces and cooked down in olive oil until they are all but disintegrated. Fresh bread crumbs are added to the mix. The result is a delicious and well textured sauce that clings to each strand of noodle, a sauce not nearly so salty as the primary ingredient of anchovies might suggest.

More substantive for a main course would be a pasta with seafood. Though the menu says shrimp and broccoli are served in a cream sauce, we asked for something without cream. Marinara was substituted and worked beautifully. Another option could be pasta with a mix of seafood. Among the pastas offered, gnocchi is plated with porcini mushrooms, asparagus and peas in a cream and tomato sauce. Angel hair pasta comes with herbs, grated parmesan cheese and a light tomato sauce, while mostaciolli is matched with sauteed peppers and oil.

Several meat, poultry and seafood selections round out the menu, which, though fairly short when matched to some Italian restaurants, offers diversity enough without resorting to dining clichés.

THE BUTCHER SHOP
KR 18/20
Decor 4/4   Hospitality 5/5   Food 8/10   Value 1/1

- **American**
- **Chicago/Near North**
- **$$**

358 West Ontario
Chicago
(312) 440-4900
Troubleshooter: Al Watkins
(manager)

Hours: Sun 5–9 pm, Mon–Thurs 5–10 pm, Fri–Sat 5–11 pm
Credit Cards: All majors
Reservations: Accepted
Handicapped: Accessible
Bar: Full bar with wine list heavy on California Cabernets, some imports
Smoking and nonsmoking sections: Both available
Parking: Valet

For the ultimate in do-it-yourself dining, spend an evening at The Butcher Shop, where you probably will be doing the grilling yourself. The steaks are choice grade, and vary in cost depending on their size. You'll pay a couple of bucks more if the restaurant's chefs do the cooking for you.

But, going to the grill is half the fun. Working at a hickory charcoal pit, you'll have a full array of spices and seasonings to put on your steak, and of course, the utensils needed to do the grilling. Chances are you'll strike up a conversation with other people who have the same thing on their minds as do you . . . namely, how good that steak is going to taste after 20 minutes or so over the coals. And, if you should have a problem, either your waiter or one of the grillmen will be there to help. All dinners come with a handsome salad and baked or au gratin potato.

There are a couple of other dinner choices on the menu beside the steak. Marinated chicken brings two boneless breasts that are grilled over charcoal at market price. Lamb chops are a recent addition, while fresh fish, which can vary from day to day depending upon availability, is also priced at market.

Desserts are typically All-American, and include apple pie hot from the oven, or tangy cheesecake.

CAFE ABSINTHE
KR 17.75/20
Decor 3.5/4   Hospitality 4.5/5   Food 9/10   Value .75/1

- **American Eclectic**
- **Chicago/Northwest**
- **$$$**

1954 West North Avenue
Chicago
(773) 278-4488
Troubleshooter: Gene Welch
(manager)

Hours: Sun 5:30–9 pm,
Mon–Thurs 5:30–10 pm, Fri–Sat
5:30–11 pm
Credit Cards: Visa, MC, Diners,
Amex
Reservations: Recommended
Handicapped: Accessible
Bar: Full service
**Smoking and nonsmoking
sections:** Both available
Parking: Complimentary valet

I guess there is something to be said for a restaurant that you enter from an alley. Of course, there is valet parking to smooth the way at Cafe Absinthe. This Bucktown brasserie brings the uptown crowd downtown.

In the old days, this would be called "slumming," a not very PC term today. And, in fact, with the gentrification of the Bucktown/Wicker Park/Ukrainian Village area, Cafe Absinthe fits right in. The restaurant is housed in a rather deep room with an open kitchen all the way back. One wall expanse is bare brick, pretty much left to itself. The other is embellished with cloth panels and swag curtains. Starched white table cloths are topped with butcher's paper.

These sort of signals really do not prepare a proper expectation for the Cafe Absinthe brand of cooking. It is contemporary, without shock, imaginative without contrivance. The menu changes daily, so what we tasted may or may not be served when you visit.

Among appetizers, gravlox is cured with pernod, a safe replacement for the restaurant's namesake beverage, banned for most of this century from the United States. Among hot appetizers, goat cheese was wrapped and baked in a delicate puff pastry at rest in a sweet fig compote. Hardly anything is more sybaritic than figs, which were well used in this creation. Other selections from the appetizer board might include scallops sautéed with vegetables, a house country paté traditionally presented with cornichons, and not so traditionally with marinated apricots.

Entrees are similarly inspired. A black angus strip steak might be given a mushroom and roquefort cheese sauce instead of the usual red wine demi glace. Free range chicken is said to be a specialty of the house, and deservedly so. I tasted it with caramelized onions and a lemon, garlic and mustard rub. Even with the skin stripped away for calories' sake, it remained delicious, almost succulent.

Venison is given hearty treatment, seared to your taste, then plated with acorn squash garnished by snow peas. Added to the platter is a sweet potato purée and a rather fruity wheatberry sauce.

From a selection of seafood, yellowfin tuna might be grilled and served with small rock shrimp and red pepper coulis. Roasted salmon has been accompanied by sautéed escarole whose slight tart accent sets off against the fish. Wholewheat crepes are stuffed like blini, not with sour cream or caviar, but with a mix of leeks, nuts and cheese as binder.

As dressy as the food and its presentation is, Cafe Absinthe is the sort of place where patrons are seen in everything from t-shirts and jeans to double breasted business suits.

CAFE BA-BA-REEBA
KR 20/20
Decor 4/4   Hospitality 5/5   Food 10/10   Value 1/1

- **Spanish Tapas**
- **Chicago Mid-North**
- **$$**

2024 North Halsted
Chicago
(773) 935-5000
Troubleshooter: Manager on duty

Hours: Lunch Tues–Fri 11:30 am–2:30 pm, Sat 11:30 am–3 pm (closed for Lunch during January and February), Dinner Mon–Fri 5:30–11 pm, Sat 5 pm–midnight, Sun noon–10 pm
Credit Cards: All majors
Bar: Full service features over 50 Wines, with special emphasis on Spanish varietals
Reservations: Taken at lunch, with limited reservations for dinner; none accepted for outdoor patio dining
Handicapped: Accessible
Smoking and nonsmoking sections: Both available
Parking: Valet at night

Tapas are Spanish appetizers, but there is hardly a way to describe their variety until you taste them. Created from meats, seafood, cheeses and vegetables, many tapas can be sampled to create a complete meal. The idea is to build as you go along, following individual tastes and appetite.

Although the idea behind Tapas dining involves small tastes of many different foods, you still might want to try an entree. The clincher is *paella*, a classic Spanish casserole that combines chicken, Spanish sausage, mussels and shrimp with saffron and baked rice. It's a splendid treat!

Desserts range from a stylized Spanish version of Italy's *tiramisu* called *bizochco birracho*, to homemade ice creams plus chocolate hazelnut cake, baked bananas in a thick caramel sauce, paoached pear, warm apple cobbler and, of course, traditional Spanish *flan*.

CAFÉ BOLERO
KR 18/20
Decor 3/4   Hospitality 4.5/5   Food 9.5/10   Value 1/1

- **Cuban**
- **Chicago/North**
- **$$**

2252 North Western Avenue
Chicago
(773) 227-9000
Troubleshooter: Juan Gonzales
(owner)

Hours: Daily 11 am–11 pm
Credit Cards: All majors
Reservations: Recommended
Smoking and nonsmoking sections: Separate nonsmoking area
Handicapped: Accessible
Parking: Street or lot across the street

For a different twist on Latin American dining one of the best spots in town has to be Café Bolero. There's nothing especially fancy about this Cuban restaurant, but it is cozy and comfortable. Dining can be as simple as a roasted pork sandwich and as elaborate as a fine *Paella Valencia*.

The Paella is truly extraordinary, and requires anywhere from 45 minutes to an hour for its custom preparation. Be sure to order it at the same time you do drinks and appetizers. It is well worth the wait. The rice is simmered ever so slowly in a chicken broth. Saffron is a primary seasoning, adding a bright yellow color as well as its unmistakable flavor. As the rice absorbs the liquid it begins to plump and becomes chewy. Somewhere along the way, fresh seafood, primarily shell fish including shrimp, mussels and a small lobster are brought into play to steam along with the other ingredients. There are a variety of seasonings that can be added depending upon the preference of the chef in any given preparation. That at Café Bolero is spectacularly delicious. It is presented in a deep pan, mounds of yellow rice topped with an abundance of seafood and chicken. This is easily one of the best versions of Paella I have had, and I cannot praise it too highly.

There are so many other delicious selections to be had at Café Bolero. Begin with some tapas appetizers such as fried plantain, similar to bananas but without the characteristic sweetness. Be sure to order black beans, which is a Cuban national dish. The beans are simmered in a thick sauce, and taste sweeter than one might expect of beans.

Try an empanada, a half moon shaped pastry filled with ground beef or chicken pieces. A stuffed tortilla is kind of like a Cuban stacked omelet, while steamed mussels in white wine sauce remind diners of Cuba's European culinary heritage.

While Paella would always be my first dinner choice at Café Bolero, there are other worthy contenders. Cut up chicken pieces with rice is another national classic. There are several beef entrees, including a grilled Cuban style steak with onions, and a simple, but flavorful strip steak. Whole red snapper often leads the list of fresh fish, in this case deep fried, rather than grilled or broiled. There are plenty of vegetarian selections. Desserts include fresh tropical Caribbean fruits and Spanish flan.

Service is fine, in a restaurant that brings a sense of the exotic to its little corner of Chicago.

CAFE CENTRAL
KR 18/20

Decor 4/4   Hospitality 4/5   Food 9/10   Value 1/1

---

* **French**
* **Highland Park**
* **$$**

455 Central Avenue
Highland Park
(847) 266-7878
Troubleshooters: Jeff
Sassorossi (manager) or Carlos
and Debbie Nieto (owners)

Hours: Lunch Mon–Fri 11:30 am–2:30 pm, Dinner Mon–Sun 5 pm until last customer
Credit Cards: All majors
Reservations: No
Handicapped: Accessible
Smoking and nonsmoking sections: No smoking
Parking: On street, can be tight weekends
Party Facilities: Private party space available Sat and Sun afternoons for 10–70 people

---

Cafe Central has a period ambiance with mustard colored walls, mirrors with dark wood-finished frames, café lamps and curtains, a bar to the rear with a few stools for patrons, and smallish, rather close together tables that almost seem to encourage discussion among neighbors.

The menu is classic bistro, including standards such as snails in garlic and Pernod butter, country paté with mustard and cornichons, and French onion soup with croutons and a blanket of melted Swiss cheese. But, there are some innovations in keeping with the idea that a bistro should offer some regional preparations, too. A recent potato and leek soup was demonstrative of that, a creamy broth with full potato flavor, simple but delicious. A round of eggplant, in another presentation, is stuffed with creamed goat cheese, and though meant to be eaten with a fork, could almost be spread on warm French bread slices.

Among other appetizers, mussels are sweet and plump, bathed in a liquid touched with beer, seasoned with shallots and garlic. Smoked salmon is served with traditional accompaniment among a selection of other appetizers.

Traditional bistro selections lead the entree menu, along with some extensions of the concept. A recent risotto of the day was infused with field mushrooms. In a courageous decision, we were told that if the risotto were made as we asked with olive oil instead of butter and less cheese, it would destroy the concept. We ordered it with a sense of all things in moderation. Each grain of rice was chewy, the entire conception full-flavored and rich.

Roast chicken is presented as an example of comfort food at its best, with a side of mashed potatoes topped with a ribbon of crushed garlic cloves. Duck legs are prepared as a confit, given a honeyed sauce and wild rice on the side. Sautéed calf's liver, braised lamb shank, and the classic rib-eye steak and *pomme frites* add their own dimension. Salmon was recently served as a daily special, bedded on lentils. Another presentation brought seabass with a bouquet of vegetables in a delicately flavored stock broth.

CAFE MATOU
KR 19/20
Decor 4/4   Hospitality 5/5   Food 9/10   Value 1/1

- **French Bistro**
- **Chicago**
- **$$**

1846 North Milwaukee Avenue
Chicago
(773) 384-8911
Troubleshooter: Charlie Socher (owner)

Hours: Tues–Thurs 5–10 pm, Fri–Sat 5–11 pm, Sun 5–9 pm, closed Mon
Credit Cards: All majors
Reservations: Recommended
Smoking and nonsmoking sections: Both available
Handicapped: Accessible
Parking: Ample street parking

Depending on the numerous lots of boarded-up buildings on your way to Cafe Matou. Chef and Owner Charlie Socher likes to think of it as an "eccentric American neighborhood." That's as good a description as any.

Suffice to say that Cafe Matou is kind of an oasis in the midst of Bucktown, on the fringe. It has the contemporary look of bleached hardwood floor, expanses of whitewashed walls, and an eclectic collection of contemporary art, the sort of stuff that dares you to guess what it's supposed to be.

For all the *avant gardism*, Socher's menu and cooking are decidedly French bistro. The menu is studded with the familiar for those who know what bistro dining should be. Mussels in white wine, lemon and shallots with garlic and parsley, get a tang of embellishment from crushed black peppercorns, a selection of *pâtés* comes in traditional arrangement with cornichons, toast points and dijon mustard as part of the garnish. Things get a bit more daring with an appetizer of grilled chicken wings, which, thankfully, are not another version of buffalo chicken wings. The inspiration, says the menu, comes from the South of France. Each wing, or tiny leg is coated with crushed chili peppers, not so much as to shock, thanks to a touch of coriander. Tomato *concasse*, kind of the French version of salsa, and a light mustard mayonnaise or *aioli* completes the platter. Among other appetizers, grilled eggplant is strictly for eggplant lovers. Baked goat cheese, sitting like a snowy island in a red sea of tomato marinara–style sauce is great when scooped up with ragged slices of crusty bread.

Salads and soup are à la carte and lead into the main course choices. Butt steak is quite tasty thanks to a crush of black peppercorns, while a recent special rib eye got the full beefsteak *au poivre* treatment. Black peppercorns also show up in an order of roasted pork chops, thick and meaty, sauced with fresh rosemary and orange zest left to mellow in the pan juices. For seafood, the menu regularly features poached salmon with a touch of horseradish sauce and chopped mushrooms. Even better was a recent special presentation of mahi mahi with a white wine sauce and a vegetable *concasse*. Meanwhile, whitefish was raised well out of the ordinary by a mustard glaze. Other entrees regularly include a simple chicken grilled and plated with a collection of herbs and garlic confit, lamb shank, made savory with cloves, lemon zest and anchovies among its ingredients, and for vegetarians a melange of vegetables atop couscous.

Service is as Gallic as the food, the wine list exceptionally reasonable in cost.

CAFE PYRENEES
KR 19/20

Decor 3.5/4   Hospitality 5/5   Food 9.5/10   Value 1/1

- **French**
- **Vernon Hills**
- **$$**

701 North Milwaukee Avenue (facing Route 60 in Rivertree Court Shopping Center, East of Milwaukee Avenue)
Vernon Hills
(847) 918-8850
Troubleshooters: Chef Marc Loustaunau, Marie Loustaunau (hostess)

Hours: Lunch Tues–Fri 11:30 am–2:30 pm, Dinner Mon–Fri 5:30–9:30 pm, Sat 5–10 pm, closed Sun–Mon
Credit Cards: All majors
Reservations: Recommended
Handicapped: Accessible
Smoking and nonsmoking sections: Both available
Parking: Ample free parking in shopping mall lot

This family team operation has been around for a decade or so. While the chef works the stoves out of sight, his wife, often wearing a floral print dress greets and seats diners, and even some of the wait staff have been along from the beginning, or near it.

If one trait seems evident from the chef's cooking, it is his well-balanced taste for seasonings. One is not likely to be surprised by the pronounced taste of one herb over another, no sharp taste of salt, except that which underlies everything else in a given recipe. French onion soup, a classic of bistro and café dining, is a beautiful example. The stock leaves a light peppered burn on the palate, but in keeping with the overall style of cooking at Cafe Pyrenees, nothing assaults or up-sets the senses. The taste of cooked onion is at the center, a complex burst of esters, which, like fine wine, becomes apparent even after a spoonful of soup is sent down the gullet. A light blanket of cheese and crouton holds in heat and flavors as the soup is transported from kitchen to dining room.

This sense of balance exists in other appetizers. Mushroom ravioli comes on a bed of spinach in a reduced mushroom sauce that brings together the woodsy complexity of field mushrooms, chewy, dark, suggestive of a long nap within the confines of a great forest. Before you think I grow too romantic about this or other dining experiences, keep in mind that this is all a part of it, to allow the senses to overflow, to allow the imagination to be stimulated. Dining is, above all else, a romantic experience.

A similar encounter might come from a cassoulet which brings together snails and mushrooms, but in a garlic and butter sauce akin to traditional escargots. Among other choices, diners can pick from a blend of crab and lobster meat in a curiously intriguing ginger and grapefruit sauce. In another appetizer, goat cheese might be wrapped in strudel dough along with diced apples in a fruity sweet and sour sauce.

Dinners include a mixed green salad and vegetables. The Chef practices restraint in all things, including vegetables, which arrive unadorned and unseasoned so that only their natural flavor is presented.

Each evening will include Chef's Specials as recited and described by a server. The printed menu rotates periodically. Recently, grilled Norwegian salmon was plated atop lightly salted barley risotto and a pinot noir reduction as sauce. Barley is firm by nature, and presents an appropriate texture contrast to the fish. Norwegian salmon, to my taste, is the mildest of the species and gets the proper cooking time and presentation.

Among other entrees, whitefish is plated with spinach ravioli, or shrimp and scallop raviolis are set in a pool of basil sauce. There are some café classics on the short list of entrees, including Calves' Liver Lyonnaise with grilled onions and apples in balsamic vinegar, or a simple New York strip steak in your choice of bordelaise or roquefort sauce. There is no bearnaise sauce offered as an option, surprising considering the chef's roots.

Desserts include a tempting choice of pastries, chocolates and tarts, as well as fresh fruits, ice creams and sorbet.

CAFE STEFANO
KR 19/20
Decor 4/4   Hospitality 5/5   Food 9/9   Value 1/1

- **Italian**
- **Palatine**
- **$$**

2275 Rand Road
Palatine
(847) 359-6220
Troubleshooter: Stefano Panozzo (chef/owner)

Hours: Lunch Mon–Fri 11:30 am–2 pm, Dinner Sun–Thurs 5–10 pm, Fri–Sat until 11 pm
Credit Cards: All majors
Reservations: Suggested
Handicapped: Accessible
Smoking and nonsmoking sections: Small smokers' section week days, only at bar on weekends
Parking: Free in restaurant lot

I do not wish to overstate the obvious, but I believe that restaurants are defined as much by the personality of their owners as they are by their food. Cafe Stefano is a perfect example. Stefano Panozzo is the sort of owner who thinks nothing of pushing over a bar stool and sitting down at the table of diners with whom he has developed a rapport. If he isn't sitting, Panozzo is working the dining room, stopping to chat and talk with people he recognizes, or first-timers such as our party. He is a gregarious, outgoing sort of a teddy bear whose warmth is infectious.

Panozzo is his restaurant's head chef, but while he is out in the dining room it is evident that his supporting kitchen staff knows their work well. The menu is part traditional Italian and part family recipes. Some selections are personal variations using the core ingredients of good cooking.

Cavatappi alla Stefano serves as a prime example. *Cavatappi* is a small corkscrew-shaped noodle whose many surfaces are ideal for a clinging sauce. In this case it is a lightly creamed, pink tomato sauce with sliced porcini mushrooms, thin spring asparagus tips and green fresh peas. What makes this work so well is that the sauce is not overdone, not overloaded.

The cooking is not necessarily trying to replicate the finesse of a Roman dining room. Rather, it is the country, or *campagnola*, as in *tortiglioni*, a tubular pasta plated with pieces of heady Italian sausage, mild *pancetta*, Italy's version of bacon, plus fennel seed cooked down into a tomato sauce to which some cream is added for texture. Fennel is a wonderful flavor addition to this particular recipe, with its light licorice-like accent.

The country-style cooking continues with *brasato*, something which Panozzo will tell you is a family style recipe bringing together braised beef brisket plated with garlic mashed potatoes. It sounds like the sort of dinner that could be a blue plate special in most any American diner or road house.

A brief overview of the rest of the menu reveals some tempting come back choices. Chilean sea bass is grilled and served in a roasted garlic and tomato sauce. Swordfish stands up well to a vesuvio presentation with lots of garlic in a white wine sauce with peas and a side of oven-roasted potatoes. Orange roughy is given a more delicate treatment akin to a *picatta*, thanks to a white wine, caper and lemon sauce.

There are a dozen pasta selections on the printed menu, plus a nightly special or two. Many can be had in half-order portions which gives diners an opportunity to taste more than they otherwise might. Incidentally, you'll have to ask about the half portions; there is no designation on the menu.

The desserts are made in the restaurant, not by any outside purveyor, always a good sign. They include standards such as *tiramisu* and Italian custard, called *panna cotta* as well as a couple of surprises. Incidentally, Chef Panozzo is a rather talented artist in a direction other than cooking. Most, if not all of the paintings showcased around the dining room are by his own hand. It's another personal touch in a restaurant whose personality is a great part of its charm and warmth.

CALIFORNIA CAFE
KR 16.5/20
Decor 4/4   Hospitality 4/5   Food 7.5/10   Value 1/1

- **American California Style**
- **Schaumburg**
- **$$**

Southwest Section of
Woodfield Mall
Schaumburg
(847)-330-1212
Troubleshooter: Mike Jurtenes
(manager)

Hours: Lunch Mon–Sat 11:30 am–4 pm, Dinner Mon–Thurs 5–10 pm, Fri–Sat 5–10:30 pm, Sun 4:30–8:30 pm, Brunch Sun 11 am–3:30 pm
Credit Cards: All majors
Reservations: Recommended
Handicapped: Accessible
Smoking and nonsmoking sections: Both available
Parking: Complimentary valet

There are fewer and fewer reasons for suburban diners to drive into the city for a city-style restaurant. This is certainly true for those diners who have found and are enjoying California Cafe, on the southwest side of Woodfield Mall in Schaumburg. This is not a perfect restaurant, and in fact is a little heavy-handed with some of its presentations. But, overall, the food is tasty and the stylized creativity is evident.

To make a choice of appetizer easier for your party of two to four people, a *menage à trois*, as it is called, brings a wire rack which stacks three platters. One holds some very good tuna sashimi with a Chinese five spice flavor and a Vietnamese vegetable roll. For the middle level, the Asian influence continues with mild-tasting duck-filled spring rolls in a light rice paper wrap with poblano chili sauce and prickly pear vinaigrette for a little bite. The bottom platter, and best of the three, holds a pair of crab cakes garnished with a Southwestern-style black bean and corn salsa with honey and chipotle vinaigrette.

Other appetizer selections from the à la carte menu range from fried calamari presented in a large edible basket with tiny rock shrimp, smoked salmon with rock shrimp and noodles, mussels in a coconut and red curry broth and a head of roasted garlic astride tomato chutney. Portions tend to be large, so a very good Caesar salad can easily be shared among three or four diners without anyone lacking a thing.

Entrees lean toward the showy stacked look. Lamb shanks in a red wine *au jus* infused with rosemary is excellent. It comes on a bed of mushrooms and barley and a side of baby carrots. From among seafood selections, halibut is crusted with the crab meat filling used for the California Cafe crab cakes. Yukon gold potato slices, zucchini and tomato relish and an orange and ginger mustard sauce completes the presentation.

Our server's recommendation of garlic roasted chicken rubbed with thyme proved right on the mark. The only disappointment among four entrees tasted recently was an order of lemon-parsley risotto, serving as the centerpiece for large sea scallops, small rock shrimp, plump mussels and grilled vegetables. The simple fact is that lemon and parsley flavors do not marry well for good risotto.

As would be expected of a California theme restaurant, there is a good, and reasonably priced wine list. Desserts lean toward the extravagant. Service is a little slipshod, particularly on the part of back up staff who need to be reminded of diners' needs.

CALITERRA
KR 18/20
Decor 4/4   Hospitality 4/5   Food 9/10   Value 1/1

- **California Italian**
- **Chicago/Near North**
- **$$**

633 North St. Clair (in the Wyndham Hotel)
Chicago
(312) 274-4444
Troubleshooter: Tony Cavalo

Hours: Breakfast to Dinner 6:30 am–11 pm, Lounge 11–1:30 am
Credit Cards: All majors
Reservations: Suggested
Handicapped: Accessible
Smoking and nonsmoking sections: Both available
Parking: Valet at hotel entrance

I think that going to a good hotel restaurant is a little like being on vacation. That's one of the reasons it is worth searching out and finding Caliterra.

Try deliciously unusual Shrimp "cigars," chunks of shrimp in a deep-fried spring roll wrapping with fruity mustard sauce and a bit of course cut fresh cole slaw. A balsamic reduction adds to the flavors. You also might want to sample the diver sea scallops with a tasty carrot and ginger oil emulsion and peppery chili oil as part of the parade of flavors. If you like something a bit more simple and to the point, tuna tartare is a good choice, set like a timbale with avocado, cucumber and caviar working as a binder of sorts.

The menu lists only a trio of pastas, which is fine with me. That makes way for the entree specialties. Among them, is lamb loin plated with a stylized risotto that uses barley instead of rice, and perfectly sautéed *chanterelles* on the side. From among seafood selections, halibut baked in a dried porcini mushroom crust is set in a light zucchini-infused broth and a side of vegetables in the Italian style of peppery "*gardiniera*."

Because this is a hotel restaurant, the kitchen has to do double duty with room service. Couple that with a busy dining room and one or two larger parties over and above the usual deuces and four tops and things can get stacked up like O'Hare on a snowy afternoon. So, if time is an issue when you make your reservations, you might want to point that out.

CAMPAGNOLA
KR 16/20
Decor 4/4   Hospitality 3.5/5   Food 7.5/10   Value 1/1

- **Italian**
- **Evanston**
- **$$**

815 Chicago Avenue
Evanston
(847) 475-6100
Troubleshooter: Michael
Altenberg (chef/co-owner)

Hours: Tues–Fri Lunch 11:30 am–2 pm, Dinner Tues–Thurs 5:30–9:30 pm, Fri–Sat until 10:30 pm, Sun 5–9:30 pm
Credit Cards: Visa, MC, Discover
Handicapped: Accessible
Smoking and nonsmoking sections: No smoking
Parking: On street, can be tight

There are no farms in Evanston these days, except for Campagnola, whose name in Italian means "farm." The restaurant's decor is more urban chic than bucolic. Expanses of bare brick wall and hardwood floors frame diners in a rather deep room. In warm weather, an outdoor patio is tucked between neighboring buildings.

The menu offers a collection of preparations, some classic in their simplicity, others more sophisticated than the "country" theme literally suggests. Several first course starters and pizzas should please a variety of tastes. Portions are generally large enough to share, and in fact "family style" dining, as the menu puts it, is encouraged.

The pizzas range from a *margherita* with its topping of fresh tomatoes, basil and mozzarella cheese to more ornate and elaborate compositions. In the *Campagna Pizza*, roasted potatoes are bedded down with caramelized onion and fresh rosemary sprigs beneath a blanket of goat cheese. Like all the pizzas, the crust is bubbly and crisp.

Though pasta is a separate course in Italy and prelude to meat or seafood, Campagnola follows the tastes of American diners who prefer pasta as their main course. Of course, you could share a pasta or two, depending upon the number of people at your table, then go on to share the next course, too.

While cream sauces are frowned on by the diet police, there remains something very enticing about hay and straw pasta, its pale colors bathed in a cream sauce binding together bright green snap peas, pink-tinged proscuitto and the herbal underpinnings of sage. In another selection, pillows of ravioli are stuffed with a forcemeat, tossed in butter flavored with marjoram, then topped with shavings of hard parmesan cheese. But, if dietary prudence dictates a dining choice, delicate strands of cappellini topped with grilled prawns splashed in a tomato sauce infused with basil is a good selection.

For a following course, there are several selections at hand. Grilled salmon is plated with barley and roasted vegetables, while striped bass is given a light saffron and garlic broth plus small green lentils and tomato. Among other selections, roasted chicken with a hint of thyme comes atop a version of Tuscan bread salad. In this case, the cubes of bread were nicely toasted, but larger than bite size. Otherwise, the salad benefitted from a nicely acidic vinaigrette dressing.

Desserts include the usual roundup of Italian sweets. The wine list is appropriate to the menu in depth and cost. Service is good, but can be less attentive if a server is covering too many tables.

CAPE COD ROOM
KR 19/20
Decor 4/4   Hospitality 5/5   Food 9/10   Value 1/1

- **American Seafood**
- **Chicago/Near North**
- **$$$**

140 East Walton Place
(The Drake Hotel)
Chicago
(312) 787-2200
Troubleshooter: Patrick Bredin
(manager)

Hours: Daily noon–11 pm
Credit Cards: All majors, house accounts
Reservations: Mandatory
Handicapped: Accessible
Bar: Extensive wine list, many by the glass, cocktails, etc.
Smoking and nonsmoking sections: Both available
Parking: Valet
Dress: Jackets required for gentlemen

For all the intervening years since The Cape Cod Room opened in 1933, it has been one of Chicago's most well-known destination restaurants. Its name has been synonymous with the finest seafood in all those years. The red-checked tablecloths, stuffed mounted sailfish, the weather vanes, exposed wood beams and nautical decor set the stage. Though space is at a premium at the tiny nine-seat oyster bar, the restaurant becomes more expansive as you move into the dining areas.

This is a restaurant which rest heavily on tradition. Much of the menu, excluding the inevitably higher prices, remains as it has for decades. Who could go and not order the Bookbinder Soup? It is one of the few seafood specialty houses still serving lobster newburg or thermidor. But, its bouillabaisse is as contemporary as any, cajun swordfish will attract contemporary diners, and the Dover sole is among the finest. In fact, while the Cape Cod Room may look, and even feel, like part of the past, its seafood is as fresh as a light breeze on the morning tide.

THE CAPITAL GRILLE
KR 17.25/20
Decor 3/4   Hospitality 4.5/5   Food 9/10   Value .75/1

• **American**	**Hours:** Lunch Mon–Fri 11:30 am–2:30 pm, Dinner Sun–Thurs 5–10 pm, Fri–Sat until 11 pm
• **Chicago**	
• **$$$**	**Credit Cards:** All Majors
633 North St. Claire Street	**Reservations:** Recommended
Chicago	**Handicapped:** Accessible
(312)-337-9400	**Smoking and nonsmoking**
Troubleshooter: Gary Gueites	**sections:** Both available
(manager)	**Parking:** Valet $7

If The Capital Grille were not as good as it is, this would be a very pretentious restaurant. It's a place heavy with what is meant to look like old wood panels and molding, patterned carpeting (the kind that speaks of old money), and just so no one misses the point, most open wall space has an oil painting of some long gone robber baron or turn of the century tycoon.

In short, the message is power dining on steaks, lobster, and other cuts of meat and seafood. Service is a lot of bowing and scraping, but extremely knowledgeable. When I asked about a good cabernet sauvignon by the glass, our server demurred, suggesting no such animal existed. Either he was being honest, or trying to push our party into popping for a full bottle.

Once you have checked your bank balance and made sure you are not too close to your credit card max-out, it's time to begin ordering some food. Nothing is going to surprise or suggest cutting edge cookery. To get started, try lobster and crab cakes, really in a portion large enough to make an adequate sized entree for most people. Two cakes are plated with appropriate garnishes and, while expensive, you do get your money's worth. These crab cakes are mostly lobster and crab with only enough filler to bind things together so they don't fall apart. Among other first course choices the selection runs from a serving of beluga caviar for big spenders or, when you want to impress your date, to shrimp cocktail which brings five large prawns to the table, as well as clams and oysters on the half-shell and a bevy of other extravagant tidbits.

Soup and salad courses are à la carte, but you really didn't expect otherwise, did you? The Caesar is everything this salad should be, while the onion soup is served in a deep two-handled cup with a rich layer of cheese over a deeply flavored soup broth.

For entrees, steaks and chops are the real heart of the matter. The filet I tasted was genuinely excellent, cooked medium with a light pink center as I had requested. In fact, the steaks here are so good, it would be a mistake to use any sort of steak sauce. Cuts and portions range from a ten-ounce filet mignon, up to a 24 ounce porterhouse. Lobsters range in size from 2 to 5 pounds and are priced at market. As for fresh seafood, the choices are impressive, and include blackened tuna with a New Orleans–style remoulade sauce, grilled swordfish which is the next best thing to eating meat without eating meat, grilled Norwegian salmon, which to my taste beats Pacific salmon without even raising a sweat, and giant shrimp scampi that make you wonder why they even call them "shrimp."

The menu's signature dish is a veal chop with roquefort butter sauce, but even without the sauce, this is prodigious eating. The pork chop comes in a double-cut portion, as do the lamb chops. Side dishes are similarly prodigious and include a one-pound baked potato as well as a towering plate of cottage fries and fried onions. Roasted mushrooms in wine sauce are a little salty; a platter of seasonal vegetables is likely to please strict vegetarians who are otherwise wondering what they are doing in The Capital Grille in the first place. As for desserts a classic *crème brûlée* is tempting.

CARLOS'
KR 20/20
Decor 4/4   Hospitality 5/5   Food 10/10   Value 1/1

• **French**	**Hours:** Sun–Mon, Wed–Fri 5–9 pm, Sat 5–9:45 pm, closed Tues
• **Highland Park**	**Credit Cards:** All majors
• $$$	**Reservations:** Required
429 Temple Avenue	**Handicapped:** Accessible with assistance up two entrance way steps
Highland Park	
(847) 432-0770	
Troubleshooters: Carlos Nieto, Deborah Nieto (owners)	**Smoking and nonsmoking sections:** No Smoking
	Parking: Free valet

In its nearly two decades, Carlos' has had at least seven chefs. That's not unusual in the restaurant business. But, Carlos' has managed a continuity thanks to hard work and perserverance. Yet, there is a sense of whimsy. The food and dining is a serious culinary endevour, but there is no pomposity, no posturing nor pretense by the restaurant's staff.

These days, a lighter, more contemporary French food is being prepared for diners at Carlos', with embellishments that do honor to the main course selections. Consider an entree which brings together lobster, Manila clams and mussels set in a saffron seasoned seafood broth reduced almost to something between liquid and glaze. Baby vegetables add color and texture to the setting. The saffron is not so strong as to overpower the light and delicate flavors of the three shellfish which are at the heart of the composition. The portion is sensible, not overwhelming.

That is the way of all flesh and seafood at Carlos'. Still, one does not leave with a sense of undernourishment, to be sure. Venison loin is grilled and set out in its own *au jus*, intensified with a red wine reduction, but softened at the same moment with the juice squeezed from parsley.

Among other meats, filet mignon is set on a sauce combining red wine and blue cheese, while a smattering of puffy dauphin potatoes is set to one side of the platter. The lily, or in this case, the filet, is gilded with an herb crust, hardly noticed in the presence of the blue cheese.

From a selection of fowl, grilled duck breast has been sliced and set upright, leaning together on a savoy cabbage and red onion cake bound with a confit of shallot. A delicious port wine and truffle emulsion is an embellishment, as is a small asparagus salad.

During our most recent visit, my willpower crumbled like a pastry crust in the face of three desert trays, each offering special treats from classic *crème brûlée* to *tarte tatin* to the symphony of chocolate ganache, truffles, mousses and more. In its time, Carlos' has had some valleys, but without valleys, there are no peaks. The restaurant is at the top of one now.

CARMINE'S

KR 17/20

Decor 4/4   Hospitality 4.5/5   Food 7.5/10   Value 1/1

- **Italian**
- **Chicago/Near North**
- **$$**

1043 North Rush Street
Chicago
(312) 988-7676
Troubleshooter: Benny Siddu
(general manager)

Hours: Lunch 11 am–3 pm,
Dinner Mon–Thurs 4–11 pm,
Fri–Sat 4 pm–12 midnight
(regular menu), Tues–Sat until
1:30 am (late night menu)
Credit Cards: All majors
Reservations: Recommended
Handicapped: Accessible with
elevator
Bar: Full service with jazz on
weekends 6:30 pm–1 am, piano
during the week
**Smoking and nonsmoking
sections:** Both available
Parking: Valet

I leaned back in my chair, took a deep breath and said to no one in particular, "I feel as if I had just eaten at a Roman orgy!" A companion quickly brought me back to reality. "This is Chicago," she said. "You're on Rush Street!"

Indeed I was, at Carmine's. The restaurant is on two levels. The first is a spacious bar and lounge; the serious eating goes on upstairs. To really get a taste of what is available, you should come with a larger party; six is about ideal. The menu presents a strong list of seafood appetizers ranging from ahi tuna carpaccio served with a spicy jalapeño pepper sauce to clams and oysters from the raw bar, to various combination fish salads.

You'll not go wrong by ordering the house specialty chopped salad. The menu says it is portioned for two. Actually, one order was enough for the six at my table, with some actually left over. It's a tasty mix of fresh greens, shrimp, artichoke, hearts of palm, mozzarella cheese and other goodies in a flavorful vinaigrette or peppercorn dressing that is so good you might want to mop up plate remainders with a hunk of foccacia or other breads served at each table.

The temptation at a restaurant like Carmine's is to over order. Though our waiter informed us that one salad would be enough, he did not prepare us for the humongous entrees. One for each person proved wasteful, except for that saved to take home.

Selections are mostly a win/win situation. Cavatelli with buds of garlic, spinach, roasted peppers and mushrooms is as good as it gets. These are lighter cavatelli, not the fat, chewy and dense kind one might expect.

Other pastas include traditional versions of spaghetti *carbonara* or fettuccine alfredo. The *zuppa di pesce* may seem traditional from the menu description, but I have never had anything like it elsewhere. Aside from the astounding portion, the selection of shellfish, finned fish and spaghetti was bathed in a sauce with a definite and flavorful nautical bite. The only flaw was soft-fish that may have been around the kitchen a little too long, like an unwelcome guest.

More successful was an order of seafood risotto, which can also be served with chicken. Carmine's namesake steak is a 14-ounce cut sirloin butt served with brine marinated peppers and roasted potatoes. The menu goes on and on, but if you have room for dessert, choose *tiramisu*; one portion feeds six.

CARSON'S
KR 18/20
Decor 4/4   Hospitality 4/5   Food 8/9   Value 2/2

- **American/Ribs/Steaks**
- **Chicago/Near North (and Suburbs)**
- **$$**

612 North Wells
Chicago
(312) 280-9200
Troubleshooter: Manager on duty
Other Locations
5970 North Ridge, Chicago; 773-271-4000
8617 Niles Center Road, Skokie; 773-675-6800
400 East Roosevelt Road, Lombard; 630-627-4300;
Private Party Facilities
5050 North Harlem Avenue, Harwood Heights (near O'Hare Airport); 708-867-4200
200 North Waukegan Road, Deerfield; 847-374-8500

Hours: Sun noon–11 pm, Mon–Thurs 11 am–midnight, Fri 11–1 am, Sat noon–1 am
Credit Cards: Amex, CB, Diners MC, Visa
Handicapped: Accessible
Smoking and nonsmoking sections: Both available
Parking: Valet

Say "ribs" in Chicago, and the automatic response from most people is Carson's. Though not everyone would agree that these are the very best ribs (a subject open to endless debate which will be foregone here), those at Carson's are certainly the best known.

The reason these ribs win such accolades is the sauce, a pungent, spicy sweet brew with a smokey aftertaste that rib lovers savor. The sauce's two stage preparation is part of the secret. In step one, a popular commercial base is doctored with as many as 8 spices and seasonings, plus a liberal helping of brown sugar. Then, this is slathered on the ribs, which are now slow baked in specially designed electric ovens. Essentially pre-cooked, the ribs are finished beneath the open flames of a gas broiler. Again, they are washed with more sauce, this time without the brown sugar to avoid burning.

In addition to the ribs, Carson's serves some of the best steaks around. They range from a 22-ounce New York cut sirloin to smaller cuts for lesser appetites. Dinners come with salad or slaw, potatoes in your choice of style and rolls with butter, making this one of the better bargains.

If you crave the barbecue flavors, but your taste does not run to ribs, order the whole roasted barbecued chicken.

Seafood is limited to orange roughy which is broiled.

CARZZ GRILLERIA
KR 19/20
Decor 4/4   Hospitality 5/5   Food 9/10   Value 1/1

- **American**
- **Naperville**
- **$$**

216 South Washington Street
Naperville
(630) 778-1944
Troubleshooter: Manager on duty

Hours: Lunch Mon–Fri 11:30 am–2:30 pm, Dinner Mon–Thurs 5:00 pm–9:30 pm, Fri–Sat 5–10:30 pm, Sun 4–8:30 pm
Credit Cards: All Majors
Reservations: Taken Fri and Sat only for parties of four or more
Handicapped: Accessible
Smoking and nonsmoking sections: Both available
Parking: In three story garage behind restaurant, or limited on street

Sometimes, if you listen closely, what seems like noise is actually music. I heard the music at Carzz Grilleria. When you listen closely, you too can hear the percussive sound of china and glass, the cymbals of silver on silver all painted against the high and low octaves of the human voice.

What does this have to do with dining, you might ask? Well, to me it suggests the pleasures of the table, sometimes a murmur, sometimes a loud tympanic crescendo. In the case of Carzz Grilleria, it means people are having a good time enjoying the good food. The word funky comes to mind.

The restaurant is decorated with a collection of wine posters, neon tubed accents and banquettes in tropical pastels. The menu leans toward New Orleans, though inexplicably an occasional Hawaiian influence is found. Sometimes, they are even combined, as in a recent special of mahi mahi, a Pacific fish, treated to the spice and pepper of blackening. Yellow fin tuna gets similar treatment and is a regular menu presentation, plated with nova lox cured with tequila, a mound of herbed rice, known as dirty rice in less refined circles, and a julienne of fresh sauteed peppers, zucchini and carrots.

In the case of another menu selection, amberjack, this one fished from the south Atlantic, blackening again is at the heart of the preparation. Amberjack is a meaty fish and stands up well in combination with a shrimp salsa, plated with light green parsley linguine infused with enough garlic to make taste buds snap to attention. A side of veggies completes the colorful plating.

Not all seafood is blackened. Salmon is grilled, and given an unusual accompaniment of green grapes and mangos brought together in a course concasse, or as the menu calls it, a relish. Like everything else we tasted, the flavors are bold, but not too overstated. Rather than suggest there is contrivance at work with these recipes, I accept it more as dauntless imagination on the part of the chef.

Other entrees on the menu are described with mouthwatering abandon. Just read of the cherry chicken, topped with dried cherry and currant sauce, or even better, nut-crusted chicken. In this case, breasts are rolled in an assortment of fine chopped nuts, basted with barbecue sauce and plated with O'Brian potatoes and a grilled banana. If that sounds yummy, consider cajun duck breast. This gets a topping of dried apricot and cabernet wine sauce. Sounds even yummier, doesn't it?

CATCH 35
KR 19.5/20
Decor 4/4   Hospitality 4.5/5   Food 10/10   Value 1/1

- **Asian Fusion Seafood**
- **Chicago/North Loop**
- **$$**

35 West Wacker Drive
Chicago
(312) 346-3500
Troubleshooter: Ross Olson
(co-owner)

Hours: Mon–Fri Lunch 11:30 am–2 pm, Dinner Mon–Sat 5–10 pm, Sun 5–9 pm, Brunch Sun 9:30 am–2 pm
Credit Cards: All majors
Reservations: Suggested
Handicapped: Accessible
Smoking and nonsmoking sections: Both available, cigars permitted in lounge
Parking: Valet in evenings, $7

Chances are you are not going to want a big, heavy dinner before your next evening of theater. Seafood at Catch 35 fits right in. In fact there is something almost theatrical about this excellent seafood house and its art deco ambiance. A large cocktail lounge, usually with a pianist on hand is just off the main entrance. The dining area is further back, terraced so that you go up a succession of levels to the one where you and your party will be seated.

The dining room is done up in copper and earth tones with large seafood murals which remind me of Depression-era public works art, except that instead of muscular workmen and the bridges they are building, these murals depict lobsters, crabs and other denizens of the briny deep.

Chef Eck Prukpitikul is from Thailand which explains the pan-Asian touches which stud the menu. It changes from day to day, so what you read about here may or may not be prepared exactly as described when you visit.

The fresh oysters and clams are clearly marked by type and availability on the printed menu for those who enjoy letting a few of the raw bivalves slide down the gullet, perhaps helped along by a crisp and cold martini or iced vodka. Next, a selection of appetizers catches the attention of hungry patrons. Fried calamari is crisp, served with a freshly made tartar sauce. You could order a trio of Asian satay and shrimp and pork-filled *dim sum* to get a little more variety. Steamed mussels have recently been served in an intensely flavored lemon grass broth with a tropical salsa accompaniment.

Panamanian fish chowder is a house specialty, thickened with a forcemeat of seafood and chunks of soft-fish in a tomato-based spice broth. Salads include a standard mix of greens, a couple of versions of Caesar and beefsteak tomatoes with mozzarella with a drizzle of basil vinaigrette.

There are a couple of steaks for those who absolutely refuse to eat fish. Grilled lobster tails may not be fresh, but they are large and meaty. Whole live lobsters are usually available.

For lovers of soft-fish, the list is varied, as are the cooking styles and saucings. Yellow fin tuna has been served in a steak cut, cross hatched from the grill with a mild ginger and sesame sauce; as with all entrees, a bouquet of fresh cut vegetables fills out the serving platter.

The chef's talents shine with a trio of stir-fried selections whipped together in a wok. Asian noodles are the foundation for a couple of other Oriental-style preparations, including not often seen diver scallops with a sauce that brings together sweet tamarind's tropical bite with that of pepper.

Oven-baked or blackened fish provide two of the other cooking styles readily at hand on the dinner menu. As good as all this is, the listing of house specialties usually draws my attention, especially at better seafood houses. The Catch 35 listing has brought together soft-shelled crabs with a spicy Szechwan glaze, grilled red snapper with garlic basil sauce and seared sea bass with ginger-scallion sauce and jasmine-scented rice among a list of offerings.

While much of the menu is touched with a kiss of the Orient, the desserts are by and large American and Continental through and through. Choices include *crème brûlée* with a praline crust, chocolate mousse in a *touile* cookie basket, and old-fashioned deep dish apple pie, plus homemade ice creams, sherbets, fruits and other temptations.

CENTRO
KR 18/20
Decor 4/4   Hospitality 5/5   Food 8/10   Value 1/1

- **Italian**
- **Chicago/River North**
- **$$**

710 North Wells Street
Chicago
(312) 988-7775
Troubleshooters: Alex Dana (owner), Jonathan Young (manager)

Hours: Lunch Mon–Fri 11 am–5 pm, Sat noon–5 pm, Dinner Mon–Sat 5–11 pm, Sun 4–10 pm
Credit Cards: All majors
Reservations: Taken only between 5–6:30 pm, waits can be considerable
Handicapped: Accessible
Bar: Full service, good wine list
Parking: Valet, nearby lots or street space available

Crowded, noisy, congenial are the words that most quickly come to mind about Centro. The cooking style leans firmly to Southern Italy, with an emphasis on pasta and seafood. Portions are lavish and handsomely served. The umbrian bread salad, in which the various ingredients of fresh bright red tomatoes, red onion, basil, olives, slices of cheese and salami, plus olive oil, garlic and oregano comes out looking more like a sandwich than a salad. It could easily be a light supper for one or two.

Something heartier would be the sausage and peppers in similar gigantic portion. In fact your waiter may very well issue a caution about portion size, adding that leftovers could easily be packed to take home. Start with a *foccaccia*, the thick Sicilian round bread, topped with tomato sauce and cheese much like a pizza, and accompany it with delicious stuffed eggplant. The sliced eggplant is lavished in an egg batter, deep-fried to a golden color, then stuffed with a filling of ricotta cheese; the ever present red sauce adds bite and color.

Speaking of sauces, the house special brings rectangular sheets of flat *papparadelle* noodles in a chunky red sauce which is just a little too harsh. There's nothing like good *cavatelli*, the finger-shaped noodle dumplings that have a special homemade quality. *Cavatelli* with broccoli is served in oil and garlic or baked with a blanket of Mozzarella over lighter ricotta and the ever-present red sauce. It is a wonderful flavor and texture combination. Several other standards include linguini in various sauces with shrimp, clams, mussels or calsmari. For something with bite, try *fusilli à la arrabiata*, corkscrew noodles in a peppery sauce that seems to leave the flavor of pimento on the tongue, in addition to the chili peppers that give the heat.

One could do fine without ordering an entree, but several are listed, including chicken or veal vesuvio, the indigenous Chicago contribution to the Italian-American larder. The latter brings thin scallops sautéed in olive oil and garlic. Though not as robust as chicken vesuvio, it still is delicious in its own way.

For dessert, the usual suspects include *tortoni*, *cannoli*, several styles of cheesecake, *zuppa Inglese* and a creamy *tiramisu* which needs a bit more unsweetened cocoa and coffee presence.

CHARLIE TROTTER'S
KR 20/20
Decor 4/4   Hospitality 5/5   Food 10/10   Value 1/1

- **French/American/ Eclectic**
- **Chicago/Near North**
- **$$$**

816 West Armitage Avenue
Chicago
(773) 248-6228
Troubleshooters: Charlie Trotter (chef/owner), Mitchell Schmieding (director of operations)

Hours: Tues–Thurs 5:30–10 pm, Fri–Sat 5:15–11 pm
Credit Cards: All majors
Reservations: Required
Bar: Full bar seats five in a small reception area
Smoking and nonsmoking sections: Entire restaurant is nonsmoking
Parking: Valet and tight street parking
Dress: Jackets required for gentlemen
Party Facilities: Private party facilities available for up to 36 in second floor dining room

Like leather against lace, like cold marble against soft silk, like taut muscles bulging beneath soft flesh, there seems to be a dysfunctional verisimilitude about fine dining in a restaurant's kitchen. But, when the kitchen is that of Charlie Trotter's, the formally set table for four to six guests with a crisp line of starched white linen defining the square of the table top, the graceful stemware with its floral bouquet, the glint of silver polished to the highest sheen reflected in the overhead kitchen work lights and the decorative chinaware meant to showcase that which will be the true center of attention, the certainty of diners receiving the finest of the culinary art is perfectly realized.

Those who decide to opt for the kitchen will be able to see firsthand the quiet authority. There is no shouting for orders, no confusion . . . only an orderly succession of orders placed and orders taken.

Like diners in the formal dining rooms, those in the kitchen will spend the next few hours savoring the likes of the chef's brilliant creations. Selections will change nightly, but rest assured, the experience will live on in memory long afterward. The Chef's Table is usually booked as much as six months in advance, so if you are interested, plan ahead.

As for the formal dining rooms, there are two *degustation* menus: The Grand Menu, or the Vegetable Menu. The selections change nightly. A recent choice included yellow fin tuna for a first course, plated with pieces of lobster and a garnish of daikon sprouts, jicama, cinnamon cap mushrooms and a shellfish vinaigrette dressing. Next might come

Japanese-style yellowtail paired with bok choy and a ginger infused soy sauce. Main course selections on the Grand Menu could include locally farmed rabbit roasted with salsify, braised red Swiss chard and shitake mushrooms mixed into quinoa, with the juices from the rabbit serving as a sauce. In another recipe, beef tenderloin might be plated with braised cabbage, brussels sprouts and a potato puree, again using the natural meat juices. The Vegetable Menu recently brought diners a pair of risottos, saffron and red wine–infused, with roasted porcini mushrooms, a mince of celery and fennel. In another vegetable recipe, Trotter creates a torte of wild field mushrooms and root vegetables with a reduction of trumpet mushrooms and red wine emulsion for his sauces.

Trotter may also prepare a carpaccio of red snapper instead of tenderloin in a style of sashimi that uses a mix of Asian noodles for texture, and a sesame oil–flavored mayonnaise. Or, consider his use of wild mushrooms in a stylized ragout that serves as binder for diced cubes of sweetbreads in a leafy spinach wrap.

It becomes clear that Chef Trotter's conceptions are based on a confluence of tradition and that spark of ingenuity that marks the chef/owner and his kitchen staff with more than commonplace ability.

Desserts are not to be overlooked. Blueberries may be showcased on a fresh tarte dough, held in place by amaretto sabayon. But, it is the baked chocolate mousse that is truly unforgettable. Baking gives the mousse a heavier character. It comes with a chocolate wafer that stands high over the platter much like a goosenecked *tuile*. The finishing touch is an intense burnt caramel sauce that simply could not be better.

CHEZ JOEL
KR 17.5/20
Decor 3.5/4   Hospitality 5/5   Food 8/10   Value 1/1

- **French Bistro**
- **Chicago/Near South**
- **$$**

1119 West Taylor Street
Chicago
(312) 226-6479
Troubleshooter: Chef Joel

Hours: Lunch Mon–Fri 11 am–3 pm, Dinner Mon–Thurs 5–10 pm, Fri–Sat 5–11 pm, closed Sun
Credit Cards: All majors
Reservations: Yes, especially Fri and Sat night
Handicapped: Accessible
Smoking and nonsmoking sections: During the week smoking tables are available in the dining room, on the weekends smoking is allowed in only the bar area.
Parking: Valet or street space

Culinary history tells us that French cuisine actually owes its origins to the Italian Renaissance. So, what comes around goes around at Chez Joel, a French bistro in the heart of the Little Italy neighborhood.

The menu follows the well-established tradition of French bistro listings, added to by nightly specials recited by a server whose French accent might be as thick as the layer of melted cheese atop a crock of French onion soup. That soup, by the way, is loaded with onions wilted into a seasoned stock with a flavor complex, but not so much as to alter the character of the soup.

Among other first course selections are typical classics such as salmon fume with creme fraiche and toast points, duck and liver paté, snails in garlic butter with Pernod and a codfish potato brandade. Sea scallops are a standout, in a yellow saffron broth set on a bed of leeks. More than half a dozen salads are offered on the à la carte menu, among them endive with Granny Smith apples and their natural accompaniment, Roquefort Cheese. In another salad, honey mustard dressing sets the tone for a mix of arugula, endive and frisee with toasted pecans and dried figs.

As for entrees, duck breast with a leg confit is plated with potatoes galette in a fruity cassis and port wine sauce. While a fricassee of wild mushrooms added some substance and flavor depth, the duck was really too fatty to be a complete success. On the other hand, there is nothing wrong with the house version of steak frites. The fries are shoestring slim and crisp, though I did hear someone at an adjacent table complain their fries were soggy. As for the steak, it's 10 ounces of grilled sirloin seasoned with a brush of garlic butter. The flavor is deep and satisfying, as I imagine some companion steaks with crushed peppercorns must be.

Among other meats, braised lamb shank is plated with the same mushroom fricassee that accompanies the duck, with a side of mashed potatoes added to underscore the comfort of this French bistro comfort food.

Fresh seafood will vary from day to day with the whim of the chef and availability. Bouillabaisse has been one recent selection, with a generous helping of lobster, crabs and other seafood in a broth which strikes me as a bit under-flavored. Toast brushed with aoili brings in more taste to the proceedings.

Desserts are like so much else, typically French and rich. The wine list is good, with several choices by the glass.

CHICAGO BRAUHAUS
KR 17/20
Decor 3.5/4   Hospitality 5/5   Food 7.5/10   Value 1/1

- **German**
- **Chicago/Mid-North**
- **$$**

4732 North Lincoln Avenue
Chicago
(773) 784-4444
Troubleshooter: Harry Kempf
(owner)

Hours: Sun–Mon, Wed–Fri 11–2 am, Sat 11–3 am, closed Tues
Credit Cards: Amex, Diners MC, Visa
Reservations: Suggested
Handicapped: Accessible
Smoking and nonsmoking sections: Both available
Parking: In nearby lots or street can sometimes be tight

Chicago Brauhaus is large and open, as one might expect of a brauhaus. The beer flows amply from spigots behind the long bar. A band plays most nights with tunes that can range from Beer Barrel Polka or Lili Marlene, to soft rock. And, on warm summer nights, it is not unusual for a musician to pick up his trumpet and lead a couple hundred people or more out the front door of the restaurant in a sort of Teutonic conga line up and down The Lincoln Mall like some modern Pied Piper.

As for the food, one finds the typical German cooking like *kassler ripchen*, assorted sausages and sandwiches. Full dinners include soup or salad, potatoes, vegetable or applesauce depending upon entree, and one of the better bread basket selections you will find anywhere. In fact, the temptation is to keep nibbling away at the delicious pumpernickel or other breads that can come your way. Something similar can be said for the liver dumpling soup which is offered with dinners. The broth is clear, the small dumplings lightly seasoned.

Saurbraten is curiously more like a Yankee pot roast without the spicy bite from this marinade of crushed gingersnaps, bacon and vinegar. Still the meat is tender and tasty, if not all that flavorful. *Weiner schnitzel* comes off a better choice to my way of thinking. The crust is golden and succulent, the veal moist and tender. Roast duckling gets traditional treatment with a side of spaetzle that taste homemade, not from the box. As with other entrees, you could choose a plump potato dumpling instead. From specials, in addition to what is on the menu, roast goose is crispened to a golden color and the skin and pulls easily away from the flesh. The bird comes with a brown gravy that can be poured over the goose, but it tastes so good just the way it is, no embellishment is needed.

From a selection of desserts, apple strudel is a fine finish for the evening's offerings.

CHICAGO CHOP HOUSE
KR 16.5/20
Decor 3.5/4   Hospitality 4.5/5   Food 7.5/10   Value 1/1

- **American**
- **Chicago/Near North**
- **$$$**

60 West Ontario
Chicago
(312) 787-7100
Troubleshooter: Susan Gayford (manager)

Hours: Lunch Mon–Fri 11:30 am–4:30 pm; Dinner Mon–Thurs 4:30–11 pm, Fri 4:30–11:30 pm, Sat 4–11:30 pm, Sun 4–11 pm (bar open daily until midnight)
Credit Cards: All majors
Reservations: Suggested
Bar: Handsome long bar evokes 19th century Chicago, good wine list, piano bar
Smoking and nonsmoking sections: Both available
Parking: Valet

Chicago Chop House is splashed with antique-style photographs and etchings of the city's history. The first floor is occupied by one of the best looking bars in the city, a serpentine affair that wraps its way around, just inviting conversation. The main dining room is up a flight of stairs, lined with more photographs, on the second floor.

The menu is straightforward without much in the way of frills. Beef is the big item here. I use the word "big" with all deliberateness, since the restaurant actually serves a 64-ounce porterhouse steak or a 48-ounce version for a few dollars less.

The still large, but by comparison, considerably more modest T-bone or smaller cuts of filet mignon and the tried-and-true New York strip are all featured, as is traditional roast prime rib and other assorted chops.

Seafood includes swordfish, Dover sole and French fried jumbo shrimp in a beer batter, as well as a few other choices. The restaurant is a big favorite with conventioneers and other tourists, but plenty of time is allowed to linger between courses and even after dinner, which is a positive note about hospitality.

CHICAGO FIREHOUSE
KR 20/20

Decor 4/4   Hospitality 5/5   Food 10/10   Value 1/1

- **American**
- **Chicago/Near South Loop**
- **$$$**

1401 South Michigan Avenue
Chicago
(312) 786-1401
Troubleshooter: Matthew
O'Malley (owner)

Hours: Lunch Tues–Sat 11:30 am–2 pm, Sun 11:30 am–4 pm; Dinner Tues–Thurs 5–10 pm, Fri–Sat Dinner 5–10:30 pm, Sunday Dinner 4–9 pm
Credit Cards: All majors
Reservations: Recommended
Smoking and nonsmoking sections: Separate nonsmoking area, smoking only at bar
Handicapped: Accessible
Parking: On street or valet, $6

There's much of the old firehouse look left over, complete with brass fire poles, tin ceilings, the polished surfaces of fire glazed tile brick walls. This somewhat harder look is softened by fine linen napery and fabric walls in the main dining room.

You won't find the likes of firehouse chili, but the grilled vegetable terrine is a good example of the contemporary twist given to most of the choices on the Chicago Firehouse menu. In this case, roasted vegetables are fanned out, rather than stacked in a conventional terrine. Sweet onion marmalade adds a distinctive touch, while a mini sandwich of goat cheese spread between toasted garlic croutons adds some panache.

Among other first course choices the house cured smoked salmon is served as a wedge, not in thin slices. Goat cheese appears again along with roasted garlic cloves as part of the presentation. The crab cakes are nothing to crab about. They are about as close to 100% crabmeat, with little if any breading filler except what might be needed as a binder. The taste is fresh and delicious.

A choice of ala carte soups and salads includes a wedge of crisp iceberg lettuce with cream blue cheese dressing and Maytag blue cheese crumbles. Say what you will about head lettuce, but it certainly has found its place on this menu.

As for entrees, there seems to be a winner everywhere you turn. Monk fish is often called mock lobster. It has a similar meaty texture, if not quite the sweetness of the real McCoy. In this presentation a large piece of monk fish is roasted, then set out with a julienne vegetable array including tomatoes, fennel and spinach in a light lobster broth on a bed of garlic mashed potatoes with a sprinkling of fried leek over the top. I really like the imagination in this one.

Other selections include pot roast loaded with mushrooms, carrots and other root vegetables in a natural pan gravy. Seafood choices include a pan fried rainbow trout in brown butter with lemon and capers, or grilled salmon in a coriander crust with apple chutney and cider sauce.

Desserts involve some rich American beauties. The wine list is excellent, and fairly priced. If the cooking were this good at the city's real firehouses, it would be tough to get anyone out during meals even for a five alarmer.

CHICAGO KALBI
KR 17.5/20
Decor 3/4   Hospitality 5/5   Food 8.5/10   Value 1/1

* **Korean**
* **Chicago/North**
* **$**

3752 West Lawrence Avenue
Chicago
(773) 604-8183
Troubleshooter: Chyo Tozuka

Hours: Mon–Sun 5 pm–1 am, closed Tues
Credit Cards: All Majors
Reservations: Recommended
Handicapped: Accessible
Smoking and nonsmoking sections: Both available
Parking: Street

Korean restaurants abound in Chicago. One of the more inviting is Chicago Kalbi. Like many of the others it is a storefront restaurant, but larger than some. There are even private booths for special parties. Most tables have a well for a brazer which is used to grill the several beef, chicken and shrimp entrees listed on the menu. Korean food is easy for beginners to enjoy; so much of it is like a good old American barbecue.

But, Korean food also has its exotic side. This is particularly true with its most popular side dish, *kimchi*, a pickled and spiced cabbage which is one of only several vegetables brought in an array to each table when entrees are ordered. Along with *kimchi*, small platters are set down with cold spinach, mung beans, a spiced turnip, a soy bean sauce and seaweed, just to name a few.

The menu is printed in both Korean and English, which makes Chicago Kalbi a hospitable restaurant for people of both cultures. And, many servers are fluent enough in English to answer specific questions. If they aren't, the restaurant's hostess, a charming woman named Chiyo (like the Chia pet, she jokes) greets diners, many with hugs who are obviously regulars.

Among appetizers, steamed or fried dumplings are similar to those offered in most Chinese restaurants and may be a good starting point for first time diners at a Korean restaurant. The dumplings are plumped with a filling of ground meat and vegetables. A single order should be enough for three or four diners. You might also order *gul-chin*, a large pancake stuffed with scallions and cut-up bits of cooked oyster. The pancake is served in squares for easy snatching with chopsticks or, if you prefer, a conventional fork. Eaten plain they are delicious, though a light soy and sesame sauce can be added.

There are other appetizers, such as tripe or raw liver with garlic sauce, a bit too exotic for most American palates. Moving to entrees, even though the names of entrees are foreign, choices such as the house name sake, *kalbi*, are as familiar as barbecue beef short ribs. Another selection, *bulgoki*, is nothing more than thin strips of beef, which, like the *kalbi*, are meant to be grilled on the open brazer. Other selections range from sliced squid or shrimp, to organ meats popular with Koreans, such as beef tripe, heart or liver.

For the less adventurous, a combination dinner could be the best way to go. We ordered one that included *kalbi*, chicken and shrimp and in no time at all we had everything sizzling over hot coals. It makes the restaurant a little smokey when several tables at a time are going full blast with cooking, but that's just part of the local color.

CLUB LUCKY
KR 18/20
Decor 3/4   Hospitality 5/5   Food 9/10   Value 1/1

- **Italian**
- **Chicago/Near Northwest**
- **$$**

1824 West Wabansia
Chicago
(773) 227-2300
Troubleshooter: Jim Higgins
(owner)

Hours: Sun 4–10 pm, Lunch Mon–Thurs 11:30 am–4:30 pm, Dinner 5–11 pm, Fri–Sat 5 pm–midnight
Credit Cards: All majors
Reservations: Usually not taken
Handicapped: Not accessible
Bar: Full service
Smoking and nonsmoking sections: Both available
Parking: Valet and street

If it's "retro" dining you want, then its "retro" you get at Club Lucky. The look is right out of the 1950s. Yes, Club Lucky is another Italian restaurant, but like its decor, the style is more a throw-back than cutting edge. You don't worry about eating a pasta as a separate course here; there's no pecking order to the dining, just good food the way Italian restaurants used to be.

Well, maybe not quite, since there is an open kitchen and separate preparation area where an array of salads and antipasti are laid out to tempt diners. It's basically à la carte but some courses are large enough to share a single order. For example, an antipasto platter has been bringing out smoked and rolled eggplant, Sicilian olives, a small slice or two of Prosciutto, a little cheese, asparagus spears, and whatever else might be at hand, all in a light dressing that serves to underscore, not obscure. Other appetizers range from a cold fish salad to fried or grilled calamari and the ever-present Italian restaurant specialty, baked or fresh clams.

Sometimes, soup is a preferred starter. Pasta fagioli is not as two-fisted or hearty as some, but its basic stock provides the underpinnings for a good flavor.

The pastas number only a few. Among them, eight finger cavatelli, not the name of a wrestling opponent of Hulk Hogan, is a delicious extruded and chewy dough sauced in a thick marinara to which a lavish amount of grated cheese is added. While cavatelli represents one extreme, the other is found in the light and delicate cappellini, known as angel hair. The thin noodles are sauced with a chop of eggplant, sweet red peppers, olives and capers in a slightly sweet tomato-based sauce. But, rather than bathed in sauce, the pasta is more accurately kissed and refreshed.

Among entree selections beef tenderloin is literally tender enough to be sliced with a fork. It is served with roasted red peppers and tomatoes along with garlic and chives. Beef eaters will love this one. Other house specialties include a delicious version of chicken vesuvio, eggplant parmigiana, veal Francese, which is lightly breaded and sautéed in butter, lemon and white wine, as well as a handful of other Italian standbys. Fresh fish is part of the rotating daily specials, and is usually served with a side of fresh vegetables.

COCO PAZZO
KR 18/20
Decor 4/4   Hospitality 4.5/5   Food 8.5/10   Value 1/1

- **Italian**
- **Chicago/River North**
- **$$$**

300 West Hubbard Street
Chicago
(312) 836-0900
Troubleshooter: Jack Weiss
(co-owner)

Hours: Sun 5–10 pm, Lunch Mon–Fri 11:30 am–2:30 pm, Dinner Mon–Thurs 5:30–10:30 pm, Fri–Sat 5:30–11 pm
Credit Cards: Amex, Diners, MC, Visa
Handicapped: Accesible
Smoking and nonsmoking sections: Both available
Parking: Valet

The very name of the Italian restaurant Coco Pazzo suggests a degree of whimsy. But, amidst that whimsy, which includes a preoccupation with baking potatoes as a decorative theme, there is some very serious and creative cooking presented to diners.

Coco Pazzo is about as far as you can get from a "mom and pop" red tomato sauce Italian restaurant. In keeping with contemporary trends, the menu stresses some traditional items, but in very imaginative ways. For example, polenta, which begins as nothing more than cornmeal mush, is blended into a creaminess with fontina cheese, topped with mushrooms, tomato and garlic, then bathed in a light drizzling of truffle-infused olive oil. The consistency is so light, one would not imagine this to be polenta, with its hard mealy grains.

Something a bit more direct, yet not without creative flair, is another antipasto, eggplant parmigiana. In this case, slices of the eggplant are covered with mozzarella and slices of tomato, then baked in the restaurant's wood-burning oven. The flavors are mellowed, easy on the palate. Another selection that reflects how good a simple direct approach can be is the antipasto platter. Here, roasted and grilled vegetables are served largely unadorned by anything but a light dressing of olive oil, and perhaps a little in the way of fresh herbs. Somewhat less interesting is the restaurant's version of frito misto, the popular collection of fried seafoods. There's nothing wrong with the concept, nor is there anything particularly imaginative.

For much of the cooking, the wood-burning oven, which is at the center of Coco Pazzo's open kitchen, figures prominently as more than mere decor. One of the tastiest entrees is chicken, pounded flat and cooked on the grill, then presented in a balsamic vinegar-based sauce that includes herbs, and peppers. Delicious roasted potatoes and fresh seasonal vegetables accompany the presentation.

While several pastas are on its menu, the restaurant also does a daily risotto. Service is both knowledgeable and attentive, though you might have to send up a flair to attract a waiter's attention from time to time. The wine list is serious, somewhat pricey. Tables are spaced far enough apart to afford some privacy in a large room with high ceilings, open duct work and bare brick walls.

COCO PAZZO CAFE
KR 19/20

Decor 4/4   Hospitality 5/5   Food 9/10   Value 1/1

- **Italian**
- **Chicago/Near North**
- **$$**

636 North St. Clair Street
Chicago
(312) 664-2777
Troubleshooter: Jack Weiss
(co-owner)

Hours: Lunch Daily 11:30 am–4 pm, Dinner 4–10:30 pm
Credit Cards: All majors
Reservations: Suggested
Handicapped: Accessible
Smoking and nonsmoking sections: Smoking in designated area
Parking: Valet at dinner $8

You may remember this restaurant when it was called Il Toscanaccio. The people who own Coco Pazzo Cafe, are very candid about why they changed the name; it was too hard for its customers and would-be customers to pronounce.

Though the name was changed, the decor is as inviting as ever. Seating is at country style tables and ladder-back chairs set on a red tile floor. Service is quite knowledgeable, and extremely cooperative. We had problems with not one, but two bottles of wine. No questions asked, they were replaced until a third bottle yielded something acceptable.

Seafood and vegetables make a strong presence on the menu. A table in the center of the dining room is topped with platters of roasted vegetables, including peppers, eggplant, zucchini, plus beans and more. A light fresh drizzle of olive oil, and a smear of basil-infused olive oil adds decoration and flavor.

White beans are an important part of the Tuscan way of cooking, and they make their presence on selections that include grilled shrimp with beans and arugula, as part of a large chopped vegetable salad or in a recent evening's fish special. Chilean sea bass is roasted in parchment with shrimp, potato cubes and whole shrimp and a smattering of fresh cut herbs. It's a simple, clean flavor, one complimented by a simple, clean wine.

But, Coco Pazzo Cafe is not without some more assertive cooking. Among pasta selections, choices include hearty lasagna bolognese, spaghetti with crushed red pepper to charge up its basic tomato and olive oil sauce, or rigatoni with spicy sausage, plus dots of green peas in a parmesan cheese and cream sauce. On the mellow side, gnocchi, lighter than one might expect, gets tomato sauce with basil while sautéed mushrooms are at the center of an order of wider ribbon pasta called *taggliolini*. Freshly prepared risotto can change daily. Recently it was redolent of fresh snippings of rosemary, the grains of large plumped rice chewy, but not sticky or even gummy.

From among meat, poultry and seafood selections *polletto* "devil style," brings a marinated and roasted cut-up chicken with roasted potatoes and broccoli rabe, while an evening's special listing included *chicken Milanese*, far from Tuscany on the map of Italy, but as welcome as could be at our table. Desserts include a chocolate layer cake of lady fingers, chocolate mousse and mascarpone cheese, and a delicious, not too sweet *panna cotta*, a creamy custard made without eggs, but rich in cream and fresh vanilla, with accents of burnt sugar caramel. Expect to spend about $60 a couple for three courses, plus tax, tip and drinks.

CoCoRo
KR 19/20
Decor 4/4   Hospitality 5/5   Food 9/10   Value 1/1

- **Japanese**
- **Chicago/River North**
- **$**

668 North Wells Street
Chicago
(312) 943-2220
Troubleshooter: Nori Muzuuhi (manager)

Hours: Lunch Mon–Fri 11:30 am–2:15 pm, Dinner Mon–Thurs 5:30–10 pm, Fri–Sat until 11 pm, closed Sun
Credit Cards: All majors except Discover
Handicapped: Accessible
Reservations: Recommended
Smoking and nonsmoking sections: Both available
Parking: Valet $7

The word *CoCoRo* suggests aromas or perfumes in the Japanese language and in a sense that is appropriate. The steaming pots of *sukiyaki* or *shabu shabu* send up their sweet smells. You may already be familiar with *sukiyaki*, a casserole of simmered Oriental vegetables, translucent golden noodles and thin slices of beef. To think of boiled beef would get the whole idea of this delicious table-cooked dinner all wrong. The correct concept is more an intermingling of flavors, a medley of textures in the best sense of balanced dining, which is much of what Japanese cookery is at its very essence.

Like *sukiyaki*, *shabu-shabu* is a one-pot dish prepared at your table. In this case, however, its preparation is more like fondue, in that diners will do their own cooking, though with help or guidance from a server if need be. This sort of communal aspect makes much Japanese dining, especially at CoCoRo, a very social experience.

There is much more to the restaurant's menu than the *nabemono*, or one-pot, style of cooking. The selections will be familiar to all but the most inexperienced visitor to a Japanese restaurant, and even in that situation, servers appear to be more than ready to help and translate where the menu is less than explicit.

Certainly *sushi* and *sashimi* are important options, each piece deliciously hand crafted. These small Japanese finger foods can be ordered by the piece, or in various combinations that make them a welcome appetizer platter for a few people, or a single dinner selection for one diner.

One of the more handsome presentations is had in CoCoRo's version of a *bento* box. This lacquered open container is sectioned off into cubicles, kind of like a three dimensional Mondrian painting. Each cubicle contains something to eat, perhaps tempura vegetables or shrimp, teriyaki chicken, or fish depending upon the main course a diner has chosen.

Though CoCoRo seems to be a restaurant where visiting Japanese business people feel comfortable and at home, that aspect of the restaurant's hospitality makes it an authentic and delicious dining option for Chicagoans who may or may not be familiar with Japanese dining.

COSTA'S
KR 17.5/20
Decor 4/4   Hospitality 5/5   Food 7.5/10   Value 1/1

- **Greek**
- **Chicago/Near West**
- **$$**

340 South Halsted
Chicago
(312) 263-9700
Troubleshooter: Manager on duty

Hours: Sun–Thurs 11 am–midnight, Fri–Sat until 1 am
Credit Cards: All majors
Reservations: Accepted
Handicapped: Accessible
Smoking and nonsmoking sections: More than half of dining space is non smoking
Parking: Free valet

While Costa's has not reinvented the wheel, it is welcome and inviting, with an easy-to-like menu. Ruddy tile floors, window treatments and wood beam accents set the tone. A grand piano stands over in one corner room in its own nook, ready for nightly entertainment.

The menu is familiar to anyone who knows the Chicago brand of Greek dining. So, there is *saganaki*, a burst of flame and the traditional cry of "*Oppa!*" resonating through the dining room. Grilled calamari is tender and fresh, stuffed with a mild cheese, plated with a course cut of cabbage and herbs much like a cole slaw. The flavors compliment each other. Perhaps even more flavorful is grilled quail, with garlic and wine worked together into a pungent glaze. A couple of dozen more hot and cold appetizers are ready and waiting, roasted peppers, pork tenderloin in lemon and wine sauce, fried zucchini with garlic sauce, homemade sausages, olives, seasoned yogurt and cheeses among the choices. Costa's version of salmon roe salad, called *taramasalata*, is too salty, but its companion spread, roasted eggplant, is tangy and flavored just right.

Diners can order from a broad choice of salads or skip that course and go right on to entrees which include the traditional baked casseroles, *pastichio* and *moussakas*. The *moussakas* is layered high with ground meat, eggplant and bechamel sauce. Its foundation is potatoes, not whipped as is often the case, but roasted and tiered in firm slices whose texture contrasts with the creamy bechamel.

Charcoal grilled chicken, just one of several chicken choices, is perfect. The chicken is boned and cut up into smaller pieces, with an infused flavor of lemon juice that only brings out the delicious grilled taste. From among other traditional Greek choices, spinach pie is plump at the center with a light and flaky phyllo crust. Several skewered meats or fish, steaks and Greek lamb chops round out the menu.

Service is fine, the wine list reasonably priced and unusually well rounded compared to many Greek restaurants. The desserts include a sinfully delicious and moist *baklava*.

COUSIN'S
KR 17.5/20
Decor 3.5/4   Hospitality 4.5/5   Food 8.5/10   Value 1/1

- **Turkish**
- **Chicago/North**
- **$**

5203 North Clark Street
(773) 334-4553
Troubleshooter: Manager on duty
Other Location
2833 North Broadway
773-880-0063

Hours: Mon–Thurs 11 am–11 pm, Fri–Sat 11 am–midnight, Sun 11 am–10 pm
Credit Cards: Visa, MC, Amex
Reservations: Accepted
Handicapped: Accessible, but washrooms are up two steps
Smoking and nonsmoking sections: Both available
Parking: On street, can be tight

Cousin's is a narrow storefront with handsome decor that makes good use of arabesque and geometric design. Seating can be at low round metal tables, which requires a bit of nimbleness, or at conventional tables.

The menu changes seasonally. As with so much ethnic dining, it's best to go with a small group, so that you can taste more of what a restaurant has to offer. Cousin's makes it easy with a "sample tour," as it is called, which combines four of the several appetizer selections. The *baba ganoush*, a puree of roasted eggplant, garlic and seasonings is delicious, the humus, a chickpea puree, is mild and savory. *Falafel*, deep-fried balls of seasoned chickpea dough, are spicy, while *dolma*, wrapped grape leaves stuffed with rice and ground meat are deliciously touched with mint for an unmistakable flavor accent.

Among other appetizers, the selection includes pancakes made of grated zucchini paired with a garlic infused yogurt called *jajik*, as well as truly superb eggplant, split open and stuffed with a filling of peppers, onions and pine nuts among its ingredients.

It would not be wrong to make an evening's meal from a broad selection of appetizers, but then you would be denied some of the delicious entrees. Truth to tell, the restaurant's specialty, *chicken doner*, plated with dilled rice, is nothing more than conventionally grilled chicken breast, skinned and cut into strips. Better, when it is available, might be chicken or lamb *adana*, in which the respective meats are ground, seasoned and grilled, then laid out like plump little tubes of sausage, though without the casings.

Speaking of lamb, it comes in several recipes; one of the best is in a casserole with a variety of vegetables; a similar dish, made with portobello mushrooms as a substitute for meat is flavorful, but lacks the deeper richness that lamb brings to the recipe. Cousin's serves several vegetarian dinners, by the way. One of the best is vegetable moussaka, which uses eggplant slices as layers much the way noodles are used in lasagna. Desserts include a sensually sweet and honeyed baklava.

CRAWDADDY BAYOU
KR 17.5/20
Decor 4/4   Hospitality 4.5/5   Food 8/10   Value 1/1

- **American/Cajun-Creole**
- **Wheeling**
- **$$**

412 North Milwaukee Avenue
Wheeling
(847) 520-4800
Troubleshooter: John Liautaud
(owner)

Hours: Sun–Thurs 5–10 pm, Fri–Sat 5–11 pm
Credit Cards: All majors
Bar: Full service with live zydeco bands
Reservations: Suggested
Handicapped: Accessible
Smoking and nonsmoking sections: Both available
Parking: Free in lot, valet available

The idea at Crawdaddy Bayou is to recreate the Cajun dining experience as much as possible. The restaurant is large, with a dining room adjacent to the bar, where a zydeco group performs just about every night. The food and music go well together.

Appetizers include a trio of soups: excellent corn and shrimp soup, a thick, rich and spicy chicken and sausage gumbo, and a chock full of shrimp and crawfish tails, seafood gumbo with a cajun tabasco, wine and tartar sauce for some down-home accent.

Other appetizer selections range from raw oysters to crab-stuffed mushrooms, to a seafood skillet *fondeaux* that serves two to three people and brings together spinach, shrimp, crawfish and scallops topped with a buttery crab-flavored sauce with jack cheese melted on top.

From among entrees, the menu highlights a shrimp and/or crawfish boil with corn and red skin potatoes. Pit-roasted chicken, pork and beef choices are also highlighted. I would have thought that they would be basted in barbecue sauce during the cooking, but that was not the case, at least for an order of chicken. Nevertheless, a cup of sweet and tangy sauce comes on the side and makes for some "lick your lips" kind of eating, right down to the bone.

Among seafood, fried catfish is plated with much too salty sweet potato fries and tartar sauce. Blackened catfish is excellent, with just the right amount of spice, and a side of red beans and rice. Grilled tilapia is glazed with brown butter crawfish sauce. Crawfish *etoufee* is as good as it gets, smothered in its tangy *roux* thickened sauce. The *etoufee* can be ordered alone, or paired with batter-fried popcorn crawfish tails for a bit of delicious variety. Desserts include various sundries, sweet potato pie with pecan crust among them.

CUCINA BELLA
KR 17/20

Decor 3/4   Hospitality 5/5   Food 8/10   Value 1/1

- **Italian**
- **Chicago/Mid-North**
- **$$**

543 West Diversey Parkway
Chicago
(773) 868-1119
Troubleshooter: Mark Donaway
(chef/owner)

Hours: Lunch Mon–Sat 11 am–5 pm, Dinner Mon–Fri 5–10 pm, Sat 5–11 pm, Sun Brunch 11 am–3 pm, Dinner 5–9 pm
Credit Cards: All majors
Reservations: Accepted
Handicapped: Accessible
Smoking and nonsmoking sections: Smoking in the dining room
Parking: Validated one hour parking at Market Place Food Store, 521 West Diversey, otherwise parking on street can be tight

The decor of Cucina Bella suggests a homey, Italian-style of comfortable dining, and that's what chef Mark Donaway and his kitchen staff deliver. Mismatched chairs, clay flower pots serving as container for foccacia bread, and a catchall of kitsch imply a sense of whimsy mixed in.

Even before diners have a chance to order from the menu, a server will bring out a hammered aluminum platter of antipasti. The selection might include tight little rollups of prosciutto, along with an array of prepared vegetables, a flavored rice, and intensely flavored sun-dried tomatoes. When it gets down to the actual ordering of dinner, *arancini*, from the list of Chef's Specialties, makes for as good a beginning as any. *Arancini* are deep-fried rice balls, bound in a crust with peas and often sausage among its other ingredients. Served piping hot, with a warmed marinara they are the epitome of the Italian comfort food which is at the heart of Donaway's approach. Other first course choices include such classics as Tuscan bean salad or melon and prosciutto, to the chef's take on scallops in a tomato cream sauce with walnuts, or fried ravioli with pesto and marinara.

For a pasta course *penne putanesca* explodes with the flavors of capers and olives, as well as mild peppers and garlic in a light tomato-based sauce. In another pasta, spinach fettucini is given a light saucing of sun-dried tomatoes and olive oil, while rigatoni could come in a much richer and indulgent walnut gorgonzola cream sauce. Several other selections round out the pastas, which if appetite suggests, can lead nicely into main course dining. Selections include various styles of chicken, seafood, even a vesuvio version of pork chops. But, the highlight of the menu may be Cucina Bella's *torte rustica*. Think of a pie with lattice pastry crust on top and you get the picture. Inside is a variety of cooked vegetables, their flavors married to a light tomato cream sauce. The torte can be had with sausage, or without as you prefer. Homemade desserts include gelatos, a chocolate indulgence or two and usually a fruit crostada, or tart, but without the custard.

CYRANO'S
KR 18.5/20
Decor 3.5/4   Hospitality 5/5   Food 9/10   Value 1/1

- **French Bistro**
- **Chicago/Near North**
- **$$**

546 North Wells Street
Chicago
(312) 467-0546
Troubleshooters: Didier Durand and Jamie Peller (owners)

Hours: Lunch Mon–Fri 11:30 am–2:30 pm, Dinner Mon–Thurs 5:30–10 pm, Fri–Sat until 11 pm
Credit Cards: All majors
Reservations: Preferred
Handicapped: Accessible
Bar: Full bar with good selection of lesser known regional French wines
Smoking and nonsmoking sections: Both available
Parking: Valet available

Cyrano's is simply decorated as a bistro, with mustard yellow walls, a well-tended bar, and gilt-framed mirrors to break the monotony. Tables are covered with butcher's wrap, freshened for each new seating. Service is very French, and of course, so is the menu.

Chef and co-owner Didier Durand, whose way with *haute cuisine*, is well-known to Chicago gourmands, is not cooking down, so much as he is cooking more directly and simpler. His menu is bistro fare, with onion tarts that have a crust so flaky it crumbles like the ego of a broken hearted lover, steak and fries, and roasted chicken at its core. But, there are some surprises, such as the appearance of ostrich paté or ostrich bourguignon with beef and vegetables.

For starters diners find a dozen or so choices such as house-cured gravlox with fennel remoulade, snails in garlic butter, even duck rillette, the fat cooked down and worked into a paste with the meat, and served with horseradish and other garnishes.

Ratatouille, served cold with croutons and an olive tapanade is classic. Grilled venison sausage is spicy and delicious, wonderful with a cold beer to accompany it and the mild potato salad which shares the platter with the sausages.

The à la carte menu highlights the restaurant's rotisserie seasoned chicken, provencal-style rabbit and crispy duck. The chicken comes in cut-up pieces, moist, wonderfully seasoned.

Elsewhere among entrees, choices range from a traditional-style bouillabaisse to veal sweetbreads sautéed to a crisp. From among seafood choices, there is deliciously seared sea scallops, the large firm rounds plated with mashed potatoes and served in a light, non-intrusive, lemon butter sauce. A fresh fish is featured daily and recently it was escolar, a firm white fleshed seafood bedded on lightly seasoned rice.

Desserts run the gamut from the elegant simplicity of fresh fruit to the richness of bread pudding with caramel sauce, tarts and other confections.

D & J BISTRO
KR 18.5/20
Decor 3.5/4   Hospitality 5/5   Food 9/10   Value 1/1

- **French**
- **Lake Zurich**
- **$$**

466 South Rand Road
Lake Zurich
(847) 438-8001
Troubleshooters: Dominique and Jacqueline Ligeai

Hours: Lunch Tues–Fri 11:30 am–2:30 pm, Dinner Tues–Fri 5:30–9 pm, Sat 5–9 pm, Sun 5–8:30 pm
Credit Cards: Amex, Diners, MC, Visa
Reservations: Accepted for parties of 4 or more weeknights, and for all parties Fri and Sat nights
Handicapped: Accessible
Smoking and nonsmoking sections: No smoking in restaurant
Parking: Plenty of free parking

The waiter was from Paris, the wine was from St. Emilion and the food was from Heaven. If that's an exaggeration, it's only a minor one. D & J Bistro has been around for more than two decades, somewhat a pioneer of bistro cookery, especially in the far Northwest suburbs.

Like good restaurants everywhere, the menu changes regularly with season and availability. But, there are standards to be enjoyed year round. At the top of that list is the classic *steak frites*, which, as the menu points out is, "a Parisian Bistro Classic." Some restaurants cook a ribeye or butt steak; D & J Bistro uses a 9-ounce New York sirloin which gives up some flavor as it acquires more tenderness. A glaze of shallot butter is brushed across the top of the meat which shares its platter with a mound of potato fries which seems almost large enough to have cleaned out every potato field in Idaho.

Another regular standard is the pork tenderloin, in this case crusted with black peppercorns and served as a comfort food entree with a side of mashed potatoes. There is always a version of *paella*. Strictly speaking, of course, *paella* is Spanish, not French bistro cooking. But, it still fits right in, largely because it is so very tasty.

Turning to seafood, the seared tuna is not to be missed! Before the sizable tuna steak is cooked, it is dredged in what may be a cornmeal crust with dijon mustard, sliced into wedges, much like a cut of good meat, and quickly seared side to side in a hot pan. The mustard flavor is rather understated, so what remains is that contrast of textures between the body of the fish and its crumb coating. Steamed baby bok choy is plated with Japanese influenced miso sauce adding color and flavor balance.

Other entree selections include grilled lamb loin, saddle of rabbit, pan roasted veal loin chop and boned chicken with a forcemeat of spinach and portobello mushrooms enriched with goat cheese.

Desserts include a rather interesting banana Napoleon and a very tasty nut tart, made with a filling of nuts and topped with a scoop of vanilla ice cream, which in turn has been coated with ground nuts.

DANIEL J'S
KR 17.5/20
Decor 3.5/4   Hospitality 4.5/5   Food 8.5/10   Value 1/1

- **American Eclectic**
- **Chicago/Mid-North**
- **$$**

3811 North Ashland Avenue
Chicago
(773) 404-7772
Troubleshooters: Jack and
Mary Jones (owners)

Hours: Sun 5–9 pm, Tues–Thurs 5:30–10 pm, Fri–Sat 5:30–11 pm, closed Mon
Credit Cards: All majors
Reservations: Highly recommended
Handicapped: Accessible
Smoking and nonsmoking sections: Both available
Parking: Street

This storefront setting is crowded with tables for two or four, none more than a few feet away from each other. Tables are covered with butcher's paper, typical for this sort of bistro. Just as the restaurant is small, so too is its menu. There are less than half a dozen appetizers and only a few more entrees.

The menu is eclectic American, with a few Mediterranean touches. Try one of the appetizer pizzas, enough to get a table of four started on their way. On one a quartet of cheeses is melted over sun-dried tomatoes. On another, grilled vegetables and pesto make up the topping, with blots of goat cheese in a combination that may not win any awards for originality, but that brings out these well-matched flavors.

Other appetizer selections can be equally tasty. Try baked crab cakes, two silver dollar-sized rounds about an inch thick plated with chive butter sauce. Wild mushroom quesadillas are just as you might infer. A platter of half a dozen quesadillas is served, each folded over a stuffing of mushrooms bound together with a bit of melted cheese. They can be enjoyed as is, or dabbed with a bit of tomatillo relish or salsa.

Good flavor is similarly at the heart of entrees. Some daily specials sell out early, testament more to popularity, I think, than poor kitchen planning. But, when available, pappardelli noodles hit the spot in a duck confit broth with flavor accents from mushrooms, shallots, tomato, a bit of lemon zest and basil or other herbs. More herbaceous than one might expect is linguini and seafood. In this recipe, the red sauce is freshened with abundant basil, adding a sweet spiciness to the tomato-based sauce. A small lobster sits atop the pasta, along with a selection of clams, shrimp, calamari rings and small pulpy whole baby squid.

Elsewhere on the seafood track, salmon is presented with an Oriental flourish, though red pepper adds some zing to basic ginger soy sauce. Mahi mahi draws on its Polynesian origins with a garnish of fresh coconut, pineapple and macadamia nuts. For meat eaters, pork tenderloin is roasted with herbs, napped with a dark demiglace and accompanied by slices of sugar-baked apples and a potato pancake. Beef tenderloin comes grilled with a selection of mushrooms plus shallots in a zingy Zinfandel wine-based peppercorn sauce.

Desserts include several homemade ice creams and sherbets. the biting fruit flavors of the sherbets can be a surprise. Crème brûlée, chocolate confections and other whims will show up as well. The wine list is concise and reasonably priced.

DAVID'S BISTRO
KR 18/20

Decor 3/4   Hospitality 5/5   Food 9/10   Value 1/1

- **American**
- **Des Plaines**
- **$$**

623 North Wolf Road
(corner of Wolf and Central
in the Norwood Plaza)
Des Plaines
(847) 803-3233
Troubleshooter: David Maish
(chef/owner)

Hours: Lunch Tues–Fri 11 am–2:30 pm, Dinner Tues–Thurs 4:30–9 pm, Fri–Sat until 10 pm, Brunch Sat–Sun 7 am–2:30 pm
Credit Cards: All majors
Reservations: Suggested
Handicapped: Accessible
Smoking and nonsmoking sections: Smoking at bar
Parking: Ample in lot

To one side there is a hearing aid shop, to the other a travel agent. Just a few doors away, there's a billiard parlor. This is life in the world of suburban strip malls, where almost anything can be found next to anything else. So, it should be no surprise to find an ambitious American bistro right here amidst the hurley burley of such commerce. But, it is.

Chef/Owner David Maish may be the only restaurateur to display his high school diploma in his dining room. It's superfluous; his food speaks volumes. By and large, Maish's cookery lives up to his descriptions, which is to say that he tends toward the elaborate. Start with an appetizer, perhaps smoked duck inside ravioli whose dough has been accented with pesto all set out in a mushroom cream sauce. In another selection, scallops are sautéed, plated with braised endive and gruyere cheese and set in a ginger soy broth. Pan Asian, French, Italian and the American Southwest are just a few of the influences which show up on the menu.

With some choices, Maish gets right to the heart of the matter without any frou-frou. His chicken paté is a smooth creamy blend that just begs to be spread thickly on toast wedges. By itself, the paté is just a hint salty. But, dab on some sharp dijon mustard and flavor balance is restored. In addition to the listed appetizers, the menu offers several pizzas; their California/Wolfgang Puck influence is clear.

Entrees run the gamut that includes half a dozen pastas as well as the more complex aspect of Chef Maish's repertoire. In one sense, it almost seems that the cooking is pushing a cutting edge, but on balance it really involves the logic of ingredients that seem to have a natural affinity. That's certainly true of pork tenderloin which is embellished with a fruity combination of dates and apples, plus sharp tasting gorgonzola cheese, all worked together into a sauce. Roasted potatoes (the menu lists them as "maished") dappled with rosemary finishes the plating.

For purists, there is the classic bistro steak and fries. In this case, a large rib eye is topped with garlic herb butter. Other special entrees include boned duck breast with Calvados brandy glaze. Dried black currants, sweet potato chips and roasted potatoes finish the plate. There are always a couple of seafood selections on the printed menu, plus nightly specials. Recently, grilled swordfish was coated with crushed pine nuts. On the printed menu, the swordfish is grilled and plated with mango salsa plus what the menu calls "rattlesnake" beans and blackberry puree. Tilapia gets more of a spicy Cajun seasoning touch and andouille sausage as part of its presentation.

Desserts are typically elaborate, but as familiar as bananas foster or crème brûlée. The wine list is fairly short and moderately priced. Service is casual and friendly in a setting which is just about the same way. David's Bistro might not have all that curb appeal that real estate sales people talk about, but once inside, there's appeal aplenty.

DAVIS STREET FISH MARKET
KR 17.5/20
Decor 4/4   Hospitality 5/5   Food 7.5/10   Value 1/1

• **American Seafood**

• **Evanston**

• **$$**

501 Davis Street
Evanston
847–869–347
Troubleshooter: Manager on duty

Hours: Daily 11:30 am–11 pm, Fri–Sun Country Breakfast 8 am–2 pm
Credit Cards: Amex, CB, Diner's, MC, Visa
Reservations: Only for parties of 5 or more
Handicapped: Accessible
Bar: Full service, limited wine list, many domestic beers
Smoking and nonsmoking sections: Separate smoking and nonsmoking seating
Parking: Street parking can be tight

Sometimes I get to thinking that ordering fish in a restaurant is like buying insurance. I mean, I must have ten different policies: whole life, half life, universal, home, auto, . . . you name it . . . and I've probably got it. And, I couldn't tell you what any of them mean.

A competent insurance agent is important to me, to explain all of the cash values, and surrender values, and anything else in the small print. And, that's why a good server in a fish restaurant is as important to me as what's on the menu. I like knowledgeable explanations to help sort through all the different kinds of fish. So, here's the point. I like Davis Street Fish Market because of a waitress who probably forgot more about fish than the old man and the sea ever knew. Selections are all listed on two large blackboards, and when anything becomes sold out, bingo . . . out comes some guy with a large eraser at the end of a stick . . . and wipes out the price. That way you know you won't be able to order any red haired barracuda or whatever. But hold on for a minute! Our waitress was better than the blackboard. She could talk about which fish were oily, and which were drier . . . . which fish were firm, and which were flaky. She probably knew which could do the back stroke.

Among eats, shrimp and crawfish *etoufee* is served in a large soup tureen, all rich and buttery, the kind you want to savor down to the last drop. For dessert, I wasn't so impressed with the Lone Star cheesecake, even if it was made with the most famous beer out of Texas. But, I did like the pecan pie, which is about as southern as you can get without an accent.

DEER PATH INN
KR 17.5/20
Decor 4/4   Hospitality 5\5   Food 7.5/10   Value .75/1

- **American Classic**
- **Lake Forest**
- **$$$**

255 East Illinois Road
Lake Forest
(800) 788-9480, (847) 234-2280
Troubleshooter: Alain Rochelemagne (food & beverage director)

Hours: Breakfast Mon–Fri 6:30–10 am, Sat–Sun 7 am–10 pm, Lunch Mon–Sat 11:30 am–2 pm, Sun Brunch 11 am–1:30 pm, Dinner Sun–Thurs 5–9 pm, Fri–Sat 5–10 pm
Credit Cards: Amex, Diners, Discover, MC, Visa
Reservations: Suggested
Handicapped: Accessibility limited
Smoking and nonsmoking sections: No smoking in dining room, smoking permitted in Pub
Parking: Free in adjacent lots

There is a cachet of exclusiveness about The Deerpath Inn. The Inn in its present form goes back to 1929, when the hotel and restaurant were built, but the name itself can be traced back well into the last century. For all of that, the hotel and restaurant are gracious and welcoming. The building (you may skip down to the next paragraph if you don't want the history lesson) is patterned after a half beamed and timbered 15th Century English mansion in the town of Chiddingstone. The public rooms reflect that Olde English sensibility about furnishings, stone fireplace, antiques, ancestry portraits, and even the Union Jack flying out front along side the Stars and Stripes.

Dining at The Inn is an experience in food preparation the way it used to be.

Grilled filet mignon comes with not one, but two rich sauces, and when was the last time you actually saw béarnaise sauce offered in any of today's contemporary restaurants? The other sauce, bordelaise, is the classic reduction of claret and the meat juices, perhaps the marrow, shallots and herbs. In the case of a black angus rib chop, green peppercorn sauce is the accompaniment along with a bouquet of sautéed field mushrooms. Rack of lamb gets a cream-based dijon mustard sauce instead of mint.

To be the saucier's apprentice here would be a real education. In another entree, a lobster and basil sauce is created, most certainly cream-based to establish the medium, for a presentation with grilled chicken breasts and large shrimp (forgive the oxymoron), plated on fettucine with fresh basil garnish. The pairing of the chicken and shrimp may seem odd, but in fact works quite well. And, even without too much of the sauce, there is enough flavor to hold a fastidious diner's interest.

For seafood, the menu choice is Dover sole done in the traditional manner with a *buerre blanc* sauce and toasted almonds. One nightly special brought Chilean sea bass to the table, predictably in a rich and buttery-based sauce which underscored the natural buttery taste of the fish itself.

The restaurant's wine cellar is commensurate with this level of dining, as is the service. The Deer Path Inn seems more geared to business than social entertainment, though if the desire is to capture a moment out of the past, The Inn should more than meet that requirement.

DELEECE
KR 16/20
Decor 4/4   Hospitality 5/5   Food 6/10   Value 1/1

- **American Eclectic**
- **Chicago/Mid-North**
- **$$**

4004 North Southport
Chicago
(773) 325-1710
Troubleshooter: Lynne Wallack-Handler (owner)

Hours: Dinner Sun 5–9 pm, Mon–Thurs 5:30–10 pm, Fri–Sat until 1 am, Brunch Sun 10:30 am–2:30 pm
Credit Cards: Amex, Diners, MC, Visa
Reservations: Suggested, especially weekends
Handicapped: Accessible
Smoking and nonsmoking sections: Both available
Parking: Street parking can be tight, especially when Cubs are home

Though things can be somewhat uneven, Deleece certainly lives up to its name. The food is delicious, savory, desire-fulfilling. But, that is not to suggest that all is perfect. The menu seems to concentrate on doing a few things well, rather than trying to be all things to all comers. Grilled calimari is as tender as this fleshy seafood can become, with a clean fresh taste. The calamari sits on a painted pool of pureed poblano peppers whose cool green color encircles red dabs of pureed tomato.

Another appetizer is even more flavorful. Quesadillas suggest cheese, but that's not all that is stuffed inside the tortilla wrappings. Sautéed portobello mushroom strips provide the lion's share of the flavor, accented with grilled onions and roasted sweet peppers for a delicious taste combination.

Other first course selections include oriental-style pot stickers, Italian bruschetta and good old American butter lettuce salad, albeit jazzed up with sherry vinaigrette dressing enhanced with spicy walnuts and enough goat cheese to contribute its essence.

Things begin to get a bit shaky among entrees. Pastas can be far too oily. In one, angel hair pasta is sauced with a concasse of roasted peppers, sweeter than usual sun-dried tomatoes as well as the usual suspects, garlic, parmesan cheese and a sprinkling of herbs, whose flavors can be generally overwhelmed by all else. Another pasta choice, linguini, might be served with not enough asparagus to taste, though the flavor of feta cheese and salty kalamata olives come storming through, while mushrooms do a sidestep to get out of the way. A decidedly Greek influence pervades this particular pasta and is served well by it.

Salmon lovers will relish the portion served at Deleece with a chiffonade of fennel plus capers accented by dill and some lemon juice. Other entrees include three versions of chicken, a vegetarian asparagus ravioli, a traditional pork chop and skirt steak with pan-fried angel hair pasta.

DIXIE KITCHEN
KR 17.5/20
Decor 4/4   Hospitality 4/5   Food 8.5/10   Value 1/1

- **New Orleans/ Cajun/Creole**
- **Evanston and Chicago/South (Hyde Park)**
- **$**

825 Church Street
Evanston
(847) 733-9030
Troubleshooter: James Pinatowski
Other Location

5225 South Harper (in Hyde Park), Chicago; 773-363-4943; Hours: Sun–Thurs 11 am–10 pm, Fri–Sat 11 am–11 pm; Credit Cards: All majors, Reservations: First come first serve; Smoking and nonsmoking sections: Both available; Handicapped: Accessible; Parking: Meters on street; Troubleshooter: James Wallace

Hours: Sun–Thurs 11 am–10 pm, Fri–Sat 11 am–11 pm
Credit Cards: All majors
Reservations: Recommended
Handicapped: Accessible
Smoking and nonsmoking sections: Both available
Parking: ½ block away or on street at meters

Dixie Kitchen looks exactly as you might expect. Its walls are filled with photos and drawings, as well as advertising billboards and signs, all suggestive of the South. The floor is checkerboard green and white tile. There is a bit of gingerbread scallop woodwork. And, of course, there is the food . . . the short list of Southern Delta and cajun cooking that still manages to cover most bases.

For instance, there are fried green tomatoes, about which the menu boasts . . . "movies are made of this." People often ask me if I cook. I sure have made my share of fried green tomatoes. The trick is to start with a really hard green tomato, slice it thin, dredge it in a good breading and let it fry in a good pan fat. Then, eat 'em up while they are still blazing hot. You could add some remoulade or hot sauce to them, but the best fried greenies are delicious right from the pan. And, with that, I have described the fried green tomatoes at Dixie Kitchen. My own recipe for breading might be a little different, but these are still good for starters.

So too are breaded oysters, though they could be better if the oysters were fresh, not frozen as I suspect these might be. There's no complaints about the gumbo, or the jambalaya, both classic Dixie stews enriched with Louisiana's andouille sausage. The difference between a gumbo and a jambalaya, by the way, has a lot to do with seasonings. Gumbos have filé, a clearly identifiable spice, whose flavor is barely evident in the Dixie Kitchen version. That might be as it should be, since the idea is to bring in a blend of tastes, with nothing overpowering.

One of my favorite Delta dishes is crawfish etoufee. This begins with a roux of flour cooked down with butter which acts as a thickener. The cooks at Dixie Kitchen cook theirs until it becomes dark brown and caramel colored. Small whole crawfish out of their shells are cooked in a mix of peppery seasonings, then plated with white rice. Etoufees are mild on the taste buds, hardly a palate shocker, but satisfying and delicious. The Dixie Kitchen version speaks to that description. Shrimp Creole is a rather straight ahead recipe, whole prawns in a tomato based sauce.

Getting away from fish and seafood, there's chicken fried steak, a truck stop favorite in any small town up and down the blue veined highways of the South. Nasty for the arteries as they might be, it's choice, basic American country-style eating. Other menu selections include a couple of versions of catfish, blackened in the skillet or deep fried, and some typically Louisiana Po' Boy sandwiches, plus a nod to the Low Country with North Carolina pulled barbecue pork.

A trio of desserts, bread pudding with whiskey sauce, peach cobbler and pecan pie round out the menu. Service is cordial and quick.

DON ROTH'S IN WHEELING
KR 18.5/20
Decor 4/4   Hospitality 4.5/5   Food 9/10   Value 1/1

- **American**
- **Wheeling**
- **$$**

61 North Milwaukee Avenue
Wheeling
(847) 537-5800
Troubleshooter: Manager on
duty

Hours: Lunch Mon–Fri 11:30 am–2:30 pm, Dinner Mon–Thurs 5:30–9:30 pm, Fri 5–10:30 pm, Sat 5–10 pm, Sun 4–8:30 pm
Credit Cards: All majors
Reservations: Suggested
Handicapped: Accessible
Bar: Full service, excellent cocktails, good wine list emphasizes American
Smoking and nonsmoking sections: Both available
Parking: Free in lot

You may be into spa cuisine, and doing health club workouts three times a week. You count calories, watch cholesterol, are into aerobics, and maybe even really do like Richard Simmons! But, tell the truth, now. Aren't there times when all you really want is a big hunk of meat?

There . . . I've said it, and I know that as you read this you are nodding your head and thinking about a thick cut of prime rib, or a tender eye of the round filet, and maybe even a 16-ounce sirloin.

If you are with me this far, then go a little further, out to Don Roth's In Wheeling. It is a homey sort of place, a huddle of smaller dining rooms clustered about. There's nothing trendy or modern about the art or other decor. The dominant theme is the memorabilia of Big Band going back to the 1920s and '30s at the original Blackhawk restaurant in the Loop. You could even ask the bartender for a Manhattan or a Rob Roy, and he'll know what you're talking about.

The menu is straight ahead American, featuring steaks, ribs, chicken, prime rib and fresh fish selections of the day. The onion soup is the genuine article with a thick layer of melted cheese blanketing the crock in which the soup has been baked and is served.

As soon as diners are seated, your waiter or waitress will bring out some toasted buttered rye rounds, the kind that are virtually irresistible for snacking. Then, once you have ordered, you can get the standard house salad complete with baby shrimp, or glide on over to one of the best salad bars around. There isn't a thing they haven't thought of for it. As for those entrees, a filet comes cooked to your specifications. Though the restaurant's reputation is built on solid pilings of beefsteak and prime rib, the seafood choices also win high marks. Norwegian salmon with an herb butter sauce or grouper fished from warm Caribbean waters, or whitefish from Lake Superior are regularly featured.

Desserts can include some real favorites such as pecan pie, cheesecakes, really big ice cream sundaes with hot fudge sauce.

DON'S FISHMARKET
KR 17/20
Decor 4/4   Hospitality 4.5/5   Food 7.5/10   Value 1/1

• **American Seafood**	**Hours:** Lunch Mon–Fri 11:30 am–2:30 pm, Dinner Mon–Thurs 5–10 pm, Fri–Sat 5–11 pm, Sun 4–9 pm
• **Skokie**	
• **$$**	
9335 Skokie Bouevard	**Credit Cards:** All majors
Skokie	**Reservations:** Suggested
(847) 677-3420	**Handicapped:** Accessible (one step up)
Troubleshooter: Bob Pasko	
(general manager)	**Smoking and nonsmoking sections:** Both available
	Parking: Free lot, valet on weekends

Don's Fishmarket fills a rather difficult niche as a mid-priced fish restaurant. For more than servicable fare in a pleasant, if predictable, atmosphere, it's a guaranteed come back restaurant.

That decor has been polished up since the opening days more than two decades ago. But, the description I wrote then more or less holds true today, ". . . typical fish restaurant à la Chicago; a recreation of a New England fish shanty with the usual trappings of weathered board, nautical fittings, polished wood tables and captain's chairs." In today's parlance that might read, ". . . more Winslow Homer than Homer Simpson."

The menu changes quite often, but there are some tried-and-true standards available most of the year, if the catch is any good. Among them is the Cape Cod–style lobster and clam bake, though the designation on the menu might change depending upon the theme of the month. You get a 1¼-pound lobster, which you can actually upgrade to 1½ pounds or larger for a few dollars more. The whole lobster sits in the pot radiating its bright red color. If you didn't know it before, you now know why sitting in the sun too long can make you look like a lobster.

Along with this king of crustaceans is a bevy of mussels, oysters and clams, a few shrimp in the shell, plus half an ear of corn and some new potatoes. The problem with "in the pot" dishes like this is that the components tend to get overcooked. They sit in a pool of hot water and simply continue to cook for several minutes after the pot is taken from the stove.

There is a wide array of other fresh seafood on the Don's Fishmarket menu, most of it tantalizingly good. By the way, beef eaters will enjoy the succulent 8 ounce filet mignon, which, like all dinners, comes with a choice of soup, or an excellent house salad, and a side garnish of vegetables.

The wine list is one of the more reasonably priced, with many noteworthy and admirable bottles for under $25. Your server will try to tempt you with selections from the dessert tray, and "tempt" is the operative word here.

DOVER STRAITS
KR 17/20
Decor 3.5/4   Hospitality 5/5   Food 7.5/10   Value 1/1

- **American Seafood**
- **Mundelein and Hoffman Estates**
- **$$**

Route 45, just East of Route 83
Mundelein
(847) 949-1550
Troubleshooters: Bill, Arthur and Aris Metropulos (owners)
Other Location
1149 West Golf Road, Hoffman Estates; 847-884-3900

Hours: Lunch Mon–Fri 11 am–3 pm, Dinner Mon–Fri 3–11 pm, Sat 4 pm–midnight, Sun 2–10 pm
Credit Cards: All majors
Reservations: Suggested week nights, required on weekends
Handicapped: Accessible
Bar: Lounge entertainment for listening and dancing Tues–Sat (no cover, no minimum)
Smoking and nonsmoking sections: Both available, main dining room is nonsmoking
Parking: Free in large lot

Dover Straits has been in business for 21 years with a tried-and-true nautical decor of dark wood, mock pier pilings, heavy ropes, marlins, swordfish and other trophy fish on the walls (I suspect they are plaster, not real), captain's chairs and the like. It may not be the latest in hip and trendy, but that's not what Dover Straits is all about.

The menu is a bit anachronistic with the likes of shrimp de johnge and oysters rockefeller on the menu. The menu has also picked up on trends, including that 1980s rage, blackened seafood.

The point is that Dover Straits gives diners a rather broad selection of popularly priced seafood. And, much of it is well prepared and presented. Some listings are quite imaginative, such as marinated and grilled calamari with a topping of chunk lobster meat and béarnaise sauce. On the other hand, ceviche is simplicity itself. A collection of shrimp, scallops, chopped clams, lobster and calamari is marinated in lime juice, whose acid virtually "cooks" the seafood. Using a classic approach, the fish is flavored with a tangy tomato and cilantro sauce.

The menu is a varied list, especially for entrees which include a list of house specials, another called "Captain's Selections," to lists of seafood and pasta. Meat eaters will find a selection "for the landlubbers" while those who cannot make up their minds can pick from that old restaurant standby, "surf and turf."

The varieties of seafood choices are fairly extensive, too. Heading the list is the house namesake, Dover sole, one of the most delicate and expensive fish found on any restaurant menu. In the Dover Straits version, the fish lives up to its expense, and its reputation. Dover sole is prepared virtually the same everywhere in a now traditional manner. The fish is sautéed in butter (though if you ask, they will broil it without butter). As busy as Dover Straits can get, a server will still offer to bone the fish table-side, presenting the flat fillets with a smattering of toasted almonds, if that happens to be the presentation of the evening.

Walleye pike, always a wonderfully flavored fish, is stuffed with cornbread crumbs, crab meat, tiny bay shrimp and scallops. A citrus cream sauce is layered on top. Sea bass has recently been prepared Cajun-style, which is to say, blackened with a topping of red, yellow and green peppers, onions and shrimp. It seems a bit more than sea bass really needs, but it also demonstrates the ideas ruminating in the Dover Straits kitchen.

The wine list is reasonably priced and service is friendly, knowledgeable and accommodating within the somewhat casual framework of the restaurant. In other words, this is not a fussy sort of place where words like "gourmet" and "connoisseur" are bandied about. It is rather, an Accessible, unintimidating, comfortable restaurant, with generally good food at reasonable cost.

Dragon Inn North
KR 17.5/20
Decor 4/4   Hospitality 5/5   Food 7.5/10   Value 1/1

* **Chinese**
* **Glenview**
* **$$**

1650 Waukegan Road
Glenview
(847) 729-8383
Troubleshooter: Jeanette Sih
(owner)

Hours: Sun noon–9:30 pm,
Mon–Thurs 11:30 am–9:30 pm,
Fri 11:30 am–10 pm, Sat 5–
10 pm
Credit Cards: Amex, MC, Visa
Reservations: Accepted
Bar: Full service
Handicapped: Accessible
**Smoking and nonsmoking
sections:** Both available
Parking: Free in lot

One question I'm often asked is where do I like to go when I am not reviewing restaurants. Frankly, there are so few such times when the meter isn't running, the question becomes almost hypothetical. But, on that list of restaurants I do return to for one reason or another, Dragon Inn North ranks up there. Low ceilings and beautiful Oriental art works help to shut away the outer world.

The menu is extensive, as one would expect from a better Chinese restaurant. Diners will find familiar items. True, the egg rolls may not be among the best; they tend to be a bit dry, as even the fried wonton can be on occasion. But the *kwoh te*, those delicious morsels of steamed dumplings are top notch, as are shrimp toast with its moist, creamy filling, and flavorful, tender onion pancakes. Among soups, sizzling rice always brings a warming pleasure to the table.

The restaurant serves up its share of Cantonese cookery if that is what you crave. But, many astute diners prefer the Mandarin, Hunan and Szechwan style for its greater challenge and depth. A good example could be Hunan sizzling lamb, beef, chicken or shrimp. The meat of your choice is grilled in the kitchen, then brought out to the dining room. There, a waitress will quickly transfer it onto a stove-hot metal platter with crispy white rice noodles. The meat instantly begins to sizzle, giving the dish its name. A somewhat spicy thick brown sauce tops the food.

Moo shu, either meat or vegetarian, has been a constant choice over the years, as is chicken with cashews. Among other favorites is General Tso's chicken, the Dragon Inn North version is more sweet than spicy hot, but make no mistake that the peppery underpinnings are there. Among other favorites is vegetarian spring rolls, with a crisp, delicate wonton wrap. And, when shipments are available and fresh, stir-fry Dover sole with crunchy Oriental vegetables is a major treat.

For dessert, there are a couple of ice creams as well as the ubiquitous fortune and almond cookies.

ECHO
KR 18.25/20
Decor 3.5/4   Hospitality 5/5   Food 9/10   Value .75/1

- **American Eclectic**
- **Chicago/Near Northwest**
- **$$**

1856 North Avenue
Chicago
(773) 395-3475
Troubleshooter: Sean Herron
(co-owner)

Hours: Mon–Thurs 5:30 pm–midnight, Fri–Sat 5:30 pm–1 am, Sun 5–10 pm
Credit Cards: Visa, MC
Reservations: Recommended
Handicapped: Accessible
Smoking and nonsmoking sections: Both available
Parking: Valet $6

Echo is very trendy, on the edge of edgy with its dark colors, low industrial look and somewhat close-together tables. In fact, if you happen to be seated too close to the bar, you might have to cope with cigarette smoke.

With that aside, Echo is a comfortable and convivial setting for what used to be called grazing. The portions tend to the small size to afford diners the opportunity to do some sampling. Among chilled selections, noodles in a spicy peanut sauce suggests the Asian influences that pepper the menu. So, too, you will find a handsomely presented and prepared tuna trio, the only plating on the menu actually designed and priced for two people. Tuna in a California maki role, as tartare and in slices of tuna sashimi are set with pickled ginger, wasabi and daikon radish plus a syrup reduced soy sauce for flavor accent. It is light and refreshing.

Not all selections need be Asian, however. There is a peppered venison carpaccio for the brave and a grilled vegetable tian for the not so brave. Thin strips of smoked onion and greens are layered with a rosemary-infused coulis. I have not a clue how the chef does it, but it works deliciously.

There are some other cold selections including an array of oysters, reminiscent of the delicious chilled bounty served when the space occupied by Echo was another restaurant, named Starfish with the same owners. Flipping the menu to the hot side are temptations like a blue cheese and caramelized onion tart with a coulis of smoked tomatoes, simple grilled beef in a red wine and thyme au jus or quail stuffed with a force of spinach and bacon set on saffron risotto among other ingredients.

The Asian-Fusion influence reappears in black bean potstickers. The beans fill these little morsels that include the southeast Asian flavor accents of cilantro, ginger and lemon grass. These are finger foods that can be dipped into soy sauce or brushed with a spiced relish sambal. Taste an order of pan-fried shrimp cake, a demonstration of the eclecticism on the Echo menu. You'll find nuggets of star anise along with glazed slices of pineapple.

There was one disappointment among our tastings, the intriguingly named Two Soups, One Bowl. It's nothing more than a tomato broth swirled across the more dominant smoked onion and potato cream soup.

E.J.'S PLACE
KR 17.5/20
Decor 4/4   Hospitality 5/5   Food 7.5/10   Value 1/1

• **American**	**Hours:** Mon–Thurs 3:30–10 pm, Fri–Sat 3:30–11 pm, Sun 3–10 pm
• **Wilmette**	
• **$$**	**Credit Cards:** Visa, Amex, Diners, MC, Discover
10027 Skokie Boulevard	**Reservations:** Reccomended
Wilmette	**Handicapped:** Accessible
(847) 933-9800	**Smoking and nonsmoking**
Troubleshooter: E.J. Lenzi	**sections:** Both available
(owner)	**Parking:** Free valet service

E.J.'s Place is like one of those North Woods restaurants that dot Wisconsin, except the food is better . . . lots better.

The reason may be that despite its knotty pine look and wood-beamed ceiling, E.J.'s is a rather citified restaurant plopped down in a North Shore suburb. This is a third generation restaurant that can trace its roots back to Gene and Georgetti's, not bad restaurant roots at that. The menu leans toward oversized portions of meat, chops, seafood and some Italian-American specialties. Try the linguini with white clam sauce for a sample of the pastas, rich with garlic and parsley, loaded with chopped fresh clams.

If any problems exist, it may be that this and some other selections come from the kitchen too oily. Even escolar, a meaty, firm-fleshed fish is plated on spinach and radicchio which has been so highly oiled that it tends to cancel out whatever reduced calorie benefits diners look for when ordering fish. Tasty, of course, but a tad on the rich side.

But, the customers know what to expect and get it in great abundance. The grilled calamari we ordered were a little rubbery, but still enjoyable, bathed in a light tomato-based sauce probably enhanced with white wine, maybe some pepper flakes and parsley. Other appetizers range from crab cakes to baked clams or fresh raw oysters, as well as such standbys as shrimp cocktail and a mixed antipasto platter.

All entrees include a choice of soup or salad. Though the salad is simple iceberg lettuce, the dressings are so delicious that it hardly makes a difference what kind of greens are used. Among those entrees, chicken vesuvio is an explosive presentation, the platter heaped with roasted potato wedges sitting atop an enormous portion of cut up pan-sautéed chicken. Veal, pork or lamb chops hot from the broiler, or any of four cuts of steak are similarly generous eating.

You could order sides of mushrooms, spinach or broccoli, or even baked, hash brown or garlic mashed potatoes, but a large platter of cottage fried potatoes accompanies all meats and seafood. They are like eating fresh cooked potato chips and as someone once said . . . "you can't eat just one."

EL CUZCO
KR 16.5/20
Decor 3.5/4   Hospitality 4/5   Food 7.5/10   Value 1/1

- **Peruvian**
- **Palatine**
- **$$**

40 West Palatine Road
Palatine
(847) 705-5032
Troubleshooters: Lorenzo and Andy Fernandez (owners)

Hours: Tues–Thurs 11 am–9 pm, Fri until 10 pm, Sat 2–10 pm, Sun 2–9 pm
Credit Cards: All majors
Reservations: Accepted
Smoking and nonsmoking sections: Both available

Short of a visit to Lima, El Cuzco brings a taste of the Andes to the Illinois flatland. The Incas made Peru the heart of their Andean kingdom. One gift the New World acquired from the Old was the potato. Thus, the tuber shows up in several interesting incarnations at El Cuzco. In one, they are served with a cheese sauce, in another a nut sauce. In yet another they are deep-fried and stuffed with savory seasoned ground beef. One thing they have in common is that no matter how they are presented, they neither look nor taste like the common baked potato that is so central to North American dining.

The unusual continues with Peruvian-style *ceviche*, or as the Peruvians call it *cebiche*. In either spelling, orange roughy is cooked by the acidic effects of lime juice. In one version, shrimp is added to the mix, both of which are garnished with onions, lettuce, corn and potatoes.

Adventurous diners will find beef hearts, while more traditional tastes should be pleased by the El Cuzco version of beef tenderloin. The tender meat is plated in a sauce more akin to a wine rich gravy, and accompanied by Peruvian style mashed potatoes, which are more like a potato whip or puree.

Among other choices, chicken and potatoes, called cau cau chicken is reminiscent of chicken à la king, a somewhat starchy, bland concoction, despite its fresh yellow coloring. Chicken shishkebab brings two large skewers, the chicken seasoned with a flavorful spicy rub, served with onions, green peppers and tomatoes with a side of fresh steamed rice. One of the most interesting entrees is Peruvian-style fried rice with a selection of mussels, shrimp, grilled calamari and scallops. The menu's depth extends to several other fashions of fish, chicken and meat, plus an array of desserts, most with Peruvian influence.

ELI'S THE PLACE FOR STEAK
KR 17.5/20
Decor 4/4   Hospitality 5/5   Food 7.5/10   Value 1/1

- **American**
- **Chicago/Near North**
- **$$$**

215 East Chicago Avenue
Chicago
(312) 642-1393
Troubleshooter: Julie Weaver (general manager), Marc Schulman (owner)

Hours: Lunch Mon–Fri 11:30 am–2:30 pm, Dinner Mon–Sun 4–10:30 pm
Credit Cards: All majors
Reservations: Suggested
Handicapped: Accessible
Bar: Full service bar and piano lounge
Smoking and nonsmoking sections: Both available
Parking: Discounted in building garage
Party Facilities: Private dining room for 30–100 guests

Eli's Cheesecake is probably more famous than the restaurant. But, this is where it all began. No one would ever call this restaurant especially modern or imaginative, though there has been remodeling that opens a view to Chicago Avenue, a playlot park named in memory of its foudner, Eli Schulman, and the Chicago Museum of Contemporary Art. Sure, the interior is glitzy, even garish by today's restaurant standards. But, the quality is enduring.

Though "steak" is part of the restaurant's name, my favorite has always been Calve's Liver Eli. It's as sweet and tender as you can imagine, the kind of dining that might even make a liver lover out of someone who refuses to touch the stuff. Thin slices are sautéed with sliced onions, green peppers and mushrooms. No, it's decidedly untrendy, but what a treat it can be!

As dining tastes have evolved, Eli's has also become a place for seafood. The selections are not numerous, but they are prepared with the same fastidious care that marks the restaurant. In a reflection of contemporary tastes, salmon is seasoned with pesto, though the menu turns "retro" with a classic version of shrimp de jonghe in garlic butter, sherry and bread crumbs.

All dinners include Eli's lavish bread and matzo basket, an iced relish tray, salad and potato. And, of course, for dessert there is the famous cheesecake served exactly as it always has been and where it all began.

ERIE CAFE
KR 18.5/20
Decor 3/4   Hospitality 4.5/5   Food 10/10   Value 1/1

- **American**
- **Chicago/Near North**
- **$$$**

536 W. Erie Street
Chicago
(312) 266-2300
Troubleshooter: Ron Lenzi, Sr. (owner)

Hours: Mon–Sat 11 am–11:30 pm, Sun 3–11:30 pm
Credit Cards: All majors except Discover
Reservations: Suggested, especially weekends
Handicapped: Accessible
Smoking and nonsmoking sections: Both available
Parking: Free valet

Opening another steak house in Chicago may seem culinary redundancy, but when it is as good as Erie Cafe, why quibble? Erie Cafe has what in art might be called a strong provenance or in horse racing, good breeding. Its owners are part of the Gene and Georgetti restaurant family.

While there is a certain clubiness at G&G, something else seems to prevail at Erie Cafe. Service is as professional as can be. There's not an actor in sight unless he is among the customers. If anything, service might be too good. Dinners seem pegged to the clock; one can be in and out in 90 minutes or less. When we asked for things to be slowed down, we were told that entree preparation had already begun. And, when dinner was over, our waiter, who otherwise was exemplary, left the check before we asked for it.

With that said, it should also be noted that there are no quibbles or complaints about the food and its quality. The menu lists five different cuts of beef from the mighty T-bone to the hand-high filet mignon. Our waiter volunteered the information that the strip sirloin had the best flavor of the lot, though the filet mignon was more tender. He was right on the money. The filet was thick and tender, a beautiful cut of beef, charred to a hard crust on the outside, still warm and pink in the center. The sirloin was also tender, and because it is a bit fattier piece of meat, more flavorful.

Dinners come with a basic, but flavorfully dressed iceberg lettuce salad and a side of the most fantastic cottage fried potatoes I have ever tasted. These are crisp, but still with a potato, not a potato chip quality. Among side vegetables, the sautéed spinach with garlic is as good as it gets. Other entrees include huge portions of chicken vesuvio, or a green and red pepper version called chicken à la vorda, as well as a selection of other chops and poultry.

ERWIN
KR 19/20
Decor 3.5/4   Hospitality 5/5   Food 9.5/10   Value 1/1

- **American**
- **Chicago/Mid-North**
- **$$**

2925 North Halsted Street
Chicago
(773) 528-7200
Troubleshooters: Cathy and Erwin Drechsler (owners)

Hours: Tues–Thurs 5:30–10 pm, Fri–Sat until 11 pm, Sun Brunch 10:30 am–2:30 pm, Dinner 5–9:30 pm
Credit Cards: All majors
Reservations: Encouraged
Handicapped: Accessible, except for steps at the front entrance
Smoking and nonsmoking sections: No smoking in restaurant
Parking: Valet

Erwin Drechsler is probably not the first person to come to mind when listing Chicago's celebrity Chefs. But, I think he could rank right up there with them. His restaurant, Erwin, is a jewel.

It's not the look of the restaurant which is rather simple, maybe even a little old-fashioned. It is Drechsler's cooking, an American-style that is inventive without being flamboyant, imaginative without being contrived.

The menu changes from time to time as he works out new ideas, but they are always grounded in sound fundamentals of cooking. He does not let his ideas get beyond reality, or a knowledgable and expectant diner's anticipations.

One of his best appetizers is a caramelized onion tart. It takes on a tangy sweetness, enhanced by dabs of Danish blue cheese, their natural accompaniment of walnuts, and a touch of sage. These toppings are set out as if the tart were a pizza instead of the buttery rich pastry it really is.

Other first course starters include lovely lamb and arugula salad and grilled shrimp and mussels in a light curry and basil broth. Dreschler's talent is manifest in the way he not only marries logical flavors, but in their extraordinary balance of taste and texture. There is at the same time, a restraint in his cooking that gives his dishes a patina of authority based on logic.

Consider pan-roasted walleye pike, which Drechsler takes out of its North Woods setting and sets in a corn and fava bean broth whose easy flavors work so nicely with the mild tasting fish. Other seafood includes salmon, perfectly flaked from the wood-fired grill, and given a bit of Asian accent with tastes of ginger and a light Japanese-influenced miso broth.

Roasted chicken climbs out of the ordinary catagory with bits of proscuitto for flavor accent along with a bed of spinach-infused spaetzle and a fundamental garlic sauce. Flank steak is grilled over a wood fire and plated with tangy barbecue sauced black eyed peas, a reduction of vidalias and stilton, the best blue cheese of them all, which brings a wonderful complexity to this recipe.

Desserts exploit the American continent with such choices as Michigan sour cherry pie, peanut butter mousse cake and the house brownie sundae that packs walnuts, sliced bananas, coconut-glazed ice cream and chocolate sauce as the end of the meal laignaippe.

Erwin's wine list is excellent as is the cheerful and friendly service.

ETHIOPIAN VILLAGE
KR 17/20
Decor 4/4   Hospitality 4/5   Food 8/10   Value 1/1

• **Ethiopian**	**Hours:** Mon–Fri 3:30–11:30 pm, Sat–Sun 1 pm–midnight
• **Chicago/Mid-North**	**Credit Cards:** Diners, MC, Visa
• **$**	**Reservations:** Accepted, suggested on weekends
3462 North Clark Street	**Handicapped:** Not accessible
Chicago	**Parking:** Street parking can be tight
(773) 929-8300	
Troubleshooter: Brahne Shifer (owner)	

From the moment you open the front door and inhale the aromas of exotic spices and seasonings, it becomes apparent that dining at Ethiopian Village is going to be an exotic experience. The restaurant is typical storefront size, with a handful of tables covered with earthtone, floral print cloths. The walls carry out the same color theme, as they showcase a few examples of Ethiopian arts and crafts.

After the initial assault on the olfactory senses, the next thing that diners will notice is a lack of silverware. That is not an oversight; Ethiopian food is meant to be taken in hand, usually wrapped inside a piece of the flat, almost rubbery bread called *injera*. The idea is to tear off a large piece of *injera* and use it to pick up foods set out on a central platter. Ethiopian Village serves several combination platters, ideal for two or three people, and so reasonably priced that they are difficult to ignore. One combination brings vegetables set around orange roughy that has been boned, cut into bite-size pieces and stewed. The roughy in the portion we were served had a stronger taste than I prefer, which suggests that this normally mild fish might not have been as fresh as it could have been. Otherwise, its spiced peppery sauce was excellent. The vegetables that could accompany this or other combinations, such as one centered around chicken or beef, is usually given a combination of spices, all of which leave an exotic sensibility on the tongue. Oiled greens are mild, in contrast to lentils at one side of the platter, or pinto beans set directly across.

The combination platters are set out on a thinner version of *injera* than that used to pick up foods. Still it makes a delicious edible doily of sorts. In addition to the four or five combinations, there are several à la carte selections that can be ordered. A taste of lamb came with green beans and potatoes, while beef was aromatically spiced with cinnamon, perhaps a little cloves or nutmeg in the mix, which found the chunks of meat in a dark gravy. Among appetizers, be sure to order a dumpling filled with lentil beans, best when dipped into a little of the *berbera*, a traditional curry-like sauce as common to Ethiopian tables as are catsup and mustard to ours.

Ethiopian Village also serves a bargain priced vegetarian buffet which includes many of the same selections found on the combination platters. Service tends to be a little bit casual, but that more or less fits in with the entire mood of the dining experience.

EVEREST
KR 20/20
Decor 4/4   Hospitality 5/5   Food 10/10   Value 1/1

- **French**
- **Chicago/South Loop**
- **$$$**

440 South Lasalle Street, 40th Floor
Chicago
(312) 663-8920
Troubleshooter: Jean Joho (chef/owner)

Hours: Tues–Thurs 5:30–9 pm, Fri–Sat 5:30–10 pm
Credit Cards: All majors
Reservations: Mandatory
Smoking and nonsmoking sections: Both available
Parking: Complimentary for dinner patrons in One Financial Place
Dress: Jackets and ties requested for gentlemen

The character of greatness is demonstrated in several ways. One is consistency. In the case of restaurants, where management changes and chefs come and go, it can be an elusive goal. But, by any definition or standard, Everest is and remains a great restaurant.

Chef Jean Joho has been in firm control of its kitchen since the beginning. His mark is on not only the menu, or even the china, where his initials are embossed. His mark is on the cuisine from conception to preparation and plating.

Our recent visit posed what could have been some thorny problems. One of our party was a strict vegetarian, while the rest of us were concerned with eliminating as much fat and cholesterol from our dining as possible, within the context of what would draw a diner to Everest.

This meant that some alterations were sought in preparation. There is a lesson in this, and that is that the better the restaurant, the more willing it should be to accommodate a patron's special needs. In the case of Everest there was no need to worry.

Our evening began with the presentation of a succession of *amusés*. The first was a bite-sized portion of caviar sitting atop a potato fondant. Each portion was presented on a silver teaspoon; its elegance spoke volumes. Next came barnacles marinated in a brine of lemon juice and herbs. Don't think of the creatures which grow on the under hull of ships. These are farm-raised barnacles. Taste and texture were similar to Mexican ceviche, the presentation was elegant.

Like many great French restaurants, Everest features a multi-course degustation, a three course pre-theatre dinner, and the regular à la carte menu. Consider a consomme of wild mushrooms, flavored with bits of smoked duck. Chef Joho's menu reflects his Alsatian heritage. So, risotto, though Italian in origin, may be prepared with an Alsatian reisling wine broth to showcase boned morsels of frog legs. And, though references to that region of France dot the menu, Chef Joho is firmly insistent that his primary ingredients be American. Thus, farm-raised venison from upstate New York, Maine oysters, Pennsylvania lamb or Wisconsin veal will be at the center of some entrees. In one particularly delicious appetizer, a terrine of smoked herring and caviar is bound with creamed potato. Meeting one request that no butter or cream sauces be used, the Chef diverted from lobster as listed on his menu and prepared a cabernet wine–based sauce, accenting the flavor with bits of Alsatian-style red cabbage and bacon.

Service is on the mark, always courteous and informed. The dining room is handsome in its own right, and for many tables offers a view of the western horizon from the restaurant's 40th floor vantage.

FAHRENHEIT
KR 20/20
Decor 4/4   Hospitality 5/5   Food 10/10   Value 1/1

- **American Chic**
- **Chicago/Bucktown**
- **$$$**

695 North Milwaukee
Chicago
(312) 733-7400
Troubleshooters: Gino and
Tom Marchetti

Hours: Sun–Fri 5:30–10 pm,
Sat 5:30–10:30 pm, Bar is open
5:30 pm–2 am
Credit Cards: Visa, MC, Amex
Reservations: Mandatory
Handicapped: Accessible
Parking: Valet $7

I'm not really sure why the owners of Fahrenheit, gave their restaurant that name. Maybe because the restaurant looks so cool, it has become a trendy diner's hot spot. The restaurant uses broad sections of padded vinyl in blue and related soft pastel shades to cover its walls from floor to high ceilings. It is minimalism to the max; I don't think vinyl has gotten this much respect since the days of the Chevy Bel Aire convertible.

Diners come in all ages, from seniors down to infants; dress ranges from t-shirt tops to double-breasted suits. It's a noisy, but convivial mix whether one is standing in the crowded bar, or seated in the main dining area, with its open kitchen all the way back. Well, not quite . . . the restrooms are farther back.

The menu is stylized upscale American chic. Soft-shell crabs are served as an appetizer, stacked like a BLT sandwich with spicy cole slaw and mayonnaise. Gazpacho is a rich red bowl of striking flavors typical of this chilled soup; fish around and you'll find a bit of lobster *timbale* down there at the bottom of the bowl. Ratatouille is served with scoops of goat cheese and a couple of black olive crisp breads on the platter. Seared sea scallops are absolutely flavor explosive, buttery and warm with basil and balsamic vinegar sauce.

There are several more appetizers and about a dozen entrees. Seafood fans will get a bang from the delicious sautéed swordfish, a big chunky cut roasted with slivers of tomatoes, artichokes and leek. Rounding out a trio of fish are roasted halibut with an herb, pancetta and basil butter sauce, or salmon sautéed with wild mushrooms in soy and crusted with scallions and fresh ginger.

The big treat for meat eaters could be a grilled veal porterhouse with macaroni and cheese. Did I mention that the cheese is *gruyere?* Venison comes grilled on the bone as a big meaty chop with a fat corn blini, perfect for soaking up the tart tastes of a dark cherry compote. But, for about half of what either of those will cost, you could order skirt steak. This delicatessen standby works amazingly well when dressed up with a béarnaise sauce to compliment the meat's own juices. Creamed spinach and *au gratin* potatoes complete things.

Among dessert choices, *plum crostada* has a delightfully light and flaky butter crust which supports a scoop of tart plum sherbet, sauced with cooked plums. It was plumy, to say the least.

FILIPPO'S
KR 18.5/20
Decor 3.5/4   Hospitality 5/5   Food 9/10   Value 1/1

- **Italian**
- **Chicago/Mid-North**
- **$$**

North Clybourn
Chicago
(773) 528-2211
Troubleshooters: Annette Simon and Filippo Del Pret (owners)

Hours: Sun 5–10 pm, Mon–Thurs 5–11 pm, Fri–Sat 5 pm–midnight
Credit Cards: All majors
Reservations: Suggested
Handicapped: Accessible
Smoking and nonsmoking sections: Separate smoking and nonsmoking seating
Parking: On street or in theatre lot across the street after 6 pm

---

The decor may be faux neo-classic, but the hospitality is genuine at this small storefront restaurant. The room is neatly appointed with suggestions of Renaissance Italy coupled with a contemporary sense of minimalist accent. The collection of crockery and chairs may seem randomly eclectic, but it really is all too perfect to be put together by chance.

The cooking is as well-designed as the decor, and perhaps just as studied. This is Italian food well-suited to contemporary tastes and needs. And, though the menu does not say so, virtually anything can be ordered in half portions. That's fine not only for small appetites, but for those who might be inclined to taste more than one or two items from each course.

One could begin with a selection of roasted vegetables, slices of eggplant, zucchini, bright orange carrots and zippy red, yellow and green peppers. A clean tasting wine, red or white, makes a good accompaniment to such simple beginnings. Other appetizers include sautéed mushrooms in white wine with garlic, an ample portion of fried calamari, classic carpaccio, the paper-thin slices of beef, almost shimmeringly translucent.

Salads are generously portioned, piled high in bowls that showcase a mix of greens in one, tomatoes and mozzarella in another, or blue cheese, prosciutto and tomatoes in yet another.

Filippo's offers a quartet of risotto preparations and nearly a dozen pastas for the next course. Risotto with portobellos is intensely flavored, perhaps a bit too highly peppered. But, pairing it with a pasta such as *spaghetti Adriatico* brings a sense of balance. The spaghetti is sauced with cherry tomatoes, olive oil and garlic, complimented by large meaty shrimp and tender sea scallops.

Seafood is somewhat limited. Salmon was one nightly special, while red snapper, broiled and stuffed with fresh herbs was another choice. From a selection of poultry, roasted chicken and an accompaniment of quartered potatoes is deliciously seasoned with rosemary and sautéed in olive oil with lemon juice, wine and garlic. It may sound like standard Chicago Chicken Vesuvio, but there is something more elusive, more subtle in the flavors. A handful of other chicken entrees round out the selections, along with a pair of veal recipes. Scallops in sage sauce are topped with sliced mushrooms and melted mozzarella in one creation; breaded veal chop is sauteed and plated in fennel sauce in the other.

Desserts include flourless chocolate cake, an Italian version of crème brûlée, gelato, and that old standby, *tiramisu*. There is a good wine list, which like menu selections, is reasonably priced.

Flatlander's
KR 19/20
Decor 4/4   Hospitality 5/5   Food 9/10   Value 1/1

- **American Brew Pub**
- **Lincolnshire**
- **$$**

200 Village Green (Milwaukee Avenue and Route 45) Lincolnshire
(847) 821-1234
Troubleshooter: Manager on duty

Hours: Mon–Thurs 11 am–midnight, Fri–Sat 11–2 am, Brunch Sun 10 am–2 pm, Dinner Sun 3:30–10 pm
Credit Cards: All majors
Reservations: Accepted, and suggested on weekends
Handicapped: Accessible
Smoking and nonsmoking sections: 100% nonsmoking
Parking: Ample, including free valet parking

Flatlander's is big, even cavernous. Think of Noah's Ark. Now, think of Noah's Ark upside down. That about does it. Everything's oversized inside, too. The booths for four people easily seat six. The platters are big. The central fireplace is big. It's even a big, long walk to the restroom.

With all this in mind, it only follows that portions would be big. Not to worry; they are! And the food is pretty good, too. The food is more than pubgrub. Yes, you will find burgers, big ones of course. In addition to the hamburger, there are ostrich burgers and buffalo burgers, and to complete the lineup, turkey burgers, too. Other sandwiches stud the menu. Among them is a two-handed Sheboygan pork brat steamed in the house brew, then grilled. A pork chop sandwich may be even bigger, while other choices range from different styles of grilled chicken to a Reuben with peppered pastrami and all the fixings to go with it.

While sandwiches are virtual meals, the dinner platters are not to be ignored. You could begin with an appetizer sampler which brings a platter of mixed nibbles. Among individual choices chicken wings are the standard buffalo issue with blue cheese and a hot red pepper glaze. More unusual might be pieces of duck tenderloin breaded and fried and served with a honey mustard dipping sauce.

Dinners come with a trio of freshly baked breads in unlimited supply, a choice of house or Caesar salad, and enough side garnishes, and usually a vegetable or other addition to the platter. For instance, an order of turkey marsala brings twin cuts from the breast that have been grilled, then doused with a mushroom and marsala wine sauce. Add to that a large heap of garlic mashed potatoes, sage stuffing, and a necklace of fresh steamed vegetables. I think if you ate it all, they'd have to carry you out feet first.

The same thing is true of other entrees, though some seafood seems a little more in proportion. Mahi mahi was recently served with an herb and garlic butter, but even plain without the sauce, the fish was tasty and fresh. The plate was finished with a mild flavored couscous (our server's description of the couscous as "puffed rice" gave me visions of breakfast). A dozen or so other seafood and chicken selections share menu space with several pastas, steaks and chops.

As for pasta, you'll find the usual suspects, as well as some a little different. Try rock shrimp and roasted barley prepared as if it were ar-borio rice for a risotto. This is a steamy casserole overflowing with shrimp and fleshed out with strips of portobello mushrooms, snow peas, peppers and baby corn.

FOODLIFE
KR Not Applicable

- **Eclectic**
- **Chicago/Near North**
- **$**

835 North Michigan Avenue,
Water Tower Place,
Mezzanine Level
Chicago
(312) 335-3663
Troubleshooters: Jeff
Winograd, Chirs Favero
(managing partners)

Hours: Mon–Sat Juice, Espresso bar and Bakery 7:30 am–10 pm, All other stations 11 am–10 pm, Sat 9 am–8 pm, Sun Juice, Espersso bar and Corner bakery 7:30 am–9 pm, All other stations 11 am–9 pm
Credit Cards: All majors
Reservations: None taken
Handicapped: Accessible
Smoking and nonsmoking sections: No smoking
Parking: Avaialble in Water Tower underground garage

In a setting of cobblestone paving, large spreading branched trees and flowering shrubs, admittedly artificial, shoppers at Water Tower Place can stroll from area to area finding an array of different items. I do not suggest that the cooking one finds here is equal to the best sit-down restaurants. A vegetarian version of bolognese sauce is too watery, pastas are not cooked to order, except for a final dousing in hot water, and seasonings on some recipes which one would expect to be full-flavored are somewhat duller, perhaps as a nod to a broader dining public than that which would seek out specialty restaurants.

The emphasis is on variety and convenience. Diners are given a plastic card with a magnetic strip. Each time an order is placed at one of the food stations, the price is tallied. After dining, you check out at a cash register; though Foodlife is self-service, a modest tip is included in the cost to cover table bussing and counter personnel.

It is not the usual restaurant which allows diners a sample taste of this and that. Browsing at one station, where roasted vegetables, couscous, chicken chili, grilled chicken and other foods were on display, a server offered us tastes of whatever we chose. That sort of generosity pays vast dividends in good will and customer satisfaction.

A Mexican station features several tacos, burritos, and similar regional fare. We tasted a delicious fish taco, several large pieces fried, given a light pepper sauce with some complexity, but no real heat and served with a side of unexpectedly spicy Spanish rice and mild dark beans in a thick dark sauce. For those who care about such things, diners can even get a soybean cheese derivative of Monterey Jack for heart healthy dining. Incidentally, at virtually all stations, there are choices for those who care to limit intake of fats, calories and cholesterol. At the dessert station, for example, amidst the chocolate chimichangas and cheese cakes, is simple angel food with fresh strawberry sauce and sliced berries.

At another station we tasted Chinese steamed dumplings filled with chicken and shrimp in a salty soy ginger sauce. A pizza station offered several styles of deep dish or thin crust. Yet another food station offers a number of whole grain recipes for strict vegetarians. There is even a meatless burger at the Foodlife version of a burger shack, right along side the more conventional hamburger sandwiches.

FRIDA'S
KR 17.5/20
Decor 4/4   Hospitality 5/5   Food 7.5/10   Value 1/1

- **Mexican**
- **Chicago Northwest**
- **$$**

2143 North Damen Avenue
Chicago
(773) 337-4327
Troubleshooter: Sandy Dranias

Hours: Sun–Thurs noon–10 pm, Fri–Sat noon–11 pm
Credit Cards: All majors
Reservations: Taken
Bar: Full bar, tequila specialty drinks
Handicapped: Accessible
Smoking and nonsmoking sections: Both available
Parking: Free in private lot

Frida's is named, not for its owner, but for Frida Kahlo, wife of Mexico's most famous artist, Diego Rivera, and a prominent artist in her own right. Thus, with whitewashed walls, high ceiling and an atrium-like decor, the restaurant is also a museum setting for examples of contemporary art and photography.

Its menu showcases the gastronomic art with considerable success. Start with grilled calamari in a pulpy sauce of peppers and garlic. In a variation on traditional Mexican cooking, there are tortillas wrapped and filled with a filling of mushrooms and mild white cheese, flavored with a wild herb called *epazote*. In another variation, flautas are filled with a purée of tomato and cheese, topped with avocado cream sauce. Other selections include a more traditional rendition of Mexican-style marinated seafood cooked in citric acid, called ceviche, even Middle Eastern humus, though far from Mexican, seems to fit in if only for its popularity.

Entrees might include a fusion of Mexican and Italian influences in fettuccine with mushrooms and mild chili sauce, though not so mild that it can be ignored. There are several fish choices ranging from shellfish in a light cream sauce, to blackened catfish, grilled shark and salmon as well as classic red snapper veracruzana. Among the restaurant's meat selections are barbecued ribs, which may not seem too Mexican, at least until the sauce is tasted. The roots may be a traditional sweet tangy tomato-based creation, but the addition of Mexican hot peppers adds a distinctive, and welcome bite. Incidentally, the same saucing is used with roasted chicken and works to perfection.

Diners may not think of turkey as a part of Mexican cooking, but the bird is used in *molé poblano*, perhaps the most famous of all dishes handed down from the Aztecs. There are as many *molés* as their are cooks to prepare them, though chocolate is at the heart of the deepest flavored. The sauce is slightly bitter, with just a hint of hidden sweetness. Thick slices of turkey medallions are like islands in a *molé* sea.

Desserts include flan, flourless chocolate cake and mango cheese-cake.

FROGGY'S
KR 19/20
Decor 4/4   Hospitality 5/5   Food 9/10   Value 1/1

• **French**

• **Highwood**

• **$$**

306 Greenbay Road
Highwood
(847) 433-7080
Troubleshooters: Gregg Mason (owner), Chef Thierry Le Feuvre

Hours: Lunch Mon–Fri 11:30 am–2 pm, Dinner Mon–Thurs 5–10 pm, Fri–Sat until 11 pm
Credit Cards: CB, Diners, Discover, MC, Visa
Reservations: Accepted only for parties of 6 or more
Bar: Full service, small lounge, large wine list highlighted by more than 50 California chardonnays
Parking: Ample free parking on street or nearby lot

After all these years, instead of growing stale, Froggy's is as fresh as ever. True, it may no longer be the impudent bistro it once was, but the maturity of age has worked well toward the restaurant's ever continuing appeal. The dining room is appointed in a well-mannered style, more formal than casual.

The menu is never static, though to be sure, some standards, such as duckling à l'orange or rack of lamb with a demiglace reduction of red wine coupled with light mustard, pay tribute to French classical cuisine, though with a contemporary touch.

Among hot appetizers, could be ravioli filled with a fine grind of smoked chicken, plated with flavorful shitake mushrooms resting in a creamy textured sweet bell pepper sauce. Other appetizers might include a vegetable gateau centered on carrots and asparagus napped on a tomato coulis.

Eye appeal is nearly as much of an attraction as the foods themselves, as ingredients are carefully plated on decorative china. In one nightly special, slices of venison were ringed over a deeply intense red wine sauce that stood up to the slight gaminess of the meat. In another entree, boneless breasts of quail and chicken came paired in a classic based vigneronne sauce, which as its name suggests, uses grapes, in this case prepared with a few shallots in a red wine demiglace.

Salmon has been presented with an herbal sauce, while whitefish came in a basil and cream sauce combination. More substantial might be yellowfin tuna sauteed, then plated with a sauce of green peppercorns and red wine. Mindful of diners' individual needs, many selections can be adjusted for a low cholesterol diet.

FRONTERA GRILL
KR 17/20
Decor 3.5/4   Hospitality 4.5/5   Food 8/10   Value 1/1

- **Mexican**
- **Chicago/Near North**
- **$$**

445 North Clark Street
Chicago
(312) 661-1434
Troubleshooters: Rick and
Deanne Bayless

Hours: Lunch Tues–Fri 11:30
am–2:30 pm, Sat Brunch 10:30
am–2:30 pm, Dinner Tues–Thurs
5:20–10 pm, Fri–Sat 5:30–11 pm
Credit Cards. All majors
Reservations: Only for parties
of 5–10 people
Handicapped: Accessible
Bar: Service bar for wine, beer,
fresh lime juice margaritas
**Smoking and nonsmoking
sections:** separate smoking and
nonsmoking seating
Parking: Valet during dinner
hours, public lot across the street

At Frontera Grill, Chef/Owner Rick Bayless and his wife Deanne explore
the multiplicity of Mexican cuisine possibilities. The restaurant is crowded,
noisy, and on the cutting edge of fashion in contemporary dining. You might
even say there is a certain boisterous character, without being rowdy, but just
enough so as to suggest the popular imagery of a cantina.

Diners will see some familiar items on the menu, but any similarity
to conventional Mexican cooking stops there. The guacamole is thick,
chunky, with the full flavor of avacado and a hint of seasonings. Chicken
taquitos are thin fingers of crisp dough around a filling of seasoned
minced chicken, all of which is topped with dollops of a fresh sour cream
unlike any I've tasted before.

Try the appetizer platter which brings with the taquitos and qua-
camole, some small quesadillas and ceviche tostados. The ceviche is cool-
ing, with the raw bite of lime juice. A bit of cilantro and other herb
seasonings makes this a distinct winner. By, the way, you might also
want to sample a platter of *sopes* if your party is large enough. *Sopes*
are cornmeal tarts, each with a different filling or topping. In this case,
Frontera Grill serves them with plantain and sourcream, guacamole,
chorizo and chicken in molé sauce.

Among past entrees has been duck breast in a green pumpkin seed
molé. As in fashionable French restaurants, pieces of the duck breast are
slightly pink, bathed in a thick, but not heavy sauce that compliments the
flavor of the poultry. The platter also comes with Mexican rice, small
rings of zucchini and chayote.

Grilled baby chicken is partly deboned, the bird marinated in a collection of sweet spices and garlic. Dinner choices also include a vegetarian stew packed with corn, black beans and marinated cabbage among its components. The dessert list replaces familiar flan with a different style of fruit custard, fresh ice creams and other sweets.

GABRIEL'S
KR 19/20
Decor 3.5/4   Hospitality 5/5   Food 9.5/10   Value 1/1

- **French/Mediterranean**
- **Highwood**
- **$$$**

Green Bay Road
Highwood
(847) 433-0031
Troubleshooter: Gabriel Viti
(chef/owner)

Hours: Tues–Sat 5–10 pm
Credit Cards: All majors
Reservations: Required
Handicapped: Accessible
Smoking and nonsmoking sections: Both available
Parking: Free parking on street can be tight, or in lot behind the restaurant

When it comes to defining a cooking style, that of Chef/Owner Gabriel Viti at his handsome Highwood restaurant is, in a word, "robust." He does not shy away from intense, up-front flavors, the kind that fill your mouth, leaving no room for doubt or hesitation. If his were visual rather than gustatorial art, there would be no doubt about colors and patterns.

The restaurant has a stylish contemporary flair, but like the cooking, not cutting edge. As contemporary as the dining room looks, there is still room for glass panels with art deco–style etchings. Broad, muted stripes mark the upholstered and comfortable seating at tables or banquettes.

Like most newer restaurants, Gabriel's is a noisy environment, with little in the way of sound damping wall coverings. But, it is elegant in a restrained and almost formal manner reflected in the excellent and attentive service.

Viti is open to a number of menu ideas, among them salmon pastrami. The flavor is reminiscent of pastrami, thought the texture is clearly that of fresh, cured salmon. Slices are arranged on a bed of arugula, splashed with a good balsamic vinaigrette.

Elsewhere among the hot and cold listing of appetizers, chicken liver mousse is wrapped in a brioche crust, a Greek influenced shrimp is served with tomato-tinged horseradish sauce, while wild mushrooms are cooked down into a ragout with asparagus, shallots and cream for a rich sauce. With a nod to the classics, beef carpaccio is presented with shavings of parmesan cheese and a brushing of glistening extra virgin olive oil. With a bow to French cuisine, snails are sautéed in garlic butter and presented out of their shells on a bed of spinach. An extra flourish of garlic underscores Viti's sturdy approach to the culinary art.

There are some delicious Italian selections. Risotto is prepared with smoky chunks of chicken, plus spinach and roasted red peppers. In another pasta selection, rigatoni is served with spicy Italian sausage and a tomato basil sauce. From other choices, finger-length penne is the foundation for asparagus, melted mozzarella cheese and a rich tomato and garlic cream sauce. Linguini and shrimp with asparagus and tomatoes is a bit more delicate and lighter in approach and style.

Gabriel's meat and seafood selections are right out of the fine dining repertoire of Chef Viti. Venison is a wonderful alternative to beef for those who watch fat and cholesterol. The recipe here brings roasted slices of meat with a mound of butternut squash purée and a syrupy reduction of port wine and meat juices for a wonderful sauce. Another hard-hitting winner is the grilled veal chop. This lovely cut of meat is plated with mushrooms and a perfumed rosemary sauce. Capon, which to my way of thinking brings variety to ordinary chicken, is rolled with slices of prosciutto and mushrooms, while a handsome rack of lamb is presented at the table with a side of ratatouille and the lovely scent and flavor of thyme sauce.

As for seafood, Chilean sea bass has been roasted in a paper wrapping to hold in its liquids. A simple lemon and herb vinaigrette adds some flavor. Other fish selections include roasted salmon and scallops with lemon sauce and a whole roasted trout that is literally wrapped in a broad slice of pancetta and plated with mushrooms for a decidedly different take on this popular fish.

GANDHI INDIA RESTAURANT
KR 17/20
Decor 3.5/4　　Hospitality 4/5　　Food 8.5/10　　Value 1/1

- **Indian**
- **Chicago/Far North**
- **$$**

2601 West Devon Avenue
Chicago
(773) 761-8714
Troubleshooters: Nand Kishore (owner), Kamlish Kishore (manager)

Hours: Lunch Daily 11:30 am–3:30 pm, Dinner Sun–Thurs 5–10 pm, Fri–Sat 5–11 pm
Credit Cards: All majors
Reservations: Accepted
Handicapped: Accessible
Smoking and nonsmoking sections: Both available
Parking: Street

More so than many other cuisines, Indian is depends on a bouquet of spices and seasonings for its very substance. It is these seasonings, turmeric, cardomom, saffron and others that makes a firm statement on what this restaurant is all about. The Gandhi menu explains most of the dishes, which makes this a welcome stop for the experienced or beginner in the Indian way of dining.

Start with a combination platter of appetizers for a preview. Much of Indian cooking can be picked up and eaten out of hand if you choose. Try the deep-fried *pakoras* and *samosa*; *pakoras* are made with spiced chickpea flour, formed into hollow dumplings into which are stuffed a mix of vegetables. The samosa are potato-based, also deep-fried and savory. Then pick up a piece of the chicken *tikka*, roasted in the tandoori ovens which have become standard equipage for Indian restaurant kitchens. Similarly tasty are the Indian shishkebabs, cubes of lamb given a deep charcoal roasting. Diners can order a prearranged dinner or à la carte and let your own tastes and instincts be your guide. Incidentally, curries can be mild or hot; those at Gandhi seem to be somewhere in between. By the time you have your table spread over with a multitude of dishes, you may notice that each will have its own distinct flavor. There is no paucity to seasonings here, nor is there a sameness.

GAYLORD
KR 17/20
Decor 3/4   Hospitality 5/5   Food 8/10   Value 1/1

• **Indian**

• **Chicago**

• **$$**

678 North Clark Street
Chicago
(312) 664-1700
Troubleshooter: I. Puri
(general manager)

Hours: Lunch Mon–Fri 11:30 am–2:30 pm, Sat–Sun noon– 3 pm, Dinner Nightly 5:30– 10 pm
Credit Cards: All majors
Reservations: Suggested
Handicapped: Accessible
Bar: Full bar features about 30 different wines and a good selection of beers
Smoking and nonsmoking sections: Both available
Parking: Valet at night or available on street or in lot across from restaurant

---

Gaylord India was Chicago's first important Indian restaurant. It features a northern style of Indian cuisine, with striking Moghul influences. Much of the cooking is characterized by the use of *tandoors*, large clay urns used as ovens. Hot coals line the bottom, generating an intense heat. Meats are set over the coals, or laid along the sides of the urn, seal-ing in flavor and juices. A mark of the *tandoori* style of cooking is the bright red color of the grilled meats or seafood.

No beef is served because of the Hindu prohibition, but delicious chicken, lamb, prawns and vegetables are regular menu items. Naturally, because vegetarianism is so prominent in Indian dietary culture, vegeta-bles get wonderful treatment, usually in full-flavored and heavily spiced sauces. À la carte dining gives you a free hand with selections, but com-bination platters offer newcomers to the cuisine a good assortment of textures and tastes. At the conclusion of your meal, take a cup of steam-ing hot and fragrant tea, and one of the delectably sweet desserts.

GEJA'S CAFE
KR 15.5/20
Decor 4/4   Hospitality 3.5/5   Food 7.5/10   Value .5/1

- **Fondue**
- **Chicago/Near North**
- **$$$**

340 West Armitage Avenue
(773) 281-9101
Troubleshooters: John Davis (owner), Jeff Lawler (general manager)

Hours: Sun 4:30–10 pm, Mon–Thurs 5–10:30 pm, Fri 5 pm–midnight, Sat 5 pm–12:30 am
Credit Cards: All majors
Reservations: Taken Sun through Thurs only, Fri 5–6:30 pm only, Sat 5 pm only
Bar: Extensive, moderately priced list of more than 150 wines
Smoking and nonsmoking sections: Both available
Parking: Valet

Geja's Cafe is one of Chicago's most romantic restaurants. Small, quiet, intimate, couples can order from the fairly abbreviated menu, and then cook and dip to their hearts' content. Even with today's heavy em-phasis on healthy dining, fondue cookery remains popular. Meat, chicken or seafood are cooked in hot peanut oil. Dining can be as elaborate or simple as you might choose. At the top of the menu choices is the Con-noisseur Fondue, which brings aged beef tenderloin, lobster tail and large fresh shrimp. Other individual or combination dinners might include shrimp, scallops, or chicken depending on your taste.

For something lighter, though certainly no less caloric, a cheese fon-due might be the way to go. Melted cheese of your choice bubbles in the pot, into which are dipped crusty chunks of French bread. The cheese is blended with white wine and seasonings and is truly delicious. The stan-dard house dessert is, what else, chocolate, flamed with orange liqueur and served with apples, melon chunks, pineapple, sliced bananas, pound cake and marshmallows.

Adding to the romance is a flamenco guitarist and one of the better wine lists in town.

GENE AND GEORGETTI
KR 15.5/20
Decor 2.5/4   Hospitality 4/5   Food 9/10   Value .5/1

- **American/Italian**
- **Chicago/Near North**
- **$$$**

500 North Franklin
Chicago
(312) 527-3718
Troubleshooter: Tony Durpetti
(owner)

Hours: Mon–Sat 11 am–midnight; closed Sun
Credit Cards: All majors
Reservations: A must
Handicapped: Accessible
Bar: Full service, good wine list, giant martinis
Smoking and nonsmoking sections: Both available, cigars in bar only
Parking: Valet and private lot

Beef is back as king of the dinner table, with cuts thought the bigger the better. That suits customers of Gene & Georgetti just fine! The specialty is prime aged steaks, along with large portioned sides of cottage fried potatoes and an old-fashioned head lettuce salad dressed with nothing more exotic than oil and vinegar or French dressing.

Gene & Georgetti is one of the more clubby restaurants in Chicago, where it probably pays to know someone in charge, or be sure that your waiter knows you. But, the real fans of the restaurant swear by its excellence, which would explain why this has traditionally been one of the more difficult restaurants to get into on a last minute reservation.

However, once seated, service can be as good as it gets. Many of the waiters look as if they have been on duty since the day the restaurant first opened its doors sometime back in Chicago's dim early history. In fact, Gene & Georgetti is a part of Chicago's history, so whatever inconveniences may be involved in dining here are probably tolerated more than they would be elsewhere.

GENNARO'S
KR 19/20
Decor 3/4   Hospitality 5/5   Food 10/10   Value 1/1

- **Italian**
- **Chicago/Near South**
- **$$**

1352 West Taylor Street
Chicago
(312) 243-1035
Troubleshooter: John Gennaro,
Jr. (owner)

Hours: Thurs 5–9 pm, Fri–Sat
until 10 pm, Sun 4–9 pm
Credit Cards: None, cash or
checks only
Reservations: Mandatory
Parking: Valet

The truth is that if you have dinner at Gennaro's, you do it their way. To its regulars it is akin to a private club, an idea the locked front door and buzzer entry do nothing to dispel. The menu is as basic Italian as you will find, without the extravagances of fashion that mark newer restaurants. Everything is fresh, hot and homemade. Seasonings are mellow, well-married in the red sauces.

If you could look into the kitchen you would see the large cauldrons of sauces, the preparation tables for fresh homemade pastas. To really appreciate the best, order an à la carte specialty. The home made gnocchi are not to be missed, chewy potato dumplings, as pleasurable as eating can get. They come in that wonderful homemade sauce which is the backbone of much of what comes from the small kitchen.

Veal dishes are given excellent treatment from basic parmigiana to country-style with sausage. Everything is cooked to order, and dining is not to be rushed.

GIANNI V
KR 17.5/20
Decor 4/4   Hospitality 4/5   Food 8.5/10   Value 1/1

- **Italian**
- **Highwood**
- **$$**

550 Green Bay Road
Highwood
(847) 443-5515
Troubleshooter: Joe Greco
(co-owner)

Hours: Sun 5–9 pm, Fri–Sat
5–11 pm, Mon–Thurs 5–10 pm
Credit Cards: All majors
Reservations: Recommended
Handicapped: Accessible
**Smoking and nonsmoking
sections:** Both available
Parking: Valet (complimentary,
needed only on weekends)

I think I've been down this road before, but does Highwood really need another Italian restaurant? The defacto North Shore restaurant capital has its newest in a space that used to be one of its oldest. Gianni V, sits on what is the closest Highwood has to hallowed restaurant ground, the building which once housed the venerable Scornavacco's.

This is a very handsome and comfortable restaurant with its countryside Italian look including two fireplaces, open woodwork and a sense of age which is more illusion than fact. The proof is in the pudding, or the pasta when it comes to Italian restaurants. The large menu includes the basic repertoire as well as some variations on the theme. Oysters rockefeller, for instance, is the traditional version, with a substitution of sambuca, the Italian anisette liquor for traditional French pernod. Not much of an inspiration there, perhaps, nor do such nibbles as fried zucchini, steamed mussels in tomato sauce or that throwback to the 1950s shrimp de jonghe suggest anything unique.

So, maybe the idea should be not to reinvent the wheel, but to make it a little better. Their take on grilled calamari is one approach. There is not a trace of sponginess, and the natural chargrilled taste is clearly evident. One of the other truly tasty antipasti selections is a platter of grilled vegetables. They include sliced peppers, zucchini and eggplant as well as a large whole head of roasted garlic and a splotch of goat cheese. The garlic is sweet and fresh, nice to spread on the veggies or perhaps on a slice of crusty bread.

Getting down to other courses, pastas are available in only full, not half orders, which precludes the opportunity to taste a couple unless you are with a larger party. There are a dozen or so pasta selections, several in combination with seafood. Among them is linguine with red clam sauce, nicely seasoned, with all the markings of a fresh, homemade noodle cooked perfectly *al dente*. Chicken and veal choices round out the menu. *Chicken piccata*, is usually with butter, and toasted pine nuts. I asked for olive oil instead of butter. My request was met without hesitation. Two meaty pieces of chicken were accompanied by fresh steamed broccoli.

Service is very cordial. The restaurant offers a variety of wines fairly balanced between California and Italian bottlings.

GIANNOTTI STEAK HOUSE
KR 19/20
Decor 4/4   Hospitality 5/5   Food 9/10   Value 1/1

- **Italian**
- **Norridge**
- **$$$**

8422 West Lawrence Avenue
Norridge
(708) 453-1616
Troubleshooter: Vic Giannotti
(chef/owner)

Hours: Lunch Mon–Fri 11 am–3 pm, Dinner Mon–Thurs 3–11 pm, Fri until midnight, Sat 5 pm–midnight, Sun 2 pm–midnight
Credit Cards: Amex, Diners, Discover; MC, Visa
Reservations: Suggested, but not taken for parties of 2 on Fri and Sat
Handicapped: Accessible
Bar: Full bar and cocktail lounge, features live entertainment, plus Karaoke Mon night after 10 pm
Parking: Valet

For almost as long as I have been reviewing restaurants in Chicago, Giannotti's has meant some of the best in hearty, Italian food. Even considering the abundance of new Italian restaurants which are part and parcel of fashionable dining in and around Chicago, a Giannotti-run restaurant was setting the trend.

Chef and Owner Vic Giannotti has had enough practice, learning the trade when his parents ran a small West Side eatery, which led to a larger restaurant some years ago. Though the name suggests that this is a steak house (and steaks are featured), it is the sublime array of Italian, and especially Neapolitan, cooking that makes this such a special restaurant. I confess that each time I visit, I order the same things. It is a dinner selection that I think is unbeatable.

Begin with the *merluzzi*, a delicious cold seafood salad with the tang of lemon juice. Counter that with stuffed rolled eggplant. The pulp is fashioned into a crepe-like patty, floured and fried to the color of gold. Then, it is filled with a rich tomato sauce and ricotta cheese, rolled up and baked, finally to be finished with a drizzle of red sauce.

For pasta, the very best is 8 finger *cavatelli* with marinara sauce. The cavatelli, hand made nuggets of pasta dough, also can be had with fresh broccoli, olive oil and plenty of garlic. If your taste leads to other kinds of pasta and saucing, you will not be disappointed.

Among entrees I have never failed to order *veal piccante*. The meat is lightly floured, sautéed in butter and lemon juice, then topped with toasted pine nuts. This is as good as it gets!

Seafood lovers will savor swordfish vesuvio which takes the popular Chicago-Italian chicken recipe and puts it to work with meaty seafood, in the interest of both calories and cholesterol. I may be mistaken about this, but I have been told that Chicago's unique chicken vesuvio was invented by Vic Giannotti's father. Be that as it may, it is garlicky good, moist, flavorful and so many other adjectives synonymous with "delicious." The roasted potatoes swimming in the gravy like sauce are almost a meal.

Among desserts, the cheesecake is light and sweet. A cup or two of cappuccino or espresso, and nothing could be better. For anyone who loves Italian food, Giannotti's is a must visit!

GIBSON'S
KR 20/20
Decor 4/4   Hospitality 5/5   Food 10/10   Value 1/1

- **American Steak and Lobster House**
- **Chicago/Near North and Suburbs**
- **$$$**

1028 North Rush Street
Chicago
(312) 266-8999
Troubleshooters: Hugo Ralli, Steve Lombardo (owners)
Other Location
5464 North River Road, Rosemont; 847-928-9900; Hours: Daily 11 am–midnight; Credit Cards: All majors; Reservations: Suggested; Handicapped: Accessible; Smoking and nonsmoking sections: Separate smoking and nonsmoking seating; Parking: Complimentary valet

Hours: Full menu served Sun–Sat 3 pm–2 am in the bar, Dining Room Dinner Service Mon–Sat 5 pm–midnight, Sun 4 pm–midnight
Credit Cards: All majors
Reservations: Required
Handicapped: Accessible
Bar: Full bar, excellent and well-portioned mixed drinks, bar is cigar friendly, piano entertainment daily 5 pm–closing
Smoking and nonsmoking sections: Both available
Parking: Valet

The city of Chicago exists for Gibson's. Talk about a power restaurant, this bastion of prodigious portions is the epitome of everything in brawny

Chicago. If you want to see the heavy hitters chowing down, this is one place to be.

It is a "meat market" in every sense of the phrase. The bar is constantly crowded with health club yuppies and their dates. The packed dining room is a cacophony of conversation, interrupted only by the appearance of servers taking or bringing orders and dispensing drinks.

There's nothing subtle at Gibson's, nor should there be. It is a world in and of itself where, for the price of a thick steak, or a fist-sized lobster tail every customer can feel like part of the *glitterati*. All of this would not be worth the paper towels in the washroom if the food were not so good. The word "best" takes on a meaning all its own. You think all steaks are alike and all steak restaurants are the same? You haven't been to Gibson's.

The pleasure starts when your server sorts out the various cuts of meat carried out on a large platter, each cut described in terms of how it can or should be grilled. If you want pasta, try another joint. There's none to be had. Instead, you can order one of the popular cuts of beef, starting with a 7-ounce filet up to the larger cuts of porterhouse or sirloin. The meat is tender as a mother's love. Even so, you'll get a wood handled steak knife with your silverware, probably as large as the one Jim Bowie carried into the Alamo.

If you really want to gild the lily, try a side order of potato pancakes and homemade chunked apple sauce, or the double-baked potato with enough cheese whipped in to drain the entire state of Wisconsin. While the menu also lists large salads, baby back ribs and spit-roasted whole chickens stuffed with fresh herbs, the other big specialty here is lobster tail. Surprisingly, there's no whole Maine lobster, but the Australian tails are in a class by themselves. They are succulent yet meaty, sweet tasting, the kind of lobster dining that is reserved for special occasions unless you happen to own the lobster farm.

The drinks are large, as are the desserts. Devil's food raspberry mousse towers from its serving platter and can easily enough feed a table of 8. Not much smaller, is a cut of banana cream pie spilling over from its flaky crust.

We Serve USDA Prime Aged Beef   *Open for lunch May 15*

FRIDAY MAY 5, 2000

SOUP & APPETIZERS

Snapper Soup......cup 1.00............bowl...	3.50
Alaskan King Crab Claws (each).................	5.50
Home Cured Gravlax...............................	8.00
Tomato & Goat Cheese...........................	5.75
Shrimp Cocktail	15.00
Shrimp *with Spicy Marinade*.....................	9.00
Chopped Chicken Livers...........................	5.00
Crabmeat Avocado................................	9.00
Oyster Assortment.................................	10.00
Spicy Rock Lobster Cocktail......................	15.00

SALADS

Caesar..	5.50
Tomato & Scallion..................................	5.50
Garbage Salad......................................	11.75
House Salad...	1.00
Cole Slaw..	1.00

ENTRÉE SPECIALS

Grilled Atlantic Salmon
With honey, mustard & sesame vinaigrette... **22.00**

Grilled Swordfish
with cool orange sauce **22.00**

Pan Roasted Walleyed Pike
With cornmeal crust & lemon butter........... **21.50**

Pepper Steak Salad.................................	18.00
Big Big Porterhouse...............................	63.00
Small Filet *with Peppercorns*....................	24.25
London Broil...	20.00
Roasted Half Chicken *with Peppers*............	12.75
W.R.'s Chicago Cut	32.00
Mediuml Lobster Tail...........................	**60.00**
with Turf...	**82.00**
Giant Lobster Tail..............................	**75.00**
with Turf...	**102.00**

RIBS & CHICKEN

Gibsons' Baby Back Ribs..........................	15.50
Whole Spit-Roasted Chicken......................	15.75

FISH & SEAFOOD

Broiled Atlantic Salmon...........................	20.00
Planked Whitefish..................................	16.95

15% Gratuity may be added to parties of six or more.

STEAKS & CHOPS

Filet Mignon...	27.75
Small Filet..	22.25
New York Sirloin....................................	30.25
Small New York Sirloin............................	24.25
Sliced Sirloin *with Red Wine Sauce*.............	30.25
Porterhouse Steak..................................	31.75
Bone-in Sirloin......................................	33.25
Veal Chop..	25.00
Double Lamb Chops...............................	26.00
Spicy Pork Chops *with Apple Sauce*............	18.00
One Spicy Pork Chop *with Apple Sauce*.........	12.00
Chopped Steak......................................	12.75

SIDE DISHES

Asparagus *with Hollandaise Sauce*...............	6.50
Mushrooms..	5.50
French Fries...	4.75
Mashed Potatoes...................................	4.75
Vegetable Combination............................	8.00
Baked Potato..	4.25
Double Baked Potato..............................	6.00
Sautéed Spinach *with Garlic*.....................	6.00
Broccoli	4.25

BAR FOOD

Charbroiled Hamburger............................	7.75
Charbroiled Cheeseburger........................	8.25
Chicken Sandwich..................................	9.75
Sliced Sirloin Sandwich............................	12.00
Half Slab Baby Back Ribs..........................	10.00
Spit-Roasted Half Chicken........................	10.00

DESSERTS

Big Banana Dream.................................	12.50
Strawberry Shortcake..............................	10.50
Apple strudel..	7.00
Lemon Meringue Pie...............................	7.00
Texas Pecan Pie....................................	7.00
Coconut Cream Pie................................	7.00
Sherbet...	4.00
Ice Cream..	4.00
Carrot Cake..	11.75
Macadamia Turtle Pie..............................	12.50

COFFEE

Gibsons Steakhouse Blend........................	1.95
Cappuccino...	2.75
Espresso..	2.50

Cigar & Pipe Smoking in Bar Only   Gift Certificates Available   Private Dining Room Available   Carry-Out Available

5461 North River Road • Rosemont, IL • 60018 • (817) 928 0000

GIOCO
KR 20/20
Decor 4/4   Hospitality 5/5   Food 10/10   Value 1/1

* **Italian**
* **Chicago**
* **$$$**

1312 South Wabash
Chicago
(312) 939-3870
Troubleshooter: Lisa Partipilo
(manager)

Hours: Lunch Mon–Fri 11:30 am–2:30 pm, Dinner Mon–Wed 5–10 pm, Thurs 5–11 pm, Fri–Sat 5 pm–midnight, Sun 4–9 pm
Credit Cards: Amex Visa, MC, Diners
Reservations: Suggested, especially weekends, walkins accepted on space-available basis
Handicapped: Accessible, including wheelchairs
Smoking and nonsmoking sections: Separate smoking and nonsmoking seating
Parking: Valet

Now and then, in the midst of the dining routine, something very special comes along. Gioco, is a very special restaurant. Brilliantly inspired with an Italian menu as creative as the restaurant's eclectic look.

There are several dining spaces starting with the front room and its sophisticated backlit bar, or the room just along side with open kitchen. Moving deeper into the restaurant, the history of its more than 100 year old building is exploited with the warren of smaller dining rooms. The walls are exposed lath and plaster, pinpoint ceiling lamps are dim, and the glow of candles is the more prevalent source of light. In one room, antique bird cages hold candles as a striking decor statement. One wall features an antique *commedia del arte* painting of a clown, perhaps the Gioco of the restaurant's name.

Chef Joe Rosetti takes the credit for the menu which appears deceptively simple, yet is anything but naïve. Consider *cavatelli*, rolled with black pepper, porcini mushrooms and ricotta cheese contribute to the sauce, and though the menu does not say so, I sensed the perfume of truffle oil. Something else may have fooled my senses, but there is no question that this is a nuclear explosion of flavor.

You could start off with something simple for an antipasto, such as a margherita pizza. This is the classic Neapolitan style, with thin crust, light dressing of tomatoes, mozzarella cheese and bright green basil leaves. Other pizzas, not your corner carry out variety to be sure, range from those with a topping of roasted vegetables or rock shrimp to salmon or spiced sausage.

From among other appetizers grilled octopus is splendid in its simplicity, presented with nothing more than watercress and fennel, some lemon wedges and olive oil glazing the octopus.

Other seafood is exemplary. Salmon as an entree comes with a showcase of roasted red peppers and braised endive. A vinaigrette with an infusion of freshly squeezed orange juice is an exercise in creation. Or consider a cut of tuna, with a bright pink rare center. Roasted red slivered onions and a mash of turnip helps complete this presentation.

Other entrees include traditional Italian sweet sausage accompanied by mashed potatoes and grapes whose fruity sweetness would compliment not just the sausage, but a bold red wine. Veal chop is topped with *caponata*, while Gioco has its version of France's bistro steak, in this case a filet topped with melted fontinella cheese and paired with fried potatoes sprinkled with fresh rosemary.

GRACE
KR 18.5/20
Decor 3.5/4   Hospitality 5/5   Food 9/10   Value 1/1

- **American Eclectic**
- **Chicago/Near West**
- **$$$**

623 West Randolph Street
Chicago
(312) 928-9200
Troubleshooters: Ethan Asch (co-owner), Ted Cizma (chef/co-owner)

Hours: Mon–Fri Lunch 11:30 am–2 pm, Dinner Mon–Thurs 5:30–10 pm, Fri–Sat 5:30 pm–midnight, closed Sun
Credit Cards: Amex, MC, Visa, Diners, Discover
Reservations: Mandatory
Handicapped: Accessible
Smoking and nonsmoking sections: Smoking only in the bar
Parking: Valet $6.50

Chef/owner Ted Cizma has peppered his menu with game, not exclusively so, but enough that it makes Grace just a bit different. For instance, a small *amuse bouche*, or complimentary taste of wild boar could be served with a dab of fruit compote. Meantime, the full dinner menu will offer the boar crusted with herbs, plated with white cheddar cheese, polenta flavored with cinnamon and chili peppers, and a nectarine compote to complete the platter. This is only one example of the sort of complexity Cizma brings out in his cooking. Recently, striped bass has been set on a red wine reduction studded with slices of field mushrooms. Fingerling potatoes offer a mild flavor balance. The sauce is very intense, and is easily picked up by the virtually neutral tasting bass. In fact, this sort of sauce would work with most red meats. Imagine it with venison!

As it turns out, that's not how Cizma does his venison. Instead, he takes a cut of loin, slices it as if it were only a London broil, then plates it in a syrupy *au jus* with blackberry pulp and fresh cut thyme. Chanterelles add a bit more of the forest. Game inherently seems to take to fruity sauces, so it is no surprise to find a saddle of rabbit with mission figs cooked down into an intensely flavored sauce; sautéed spinach and parsnip puree complete the setting.

Even the non-game entrees are richly endowed with complex sauces and flavor combinations. Pan-roasted chicken breast gets a glaze of honey and a cornbread stuffing that includes bits of andouille sausage and sage in the mix. Grilled lamb tenderloin is paired with sun-dried cherry sauce, while a grilled rib eye steak comes with cherry and tomato cooked down into a relish; white truffles are used to flavor a potato puree.

As for seafood, halibut is set in a rich saffron and lobster bisque. Tuna steak is grilled, but left rare in the center. Warm whole wheat spaghetti is the bedding while crushed peanuts and horseradish vinaigrette contribute texture and taste.

The Grace dining room is crowded, noisy and bustling on busy nights. The din is somewhat hard to overcome. Grace is not the place to pop the question, unless you want to shout it out.

GREEK ISLANDS
KR 17/20
Decor 4/4   Hospitality 4/5   Food 8/10   Value 1/1

- **Greek**
- **Chicago/Near West**
- **$$**

200 South Halsted
Chicago
(312) 782-9855
Troubleshooter: Gus Couchell
(owner)
Other Location
300 East 22nd Street, Lombard;
630-932-4545

Hours: Sun–Thurs 11 am–midnight, Fri–Sat 11 am–1 am
Credit Cards: All majors
Parking: Free valet

The rustic Greek fisherman's look at Greek Islands makes this an appealing restaurant to while away a couple of hours when neither time nor budget permit a journey to the Aegean. During the height of the lunch and dinner hours, it's one of the more bustling stops on the Halsted Street strip. And, as with its shoulder-to-shoulder competitors, the food is abundant and fairly cheap.

A house specialty, broiled sea bass, is served with lots of oregano and fresh lemon. The fish is deftly deboned tableside, after your waiter proudly shows you the entire fish from head to tail.

In addition to the seafood, Greek Islands serves the ubiquitous array of Hellenic fare, braised lamb, loin and leg of lamb, Greek-style skewered pork called *souvlaki*, plus the casserole standbys, *pastitsio*, *moussaka* and all the rest. As with the other Greek restaurants in the neighborhood, the combination platter may not be the most delicate dining, but it is a best buy for price-conscious or bargain-seeking diners.

HACIENDA TECALITLAN
KR 19/20
Decor 4/4   Hospitality 5/5   Food 9/10   Value 1/1

- **Mexican**
- **Chicago/Near West**
- **$$**

820 North Ashland Avenue
Chicago
(312) 243-6667
Troubleshooter: Carlos Gomez
(owner)

Hours: Mon–Thurs 11 am–11 pm, Fri–Sun 11 am–midnight
Credit Cards: All majors
Reservations: Recommended, especially for weekends
Handicapped: Accessible
Parking: Valet

Hacienda Tecalitlan is as pleasant a dining environment as almost any in Chicago. As its name suggests, this is a Mexican restaurant, but with a significant difference. Inside, and out, it was constructed to recreate a Mexican courtyard.

The Spanish colonial architecture is scrupulously recreated, including two floors of arched colonnades that march around the main dining area, with its Spanish tile floor, graceful fountain, and ornate woodwork trim.

The extensive menu reflects several regions of culinary Mexico, though little is so exotic as to seem too unfamiliar to any but those who have never had Mexican food. The guacamole has a natural flavor as it is found in Mexico, without the peppery seasonings many U.S. restaurants add. Tortilla soup is in a tomato stock, enhanced with cream and a little cheese. Its taste is mellow and comforting. Among other appetizers are several versions of *queso fundido* and a pair of *ceviches*. One is made with red snapper, the other chopped shrimp. The tastes are marvelously fresh, somewhat complex, with underpinnings of lime juice, onions and cilantro.

Entrees run an all-inclusive gamut, ranging from grilled meats and seafood to burritos, *chiles rellenos* and even empanadas. Though usually thought of as Argentinean, empanadas, pastry turnovers with savory fillings, are a delicious part of the Mexican repertoire, too. Those fillings include mushrooms, spinach, chorizo, shrimp, cheese or poblano peppers. Each has its own distinctive flavor; the shrimp empanada is a standout.

Salmon veracruzana is delicious; the fish comes to the table moist and flaky. This or red snapper can also be ordered with a wealth of other traditional Mexican sauces. Meantime for meat eaters, beef fajitas are just one of half a dozen fajita entrees. Like everything else we tasted, seasonings were in balance. Even a simple recipe like chiles rellenos seems somewhat beyond the usual.

Even without the lovely setting, there is something special about the cooking. Balance and finesse are words that come to mind, though the sheer fact that this restaurant almost makes me think I'm actually in Mexico helps.

HARRY CARAY'S
KR 17/20
Decor 4/4   Hospitality 4/5   Food 8/10   Value 1/1

- **American/Italian**
- **Chicago/Near North**
- **$$$**

33 West Kinzie
Chicago
(312) 465-9269
(H-O-L-Y-C-O-W)
Troubleshooter: Manager on duty

Hours: Lunch Mon–Fri 11:30 am–3 pm, Sat–Sun bar only 11:30 am–4 pm, Dinner Mon–Thurs 5–10:30 pm, Fri–Sat until midnight, Sun 4–10 pm
Credit Cards: All majors
Reservations: Preferred for lunch, dinner reservations taken only for parties of 8 or larger
Handicapped: Accessible
Bar: Full service bar is 60'6" long (the distance from pitcher's mound to home plate), excellent and extensive list of Italian and American wines, domestic and imported beers, cocktails
Parking: Valet or ample street or lot

Meat, fish and some Italian specialties are at the heart of Harry Caray's menu. Service is cordial, with just the right amount of personality.

Right out of the batter's box, from a selection of appetizers, which includes *carpaccio*, shrimp cocktail, roasted peppers and fresh or baked clams from a longer list, try an excellent seafood salad. The portion is large enough to split for two, fresh with cold squid, perhaps some codfish, shrimp, and other seafood, all in an oil and vinegar herbed and seasoned dressing. Less successful is toasted ravioli. Toasting defeats the whole purpose of the pasta, which is meant to be tender, not crisp.

Things get back to high ground as you begin to round the bases of entrees. From a list of pastas and other Italian specialties, *spaghetti carbonara* is a solid hit. Linguine is bathed in a full-flavored sharp cheese sauce that clings to each strand of noodle. Bits of bacon are tossed into this classic recipe. A couple turns of fresh cracked pepper, and it's better than a seat in the bleachers.

If you like lamb, you'll love a trio of Lamb Chops Oreganato. These are simply broiled chops, meaty, with little or no fat, and the kind of flavor for which you'd trade away your best shortstop.

Among meat selections *veal piccante* is a major leaguer on any team. This veal, however, can be a bit light on buttery sweetness, though tender enough to easily be a two bagger. Batting cleanup are the steaks, and other chops, a full lineup from porterhouse to peppered.

Rounding third and heading for homeplate are desserts, piled high on a three layer cart, just waiting to be picked for your All-Star Team. They range from apple tarts to chocolate tortes and pumpkin cheesecakes.

HARVEST ON HURON
KR 20/20
Decor 4/4   Hospitality 5/5   Food 10/10   Value 1/1

- **American**
- **Chicago/River North**
- **$$$**

217 West Huron
Chicago
(312) 587-9600
Troubleshooter: Tom Powers
and Oz Schoenstadt (owners)

Hours: Sun–Mon 5:30–10 pm, Tues–Thurs 5:30–11 pm, Fri–Sat 5:30–midnight
Credit Cards: All majors except Diners
Reservations: Recommended
Handicapped: Accessible
Smoking and nonsmoking sections: Smoking in bar and lounge only
Parking: Valet $7

Harvest On Huron speaks to a contemporary dining audience with an upscale and varied menu, coupled with a broad selection of wines and premium spirits. This is a restaurant that is usually packed, even on week nights when other restaurateurs expect a night off.

Located in the heart of the River North art district, it is almost hip-hop hip. Style seems to mean everything, not only to clientele but to waitstaff, whose costuming, while short of Halloween, can be striking, to say the least.

Chef Alan Sternweiler is cooking on all four burners, with a menu that is almost unrelenting in its striking invention. Instead of a typical potato pancake, or even an Oriental pancake featured in some restaurants, Sternweiler has created a wild mushroom pancake, seasoned with thyme, garnished with the requisite sour cream plus crispy fried leeks as an added *lagniappe*. From among other appetizers, Sternweiler looks south of the border for an inspired creation that brings together strips of roasted duck, the cracklin's, plus blue cheese, chili peppers and a contrasting basil coulis. In yet another imaginative rendition, the menu reaches to Japan for inspiration with a platter of salmon sushi, which has a unique look with plating that includes a customary dab of wasabi mustard and snow white daikon radish slivers; the salmon is glazed with soy sauce and coriander seeds. This one is almost too pretty to eat!

Entrees run the gamut from strictly vegetarian that would please the most demanding vegan to a richly endowed pork tenderloin glazed with ancho pepper and ginger sauce, a trio of steaks, plus unusual creations of poultry and seafood. The Harvest On Huron version of filet mignon emphasizes flavors, not only of the beef, but of the side addition of portobello mushrooms, mashed potatoes and shallots. The meat is napped in a reduction of Zinfandel wine. Even something as basic as prime rib is not allowed to leave the kitchen without significant embellishment. In this case, the beef is accompanied by a roasted garlic flan and a silky smooth tomato coulis.

Anyone who thinks of walleyed pike cooked over a North Woods campfire minutes after it has been taken from a glacier spring–fed lake would probably not recognize this version. The fish is baked in a *brioche* dough crust along with a topping of mushrooms, green beans, fresh tarragon snippings and an infusion of lemon butter with lobster oil. It may be gilding the lily, but after all this is the new millenium!

Desserts are in many examples embellishment of a basic theme. Service is exemplary, and despite all of the involved cookery, the kitchen seems more than willing to accommodate special diet needs where possible.

HATSUHANA
KR 20/20

Decor 4/4   Hospitality 5/5   Food 10/10   Value 1/1

- **Japanese**
- **Chicago/Near North**
- **$$$**

160 East Ontario Street
Chicago
(312) 280-8287
Troubleshooter: Nick Nakamura
(owner)

Hours: Lunch Mon–Fri noon–
2 pm, Dinner 5:45–10 pm,
Sat 5:30–10 pm
Credit Cards: All majors
Reservations: Requested
Handicapped: Accessible
**Smoking and nonsmoking
sections:** Both available
Parking: Valet available

As popular as this restaurant is with the business and convention diners, it manages to offer a serenity that exists in few other Japanese restaurants in the city. White walls are accented with blond wood trim. Individual tables accommodate small groups, and a 25-seat sushi bar lets diners watch the sushi masters at their culinary artistry. Sushi can be ordered à la carte or in fixed price portions that offer samples of several different styles. Should you find the idea of eating raw seafood unpleasant, start with something easy such as chopped tuna and scallions, much like a seafood version of steak tartare, but with mild Oriental seasonings adding to the flavor. Then, work up to other choices, usually served in bite-sized pieces on a wedge of vinegared rice and wrapped in a sheet of dried seaweed.

Or, you might get something seasoned with a dab of hot green *wasabi* mustard and a bit of pickled ginger sliced paper thin. In addition to the selections of sushi and sashimi, Hatsuhana serves complete lunches and dinners with soup, pickled vegetables, rice and tea. À la carte selections will raise your tab, but they will also give you the chance to work through the menu and try some of the more exotic fare. Conservative diners may want to stay with tempura, lobster or steak, but whatever you choose, Hatsuhana is the best of its kind in Chicago.

HAU GIANG
KR 17/20
Decor 2.5/4   Hospitality 5/5   Food 8.5/10   Value 1/1

* **Vietnamese**
* **Chicago/Far North**
* **$**

1104 West Argyle Street
Chicago
(773) 275-8691
Troubleshooter: Manager on
duty

Hours: Mon–Thurs, Sun 10
am–10 pm, Fri–Sat 10 am–11 pm
Credit Cards: No credit cards,
but they will accept checks
Reservations: Accepted
Handicapped: Accessible
Bar: No bar, but diners may bring
in beer or wine from outside
Parking: On street, tight

The garish neon colors which splash across restaurant windows along
Argyle Street fortunately do not overwhelm some of the subtleties of
cookery which go on inside. Hau Giang is a good case in point.

The restaurant takes up two storefronts. There is not much in the
way of exotic decor inside, a few tables scattered about, a counter to the
rear. What reveals the most about Hau Giang is that a large number of
those who dine here are Vietnamese, a sure tipoff that the food represents a degree of authenticity.

Despite its tropical Southeast Asian geography, the foods of Viet-
nam are not especially spicy. Rather, there is a sometimes quiet delicacy
about ingredients and their pairings. Lettuce leaves often serve as wrappings for food to be taken in hand, or in other cases, something more
than platter dressing. Noodle dishes, an influence from neighboring
China, reflect a concern with balances in flavors and textures. Something
with noodles should certainly be part of your dinner. For a sampling of
several tastes, order pan-fried noodles with shrimp, octopus, pork and
mixed stir fried vegetables. You could add some of the mild pepper or
nuac nam, a salty fish sauce central to much Vietnamese dining.

Some preparations are deceptively simple, others reflect a greater
complexity of influences. From among nearly a dozen appetizers, one
brings a combination of shrimp and vegetables wrapped in rice paper,
another ties together beef with lettuce, cucumber and bean sprouts, also
in a rice paper wrap, delicious when dipped into a lemon oil sauce. The
egg rolls may be the most crisp I have ever tasted, their dark skins
wrapped tightly around a mix of ingredients including meat and vegetables, but with decidedly different flavor than the usual Chinese restaurant
variety.

Soups come in hearty portion. From a wide selection of choices,
crabmeat is combined with asparagus in a delicately flavored broth. Even
better is the Vietnamese version of chicken soup, loaded with chicken

pieces and vegetables in a clear broth with the flavor of cilantro for a bit of tropical freshness.

Like most, if not all menus in oriental restaurants, Hau Giang's is set up into different categories for seafood, poultry, beef, pork and vegetables. The hardest part is making up your mind. Should you choose chicken with lemon grass, as did our party, you will not go wrong. The lemon grass adds a light spiced citric flavor to the stir-fred strips of chicken. Portions are generous; we found that a couple of appetizers and soups coupled with two entrees satisfied our party of five.

HEARTLAND CAFE
KR 16.5/20
Decor 3/4   Hospitality 5/5   Food 7.5/10   Value 1/1

- **American**
- **Chicago/Far North**
- **$**

7000 North Glenwood Avenue
Chicago
(773) 465-8005
Troubleshooter: Michael James
(manager)

Hours: Mon–Fri 7 am–10 pm,
Sat–Sun 8 am–10 pm
Credit Cards: Amex, MC,
Premier, Visa
Reservations: Taken for parties
of 6 or more
Handicapped: Accessible
**Smoking and nonsmoking
sections:** Both available
Parking: Parking lot one block
North of restaurant at Glenwood
and Estes

T hough Heartland Cafe is thought of by some people as a vegetarian restaurant, that is not strictly so. Still, red meat is limited to farm-raised buffalo and fish, poultry and tofu are more likely ingredients. Food service starts with breakfast, including various styles of egg dishes, pancakes and the like and goes on all the way through dinner. Sandwiches can be made with a variety of vegetables, even fruit as in grilled almond butter–banana and raisin on whole wheat. A pita stuffed with grilled vegetables is topped with melted cheese and served with corn chips, while spinach or broccoli can be sautéed and used for another filling.

But, there are more than sandwiches. Consider their version of a pizza, which is made on a cornmeal bread dough about six inches round. You can get it topped with turkey sausage or shrimp. The kitchen will even use a soy-based cheese if you really want to watch the cholesterol. It may not be the best pizza in Chicago, but it's tasty. So too is the mixed bean chili or chicken wings, served more simply than the standard edition buffalo chicken wings.

Entrees show off more imagination, though people who have been coming to Heartland Cafe for years and have hardly seen the menu change, might not think so. Nonetheless, there's more going on here than seasoned stir-fried vegetables and tofu. Mexican-style chicken and rice brings a platter heaped high with a mix of the two main ingredients. Oddly, the flavor strikes me as more Chinese than Mexican, though the large helping of red beans brought things back south of the border. Other entrees include red and yellow pepper lasagna bound with cheese interlacing the broad lasagna noodles, grilled salmon with a spicy "pickapeppa" sauce, chicken or meatless fajitas, pan-fried or blackened catfish, from a fairly good sized list of choices. By the way, those vegetable dishes can be very tasty if an order of soba noodles is an example. Teriyaki saucing makes this sweeter than some might otherwise expect, but it really is delicious. Steamed vegetables help fill out the large serving bowl.

There are a variety of desserts including a dense chocolate cake with black walnuts. Service is casual, matching the style of the restaurant, but not without a certain charm.

HONG MIN
KR 15.5/20
Decor 3/4   Hospitality 4/5   Food 7.5/10   Value 1/1

- **Chinese**
- **Chicago/Chinatown**
- **$**

221 West Cermak Road
Chicago
(312) 842-5026
Troubleshooter: Manager on duty

Hours: Mon–Fri 10–2 am,
Sat–Sun 10–3 am
Credit Cards: Visa, Mastercard
Reservations: Taken for parties of six or more
Handicapped: Accessibility is limited
Smoking and nonsmoking sections: Both available
Parking: Validated in nearby Chinatown lot

Chinese dining is tailor-made for stretching out an evening by taking a course or selection at a time. That's how experienced diners do it at Hong Min. Begin with the hot and sour soup, savoring its peppery tang and abundance of tofu, egg threads and shredded pork in a rich savory broth. Other appetizers are the sort one expects in Chinese storefront dining. The dumplings have a silky-smooth doughy crust and are plumped with pork, or if you prefer, chicken, and the light aftertaste of ginger. Other choices range from egg rolls, to barbecue pork, to Cantonese-style fried shrimp.

There are really two menus at Hong Min, the standard multi-page Chinese restaurant listing, and another shorter printed list with some truly wonderful specials. Whole lobster is steamed in one version, grilled in another and served in a rich garlic and ginger sauce. That sauce also works wonders with shrimp, scallops or walleyed pike.

General Tso's chicken has become a popular staple on Chinese menus. It's a battered and fried chicken plunked into a complex, sweet and spicy sauce. The Hong Min version is good, though not really the best I've tasted. The batter is somewhat soggy, and the sauce rather mild. But, another chicken selection with vegetables in an oyster sauce with hints of garlic is delicious.

Among side orders, eggplant comes sliced and well-cooked in yet another spiced sauce, which like so much in the Chinese cuisine, defies description for its subtle and not so subtle flavorings.

The restaurant appears to be rather small, until you realize that a second dining room is attached. Service is good, but somewhat impersonal. Hong Min serves no alcoholic beverages, but you can bring in beer or wine. As for desserts, standard issue fortune cookies and almond cookies tell the tale.

HOT TAMALES
KR 18/20
Decor 4/4   Hospitality 4.5/5   Food 8/10   Value 1/1

- **Mexican**
- **Highland Park**
- **$**

493 Central Avenue
Highland Park
(847) 433-4070
Troubleshooter: Jim Wygonski (owner)

Hours: Mon–Fri 11:30 am–2 pm, Dinner Mon–Thurs 5–9 pm, Fri–Sat 5–10 pm, Sun 5–8:30 pm
Credit Cards: All majors
Handicapped: Accessible
Smoking and nonsmoking sections: Nonsmoking
Parking: On street, can be tight

If it is possible to be funky and a Mexican restaurant, that's what Hot Tamales is all about. There is a sense of humor in the sprightly decor with its use of bold color and stylized designs. Service leans toward the informal.

The dining can be rather serious, at least when it comes to preparation and presentation. There is no fooling around with principles of good cooking. Just taste a platter of quesadillas with goat cheese and mushrooms to get a sense of what is going on here. This is not the traditional enchiladas, burritos and tacos Mexican restaurant.

Those Mexican staples are on the menu, but treated more like gourmet dining than so called "border food." Take the namesake tamales for example. They can be ordered with a chicken and raisin, chorizo sausage, pumpkin or seafood filling. The pumpkin filling has the expected taste. But, when garnished with a hot salsa verde, sour cream and molé, all napped around a corn husk on which rests the tamale, it is evident that this is not basic *taquería* cooking. Tacos, meantime, can be stuffed with a delicious rendering of duck in one version, meat sliced from a leg of pork in another, chicken in yet another creation, or vegetarian-style.

The imaginative menu makes wonderful use of fresh vegetables. Roast corn chowder is made from a chicken stock finished with cream, endowed with kernels of corn, larger pieces of smokey ham, and slivers of hot peppers just to remind you that this is not your basic Massachusetts corn chowder.

Diners could make a meal by ordering a handful of the smaller appetizer dishes, ranging from spinach and cheese chimichanga to stylized Mexican pizza topped with chicken, black beans, green olives and sour cream. A recent fish of the day, tuna, came grilled with *chayote*, a Mexican squash with the pale color and crisp feel of jicama or turnip, but a flavor that hints of lemon. A garnish of freshly grilled vegetables completed the platter. Among other selections, grilled Cornish hen is surrounded by grilled vegetables; the hen was completed with a reddish orange achiote sauce, its flavor ever so delicate and mild.

Combination meals might bring together a large burrito stuffed with chicken, salsa and refried beans, lavished with a melted cheese topping. Among other offerings is delicious grilled *tilapia*, a mild Pacific fish bathed in a trio of chili sauces, plated with Spanish rice, asparagus and broccoli. Other fish choices will vary depending upon market availabilities, not to mention the predilections of the chef.

THE HOUSE OF NOODLE 777
KR 18/20
Decor 4/4   Hospitality 4/5   Food 9/10   Value 1/1

- **Vietnamese**
- **Chicago/North**
- **$**

1065/63 West Argyle
Chicago
(773) 561-9909
Troubleshooter: Tony Nguyen
(manager)

Hours: Sun–Thurs 9 am–8:30 pm, Fri–Sat 9 am, closed Wed.
Credit Cards: Visa, MC
Reservations: Recommended
Handicapped: Accessible
Smoking and nonsmoking sections: Smoking section
Parking: Street

Argyle Street is festooned with flag banners and its storefronts with the crisp Oriental calligraphy that identifies this otherwise typical Chicago Street as home to the city's Vietnamese commercial community. Restaurants have been part of this community from the beginning of the Vietnamese emigration to Chicago. The House of Noodle 777 (the owner says the 777 is for luck) is clearly a popular restaurant with local Vietnamese families, and though the menu might take some deciphering and servers might struggle to understand your English and you theirs, the welcome and hospitality are evident.

The menu is lengthy with choices transliterated from Vietnamese script to our more familiar alphabet. Underneath each designation is a scant description of ingredients, sometimes more idiomatic than clear. For instance, the house special is a traditional *pho*, or Vietnamese beef soup. The menu translates in English as "eye of round steak, well-done flank, fat brisket, soft tendon, bible tripe & meat balls."

In the case of Vietnamese chicken noodle soup, the noodles are bathed in a flavorful clear chicken stock enhanced with onions, lots of white breast chicken meat, spicy hot green peppers and plenty of coriander to give a delicious sweet spiced underpinning. Add some bean sprouts and leafy lettuce served up from a separate platter and it becomes almost a meal in itself. This is definitely not your grandmother's chicken soup, unless she came from Saigon.

Egg rolls are less successful. Ours had evidently been prepared earlier in the day and were kept warm, but certainly not hot, in a warming oven or steam table. Still, they had a delicate flavor distinctly different from the more common Chinese egg rolls.

From that lengthy menu, take my suggestion and order a large fried thin pancake or crepe filled with bean sprouts, shrimp and assorted sliced vegetables. Lettuce leaves can be folded around ingredients, or they can be eaten right form the crepe. One portion is easily enough for two people. The flavors are very delicate, but a tray of sauces ranging from salty *nuac mom*, or fish's gravy, to nominally hot and downright fiery is at hand on each table.

Another good choice is a stir-fried seafood and vegetable combination, rather oily, but still interesting thanks to the contrast of textures between the broad smooth noodles and the vegetables. Like the crepe, it can be seasoned with condiments at hand.

The House of Noodle 777 is right in the heart of the Vietnamese commercial strip. It's quite an adventure.

HUBBARD STREET GRILL
KR 18/20
Decor 3.5/4   Hospitality 5/5   Food 8.5/10   Value 1/1

- **American**
- **Chicago/River North**
- **$$**

351 West Hubbard Street
Chicago
(312) 222-0770
Troubleshooters: Debbie & David Schy (owners)

Hours: Mon–Thurs 11:30 am–9 pm, Fri 11:30 am–10 pm, Sat 5–10 pm, closed Sun
Credit Cards: All majors
Reservations: Accepted
Smoking and nonsmoking sections: Both available
Parking: Valet or lot

Hubbard Street Grill is as easy to like and enjoy as any restaurant I can think of. For one thing, service is engaging and amiable, not to mention knowledgeable. When a waiter thought we might be ordering too much food, he was quick to say so. Though appetizers are tempting, ordering a course might not be necessary since all dinners come with two side dishes. In fact, the menu also encourages making a meal of a selection of side dishes. For example, white beans with pasta and fennel could be matched with wilted spinach glazed in olive oil and lemon, and perhaps steamed broccoli flavored with pine nut butter, or the Grill's version of potatoes vesuvio. Each of these selections is good alone; combined, they make a full-sized meal.

More conventional entree selections have some built in pairings. For instance, the menu's mixed grill plates a generous piece of salmon with a trio of skewered shrimp and a somewhat small cut of skirt steak. The steak is basted in a peppery sweet barbecue sauce before it hits the grill. Delicious fried onions are the natural accompaniment to the meat. The salmon comes on a bed of fruited salsa; the shrimp are served with contrasting colored tiny black beans. It is an imaginative, uncontrived display.

It should go without saying that each of the mixed grill items can be ordered singly in full portion. Other entrees include a perfectly grilled filet mignon, grilled ahi tuna and an absolutely delicious grouper. The fish is treated like a piece of steak, coated with course ground cracked pepper before it is charred on the grill. An accompanying salsa marries flavors of orange and garlic with sliced olives and tomato chunks. Garlic mashed potatoes is a perfect accompaniment as one of the side dishes, though it is hard to pass up a platter of hand-cut french fries with what the menu describes as "ketchapeño." As the name suggests, it is a jalapeño pepper–spiced ketchup.

Desserts are not guilt-free, except for the mixed berries. Otherwise, chocolate cake, chocolate pudding or cheesecake are among finishing touches.

HUDSON CLUB
KR 19.5/20
Decor 4/4   Hospitality 5/5   Food 9.5/10   Value 1/1

• **American Eclectic**	**Hours:** Mon–Thurs 5–10 pm, Fri–Sat 5–11 pm, closed Sun
• **Chicago/River North**	**Credit Cards:** All majors
• **$$$**	**Reservations:** Recommended
504 North Wells Street	**Handicapped:** Accessible
(312) 467-1947	**Smoking and nonsmoking**
Troubleshooter: Stephanie	**sections:** Both available
Gerkin (manager)	**Parking:** Valet $7

When it comes to swanky, you won't find anything more so in Chicago than Hudson Club. The exterior makes an immediate statement, which gets full follow-through inside, where the decor might best be described as space age deco. The restaurant's main room is cavernous with a high vaulted ceiling and open trusses supporting it. A small side room is used for private parties.

Seating is on maroon vinyl or velvet plush; service is sharp and attentive; the food is contemporary and stylish. There are more than a few Asian-fusion accents on the menu, though no one style or region predominates. First course choices range from chilled roasted beets, Asian pear salad or tuna carpaccio to such hot appetizers as roasted butternut squash ravioli, snails with mushrooms on a bed of wilted spinach with garlic butter, baked and served in a bread crust, to the ubiquitous grilled portobello.

A sushi plate is handsome, somewhat conventional with its selection of seafood atop mounds of rice. Corn flake crusted shrimp are much more intriguing, served in a peppery Tabasco-infused broth along with slivers of fried collard greens with chive. Similarly interesting is a platter of conch fritters, maybe not as they would be served in Key West, but fresh and tasty with a papaya chutney for embellishment. One of the most interesting selections is eggplant saganaki, layered lasagna-like.

Among entrees, a recent special brought roasted white fish in a fairly small wedge, but beautifully plated with lentils and small stalks of white asparagus. A gremolada completed the presentation of flavors. Other seafood choices include seared tuna, left rare in the center, roasted Atlantic salmon with orzo pasta, sea bass and shrimp plated with currant risotto and beans in a complex carrot curry broth or fried red snapper prepared and served much as it would be in a Japanese restaurant.

For meat eaters, grilled venison is a hearty selection, as is the Jamaican-influenced jerked pork tenderloin. Ostrich meat can be tough; just look at how muscular the huge wingless birds are. Tough as it might be, ostrich steak has a delicious meaty taste. Slices are set on a bed of wheatberries, wild mushrooms and shredded brussels sprouts. It's not only an interesting flavor mix, but also compelling for its balance of texture.

Hudson Club prides itself, justifiably so, on its extensive wine list, and its service of wine flights, which gives diners the opportunity to taste several different wines in smaller portion. Desserts cater to the sweet tooth in all of us. Pear poached in zinfandel wine and glazed with tasmanian honey with a filling of creamy mascarpone cheese took the honors.

Il Jack's
KR 18/20
Decor 3/4   Hospitality 5/5   Food 9/10   Value 1/1

- **Italian**
- **Chicago West**
- **$$**

1758 West Grand Avenue
Chicago
(312) 421-7565
Troubleshooter: Manager on duty

Hours: Lunch Mon–Fri 11 am–2:30 pm, Dinner Mon–Thurs 5–10 pm, Fri–Sat 5–10:30 pm, Sat Sept–Jan (football season) noon–9:30 pm
Credit Cards: All majors
Reservations: Recommended, call for parties
Handicapped: Accessible
Smoking and nonsmoking sections: Both available
Parking: Free in adjacent lot or valet

I think the most fun I have as a restaurant critic is when I stumble across a little or lesser known restaurant which deserves far more attention than it otherwise might get. Il Jack's is that kind of restaurant. It's West Side Italian, but far from the red checkered table cloth kind.

The decor is somewhat contemporary and rather reserved with muted tones of gray, white and black, accented by splashes of pastel abstract art on the walls. It is a restaurant which should be busy on a Saturday night, but one in which we walked into without a reservation, only to find more empty tables than any restaurant owner would want to see.

And, that's too bad, because Il Jack's has some outstanding cooking. It can be as baroque in nature as one of the complex specialties of the night. Boned breast of chicken rolled around a stuffing of prosciutto and fontinella cheese, then sautéed with Grand Marnier, or as prosaic as chicken marsala or broiled veal chop. That list of nightly specials has included *risotto fruiti de mare*, a selection of shellfish, squid and baby octopus set out on a bed of simmered arborio rice. Because this was a seafood preparation, there was no cheese, which meant nothing bound the rice together in the way of traditional risotto. In a sense, this was a test of the kitchen's expertise, a test passed flawlessly. A reduced seafood stock brought some flavor intensity made even better with a squirt or two of fresh lemon juice.

Among other choices from the fairly short printed menu, 8 finger cavatelli is a standout. This is a hallmark of West Side Italian cooking in the old country style. The "8 finger" designation refers to how the cavatelli is cut out from a sheet of pasta dough. It may not really be done this way today, but legend has it that the pasta maker draws four fingers of each hand through the flattened dough to shape each noodle. With a marinara sauce, that is true marinara, it is an exceptional pasta. *Pasta putanesca*, a popular Roman recipe with a rather colorful history, is similarly flavorful, and typical of good basic Italian cooking.

The menu lists a wealth of chops and fish choices, plus a quartet of thin crust old-style pizzas which can be enjoyed individually or as appetizers for your table of two to four people. Service is accommodating, the wine list reasonably priced with some standouts for special "big spender" occasions.

IL VICINATO
KR 17/20
Decor 3.5/4   Hospitality 5/5   Food 7.5/10   Value 1/1

- **Italian**
- **Chicago/South**
- **$$**

2435 South Western Avenue
Chicago
(773) 927-5444
Troubleshooters: Ivo Marchetti, Jim Nacarato (owners)

Hours: Mon–Thurs 11 am–10 pm, Fri 11 am–11 pm, Sat 5–11 pm, closed Sun
Credit Cards: All majors
Handicapped: Not accessible
Reservations: Accepted
Parking: Street parking usually ample

The man behind the bar smiles and waves hello! I have never seen him before in my life, but he greets me almost like a long lost friend. This is Il Vicinato. The name of the restaurant fits like a glove; in Italian it means "the vicinity," "the neighborhood." This stretch of South Western Avenue parallels a similar stretch of South Oakley Avenue. It, and the streets which run perpendicular make up an old South side Italian neighborhood which has been virtually the same for decades. The neighborhood is dotted with restaurants, as well as the local church, a funeral home and a few retail and service stores. But, above all, it is where people live, as did their parents, and great-grandparents before them.

This is a restaurant review, but it is important that you know the vicinity itself. This is a neighborhood restaurant, and you don't ask more of it than is reasonable. The cooking is homestyle. The chef, a man named Ivo, welcomed me into his kitchen with the same warmth as had the bartender earlier, knowing me only as another customer. He explained how his recipes for homemade ravioli and potato dough gnocchi came from his grandmother. Though the other pastas are boxed and branded products, the sauces which flavor them are products of Il Vicinato's kitchen.

But, while a bolognese sauce may have the classic taste of Tuscany, where Chef Ivo was born, other recipes might be created on the spot. One such dish, Ravioli Roger has such a local provenance. It is named after a long time customer who, several years ago, asked for something with peas and cheese. The result was a blanket of melted parmesan covering a sprinkling of peas over ravioli, filled with ground veal, then braised beneath the broiler until the cheese melts into a creamy sauce. There's nothing complex about it, just a direct request from a customer that became a standard of the restaurant.

Though Il Vicinato shares the common staples of better Italian restaurants, it remains unique for its personalized service and presentations. This is not the cutting edge of Italian cookery or fine dining. It is a neighborhood restaurant that happens to be good enough to draw from all over.

INDIA HOUSE
KR 18.5/20
Decor 4/4   Hospitality 4/5   Food 9.5/10   Value 1/1

• **Indian**	**Hours:** Lunch Buffet Mon–Thurs 11:30 am–2:30 pm, Fri–Sun 11:30 am–3 pm, Dinner Mon–Thurs 5–10 pm, Fri–Sun 5–11 pm
• **Schaumburg**	
• **$$**	
1521 West Schaumburg Road	
Schaumburg	**Credit Cards:** All majors
(847) 895-5501	**Reservations:** Suggested
Troubleshooter: Jag Mohan (owner)	**Handicapped:** Accessible
	Smoking and nonsmoking sections: Separate seating

Though Devon Avenue is the heart of Indian dining in Chicago, there are many other worthwhile locations. India House, in Schaumburg has its roots on Devon Avenue.

The restaurant is cavernous. The decor is contemporary with accents of classical Indian art.

India House remains the only restaurant of its cuisine that I know of in the Chicago area where *tawa* and *khadai* dishes are specifically identified. The words refer to a iron griddle or plate and an Indian-style wok. The menu also includes tandoor-roasted meats and vegetables. The chicken is succulent, moist, wonderfully flavored. A selection of tandoor roasted vegetables has the tangy flavor from roasting over hot coals, but may be a little too salty. That saltiness was characteristic of one or two other vegetable dishes, the only downside to otherwise excellent cooking.

Soups can often define a kitchen's excellence or lack of it. The chicken soup called *murg ka shorba* is a perfect example, aromatic and delicious. A seafood soup is almost as good, in a creamy broth loaded with small shrimp, mussels and baby squid. I think, though, that its complexity was masked by the cream.

Among other first course choices India House serves delicious finger foods. Cashew nut rolls are crisp and take well to any number of accompanying chutneys, or as is. As I wrote back in 1995 when India House was on Devon Avenue, "Even though it has been deep-fried, there is not a trace of oiliness, only the sublime and smooth flavors of the ingredients."

Similar care is evident in the complexity of seasonings so characteristic of Indian dining. This is never boring or hackneyed food. Consider okra, with its characteristic clove seasoning among others, while something else, such as roasted potatoes have an entirely different flavor and texture. Lentils get excellent treatment in a variety of cooking styles and seasonings. The selection of curries includes seafood, ranging from salmon which is hardly ever seen in Indian restaurants, to the more usual shrimp or crabmeat.

IXCAPUZALCO
KR 18/20
Decor 3.5/4   Hospitality 5/5   Food 8.5/10   Value 1/1

- **Mexican Eclectic**
- **Chicago/Northwest**
- **$$**

2919 North Milwaukee Avenue
Chicago
(773) 486-7340
Troubleshooter: Geno Behena
(chef/owner)

Hours: Lunch Mon–Fri 10:30 am–2:30 pm, Dinner Mon–Thurs 5:30–10:30 pm,
Fri–Sun 10:30 am–10:30 pm
Credit Cards: All majors
Reservations: Suggested
Handicapped: Accessible
Smoking and nonsmoking sections: No smoking
Parking: On street, valet

At Ixcapuzalco diners will have a different Mexican restaurant experience. One full page of the menu offers some rather detailed information about the various *molés*, or indigenous Mexican sauces, featured each day as specials.

The cooking is complex, whether your choice is one of the *molés* or something else. There is a five course tasting menu of the chef's selections. Or you can choose an à la carte dinner. Begin with an appetizer portion of smoked whitefish and potato cakes and you will quickly understand the difference between Ixcapuzalco and other Mexican restaurants. Fresh thyme is used as a flavor freshener while cucumber, red onion and cilantro are combined with a touch of serrano pepper to make a salsa. Mixed greens complete the platter, set out on a cheerfully colorful plate. Among other first course choices, *masa* boats, made from the traditional Mexican corn meal batter, are filled with sample portions of chicken in red *molé*, sweet plantain, black beans with mushrooms, and smooth and creamy guacamole.

Not everything on the menu calls for a *molé*. Capon breast is fanned in slices with a delicious peppery, but not really hot red salsa. Seasoned roasted potatoes are on the side. Among seafood selections, the "day-boat catch," as the menu calls it, is a freshly seared fish fillet with a simple accompaniment of roasted garlic, olive oil, avocado slices, smoked onions and rice pilaf. If you like a fish stew, the Ixcapuzalco version is spiced with red chiles and includes mussels, shrimp, scallops and soft fish, with rice, grilled zucchini and corn kernels in the tangy fish stock.

Among other selections, roasted duck breast is given an almond and sweet spice sauce bound together with tomatoes and pickled jalapeño peppers, with just a remnant of heat. Vegetarians can order a mushroom-stuffed tamale in which mixed greens, roasted tomato, melted white cheese and sour cream complete the filling. Classic *carne asada* is on the menu for steak lovers, plated with fried plantain, sour cream, dried cheese, guacamole and black beans, while leg of lamb is given a spicy salsa that includes beer, chili peppers and roasted garlic among its ingredients.

JACKY'S BISTRO
KR 19/20
Decor 4/4   Hospitality 5/5   Food 9/10   Value 1/1

- **French**
- **Evanston**
- **$$**

2545 Prarie Avenue
Evanston
(847) 733-0899
Troubleshooter: Jacky Pluton
(chef/owner)

Hours: Lunch Tues–Fri 11 am–2:30 pm, Dinner Tues–Thurs 5–9:30 pm, Fri–Sat 5–10 pm Sun 5–8 pm
Credit Cards: Amex, Diners, MC, Visa
Reservations: Recommended
Smoking and nonsmoking sections: Nonsmoking inside, but allowed outside
Handicapped: Accessible
Parking: Valet $5

I don't know that restaurants can be treated like diplomatic embassies, but if they could, I am certain Jacky's Bistro would be a sovereign part of France. Everything is authentic and real, closer to Avignon than Evanston. Most of the servers are French, or at least speak with accents almost as thick as paté on brioche.

There are French posters for wall adornment, a small bar and a semi-exposed kitchen framed by a window that gives diners full view of the culinary orchestrations underway. The menu is not exactly extensive enough to qualify as a tour guide of culinary France, but there are certainly the expected bistro offerings and a few things more.

Begin with two categories of Starters, listed on the menu as Classic or From the Market. Similar designations categorize main course listings. Start with something as fresh as daylight, a plated assortment of the Chef's pates of the day, always freshly prepared, plated as an assortment along with a terrine that could be *charcuterie* or vegetable. French Onion Soup is sweet and tangy; aged Parmesan shavings are used for embellishment instead of more traditional gruyere.

As for chilled salads, two are outstanding. Roasted beets are at the heart of one, while I think endive salad with poached pear slices, crumbled blue cheese and pecans is the sort of creation that brings natural flavors together for comparison and contrast. Just imagine the sharpness of that cheese as it stabs at your tongue, which has been savoring the sweet tang of the roasted pears.

As for the other first course options in the "From the Market" category, crab cake is plated with a stylized *ratatouille* salad touched with mustard vinaigrette. Pan seared vegetables are coupled with a goat cheese terrine, while another selection brings a hot plate of wild mushrooms in a *fricassee*, cooked together with what tastes like sherry or a similarly fortified wine. In any event, it is another example of flavor reciprocity.

Steak and Frites is given its own menu display box so it is not easily overlooked. You can have it in the classic strip steak version as a grilled sirloin, as sirloin with cracked peppers or the ultimate indulgence, sirloin Bordelaise. Thanks to the kitchen gods that Pluton is among those chefs to appreciate the importance of saucing.

As good as it is, steak cannot really show off a chef's expertise. For that, you must taste something more complex, more involved. *Bouillabaisse* fits that to perfection. This is a more or less clear broth *Bouillabaisse*, with definite flavor accents of fennel and saffron in its basic fish stock. Cuts of soft fish, a small langoustine, shrimp, clams and mussels may be simmering in the broth, adding their good flavor, while absorbing flavors from the stock. A swirl of *rouille*, or garlic mayonnaise is added enrichment.

There are so many other choices ranging from sautéed calves liver with Lyonnaise potatoes, to braised lamb shank, perfect comfort food plated with garlic mashed potatoes, to roasted duck with wild rice and a tart citrus sauce reduction. For seafood, sautéed seabass has been served recently with Indian style Basmati rice and a side of roasted carrots. Salmon is crusted with a bouquet of fresh herbs, roasted and set on a vegetable bedding. For vegetarians, choices include risotto or roasted vegetables of the day, neither as prosaic as it sounds.

Desserts include *crème brûlee*, sorbets and meringue cookies which sandwich vanilla ice cream. Service is excellent, very informative, with good follow through on little things like freshening water glasses or keeping tableware current for each course. In addition to the regular menu, there is a chef's tasting. Ask your server for specifics. Jacky's Bistro may be an ocean away from France, but it sure seems a lot closer.

JAIPUR PALACE
KR 19/20
Decor 4/4   Hospitality 5/5   Food 9/10   Value 1/1

- **Indian**
- **Chicago/River North**
- **$$**

22 East Hubbard Street
Chicago
(312) 595-0911
Troubleshooter: Shamas Kahn
(owner)

Hours: Mon–Thurs 11 am–
10 pm, Fri–Sat 11 am–11 pm,
Sun 11 am–9:30 pm
Credit Cards: All majors
Reservations: Recommended
Handicapped: Accessible
**Smoking and nonsmoking
sections:** Both available
Parking: Valet $7

Jaipur Palace captures not only the complex subtleties of the cuisine, but it does so in an atmosphere of tranquility and beauty. Though people might think of Indian food as hot and spicy, that need not be the case. Indian snack foods such as deep-fried cauliflower and potato fritters, called *pakora*, are delicious just as they come. The same is true for *samosas*, another sort of fritter, though more akin to a pancake filled with potatoes and green peas, plus the aromatic flavor of fresh coriander. Even ground lamb patties are perfectly delicious without any additions, though to ignore the fruit chutneys or peppery, but not too hot green sauce is to ignore an aspect of Indian cookery which deserves full attention.

There is more than snack food type appetizers, of course. But, before going on to a main course selection, soup should not be ignored. *Mulligatawny* is my favorite, chicken stock with a bevy of aromatic seasonings, whose origins stem from the South of the subcontinent with roots that predate by centuries the Moghul influence in the North.

Jaipur Palace captures popular fancy with such dramatic foods as those from the *tandoor*, a deep clay urn used as an oven to grill a variety of meats, and even the puffy flat breads often used to scoop up gravies and cooked vegetables. Chicken is always moist, lamb even better. Tandoor-grilled meats are distinguished not just by flavor, but by the bright red color, a characteristic of their yogurt-based seasonings.

The lengthy menu offers much more than tandoor cooking. India is rich in spices, used to perfect effect in various lamb or vegetable stews. Indian chicken dishes, or *murghs* bring a whole new dimension to something which in other cuisines seems repetitively boring. Diners can get a taste of several menu listings with either a vegetarian or meat combination platter.

Vegetarians already know the joys of Indian cooking. Vegetable entrees and side dishes hardly miss a beat. And, unlike other regions of the Orient, desserts are important to Indian dining, whether a rich mango-flavored ice cream, fried cottage cheese balls in rose water or a deep-fried cottage cheese fritter sweetened with milk and sugar, topped with crushed pistachios.

There is a rather ambitious wine list, though I think hot tea or cold beers are better suited accompaniments. Be sure to go with a small group so you can taste and sample more of what is offered.

JANE'S
KR 19.5/20
Decor 4/4   Hospitality 5/5   Food 9.5/10   Value 1/1

- **American Eclectic**
- **Chicago/Near Northwest**
- **$$**

1655 West Cortland
Chicago
(773) 862-JANE
Troubleshooters: Jeff or Arden (owners)

Hours: Sun–Thurs 11 am–10 pm, Fri–Sat until 11 pm
Credit Cards: MC, Visa
Reservations: Taken
Handicapped: Accessible bathrooms, but there are two steps up to front door of restaurant
Bar: Full service
Smoking and nonsmoking sections: Both available, plus smoking at bar
Parking: Street parking can be tight
Party Facilities: None available

Finding a converted storefront restaurant is not very difficult. But, I know of only one converted Chicago-style cottage. And, that's not the only thing that makes Jane's unique.

The former cottage was gutted, leaving its high peaked ceiling open to create a sense of space in what is actually a very small dining area that seats hardly more than 40 or 50 people.

Considerable thought has evidently gone into the menu at Jane's, which is about as different as the restaurant's building. For one thing, while Jane's is not vegetarian, there are no beef or other red meat selections. But, there are poultry and seafood, as well as several meatless choices.

Luscious abundance of flavors comes to mind when trying to describe the food. For example, an onion tart is bound with thin slices of porcini mushrooms, tantalizing blue cheese and thyme in its sauce. The tart really does not hold together in the sense that it is in a pastry, but its flavors are virtual taste explosions. The menu also offers something as simple as humus, the popular Middle Eastern chickpea puree, served with warm triangles of pita bread. Back on the more creative side is another appetizer, Jane's version of Mexican quesadilla. It is filled with melted cheese, and plated with a sharp spicy salsa and cooling guacamole. The flavors are pronounced, yet in balance with each other.

The menu offers only three pastas and a selection of other entrees. Thai herb curry with shrimp is noted as being very very spicy, angle hair pasta with chipotle pesto, chicken and other components is only very spicy, while paparadelle with wild mushrooms is not spicy at all. But, it is delectable with an infusion of woodsy flavor from the mushrooms, set on a foundation of port wine and marsala reduced into an intense sauce.

Other entrees range from what the menu calls a garden burger or burrito with vegetables, tofu and goat cheese, to several elaborate seafood selections. Among them is a mild tasting grilled sea bass enhanced with a bouquet of herbs for seasoning set atop spicy caponata. Thanksgiving turkey has never been like that at Jane's. A well-marinated breast is grilled, then plated with a sauce infused with dried cranberries and pepper. With a bow to tradition comes mashed potatoes with a slight horseradish after taste.

Among desserts an apple tart with ice cream is excellent, but bread pudding is much too custard-like, without the texture that characterizes the best.

JILLY'S CAFE
KR 19/20
Decor 3/4   Hospitality 5/5   Food 10/10   Value 1/1

- **French**
- **Evanston**
- **$$**

2614 Green Bay Road
Evanston
(847) 869-7636
Troubleshooter: Erich Rauch
(owner)

Hours: Lunch Tues–Fri 11:30 am–1:30 pm, Dinner Tues–Thurs 5:45–8:30 pm, Fri–Sat 5:30–9:30 pm, closed Sun
Credit Cards: All majors
Handicapped: Not Accessible
Bar: Full service
Smoking and nonsmoking sections: No smoking
Parking: Street
Party Facilities: Entire restaurant available for private parties of up to 50 people

The chefs come and go, but Jilly's Cafe continues a steady course through the shoals of bistro French dining. Even though things may change behind the scenes, the front of the restaurant remains the small dining room it has always been, comfortable, cozy, handsomely decorated, though not too ornate.

A previous chef's fusion style lingers, but has been amplified with what amounts to contemporary French eclectic. Diners will find tradition mixed with adventure. For instance, among appetizers might be steamed mussels with roasted garlic. Add some chili pepper for bite, plus shallots for depth and finish with a reduction of chardonnay wine in the sauce and things become challenging and different. In another appetizer, Oriental-style spring rolls are plumped with mushrooms and dried fruits and what an exotic combination that is! Spinach and brie cheese flavor a dressing for a mix of greens whose color and texture contrasts bring more complexity, without contrivance, to the happenings.

There is a trio of à la carte salads on the menu, but dinners include a choice of soup or house salad, as well as a small sorbet intermezzo. The entree dining is as imaginative and rewarding as what has preceded. For example, the menu lists *bourride nicoise*, a variation on bouillabaisse. A collection of scallops, shrimp, mussels and soft fish fresh from the market is simmered with potatoes, garlic, white wine and seasonings, then ladled into a bowl with croutons, a fleck or two of parsley and creamy rich garlic and saffron infused *aoili*, a variation on conventional mayonnaise. This is not the kind of cooking that is left to boil away all day, but rather a delicate, yet still very flavorful creation.

Other entrees fall into a classic bistro mold, but in most cases, something unusual is added. For instance, veal *paillard* is plated with endive simmered in the natural liquid it and similar leafy vegetables throw off. A citrus-based sauce and kitchen-made noodles complete the setting. Among seafood choices, roasted salmon has been a regular entree, sometimes with red potatoes in balsamic vinaigrette among other contributing flavors. In another more current version, the salmon is baked in a crust of olive and lemon spread, then plated atop slices red potatoes with balsamic vinaigrette for bite and diced tomatoes with spinach for color.

Several contemporary pastas are regularly served. Recent selections have included penne with slices of roast chicken, radicchio, shitake mushrooms and broccoli in a light chicken-based broth. In another selection, angel hair capellini are served simply, but elegantly with diced tomatoes, roasted garlic, basil and a whiff of olive oil.

Desserts are as tempting as other courses; the wine list is reasonably priced and well thought out. Service is knowledgeable.

KAMA KURA
KR 17.25/20
Decor 3.5/4   Hospitality 5/5   Food 8/10   Value .75/1

- **Japanese**
- **Wilmette**
- **$$**

116 Central Avenue
Wilmette
(847) 256-6783
Troubleshooter: Manager on
duty

Hours: Lunch Tues–Sat 11:30
am–2:30 pm, Dinner Tues–Thurs
5–9:45 pm, Fri–Sat 5–10:30 pm,
Sun 4–10:30 pm, closed Mon
Credit Cards: All majors
Reservations: Suggested
Handicapped: Accessible
**Smoking and nonsmoking
sections:** No smoking in
restaurant
Parking: Street parking can be
tight

I wonder if there is a restaurant in the small city of Kama Kura, Japan
that might be named the Wilmette, where sturdy American food is
served? I don't know the answer to that question, but I do know that
there is Kama Kura Japanese Restaurant smack dab in the middle of
Wilmette.

The menu is fairly descriptive of what's what, though newcomers to
Japanese dining will undoubtedly want some instruction either from ex-
perienced companions or servers. Deep frying is a cooking technique
adapted by the Japanese and used to particularly good effect with the
many *tempura* selections. Tempura cooking is said to have been brought
to Japan by Portuguese traders. Whatever the origin, the results in con-
temporary dining are uniquely Japanese. Tempura foods are highlighted
by a light and airy egg batter, almost lacy in texture. The batter can be
used around most any firm vegetable or seafood. So, tempura shrimp,
squid, scallops or other seafoods are found on the menu, as are vegetable
combinations such as sweet potatoes, green beans and broccoli. A little
ginger soy sauce is used for dipping.

Japanese cooking is also characterized by sweet flavors, such as that
found in cooked spinach in sesame seed sauce called *goma-ae*. One might
not think of a sweet taste and spinach together, but it is excellent, partic-
ularly in the Kama Kura version. If you want to balance the goma-ae with
something else, an order of pan-fried dumplings will work well. These half
moon crescents taste fine as they are, though a touch of sesame soy sauce
brings a little more flavor.

A sushi or sashimi combination platter is fine for an entree main
course. They come in various sizes priced according to the number of
pieces served. Incidentally, at a time when people worry about raw foods,

and especially the freshness of seafood, Japanese restaurants such as Kama Kura are exemplary in their dedication to cleanliness and the freshest possible ingredients. Whatever platter you pick, you'll get a small portion of the spicy hot wasabi, to be used with great care, and a mound of pickled ginger slivers. Some people like to pile them right on a piece of sushi or sashimi. Actually, the ginger is meant to be eaten as a palate refresher between pieces. In either fashion, the ginger adds just a little more zest.

The menu continues with a listing of more main course selections, all served with a clear broth miso soup and rice. Entrees include full portions of tempura, chicken or beef *yakis* (a word which means grilled), yaki style salmon and the well known beef and vegetable hot pot *Suki Yaki*. The salmon is moist, flaky, perfectly broiled. The Suki Yaki is a large portion of thin sliced boiled beef in a sweet tasting broth loaded with vegetables.

There are a variety of combinations that can be ordered to give a taste of this or that. Among those combinations are either of two *bento boxes*. A bento box is a decorative enamel container with compartments separated by vertical risers. Each compartment will hold a specific food whether it be a sushi or sashimi, tempura, or one of the yakis.

KAMEHACHI
KR 18/20
Decor 4/4   Hospitality 4/5   Food 9/10   Value 1/1

- **Japanese**
- **Chicago/Old Town and Northbrook**
- **$$**

1400 North Wells Street
Chicago
(312) 664-3663
Troubleshooter: Guila Sindler (Owner)

Other Location

KR 16.5/20, Decor 4/4 Hospitality 4/5 Food 7.5/10 Value 1/1; 1320 Shermer Road, Northbrook; 847-562-0064; Troubleshooter: Manager on duty; Hours: Lunch Tues–Sat 11:30 am–2 pm, Dinner Tues–Thurs 5–10 pm, Fri–Sat 5–11 pm, Sun 4:30–9:30 pm; Credit Cards: All majors; Reservations: Accepted; Handicapped: Accessible; Smoking and nonsmoking sections: No smoking in restaurant; Parking: On street or in lot behind restaurant

Hours: Lunch Tues–Sat 11:30 am–2 pm, Dinner Tues–Fri 5 pm–2 am, Sun 4:30 pm–midnight
Credit Cards: All majors
Reservations: Requested
Handicapped: Accessible
Smoking and nonsmoking sections: Small dining section for smokers
Parking: Valet in evenings

Kamehachi, which means "Eight Turtles" according to a waitress whom we asked, serves some fairly standard fare for those familiar with Japanese cuisine. The restaurant is long and narrow, almost like a railroad car with a center aisle and tables on either side. Near the entrance, the sushi bar greets diners as they walk in. The obligatory bleached blond wood accents and Japanese wall art set the decorative tone.

Though diners will find the tried-and-true selections of sushi, sashimi, maki and the like, there are some surprises, too. From a selection of appetizers, fried eggplant is topped with a sweet miso-based sauce. Sea scallops are presented with soy and lemon butter sauce. *Yakitori*, the Japanese version of shishkebab, dumplings called *gyoza* and combinations of tofu and seafood abound.

The food quality is excellent. The dumplings, filled with a fine grind of meat, shitake mushrooms and a light seasoning of ginger come steaming hot to the table and are delicious. Eat them quickly, because they lose their heat rapidly. From a cold list of appetizers, spinach with sweet sesame sauce is easy to like, even for the beginner to Japanese cookery.

There is an à la carte selection of sushi, maki and sushimi, or combination platters that provide more economy. A typical combo is handsomely served in a lacquer box to carry out the idea that food should feed the eye as well as the mouth. For sushi beginners, Kamehachi serves a selection of all cooked seafood; "nothing raw," as the menu proclaims. But, if you savor the best sushi there is, *toro*, the belly of the raw tuna, which Kamehachi serves up fresh tasting as can be.

Japanese soba and soup courses are welcome parts of a meal. In fact, portions are large enough that a bowl of soba with vegetables, tempura or shrimp is virtually a one dish supper. *Yaki soba* is another approach to noodles, stir-fried with vegetables for a delicious and satisfying combination of flavor and texture.

Full dinners include miso soup, rice and mild green tea. *Sukiyaki* has a characteristic sweet broth, which immerses translucent rice noodles, cooked vegetables and strips of boiled beef. A combination platter brings a choice of chicken or beef *teriyaki* and a mixed grill of scallops, shrimp and other seafood on a skewer. Flavors are light and fresh.

Service can be a bit odd since, even if dining with as few as four people, you cannot be assured that all courses will arrive at the same time. But, the assistance is nonetheless friendly, characterized by an eagerness to please.

KATSU
KR 18/20
Decor 3/4   Hospitality 5/5   Food 9/10   Value 1/1

- **Japanese**
- **Chicago/Far North**
- **$$**

2651 West Peterson
Chicago
(773) 784-3383
Troubleshooters: Katshishi and Haruko Imamura (owners)

Hours: Daily 5–11 pm, closed Tues
Credit Cards: All majors
Reservations: Suggested
Smoking and nonsmoking sections: Both available
Parking: Street parking ample
Party Facilities: Private party space for up to 40 people

On the wall midway up behind the sushi bar at Katsu are strips of parchment embellished with an ornate calligraphy. What appears to be some kind of Oriental art to the unknowing eye, is in fact a menu of the various kinds of *sushi* or *sashimi* available on a given night. Katsu is that kind of a restaurant, one which draws a predominantly Japanese following of businesspeople and families with children.

It also happens to be a very welcoming place for even the newcomer to Japanese foods, a cuisine very easy for beginners to get to know. The *sushi* and *sashimi*, raw fish, with or without vinegared rice, may seem intimidating at first. So start out with something easy, such as *tomago*, which is nothing more than a wedge of cooked egg on a mound of rice wrapped in seaweed. Move on to *kappa makki*, chopped cucumber in the center of a rice roll, again bound with seaweed.

Of all the *sushi*, shrimp and tuna are probably the easiest to start with. Both are meaty, clean tasting, familiar. A mixed selection of sushi is prepared at an immaculately clean counter by the sushi chef; take a seat at the sushi bar to watch, and converse as each piece is virtually handcrafted in an age-old fashion. The finished pieces are presented on a decorative wood board with a mound of green and very hot *wasabi* mustard, plus thin slivers of pickled ginger. Use the wasabi, and a little soy sauce to perk up the taste buds, and nibble on the ginger as a palate cleanser between each piece.

The *sushi* and *sashimi* can be ordered in combinations of individual kinds or mixed varieties. Service is as cheerful as can be, and a conversation with the *sushi* chef is a delight.

Though you really can make a light meal from the sushi bar, Katsu also offers some standardized versions of cooked Japanese dinners. From among appetizers, take small beef rollups around sliced asparagus with sesame seeds. Or, try delicious fried dumplings stuffed with ground beef and vegetables. To the Italians, these would be akin to ravioli, to the Pole, periogi. In Japanese cookery, they are called gyoza, but in any language, they are delicious.

Grilled chicken, salmon or beef choices are always tasty, as is the traditional Japanese one pot meal, *sukiyaki*, a steaming broth filled with cooked leafy greens, slender translucent noodles and thin strips of boiled beef. Other selections include the house namesake, a deep-fried pork cutlet, plus various noodle soups and chowders.

KIM YEN
KR 18.5/20
Decor 3/4   Hospitality 5/5   Food 9.5/10   Value 1/1

- **Chinese**
- **Chicago/South**
- **$**

228 West Cermak
Chicago
(312) 842-7818
Troubleshooter: Mrs. Mui
(owner)

Hours: Thurs–Tues 11–3 am,
Wed 5 pm–3 am
Credit Cards: MC, Visa
Reservations: Accepted
Handicapped: Accessible
Bar: No bar service, but diners
may bring their own
**Smoking and nonsmoking
sections:** Both available
Parking: Validated two hour free
parking at nearby lot

Have you ever wondered where Chinese people go to eat in China-town? The answer is Kim Yen, a Chinese and Vietnamese restaurant. We went with friends who are regulars and got a sense and taste of what authentic Chinese dining can really be.

Kim Yen is somewhat difficult to spot since most of its signage is in Oriental calligraphy. Once inside, the first thing you may notice is the lack of English. But, you need not worry, because even though you may not be able to read a thing on the menu, or on the poster board which features daily specials, many of the staff people speak English.

You might ask for the specials and will probably come up with some wonderful treats. The style of cooking is noticeably different from the conventional neighborhood Chinese restaurant many Americans grew up with. The cooking is also different from that at the better known name Chinese restaurants, either in Chinatown or scattered about the city.

For one thing, there is a genuine subtlety to seasonings. You may know that Chinese culture strives for a balance in all things, including the culinary. Thus, flavor and textures are meant to compliment each other, without any one feature becoming dominant.

Our Chinese friends placed all the orders, so we had no idea of what to expect until things began arriving for our party of six. First came razor clams, the kind whose shell looks like the handle of an old-fashioned straight razor. They were served in black bean sauce delicately flavored with scallions and ginger. Next out was a platter of squid in mustard greens. The bitter flavor from the greens offered the contrast here. Conch and coriander followed, and again the contrast to the previous course became evident. Fresh slices of lotus root were next, plated with smoked Chinese ham, somewhat like Italian proscuitto, though drier, basted in a sweet sauce.

The next platter held oysters sitting in the valley of their large pearlized shells. Black bean sauce made a reappearance, but in this case it was decidedly mild. Yet another seafood came to the table, large sea scallops sitting on their shells like a Botticelli Venus.

We were not done; the culmination of the evening was Chinese hot pot. Unsalted broth is brought to a boil at the center of the table. Much like fondue, pieces of thin-sliced raw lamb, cuts of codfish, shrimp, Chinese greens, rice noodles and large squares of tofu are cooked for a few moments, fished out and mixed with a sauce that brings together sweetness and mild pepper oil, not so complex as to overpower. At the bottom of the pot, flavors have mingled in the broth, if not intensified. A dessert soup of sweet fungus and papaya brought a most unusual dinner to a close.

KYSOYA
KR 18/20
Decor 4/4   Hospitality 4/5   Food 9/10   Value 1/1

• **Japanese**	**Hours:** Mon–Sat 11 am–10:30 pm, closed Sun
• **Chicago/North**	**Credit Cards:** All majors
• **$$**	**Reservations:** Mandatory on weekend nights
5828 North Lincoln Avenue	**Bar:** Service bar
Chicago	**Smoking and nonsmoking**
(773) 784-6686	**sections:** Both available
Troubleshooter: Grace Jun	**Parking:** Free in private lot next to restaurant

While "pretty" is an overused and tired word, it accurately characterizes this neat as a pin, and evidently authentic restaurant. Light stained wood trim, rice paper lanterns, decorative art characterizes the dining room. To one side are a couple of *tokonama* and semi-secluded alcoves with low tables, and mats for sitting. The *tokonama* might be more favored by Japanese diners accustomed to seating arrangements that only the most nimble of Westerners might find comfortable.

Soon after arrival, a waitress brings out steaming warm towels to refresh one's hands. Cleanliness is at the heart of Japanese dining. The menu is written in both Japanese and English; there are short descriptions of each selection. The noodle dishes are usually part of a soup, a semi-clear broth which will contain a variety of ingredients depending upon what you order. *Misonabe udon* contains pieces of pork, vegetables and sliced egg, while *nabe udon* has shrimp, just as another choice might have tempura vegetables with buckwheat *soba* noodles. There are more than a dozen choices.

While à la carte dining has its attraction, Kysoya offers at least two combination dinners, simply designated Bento A or Bento B. The word *bento* refers to the stylized and decorative box in which the dinner is served. Here is where the Japanese eye for design, presentation and balance come into play. The foods in either combination are set out in small trays or bowls, depending upon what they are, inside a lacquered wooden box or tray. There is hardly any other culture that I know of that places so much emphasis on the proper manner in which foods are presented for dining.

One combination includes a generous portion of delicious chicken teriyaki, perfectly grilled, the other beef teriyaki. Also included are a side of *tempura* vegetables with a wonderfully light and airy batter coating, carefully crafted and designed vegetables, served for eye appeal as much as flavor and texture, steamed rice, plus two pieces of California maki and 3 pieces of sushi. In addition, a bowl of sunomono soup precedes the dinner, and green tea ice cream follows.

The restaurant offers several styles of sushi, sashimi and maki. They can be ordered à la carte or as a complete dinner, too. Each is handsomely crafted, delicately rolled in seaweed, formed into little cubes, or set out on mounds of rice in traditional design. Paper-thin slices of pickled ginger, and fire hot green wasabi mustard accompanies the sushi, as does a tangy soy sauce for dipping.

L. WOODS TAP & PINE LODGE
KR 18/20
Decor 3.5/4   Hospitality 5/5   Food 8.5/10   Value 1/1

• **American**

• **Lincolnwood**

• **$$**

7110 Lincoln Avenue
Lincolnwood
(847) 677-3350
Troubleshooter: Dan McGowan
(managing partner)

Hours: Tap Room Mon–Thurs 11 am–11 pm, Fri–Sat 11 am–midnight, Sun noon–10 pm, Pine Lodge Mon–Sat 5–10 pm, Sun 3–9 pm
Credit Cards: All majors
Reservations: Are taken for The Pine Lodge, not for The Tap
Handicapped: Accessible
Separate smoking and nonsmoking sections: Both available
Parking: Free in adjacent lot

L. Woods Tap & Pine Lodge looks 1950s knotty pine chic. The menu is rather straightforward with a surprisingly short list of selections. The specialties are meats and fried fish. There is a quartet of rib selections, each in a characteristic sweet sauce that still manages to leave a little bit of a sting. If you want it with even more bite, ask for the devil sauce. The BBQ Baby Back Ribs comes in a portion too large for its serving platter.

The same can be said for a charbroiled skirt steak, which seemed to stretch on for a country mile. Incidentally, this skirt steak is tender and without gristle. I suspect it could be ordered with a touch of BBQ sauce should you like to go that route.

Among seafood selections, most are deep-fried or pan-fried. Choices include fried walleye or sole as well as shrimp. However, a simple plain grilled fish is also available. Often it can be salmon, also served with a delicious BBQ sauce. The fish is planked with a swirl of duchess mashed potatoes encircling the fish.

The only entree I will not recommend is spaghetti with vegetable ragout. I ordered it more or less as curiosity. If you want spaghetti, go to an Italian restaurant. The kitchen makes a decent stab at a complex meatless sauce, but . . . enough said about that.

For starters, I don't think there can be anthing better than a chopped salad. The dressing has a light flavor of blue cheese, though a request would bring another dressing of your choice.

Desserts must be ordered when you order your entree. One portion feeds 6 or so people. The apple strudel is the house specialty, and with good reason. Incidentally, aside from dessert, the menu states there is a $3 charge to split entrees . . . and $5 if you argue about it with your server. L. Woods Tap & Pine Lodge has a sense of humor mixed in with good service and food.

LA BOCCA DELLA VERITA

KR 18/20

Decor 3/4   Hospitality 5/5   Food 9/10   Value 1/1

• **Italian**	**Hours:** Mon–Sun 5–11 pm
• **Chicago/Far North**	**Credit Cards:** All majors
• **$$**	**Reservations:** Suggested on weekends
4618 North Lincoln Avenue	**Handicapped:** Accessible
(773) 784-6222	**Party Facilities:** Private party facilities for up to 40 people
Troubleshooter: Cesare Dortenzi (owner)	

Do you remember that scene in the film *Roman Holiday* where Audrey Hepburn persuades Gregory Peck to follow custom and stick his hand into a small hole in a wall in Rome? As legend has it, if you do not tell the truth when someone asks if you love them, your hand will become stuck. The Italians call it *La Bocca Della Verita,* which literally means

"The Mouth of Truth." Chicago's La Bocca Della Verita is more than "a hole in the wall" restaurant inspired by that charming Roman attraction.

Dining here is meant to be at a pace which the Italians might call "*piano, piano.*" Each course is prepared individually, and there is no rushing of good cooking. The menu changes weekly.

In warm weather months, fresh vegetables are given prominence, perhaps as an antipasto assortment or in the case of summer tomatoes, sliced for arrangement on a plate with crumbles of blue cheese or pieces of mozzarella with a finish of extra virgin olive oil and red onions. Other selections can be more complex such as shrimp with artichoke hearts. In this case, the key ingredients are sautéed in olive oil with white wine and fresh lemon juice, then topped by slivers of fleshy portobello mushrooms. The flavors are easy on the palate, fresh, crying out for an accompaniment of a crisp white wine.

One could make a case that something simple such as bruschetta provides insight into an Italian kitchen. It was brushed traditionally with olive oil to which were added crushed garlic, chopped tomatoes and an abundant spread of olive paste. Portobello slices served as topping.

The kitchen usually prepares several pastas, and two risotto choices. Recently, risotto was enhanced with both creamy mascarpone and tangy blue cheeses and roasted red peppers, plus the customary inclusion of grated parmesan, garlic and a sprinkling of parsley.

Rigatoni à la Siciliana brings pasta tubes in consort with slices of baked eggplant, the pervasive tomato sauce, garlic and olive oil, plus crumbles of pecorino and dried ricotta cheese. Other pastas can include fettuccine with salmon in a tomato cream sauce, gnocchi in a simple tomato, basil and parmesan cheese sauce, or a rich combination that ties together a forcemeat of duck breast, sage and shallots as filling for home made ravioli napped in a light tomato cream sauce.

When available the restaurant's Dover sole is excellent, sautéed in olive oil, then baked with white wine, lemon juice and capers in what is akin to a Picatta sauce. The bitter taste of raw endive contrasted with the otherwise rich flavors. Our waitress had no objection to bringing a fresh fish to our table for inspection before we confirmed the order. Other entrees range from grilled sea scallops with radicchio and tomato sauce to roast or sauteed chicken, veal and even a portobello steak for vegetarian connoisseurs of the mushroom.

Desserts, all homemade, are as eclectic as the art on the walls. Courses are large enough to share.

LA BORSA
KR 17.5/20
Decor 4/4	Hospitality 4/5	Food 8.5/10	Value 1/1

- **Italian**
- **Chicago/West**
- **$$**

375 North Morgan Street
Chicago
(312) 563-1414
Troubleshooter: Brian McQuiad
(manager)

Hours: Lunch Mon–Fri noon–
2 pm, Dinner Mon–Fri 5–10 pm,
Sat 5–11 pm, closed Sun
Credit Cards: Amex, MC, Visa
Reservations: Suggested
Handicapped: Accessible
Parking: Free in lot

Trying to reinvent the wheel, especially in the restaurant business is an exercise in frustration, not to mention redundancy. This is particularly true with the current rage, Italian restaurants. La Borsa, while not completely unique, manages to put a fresh foot forward. The restaurant is most assuredly Italian, but before you roll your eyes and moan, La Borsa deserves a bit more attention. For one thing, there is its striking decor and location. The restaurant is built from a former railroad station, with plenty of space for dining and decoration. When weather allows for outdoor seating on the deck, diners can enjoy a spectacular Chicago skyline, not to mention the roar of an occasional train rolling slowly past. At night, instead of candles, each table is lit by a pinpoint spotlight; the effect is dramatic.

The menu is not as imaginative as the decor, but there are some surprises. Marinated eggplant makes a great appetizer. Slices are grilled, then rolled with some mozzarella cheese and topped with a spicy tomato sauce. Even tastier is an order of crab cakes resting on a bed of shredded shallots. Onion confit, worked into a marmalade, is a wonderful flavor companion for the crab cakes. Yet another selection worth noting is *castela*, a farmer's style cheese mixed with artichokes and carrots, and wrapped in spinach leaves. Tomatoes and scallions season a vinaigrette-style dressing.

From a selection of pastas, green linguine is tossed with sautéed scallops and artichoke hearts. The flavor is soft and natural. There are two risotto choices regularly offered. Saffron-seasoned mussels were recently being paired with dates. It's an idea that is best left alone. The sweet dates simply had no affinity for the mussels or saffron. Another risotto, bringing together fennel and porcini mushrooms with parmesan cheese sounds more workable. Tortellini, chewy and delicious, combine perfectly with goat cheese and garlic sauce with slices of zucchini.

Among entrees, or second course as the Italians would think of it, *osso bucco,* roasted chicken with garlic and rosemary and a fish of the day are among choices. Veal scallopini should have been like velvet; it was not as delicate as we expected, though the caramelization of onions with mushrooms and marsala wine made a terrific sauce.

LA DONNA
KR 17.5/20
Decor 3.5/4   Hospitality 4.5/5   Food 8.5/10   Value 1/1

- **Italian**
- **Chicago/North**
- **$$**

5146 North Clark Street
(773) 561-9400
Troubleshooter: Manager on duty

Hours: Mon–Thurs 11:30 am–11 pm, Fri–Sat 11:30 am–midnight, Sun 10 am–11 pm, open early Sun morning for Brunch
Credit Cards: All majors
Reservations: For parties of six or more
Handicapped: Accessible
Smoking and nonsmoking sections: Both available
Parking: Valet on Fri and Sat evenings, otherwise street parking can be tight

---

The once all Swedish Andersonville neighborhood on Chicago's far North Side has become, like so many other parts of the city, a multicultural community. This is particularly evident in the restaurants which stretch through the area, Persian, Turkish, Jordanian, Mexican, and, yes, Italian.

La Donna serves some strikingly tasty fare in a small and narrow dining room, where locals can and do linger. The menu is similar to so many other Italian restaurants, but some house specialties stand out. From a selection of first course antipasti eggplant rolled around a filling of fontina cheese is napped in a tangy sun-dried tomato–based sauce. While entrees and other courses are served on stock bone restaurant china, appetizers are plated on handsome Villery and Boche platters, perhaps a bit of decorative overkill considering the surroundings, but a handsome touch nonetheless.

Among other antipasti, a selection of grilled seafood, including calamari, octopus, shrimp and scallops is a little skimpy in size, but tasty. One of the most interesting selections is a tower of roasted vegetables including sweet potato slices, eggplant, zucchini and other available choices, layered with melted mozzarella cheese and set into a sauce of tangy balsamic vinegar and olive oil.

Soup, salad or pizza are available for following courses, or diners can move right on to pastas and entrees. La Donna follows the trend of large pasta platters, and, unfortunately, does not serve half portions. But, prices are reasonable enough that it's almost a bargain. Sauces could more accurately be termed "ragouts" for their body, their complex flavors and seasonings, and the gusto which is apparent on first taste. Try *rigatoni nunzia* and taste the luscious red tomato–based sauce, with dried ricotta cheese and a smattering of eggplant. *Pasta puttanesca* is complex in its own manner, rich with the salty taste of anchovies and capers, pocked with black olives in a quick-cooked tomato sauce. Other pastas include pumpkin-stuffed ravioli, spaghetti carbonara, a mixed seafood selection with linguini and other choices. A trio of risotto dishes is featured each day.

For a second course, or entree, choices range from fresh grilled or sautéed fish to a small filet mignon in barolo wine sauce with mushrooms, to several kinds of veal and chicken. Veal marsala is on the menu; chicken marsala is prepared by request. The sauce is winy and sweet, lavished with sliced mushrooms.

Desserts include several ice creams and sorbets, *tiramisu* and other dolci. Wines can be ordered by the glass or bottle.

LA LUCE
KR 16/20
Decor 4/4   Hospitality 4/5   Food 7/10   Value 1/1

• **Italian**	**Hours:** Mon–Thurs 11 am–11 pm, Fri 11 am–midnight, Sat 5 pm–midnight, Sun 5–10 pm
• **Chicago/Near West**	
• **$$**	**Credit Cards:** All majors
1393 West Lake Street	**Reservations:** Recommended
Chicago	**Handicapped:** Not accessible
(312) 850-1900	**Smoking and nonsmoking**
Troubleshooter: Anna Moretti	**sections:** Both available
(owner)	**Parking:** Valet $5

You may be one of the people who visits La Luce for its proximity to the United Center and the sporting events there. The other reason to visit La Luce is for its generally good food and handsome atmosphere. The restaurant is in a late 19th Century building with a high tin ceiling, bare brick walls and lots of dark, ornamental wood.

Pre-game diners have a fairly limited menu, designed more for speed and convenience than a leisurely meal. Arrive after 7 on game night, or any time on non-game days, and it's the pick of the litter from the full menu.

The cooking is pan-Italian, Sicilian, Northern, the whole culinary map. Try sausage and peppers with roasted potatoes and grilled onions as a hearty first course choice. Should you not have the taste for something quite that ponderous, *carpaccio* with capers, oil, lemon and thin shavings of parmesan cheese will work, as would sautéed mussels in marinara or white wine and garlic sauce with parsley.

Those are just some of the choices from the menu that also includes a full page of salads, some of them dinner-sized. Pastas take up two pages. Homemade eight finger *cavatelli* are given a vodka cream sauce bath, though if you ask for a simple red sauce, it tastes just as good and has fewer calories. Lasagna is thick, piled high with alternate layers of noodles, spinach and a quartet of cheeses. Risotto, ravioli, linguine and fettucine recipes are among other choices.

As for entrees, a cut of filet mignon is topped with blackened *prosciutto* and a reduced red wine and brandy sauce. Another house special, *chicken rafaello* is surrounded with grilled vegetables. The chicken is stuffed with a filling of roasted peppers, spinach and marinated artichoke hearts.

The grilled salmon is somewhat peculiar. There is nothing at all Italian about its shitake mushroom or mango sauce accompaniment. Pork tenderloin gets back more into the fold with a roll-up of *prosciutto*, spinach and provolone cheese oozing from the sides. The sauce is a standard marsala. Speaking of that, chicken marsala is another option, with shitakes; I think the sauce is much too sweet. Of course, a *limon* sauce is an alternative.

Desserts include temptations ranging from *tiramisu* to bread pudding. Service is friendly, though for our recent visit, my Italian was none too good, and our server's English was only a little better. But, maybe that's part of the charm.

LA PAILLOTTE
KR 19/20
Decor 3/4   Hospitality 5/5   Food 10/10   Value 1/1

- **Vietnamese French**
- **Chicago**
- **$**

3470 North Clark Street
Chicago
(773) 935-4005
Troubleshooter: Tanya Pham
(owner)

Hours: Sun noon–10 pm,
Mon–Thurs 5–11 pm, Sat 11:30
am–11 pm
Credit Cards: All majors
Reservations: Recommended
Handicapped: Accessible
**Smoking and nonsmoking
sections:** Both available
Parking: In the rear or on street
(tight)

Think of Clark Street as a diamond field of restaurants and you never really know when you are going to stumble upon a jewel. It happened to us again when we found La Paillotte in a storefront tucked along a strip of restaurants and other businesses.

Most of the menu is Vietnamese. The only listing that is clearly French is an appetizer of escargots. They come in what the menu describes as the chef's special basil sauce and are served with French bread.

The cooking is flawless. One example is a Vietnamese pancake, really a stuffed crepe made from rice flour filled with indigenous Southeast Asian vegetables and chicken or shrimp as you choose. The pancake is served with romaine lettuce leaves. The idea is to take up some of the pancake, wrap it in lettuce, and add a touch of tart lime dipping sauce. Sauces, by the way, are key to Vietnamese foods. The most prevalent are a semi-sweet and salty fish sauce known as *nuac mam* or the more peppery *nuac cham*. They are used the way Americans use salt, pepper and other condiments.

The dipping sauces are particularly good when used with any of the mild flavored spring rolls that come in three distinct varieties. Other appetizers include grilled quail in Chinese five spice, cut-up pieces of fried chicken breast on greens and a rather complex creation that uses shrimp paste, sugar cane and a thin vermicelli noodle among its ingredients.

The menu lists a half dozen soup selections, including *pho*, a classic noodle and beef broth, and goes on to showcase a handful of lavish salads. Entrees are exceptional with their bounty of tropical ingredients that are at the heart of Southeast Asian and particularly Vietnamese cooking. Something that sounds as simple as vegetables stir-fried with tofu is made exotic thanks to the tang of lemon grass which is part of the sauce. Other entrees run from Vietnamese stylings of chicken, beef or duck as well as seafood. And that brings things around to what may be one of the best fish preparations I have ever tasted. Sea bass is boned and steamed, set out on a bed of cellophane noodles with a touch of ginger plus mushrooms and scallions. I have never enjoyed better, fresher fish so deliciously seasoned and perfectly cooked. The sea bass alone is enough reason to visit

LAS CAZUELAS
KR 17.5/20
Decor 4/4   Hospitality 5/5   Food 7.5/10   Value 1/1

- **Mexican**
- **Chicago/Far North**
- **$$**

4821 North Elston
Chicago
(773) 777-5304
Troubleshooter: Ricardo
Caballero (owner)

Hours: Tues–Fri 11:30 am–10 pm, Sat 4 pm–midnight, Sun 3–10 pm
Credit Cards: Discover, MC, Visa
Reservations: Suggested
Handicapped: Accessible
Smoking and nonsmoking sections: Separate smoking and nonsmoking seating
Parking: Free behind restaurant or on street
Party Facilities: Private party facilities for up to 90 people

Some ethnic restaurant cuisines are so well established that it is very difficult to develop something new or original. Mexican restaurants in America often fall into the same pattern because of that. But, Las Cazuelas manages to clear that hurdle with an approach that adds a bit of comfort and sophistication, as well as some depth around a core menu.

The name of the restaurant refers to small clay crocks used in cooking. The restaurant picks up on the theme with an atmosphere that suggests home cooking, and in fact, its exterior appearance almost seems to suggest a home, thanks to wood window frames and curtains. A comfortable, homey theme continues inside, albeit with the help of white tablecloths that add a fine dining flair.

The menu incorporates several tried-and-true Mexican specialties and some surprises on a daily menu addition. The seed for something beyond the usual is planted at the very beginning with a dark sauce suggestive of molé which has been adapted for the taco chips brought out as soon as guests are seated.

A somewhat different, more traditional molé is used in the serving of roasted chicken. That's one of the entrees on a list that includes stand-bys ranging from *steak Milanesa* and *carne asada* to *chiles rellenos*, steak or vegetarian fajitas and Mexican-style pork served with potatoes and hot sauce.

Daily specials include various kinds of finned or shellfish. Recently, codfish was served veracruzana, with tomatoes, olives, onions, garlic and sliced jalapeños. Though red snapper is the usual fish in most Mexican restaurants for this particular presentation, codfish, with its distinctive flavor, stands up well as an alternative.

In an interesting appetizer, salmon quesadillas demonstrates some of the imagination at work in the restaurant's kitchen. A layer of slightly melted mild white cheese eases some, but not all of the salmon's intense saltiness.

LAWRY'S THE PRIME RIB
KR 17.5/20
Decor 3.5/4   Hospitality 5/5   Food 8/10   Value 1/1

- **American**
- **Chicago/Near North**
- **$$$**

100 East Ontario
Chicago
(312) 787-5000
Troubleshooter: Vern Wright
(general manager)

Hours: Lunch Mon–Fri 11:30 am–2 pm, Dinner Mon–Thurs 5–11 pm, Fri–Sat until midnight, Sun 3–10 pm
Credit Cards: All majors
Reservations: Suggested
Handicapped: Not accessible
Bar: Full service with extensive listing of California wines
Separate smoking and nonsmoking sections: Both available
Parking: Valet

A major redecorating job and facelift has not changed the substance of Lawry's the Prime Rib, which remains dedicated to exactly what its name implies. The prime ribs are coated with a heavy layer of rock salt and then roasted in specially built ovens. The rock salt forms a hard shell, or cover. When the meat is done to the chef's specifications, the rock salt cover is cracked open. The whole standing rib roast is place onto a domed silver cart from which it is cut and served to order.

Diners may choose from one of four cuts, ranging from the extra thick "Chicago" cut with the rib bone still in to the smaller "California" cut, which the menu says is for lighter appetites. In between are the regular "Lawry's" cut and the thinner "English" slice.

Dinners include salad, of course, with Lawry's dressing, mashed potatoes whipped with milk for extra richness, Yorkshire pudding and cream horseradish sauce for the beef. Desserts are à la carte.

The luncheon menu includes several other lighter choices aside from the cuts of prime rib, including some seafood and salads. Daily specials, plus the menu's addition of fresh fish is recognition of the fact that even in a restaurant whose very name suggests a fine cut of meat, there are some diners who would still prefer seafood.

LE BOUCHON
KR 18.5/20
Decor 4/4   Hospitality 4.5/5   Food 9/10   Value 1/1

- **French**
- **Chicago/Near Northwest**
- **$$**

1958 North Damen Avenue
Chicago
(773) 862-6600
Troubleshooter: Jean Claude Poilevy (chef/owner)

Hours: Mon–Thurs 5:30–11 pm, Fri–Sat 5 pm–midnight, closed Sun
Credit Cards: All majors
Reservations: Encouraged
Handicapped: Not Accessible
Bar: Full bar, good selection of wines by the glass
Smoking and nonsmoking sections: Smoking permitted anywhere in restaurant

Le Bouchon's food speaks of tradition, with considerable flair. The menu is à la carte and includes a house specialty, warm sausage with potatoes. The *charcuterie* is a mixed selection, mostly mild, served with dijon mustard; the potatoes tend to offer a bland balance. Other starters include a mixed salad of greens, lentils and assorted fresh vegetables on a composed platter, classic snails in individual ceramic pots with garlic butter, and a delicious salad of greens topped with shreds of duck confit. Mushroom lovers will love the collection of morels, shitakes and other varieties sautéed in butter, or as we requested, olive oil.

This is hearty eating, French comfort food, without much regard for the contemporary lighter dining trends. But, it is satisfying, as a move into the entrees suggests. Rabbit, a French bistro favorite, is accompanied with bow tie noodles in a dark woodsy sauce. The meat is tender, pulls easily from the bones, and is somewhat reminiscent of capon. There is the classic bistro steak and fries as well as frog legs with garlic, though pasta does bring the presentation somewhat up to date. Roasted fillet of salmon is perfect; roasting brings out the kind of succulence usually not associated with seafood. In this case, the fish is served with red wine sauce and onions, a typical Lyonaisse touch. Free range chicken is roasted to a delicious flavor, served with whole cloves of garlic and a thin potato wafer called a *gallette*. Usually one or two other choices will be offered in addition to the half dozen or so on the printed menu.

Desserts include a chocolate layered terrine, crème brûlée, somewhat lighter than expected, and other whims of the kitchen. The wine list reflects the country character of Le Bouchon, without regard to big names and high prices.

LE COLONIAL
KR 18/20
Decor 4/4   Hospitality 5/5   Food 8.5/10   Value .5/1

- **Vietnamese**
- **Chicago/Near North**
- **$$$**

937 North Rush Street
Chicago
(312) 255-0088
Troubleshooter: Jean Goutal and Rick Wahlstedt (owners)

Hours: Lunch Daily 11:30 am–2:30 pm, Dinner Mon–Thurs 5–11 pm, Fri–Sat until midnight, Sun until 10 pm, Lounge Mon–Fri 4 pm–midnight, Sat noon–midnight, Sun noon–10 pm
Credit Cards: All majors
Reservations: Suggested
Smoking and nonsmoking sections: Separate smoking and nonsmoking seating
Parking: Valet

Ceiling fans revolve slowly overhead and louvered shutters are drawn tight to keep out the midday heat. Potted palms stand sentry in a large dining room that could be set in tropical Saigon, not Chicago, in the 1940s, not the in the new millenium.

This is Le Colonial, where the people watching is as much a part of the show as the food. Presentations are dressy, service is chic, as is the whole ambiance. Prices reflect the Rush Street neighborhood and some portions are enormously small. But, each selection is beautifully plated and each, in its own way, is delicious. There are two soups to choose from for a first course. Oxtail has a flush, beefy taste, as would be expected. More exciting is the complex *cahn chua tom*, a clear stock swimming with whole shrimp, cut-up cubes of pineapple, tomatoes and fruity tamarind, with a bouquet of herbs and peppers.

Next comes a selection of appetizers. Translucent rice noodle wraps shrimp, ground pork and mushrooms for the restaurant's version of spring rolls. Contrast their mild, cooling flavor with grilled shrimp wrapped around sweet pieces of sugar cane, plated with soft angel hair noodles and lettuce. A touch of mint infuses each piece of shrimp, while a spicy peanut sauce brings some contrast. Among other appetizers selections of note is *banh cuon*, a Vietnamese version of ravioli, soft and cushy with a filling and flavor of mushrooms and ground chicken.

Several entrees lie ahead. One of the best is barbecued pork, sweet, tender, not overwhelmed by its sauce. More delicate is steamed sea bass with cellophane Oriental noodles and a garnish of scallions and mushrooms with a touch of ginger. Among other choices, shrimp and eggplant are sautéed together with a mild curry coconut sauce, while roasted duck has been infused with a ginger marinade, then sweetened with tamarind sauce in a small bowl to dip each tender slice. The menu has a couple of beef choices, whole red snapper in a sweet and sour sauce and elegantly simple noodles and mixed vegetables in a complex, but mild stir-fry.

Le Colonial's desserts are too tempting to be ignored. Banana tapioca pudding is lusciously creamy, while the restaurant's lemon tart is sharp and tangy, somewhat reminiscent of key lime.

LE FRANCAIS
KR 20/20
Decor 4/4   Hospitality 5/5   Food 10/10   Value 1/1

- **French**
- **Wheeling**
- **$$$**

269 South Milwaukee Avenue
Wheeling
(847) 541-7470
Troubleshooters: Jean and Doris Banchet (co-owners)

Hours: Mon–Thurs 5:30–9:30 pm, Fri–Sat 5:30–10:30 pm
Credit Cards: All majors
Reservations: Required
Handicapped: Accessible
Smoking and nonsmoking sections: Smoking not permitted
Parking: Free valet

"In five years, the Corleone Family will be out of the olive oil business." When Michael Corleone said that in *The Godfather*, it was clear that it was never to be, no matter how sincere Michael might have been.

"In five years, I will be out of the restaurant business." That's what a young Jean Banchet, in his late thirties at the time, told me several years ago. I didn't believe it, no matter how sincere the famed chef might have been at the time.

Some things are in your blood, part and parcel of who you are, whether it be a fictional Michael Corleone or a flesh and blood 100% real Jean Banchet. He, of course, never left the restaurant business. He did leave Chicago, making Atlanta his home base. But, now he is back in Wheeling to reclaim the stoves and kitchen where he earned a nearly global reputation.

Today, his cooking shows a tendency toward a more modern, contemporary flair, but he still finishes sauces with a swirl of butter or a splash or two of cream. It may not be the parade of overloaded platters which marked Le Francais back in the days when his wait staff wore tuxedos, when the dining room was dark wood, inlaid gold leaf, maroon banquettes and heavy swaged curtains. The dark wood has been replaced by blond. The silver and stemware sparkle in a room that is brightly lit; there is no squinting to read a Le Francais menu.

Take a look at the menu and it is clear how much things have evolved. A grilled vegetable terrine is wrapped in delicate puff pastry, sliced and laid out sideways on the platter. Each of its distinctive layers of color look like some edible flag of an unknown nation. But, Banchet will not let it go at that. A fascinating tomato sorbet is there, a quick reminder that the tomato is a fruit, not a vegetable. And, there is truffle oil vinaigrette, not exactly a wash, but certainly abundant enough so that the *gout de terroir*, the earthy taste of the fungus perfumes and permeates.

A showcase of salmon comes as a trilogy, unfolding the splendors of home-cured and smoked salmon, another marinated version sharp with brine, and a third, softly flavored salmon tartare.

There are several more first course choices including a selection of duck liver pate bound as a *ballotine* with crushed pistachios, *duck foie-gras* and richly endowed duck *rillette*. This practically cries out for a luscious sauternes or late harvest riesling from the Le Francis bibliography that is modestly called their wine list.

Now, consider the entrees. Chef Banchet stuffs capons with wild mushrooms and delicately flavored Amish goat cheese, roasting everything together. He splits the chicken and sets it on a platter with an array of dark green salsify, slender haricot verts, and the natural au jus of the chicken infused with fresh rosemary. A side of whipped potatoes is set in a small silvered pan.

From a selection of seafood, red snapper is sautéed and set over a stylized *paella* flavored with a light chicken *au jus*. A piece of mild sausage enriches the rice. Striped sea bass is a wonderful fish, especially in the talent-laden kitchen of Le Francais. In this case, fennel and saffron flavors are combined with the fish.

Culinary tastes have changed, and Banchet is keeping up with them, though his hand still dips into the creamery and butter pot. But, the greatest difference today is that there are so many more restaurant options for diners. The new contemporary fine dining restaurant may draw on French cuisine for inspiration, but the new chefs are looking more toward a future of innovative cooking, rather than to a past tradition. Banchet seems caught, unsure which way to turn. And, so, he tries to do both. The message seems to be that old Satchel Paige sobriquet; "Don't look back; they might be gainin' on you!"

LE LOUP CAFE
KR 16.5/20
Decor 3.5/4   Hospitality 4.5/5   Food 7.5/10   Value 1/1

- **French**
- **Chicago/Mid-North**
- **$$**

3348 North Sheffield
Chicago
(773) 248-1830
Troubleshooter: Gisele Laura
(owner)

Hours: Sun–Thurs 4–10 pm, Fri–Sat 4–11 pm
Credit Cards: MC, Visa
Reservations: Accepted
Handicapped: Accessible
Smoking and nonsmoking sections: Small smoking section
Parking: On street or limited space behind restaurant

There is no ignoring the design theme behind Le Loup Cafe. It's centered around the French word *loup*, which means "wolf." For one thing, the walls are covered with photos and prints of wolves in their natural environs. For another, the back cover of the menu features an essay on the wolf and its habits. And, just to insure the point will not be missed, diners will usually see a large wolf-like dog, actually a Siberian husky named Mystere, lounging in the side patio.

The cooking is decidedly French, with a North African punctuation. *Tabbouleh* is on the menu, right below the salad *nicoise*. Diners can select *dolma*, deliciously stuffed with rice and ground lamb, or take classic snails in garlic butter sauce. Another fascinating selection is *gateau d'herbages*. This is a lightly textured affair bringing together a spray of fresh herbs and vegetables. The flavor is mild, somewhat ethereal.

The menu lists a small collection of entrees, including a trio of vegetarian choices, plus some daily specials. One recent special was chicken à la basque, a recipe which brings together spaghetti noodles, some peppers and other seasonings into a spicy brown sauce much like a chicken ragout. Geographic or cultural origins aside, it is a delicious preparation. Similarly exotic is the restaurant's version of curried chicken. In this case, the curry is medium spicy, prickly enough to showcase its distinctive flavors. Whole chicken pieces are bathed in a cream-based sauce that clings to each savory bite.

Chicken gets considerable attention, ranging from a cajun-style preparation, to one that is North African in origin with couscous, vegetables and spicy *harrisa* sauce, to a traditional French country roasted chicken with a quartet of herbs. Other entrees include classic French beef *bourguinon* as well as pork tenderloin in a red wine sauce. Vegetarians will find dinner-sized portions of *ratatouille*, a collection of mushrooms and zucchini sautéed in olive oil, given a seasoning of fresh thyme, lemon and oregano.

Le Loup Cafe is a casual and friendly restaurant. Service is knowledgeable, without pretense. As far as the wolf in Siberian husky clothing is concerned, she's friendly and would probably lead the burglars to the silverware. The restaurant serves no alcohol, but guests may bring in their own for a $2 corkage fee.

LE TITI DE PARIS
KR 20/20
Decor 4/4   Hospitality 5/5   Food 10/10   Value 1/1

- **French**
- **Arlington Heights**
- **$$$**

1015 West Dundee Road
Arlington Heights
(847) 506-0222
Troubleshooter: Pierre and
Judith Pollin (owners)

Hours: Lunch Tues–Fri 11:30 am–2:30 pm, Dinner Tues–Thurs 5:30–9:30 pm, Fri 5:30–10 pm, Sat 5–10 pm
Credit Cards: All majors
Reservations: Required
Handicapped: Accessible
Smoking and nonsmoking sections: Both available
Parking: Ample free parking in lot

When I wrote of Le Titi de Paris twenty or more years ago, the menu was a catalog of classic French cuisine with selections such as sweetbreads in apple brandy sauce or duckling in peach sauce, veal kidneys in mustard sauce or calf's liver with onions. The cooking was not so prosaic as it may sound.

Nor, is that the case today, where the menu of this restaurant (whose name roughly translated means "The Parisian Rascal") is contemporary, if not boldly so. At the forefront is the look and comfortable feel of the main dining room. It is tailored, somewhat formal with upholstered seating and plum and gold colors.

Service can also be formal, though never intimidating. I was recognized by our server, Rolf Franz, a man who represents the best of his profession, and always seems to know and anticipate something special for his guests. And, though recognition may alter treatment in some settings, I am convinced that all diners are made to feel special.

The large printed dinner menu is extended by a collection of specials listed in a small folder, much more extensive and varied than the formal menu listing. Tuna tartare is mild tasting with a coulis of avocado. In another choice, a layered pastry of vegetable mousse includes mushrooms, carrot, celery root and asparagus, napped with fresh tomato concasse. A mushroom and artichoke terrine is among hot appetizer selections, its madeira wine sauce wonderfully indulgent.

The larger printed menu includes a shorter list of appetizers including an assortment of patés, seared tuna carpaccio, smoked Norwegian salmon and beluga caviar. A single lobster and crab cake is bedded on a julienne of leek and roasted sweet peppers, the flavors of the crab cake clearly in the forefront. In yet another selection, a bouquet of grilled eggplant, its smoked flavor predominate, plum tomatoes, and zucchini are splashed with a light rosemary and shallot vinaigrette. Each of the ingredients holds onto texture and taste.

A soup and salad can follow; the Caesar is the classic version. Then, a small sorbet intermezzo, in a beautiful glass free-form container comes as a palate refreshment. This presentation, like all else, is as elegant as the overall decor and sensibility of the entire restaurant's ambiance.

For entrees, the influence is clearly French, but with an occasional surprise. Horseradish and ginger are combined in a sauce to compliment sautéed duck breast, plated with its confit. Veal sweetbreads are a culinary link to the restaurant's origins some two decades earlier. From time to time, there are game meat selections. Antelope is a mild-flavored meat, a bit tougher than beef. It has recently been served with a calvados brandy sauce and a wild rice cake that is perfectly appropriate. More commonly seen venison is plated somewhat traditionally with roasted chestnuts and a cranberry preserve, plus a richly-flavored sauce infused with meat juices.

For seafood selections, grilled swordfish is plated with orzo in a sauce that combines small bits of shrimp and fresh basil in a butter and wine base. Other selections could include poached halibut with sorrel sauce and couscous, or red snapper and risotto in a light tomato broth.

Desserts are not for the calorie conscious. The popular favorite is a chocolate symphony, which gathers a large platter of all chocolate-based confections, pastries and the like. The wine list is one of the more prestigious among North Shore restaurants, certainly as deep and wide ranging in its search for quality and recognized greatness, especially among French and California vintages.

LE VICHYSSOIS
KR 19/20
Decor 3/4   Hospitality 5/5   Food 10/10   Value 1/1

- **French**
- **Lakemoor**
- **$$$**

220 West State Route 120
Lakemoor
(815) 385-8221
Troubleshooters: Bernard and
Priscilla Cretier (chef/owners)

Hours: Lunch Wed–Fri 11:30
am–2:30 pm, Dinner Wed–Sat
first seating at 5:30 pm, Sun at
4:30 pm
Credit Cards: CB, Diner's, MC,
Visa, house accounts
Handicapped: Accessible
Bar: Extensive wine list featuring
French and American bottlings
**Smoking and nonsmoking
sections:** Both available
Parking: Ample free parking in
lot

It has been more than 20 years or so since Chef Bernard Cretier pulled
up stakes from the city and with his wife, opened their version of a
French country restaurant. In fact, when you see their charming restau-
rant and walk inside, you could almost think you were in the French
countryside instead of nearby McHenry County.

The Cretiers' vision, I imagine, was to bring to the far suburbs of
Metropolitan Chicago the kind of restaurant which dots the small towns
of France. They have succeeded wonderfully. If anything, the restaurant,
its charm and its service have gotten better over the years.

Chef Cretier stays true to the principles of what great French cook-
ing is all about. He is not trying to recreate an Escoffier menu, but rather
the simpler, though no less ambitious, cooking that relies on the basic ar-
chitecture of the French dining experience.

The restaurant is whitewashed stucco with charming accents and the
look of a prosperous French farmhouse. At a time when too many restau-
rants are so noisy that din competes with dinner, the soft murmur of con-
versation is all one hears in the dining rooms of Le Vichyssois. That, for
no other reason, should put it on the short list of most discerning diners.

A glance at the menu begins to whet the appetite with anticipation.
Begin with a house classic, tomato and onion tart Nicoise with goat
cheese. The expected flavors are there, gentle tastes and sweet onion in
a perfect pastry. Other first course choices include some standards of the
cuisine such as snails in garlic butter, an assortment of chilled pates or a
delightful terrain of smoked salmon. Of course there is the house signa-
ture, Vichyssois in either warm or classically chilled versions. The menu's
listing of "Mushroom Cigar, Madeira Sauce," is not really the curiosity its
name suggests. A *duxelle* of field mushrooms is wrapped in a *feuilltage*

pastry, which as the name suggests, is cigar shaped. The flavorful wine sauce is perfect compliment, good enough to soak up any leftover drops with a piece of bread.

Take one of the several à la carte salads, such as one which brings together slender French beans, clots of goat cheese and tomatoes on Mesclun, all dressed with a walnut infused olive oil. Not so incidentally, entrees include a house salad which is satisfying enough that one need not order an ala carte salad unless you want something a little more elaborate and special.

Getting down to the heart of the menu and a look at the several entrees is a pleasant chore. Dover Sole is treated to a vermouth sauce, as is one of the house specials, the extravagant sweetbread *cassoulet* with oyster mushrooms and asparagus.

Tuna steak is solid enough to stand up to peppercorn sauce, not cream based as this sauce often is. Sea scallops are set in lightly seasoned Champagne sauce, while roast duck is plated with a slightly sharp, but not too assertive sherry and vinegar sauce.

Desserts are presented from a carte from which you can select three. I love the Napoleon, though the chocolate cake we tasted was a bit dry as if it had been around for a couple of days.

The wine list is fine. There is an exceptionally priced four course prix fixe dinner. Service is not only friendly, but competent and knowledgeable, perhaps the biggest improvement of the years.

LES NOMADES
KR 20/20
Decor 4/4   Hospitality 5/5   Food 10/10   Value 1/1

- **French**
- **Chicago/Near North**
- **$$$**

222 West Ontario Street
Chicago
(312) 649-9010
Troubleshooters: Roland and Mary Beth Liccioni (owners)

Hours: Tues–Sat 5–10 pm, closed Sun–Mon
Credit Cards: Amex, Diners, MC, Visa
Reservations: Mandatory
Handicapped: Not accessible
Bar: Full bar and lounge
Smoking and nonsmoking sections: Smoking only in bar
Parking: Valet available
Dress: Jackets and neckties required for gentlemen

Founded as a private club by the legendary Jovan Trboyevic, Les Nomades was sold to Roland and Mary Beth Liccioni. Now, as a restaurant opened to the public, it nevertheless retains much of its past cachet.

When he built Les Nomades, Trboyevic installed Chicago's first zinc bar, a standard fixture in Parisian bistros. A zinc bar is still there, as are handsomely framed antique travel posters. Seating is at banquettes or café tables in the tight downstairs dining room. An upstairs area is darker, more suggestive of something a bit older, even more exotic.

The cooking retains the distinctively modern quality upon which Trboyevic insisted not only here, but at two other restaurants which are now a part of Chicago dining history, Jovan and Le Perroquet. Some selections can still be found on the menu. Occasionally, a dodine of pigeon or lamb navarin will appear.

Among appetizers, grilled razor clams are mild in flavor, bedded on a melange of sliced potatoes, red onion and haricots vert with a leek coulis for accent. For an entree, selections can range from a Cassoulet rooted in French tradition to a contemporary roasted breast of duck plated with risotto and a green peppercorn sauce. Desserts continue to include a lusciously rich chocolate sorbet that virtually imitates rich ice cream in its silken smooth texture and deep, dark flavor.

L'OLIVE
KR 18.5/20
Decor 3.5/4   Hospitality 5/5   Food 9/10   Value 1/1

• **Moroccan**	**Hours:** Mon–Sun 5 pm–midnight
• **Chicago/Near North**	**Credit Cards:** MC, Visa, Discover
• **$$**	**Handicapped:** Accessible
1629 North Halsted	**Reservations:** Mandatory
Chicago	**Smoking and nonsmoking**
(312) 573-1515	**sections:** Smoking at bar
Troubleshooter: Mohamad ben Mchababcheb	**Parking:** $6

Moroccan cooking emphasizes a combination of fruits with meat and poultry, combined with bouquets of aromatic seasonings for a cuisine which is different as night and day from the more often found style of Arabic cooking as practiced in American restaurants.

A far more decorated and atmospheric restaurant than the former L'Olive reviewed in previous editions of *Chicago's Best Restaurants*, it is awash with colorful mosaics and other touches of the arabesque. The chef's cooking has an indulgent quality that feeds the senses, of sight, smell and touch, as well as taste. Though fruity sweetness runs as a common thread through several preparations, there is also a degree of complex spiciness found in the classic Moroccan sauce called *harissa*. A different sort of spice is evident in *merguez*, an indigenous lamb sausage that leaves a touch of heat on the palate. Balance that with salad that might include figs, with ginger, honey and walnuts, or tangy roasted eggplant and tomatoes with candied preserved lemon adding a combination of tart citrus bit contrasted with its underlying sugars to the mix.

Entrees are similarly complex and fall generally into three categories. The first are couscous creations, using the grain common to much North African cooking, especially Moroccan. Try couscous with chunked roasted vegetables and a seasoning of cinnamon, raisins, almonds and sweet potatoes. Couscous with shrimp draws on preserved lemon, this time diluted in a saffron-infused broth with roasted peppers. Other couscous preparations could bring roasted lamb or chicken, even calamari and scallops, into play.

The second category is *bastilla*, basically phyllo-crusted chicken or vegetarian pies. One with vegetables and goat cheese suggests a broader Mediterranean reach. The other, chicken with lightly scented rosewater, almonds and cinnamon is more typically Moroccan.

The last category at L'Olive is the *tagines*, which refers to the clay cooking pot in which ingredients are simmered and served. Roasted chicken with dried apricots, raisins and almonds is almost festive, while lamb with olives, saffron and again the preserved lemon is more complex. Desserts are typically elaborate.

LOU MITCHELL'S
KR 19/20
Decor 3.5/4   Hospitality 4.5/5   Food 10/10   Value 1/1

- **American**
- **Chicago/Near West**
- **$**

565 West Jackson, Chicago
(312) 939-3111
Troubleshooter: Helene Thanas

Hours: Mon–Sat 7 am–3 pm
Credit Cards: None
Reservations: No
Handicapped: Not accessible
Smoking and nonsmoking sections: Both available
Parking: Street or lot

Lou Mitchell's is in the breakfast business, and serves just about the best there is to find in Chicago. Hundreds of thousands of Chicagoans, and visitors to the city have been coming here for about 70 years. The restaurant employs two full-time bakers who do nothing but make fresh buns, breads, sweet rolls and other pastries from scratch. Even the jams and jellies are kitchen-made. The french vanilla ice cream is 18% butterfat, which may not make it prime for recommendation on the Surgeon General's healthy foods list, but you do have to splurge once in a while!

The restaurant's specialty is the enormous breakfasts served to Chicago's early risers. Fluffy three egg omelettes are made from double yolk eggs. If the zoning laws would allow it, they probably would raise their own chickens behind the restaurant. As it stands, the omelettes are spectacular creations, served in the individual pans in which they have been cooked.

Pancakes and waffles are among other favorites. Try rolled pancakes with apples, sour cream and genuine pure maple syrup or a fluffy-light Belgian waffle made with real malted milk. The breakfast specials are served all day, but if you prefer something more conventional for lunch, you might want the roast chicken in a barbecue-style sauce. Other choices include roast loin of pork with fresh sage dressing, baby broiled beef liver or fried fillet of sole.

But, it really is the eggs, waffles and pancakes that make Lou Mitchell's famous; if you don't try one of them, you will have missed what all Chicago talks about.

LOVELL'S
KR 17/20
Decor 4/4   Hospitality 3.5/5   Food 8.5/10   Value 1/1

- **American**
- **Lake Forest**
- **$$$**

915 South Waukegan Road
Lake Forest
(847) 234-8013
Troubleshooter: James A. Lovell III (chef/owner)

Hours: Lunch Mon–Sat 11 am–2 pm, Dinner Mon–Thurs 5–10 pm, Fri–Sat 5–11 pm, Sun 5–9 pm, Sun Brunch 11 am–2 pm
Credit Cards: All majors
Reservations: Suggested
Handicapped: Accessible with elevators available
Smoking and nonsmoking sections: No smoking in restaurant, permitted in Captain's Quarters Lounge on lower level
Parking: Free valet

Lovell's is housed in a 12,000 foot newly constructed building with all the exterior markings of a French manor house or chateau. Astronaut James Lovell, Jr. who is bankrolling the restaurant where his son, Jay Lovell, is Chef de Cuisine, has placed his mark on display with handsome and interesting artifacts and letters from his storied career. The real eye candy, however, is a stunning mural behind the main bar in the entrance foyer. It pictures four horses on a heavenly race across the sky, pulling the chariot of Apollo. The mural is fully 20 feet across and 8 feet high, a breathtaking vision of classical metaphor in a strikingly modern setting.

Plush carpeted dining rooms set the stage for Chef Lovell's cooking. There is also an enclosed porch which is particularly pleasant at sunset. Private dining rooms are upstairs, as is space for a small gathering of up to 12 in the restaurant's wine cellar. A cigar and martini bar are cozy and comfortable with handsome wood, sofas and wingback chairs for pre-dinner or post-prandial comforts.

Lovell's menu is embellished American with a somewhat Continental and definitely contemporary flair. Salmon is pan-seared and set on couscous, though the menu calls it *tabbouleh*. Tomatoes, capers and an olive tapanade provide a relish or vinaigrette. The salmon, by the way, is virtually blackened with a somewhat pronounced tasting, if not salty, crust.

With a nod to his father's endeavors, Chef Lovell's menu features what is listed as "Lovell's Famous Countdown Shrimp Creole, 'New-Orleans Style' with jambalaya rice." The tastes are more sweet than peppery, with a pleasant sense of complexity. Among meats, pepper crusted New York strip steak is plated in a syrupy wine reduction with veal stock, a fitting embellishment for the steak. A mound of curly potato fries completes the platter.

First choice selections include an only ho-hum onion soup, an excellent rendition of crab cakes with stylized salsa plus a good selection of salads, grilled vegetable terrine, a paté platter and the ubiquitous portobello mushroom, this time with risotto, spinach and a clear veal sauce.

A quartet of pastas has included fettucini with pine nut–crusted chicken and parmesan cheese. The sauce, like many others, relies on veal stock, this time reduced with pesto. Several desserts are offered each evening. One, a chocolate cake, dubbed "muca-muca," is akin to an Italian bodino, though the chocolate center is more mousse than sauce.

LUCCA'S
KR 17/20
Decor 4/4   Hospitality 5/5   Food 7/10   Value 1/1

- **Italian**
- **Chicago/Mid-North**
- **$$**

2834 North Southport
(773) 477-2565
Troubleshooter: Manager on duty

Hours: Sun, Tues–Thurs 5:30–10 pm, Fri–Sat 5:30–11 pm, closed Mon
Credit Cards: All majors
Reservations: Recommended
Handicapped: Accessible
Smoking and nonsmoking sections: Separate sections
Parking: Complimentary on Northwest corner at Southport

Some restaurants immediately convey a welcoming sense of gracious hospitality as soon as you step inside. Lucca's is just such a restaurant. Oriental rugs over a polished floor, dark wood walls, and a massive mirrored sideboard help set the scene. This is not a restaurant for power dining or a client dinner. It is one for good friends to gather, one for romance to develop and be played out.

Though its name suggests Italian dining, Lucca's is more Mediterranean, though even that focus is somewhat diffused. Consider some of the appetizers, elaborate preparations each and every one whether a feta cheese soufflé with yellow pepper *coulis* and tapenade, or a popover pastry stuffed with prosciutto, peas and basil, bound with gorgonzola cheese and plated with a sauce made of pearl onions. In another selection, calamari is stuffed with crabmeat and grilled, then served with a tangy sauce that binds capers and *craisins*. Craisins, our waitress explained, is a combination fruit of cranberries and raisins, though they show up in no food dictionary or cookbook that I know of. In any event, the flavors marry well.

Shitake pancakes are even better, crisp, thin fried batter corn cakes with basil and shredded shitake mushrooms, served with balsamic vinegar reduced to a syrup. Equally addictive is *torta livorno*, an onion tart embellished with pancetta and creamy mascarpone cheese. For less elaborate tastings, *insalata rustico* is a fine option, course shreds of radiccio with jicama, chopped portobellos and walnuts roasted in garlic oil and finished with balsamic vinegar.

Entrees can be as elaborate as are most of the first course selections, but not always successful. Macedonian lamb, as it is called on the menu, is a pungent stew with garlic croutons, spinach and seasonings. Unfortunately, the lamb was tough, and certainly too strong. A similar problem afflicted paella, in which scallops were much too fishy, though shrimp, clams and white fish mixed into the saffron-infused rice were fine. Still, one bad flavor makes the whole dish less than a complete success.

Better fortune is to be found with a couple of other selections. Sea bass is as buttery and delicious as can be, not to mention fresh and clean-flavored. It is prepared with a rub of dry ground porcini mushrooms, served with couscous and wilted greens. From the rather challenging list of entrees, our other choice, vegetable risotto proved to be largely on the mark, though certainly not as complex as many other entrees. Service could not be better, and, no matter a flaw or two in cooking, Lucca's is a fine destination restaurant for a romantic evening ahead.

Maggiano's Little Italy
KR 17/20
Decor 4/4   Hospitality 4.5/5   Food 7.5/10   Value 1/1

- **Italian**
- **Chicago and Suburbs**
- **$$**

516 North Clark Street
Chicago
(312) 644-7700
Troubleshooter: Mark Tormey
(managing partner)

Other Locations

Oak Brook Center (Lower East side next to Saks Fifth Avenue), Route 83 at 22nd Street, Oakbrook; 630-368-0300; Hours: Mon–Sat Lunch 11:15 am–3 pm, Dinner Mon–Thurs 3–10 pm, Fri–Sat 3–11 pm, Sun noon–9 pm; Reservations: Accepted for parties of 6 or more; Parking: Valet or ample parking in mall lot; Party Facilities: Private party facilities for up to 600 people

Old Orchard Center (North of Nordstrom in the Southeast corner of the shopping center) Golf Road and Skokie Boulevard; 847-933-9555; Hours: Same as Oakbrook Center location; Reservations: For parties of any size at lunch, only 6 or more at dinner; Parking: Valet or free parking in mall lot; Party Facililties: Private party facilities for up to 600 people

Hours: Lunch Mon–Sat 11:30 am–2 pm, Dinner Mon–Thurs 5–10 pm, Fri 5–11 pm, Sat 2–11 pm, Sun noon–10 pm
Credit Cards: All majors
Reservations: Suggested
Handicapped: Accessible
Bar: Full bar, call brands, fair selection of wines
Parking: Valet at dinner, plenty of lot space nearby

Maggiano's Little Italy serves up basic Italian comfort food, in the kind of portions that encourage diners to take home plenty of leftovers. Many choices come in half or full orders; both are immense bargains. The restaurant is cavernous enough to seat some 200 people, at red checkered clothed tables, of course. The floor is hand-laid mosaic tile that looks as if it has been in place for since the early 1920s, not the '90s.

As for the dining, try an order of roasted peppers, perhaps a stuffed artichoke, and maybe a portion of Corner Bakery garlic bread. When it is available, you don't want to miss one of the *crostini*, thick slices of Italian bread with a variety of toppings. One evening it was served with flavorful *caponata*, the Italian version of *ratatouille*. Other appetizers include the more conventional, though in portions that are anything but that.

Next, in true Italian fashion, should come a pasta. They are brought out in huge serving bowls, whether spaghetti in basic marinara, meatsauce or with meatballs, *rigatoni* with a somewhat too sweet eggplant and red tomato sauce, (dubbed country-style on the menu), or something a bit more fancy such as garlic shrimp with shell macaroni.

By the time you come to an entree, you might be ready to throw in the proverbial towel. But, if you have paced yourself, and left some pasta to be taken home, you now can enjoy a continuation of some extremely contented dining. Entrees are not all that unusual, as befits the theme at Maggiano's Little Italy. But, they are hardly dull. We took *chicken cammarrari*, which I am sure, neither we nor our waitress ever managed to pronounce the same way twice. A cut-up roasted chicken is at the heart of the matter, its flavor undisguised by nothing more than herbs and spices, garnished with fresh peas, mushrooms and red peppers. As with previous courses, there is more than enough to go around. But, if you must have any side dishes, try the crispy potatoes and onions, which are as delicious as they sound.

Other entrees include the usual suspects, steaks, lamb chops, various kinds of veal, and more than a causal nod to seafood, including swordfish and tuna steaks. After all this, if you still want dessert, it's there . . . and good luck. Incidentally, come with a table full of people and order family style. You won't regret it!

Mambo Grill
KR 16.5/20
Decor 4/4   Hospitality 4.5/5   Food 7/10   Value 1/1

- **Caribbean**
- **Chicago/Near North**
- **$$**

412 North Clark Street
Chicago
(312) 467-9797
Troubleshooter: Debra Nelson
(manager)

Hours: Mon–Thurs 11 am–
10 pm, Fri 11 am–11 pm, Sat 5–
11 pm
Credit Cards: All majors
Reservations: Taken for parties
of six or more
Handicapped: Accessible
**Smoking and nonsmoking
sections:** Smoking only at bar
Parking: Valet, lot or street

Mambo Grill is a rather funky sort of restaurant. The slate floor, stencils and geometric shapes that stress its ceiling design, the happy-go-lucky sort of approach, making it a comfortable place for casual drinking and dining. I even saw one waitress actually dancing her way from table to table.

The dining begins with a small mound of butter seasoned with *chipolte* peppers and honey, kind of a sweet-hot combo to spread on tacos. Then, its down to business with a selection of appetizers. Our waitress suggested the Mambo Combo to which we added a couple of à la carte choices. That combo is handsomely plated with several sample-sized appetizer portions. Sliced calamari is coated in a potato meal batter and deep-fried, a tamale corn husk is partly unwrapped exposing *chorizo*, sliced olives and a wedge of cornmeal mush, while another part of the large serving platter holds a fried cheese croquette enclosing a small strip of prosciutto. A helping of sliced dried banana chips and skewered grilled chicken rounds out the selections. A trio of condiments, peppered and milder mayonnaise, plus a mix of parsley, garlic, lemon and olive oil spread, called *chimichurra*, adds to the festivities.

Appetizers are varied enough that you might want to choose them as you would selections of tapas. *Tamal Cubano* is particularly tasty. It's a hunk of polenta topped with small marinated shrimp, olives and an olive spread to bind it together. With warm weather ahead, this will be particularly refreshing. And, while tacos are nearly as ubiquitous in Chicago as hamburgers and hot dogs, the chicken tacos at Mambo Grill are somewhat different. The chicken has been minced into a dense filling for blue corn tortillas; it comes with a side of guacamole and a spiced salsa. Even crab cakes get a Caribbean spin thanks to a creole-influenced salsa and tartar sauce accented with cilantro. By the way, connoisseurs of portobello mushrooms will get a wallop from the Mambo Grill version. A generous sized mushroom steak has been grilled and drenched with melted mild white cheese together with slices of button mushrooms. It's very rich, but a real delight.

Mambo Grill does well with its beef, including an aptly named and very tender tenderloin served Argentinian-style with the fresh tasting *chimichurra* sauce. On the seafood side mahi mahi is done veracruzana style with tomatoes, olives, even capers which puts on a little bit different twist to a classic recipe. But, *zarzuela*, a Spanish fish stew adapted to Latin American tastes, lacks the seasoned complexity of ingredients and flavors that make this such a ravishing recipe in more competent kitchens.

MARCHÉ
KR 18/20
Decor 4/4   Hospitality 4.5/5   Food 8.5/10   Value 1/1

• **French/American Eclectic**
• **Chicago/West**
• **$$$**

833 West Randolph Street
Chicago
(312) 226-8399
Troubleshooter: Manager on duty

Hours: Lunch Mon–Fri 11:30 am–2 pm, Dinner Sun–Wed 5:30–10 pm, Thurs 5:30–11 pm, Fri–Sat 5:30 pm–midnight (last reservation at midnight)
Credit Cards: Amex, Diners, MC, Visa
Handicapped: Accessible
Smoking and nonsmoking sections: Both available
Parking: Valet and street

Marché is the kind of trendy restaurant where the customers are part of the atmosphere. In a huge dining and bar space, where something is happening visually everywhere the eye turns, diners gather to enjoy the sights, the sounds, and especially the tastes.

The people-watching is great, and that even includes the wait staff, who are as eclectic as the clientele. One turban festooned waiter could be a case in point, a man in the retailing business by day, who makes a living as a waiter by night.

The menu ranges from the traditional, such as a noticeably generous crock of French onion soup crowned with a layer of melted cheese, to the changing selection of what the menu calls "beautiful soup." Recently, it was carrot in a chicken stock with a bonus of light seasonings. Elsewhere from the selection of hot and cold hors d'oeuvres, one could find grilled eggplant laced with feta cheese and tomatoes, or broiled oysters with andouille sausage, even salmon tartare. Certainly, there is no loss of creativity nor imagination.

It gets even more difficult to make a selection among entrees, considering all the temptations available. Veal sweetbreads are given a crisp sautée, then plated with a vegetable ragout of turnips and salsify. Monkfish, the so-called mock lobster, is served with cut-up tomatoes and artichokes, herbed with fresh basil in a light broth. Salmon has been given a somewhat simpler presentation, with roasted red onions and a soy sauce reduced to vinaigrette. Or consider quail with chanterelles, apricots and brandy for a finish.

Elsewhere on the menu, simple roasted chicken is not all that simple, considering the bounty of herbs rubbed into and under the skin. A bit of onion confit adds more flavor, while a large mound of classic fried potatoes makes for table-sharing nibbles.

Desserts could include a chocolate and armagnac mousse, an apple and cranberry cobbler or any of more than a dozen other selections. Chocolate pot au creme is sensually indulgent.

MARCO!
KR 19/20
Decor 4/4   Hospitality 4.5/5   Food 9.5/10   Value 1/1

• **Italian**	**Hours:** Lunch Mon–Sun noon–2:30 pm, Dinner Sun–Thurs 5–10:30 pm, Fri–Sat 5–11 pm
• **Chicago/North**	
• **$$**	
2360 Clybourn	**Credit Cards:** Amex, Visa, MC
Chicago	**Reservations:** Recommended
(773) 348-2450	**Handicapped:** Accessible
Troubleshooter: Marco	**Smoking and nonsmoking sections:** Smoking only at the bar
	Parking: Valet $6

In a wealth of riches on the Marco! menu, the risotto is a standout. Many restaurants aspire to make the best risotto. And, while it is true there are many approaches, certain factors must apply. They include the correct rice, *arborio*, the right method of cooking, which is a slow simmer, and above all, a close attention to texture and detail. This kitchen gets it just right. Several kinds of risotto are featured on the menu. Among choices is risotto with porcini mushrooms and truffle oil, or a heady version with veal, artichoke hearts and sliced portobellos in a red wine sauce. That with fresh spring asparagus and a touch of saffron is so good you might want to make it your entire meal.

Resist the temptation to over-order so that you might go slowly and savor from other courses. Start with something very unusual such as calamari stuffed with a scampi mousse and set in a pool of black ink squid sauce. The flavors are light, but easily identifiable. You might want to contrast the calamari with a terrine centered around fresh red tomatoes and a bouquet of seasonings worked into a *paté*, or maybe a simple green salad would help simplify things.

With a party of four or more, you can try one of the risotti and also a fresh pasta course to compliment it. *Gnocchi*, little finger-sized potato dumplings, are covered with a wonderfully fresh tomato sauce and just enough mozzarella cheese to make itself evident. The *tagliatelle* with duck sausage and red wine sauce worked together into a ragout is sumptuously rich. Share this one to get the most pleasure.

Among meat courses there are a couple of versions of *osso buco*. The one we tasted was rather like a stew, or even a pot roast with a selection of root vegetables and a red wine sauce. Truffle oil may have been there as the menu states, but I could not taste it.

From a choice of deserts, *nougat semifreddo* is a block of nearly frozen sweet cream bedded on a creamy vanilla sauce, while the *tartufo* is a ball of ice cream covered with chocolate sauce infused with espresso. Service is quite good; the restaurant exudes a welcoming atmosphere in a contemporary decor that mixes bare brick with 19th century cabinetry and an oversized antique wood bar.

MATSUYA
KR 16/20
Decor 3/4   Hospitality 4/5   Food 8/10   Value 1/1

- **Japanese**
- **Chicago/Mid-North**
- **$**

3469-71 North Clark Street
Chicago
(773) 248-2677
Troubleshooter: Michie Yokomori (owner)

Hours: Mon, Wed–Fri 5–11:30 pm, Sat–Sun noon–11:30 pm, closed Tues
Credit Cards: MC, Visa
Reservations: No
Parking: Street parking can be tight

Matsuya's menu reflects not so much trendy Japanese cooking as it does a way of culinary life that lasts beyond fads. Diners may order from an à la carte menu or choose combination dinners. The restaurant's specialty is fresh fish, particularly when it has been charcoal-broiled, as with mackerel or similar varieties with a high oil content. The fish choices, of course will vary depending upon availability at market. Selections at any one time might include butterfish, grouper, snapper, mahi mahi or salmon, as well as several other varieties. The whole grouper I ordered on my most recent visit came in teriyaki sauce, sweet and syrupy, but not overpowering.

Broiled eel is for more adventurous diners. Combination dinners offer a taste of this and that, including battered and fried *tempura* vegetables or shrimp, beef teriyaki and a selection of sashimi or sushi. The sushi and sashimi combination platters offer diners an excellent variety. From time to time, the sushi bar will even have *toro*, the fat belly of the tuna, and considered one of the best sushi delicacies of them all. Dinners include a small cabbage salad, delicious miso soup, rice and light green tea with a delicate woody fragrance, and dessert, usually a fruit sherbet.

McCORMICK & SCHMICK'S
KR 16.5/20
Decor 4/4   Hospitality 4/5   Food 7.5/10   Value 1/1

- **American Seafood**
- **Chicago/Near North**
- **$$**

41 East Chestnut
Chicago
(312) 397-9500
Troubleshooter: Kerri Marti

Hours: Mon–Thurs 11:30 am–11 pm, Fri–Sat 11:30 am–midnight, Sun 11:30 am–10 pm
Credit Cards: All majors
Reservations: Recommended
Handicapped: Accessible
Smoking and nonsmoking sections: Both available
Parking: Valet $6.75

Horace Greely may have advised, "Go West, young man!," but for McCormick & Schmick's, the admonition has been reversed. This popular West Coast chain of seafood houses has set up shop in Chicago in a large space with high ceilings, comfortable though close seating, lots of wood paneling and deco touches to add warmth.

The menu changes each day, as good seafood menus often do to keep up with what's fresh and current. Our waiter advised that the halibut was just flown in from Alaska and showed up in a couple of fashions. A bowl of *cioppino*, generically listed as San Francisco Stew had a delicious tang and a generous mix of shrimp, huge scallops, clams and crab legs that virtually slid from their shells with only a minimal amount of work with a cocktail fork.

Seared yellowfin tuna is excellent, rare at the core, with a spicy crust brushed with wasabi soy sauce; the Japanese theme is continued with pickled ginger as a garnish. Among other entrees, there's a bit of an Italian touch to linguini in marinara with mussels and clams, while more culinary geography is spanned with preparations ranging across the globe from Hawaii, to South America to Louisiana and more.

Among appetizers, pan-fried oysters are plump and juicy, while calamari is grilled and stuffed with a course sausage-like grind of mixed seafood, spinach and mushrooms. The wine list is quite extensive, service is good, but lacking in some attention to details.

MEI SHUNG
KR 18.5/20
Decor 3.5/4   Hospitality 4/5   Food 10/10   Value 1/1

- **Chinese & Taiwanese**
- **Chicago/Far North**
- **$**

5511 North Broadway, Chicago
(773) 728-5778
Troubleshooters: Owner or manager on duty

Hours: Tues–Thurs 11:30 am–10:30 pm, Fri until 11 pm, Sat noon–11 pm, Sun noon–9:30 pm
Credit Cards: Amex, Diners, MC, Visa
Reservations: Accepted, though not always needed
Handicapped: Accessible
Bar: No bar, but diners may bring in beverages from outside
Smoking and nonsmoking sections: Both available
Parking: On street, though there is a church parking lot right across the street, it is posted with a towing sign, and I don't suspect they would be too willing to forgive you your trespasses

My Vice President in Charge of Dining Suggestions probably deserves a raise for pointing me to Mei Shung. This is two restaurants in one, Chinese and Taiwanese.

The two menus are separate, and since we were drawn here for the opportunity to sample Taiwanese-style cookery, I hardly looked at the Chinese menu. At first glance, I thought we would be served foods very much like those found at most Cantonese-style restaurants. There is an emphasis on seafood and vegetables, but otherwise, differences are clear.

The Taiwanese cooking is spicy but subtle, complex, yet identifiable. You could start with a sampling of appetizers. Steamed beancurd leads off the menu. Beancurd, or tofu, is neutral itself, heavily influenced by the way in which it is served or seasoned. In this case, mushrooms provide the basic flavor, intense, but not overpowering. A little soy ginger sauce helps perk things up, while just the tiniest dab of pepper oil gives an added kick. We paired the tofu with a platter of noodles and mixed seafood, including shrimp, scallops and squid. The flavors were mild, always in balance.

Soup gets excellent treatment. Spicy shredded pork noodle soup is everything the name suggests, the kind of broth you'll want to go back to for second helpings from the large serving bowl.

The menu is explained in English, though without a great deal of detail. One of the most interesting selections is called prawns with spiced salt. The prawns are given a light batter coating, much like tempura, but the similarity ends with the frying. The texture is different from tempura, the complexity of spice and salt makes this an unbeatable combination.

From a selection of meats, lamb with hot bean sauce is served with a side of spinach, whose slight bitter taste contrasts against the spiced peppery aftertaste of the sauce. The menu goes on for several pages; with so many choices, Mei Shung is certainly a restaurant you will want to visit with a party of 6 or 8 friends. And, if anyone balks at the unusual tastes found on the Taiwanese menu, they can always choose from the Chinese.

MERITAGE
KR 19/20
Decor 3/4   Hospitality 5/5   Food 10/10   Value 1/1

- **Global Eclectic**
- **Chicago/Near Northwest**
- **$$**

2118 North Damen
Chicago
(773) 235-6434
Troubleshooter: Shawn Harris (owner)

Hours: Sun–Thurs 5:30–10 pm, Fri–Sat 5:30–11:30 pm
Credit Cards: Visa, MC, Amex, Diners
Reservations: Suggested
Handicapped: Accessible
Smoking and nonsmoking sections: Smoking at bar only
Parking: Valet $6

If you could savor the work of Chef John Hartoonian without knowing your surroundings, you might think you were in any of the four or five fine dining restaurants in and around Chicago which are at the very pinnacle of culinary artistry. But, Hartoonian's foods are served in a very modest surrounding. This is hardly the sort of culinary artistry that should be showcased in a small and much too noisy dining environment. It requires white tablecloths, candles, a hushed murmur of dining, the light background of fine music.

Hartoonian is a master of Asian/Fusion preparation. He understands the visual importance of proper platings and settings. He stacks some ingredients, while others he might lay out in a playful arrangement of color. Whatever he prepares, diners can be certain they are about to enjoy the work of one of Chicago's best, but little known *Chefs de Cuisine*.

Consider an appetizer, tea smoked duck spring rolls. Two are plated with a stalk of lemon grass on a bed of lettuce with a smear of chili and lime sauce, and a small pot of pickled ginger jam. The flavors are pronounced, but not overpowering. In another appetizer, lobster and crabmeat are combined into deep-fried cakes napped on a bed of roasted corn sauce with a decidedly flavorful lobster oil. You'll find almost all crab and lobster, little or no filler in these cakes.

In another first course offering, butternut squash soup, a swirl of cream infused with hazelnuts spreads out over the soup like an Oriental calligrapher's seal. Among several other appetizers, steamed mussels come in a coconut flavored broth with a bit of chili sauce for accent. This was the only weakness we found on a recent evening; the mussels were too strong.

From the selection of entrees, try roasted monkfish and you will understand exactly why this is sometimes called "mock lobster." The monkfish is meaty, with the density of lobster and a similar taste. A miso and blood orange sauce is at the flavor center, along with a savory mix of roasted root vegetables, plus shreds of fried sweet potatoes. In another entree, large scallops are roasted and served with black beans and asparagus for texture and color contrast, along with a light orange saffron oil.

Braised lamb shank may be like pot roast on a stick . . . with tender lamb barely clinging to the bone in an *au jus* accented with fresh thyme. Depending upon the entree, Chef Hartoonian uses a variety of exotic ingredients ranging from saffron to cardamom, from ginger and garlic to wasabi and balsamic vinegar.

MESON SABIKA
KR 18/20
Decor 3/4   Hospitality 4/5   Food 10/10   Value 1/1

- **Spanish Tapas**
- **Northfield**
- **$$**

410 Happ Road
Northfield
(847) 784-9300
Troubleshooters: Hossein Jamali, Francois Sanchez (owners)

Hours: Mon–Thurs 11:30 am–9:30 pm, Fri–Sat 11:30 am–10:30 pm, Sun 5–9 pm
Credit Cards: Amex, Discover, MC, Visa
Reservations: Recommended, limited reservations accepted Fri and Sat
Handicapped: Accessible
Smoking and nonsmoking sections: Both available
Parking: Free

Spanish food has its own influences, not the least of which is Moorish. Though it has been centuries since the Moors governed the Iberian peninsula, their cultural and culinary contributions can still be felt, in the way of seasonings and ingredients, one of which is that rarest of all spices, saffron.

Saffron, whose pale yellow has given its name to a delicate color as well as flavor, is at the heart of much that is traditional in Spanish cooking. That certainly includes *paella*, a casserole of slowly simmered rice in which each grain blossoms in the heat of a cooking liquid and absorbs the touch of saffron that adds wonderful taste and a distinctive color. Unlike tapas, which are small individual servings, *paella* is prepared and served in larger portions. It comes out in a copper cooking pan with a variety of ingredients depending upon which style is being prepared. *Paella mariscos*, with an array of shrimp, mussels, clams, scallops and calamari is one approach, while the traditional *Valenciana* adds chicken. Some Spanish cooks make one that includes *chorizo* sausage, but like American clam chowder or jambalaya, there is no one true recipe.

While, in my opinion, *paella* should be at the center of dining at Meson Sabika, the evening begins with tapas. Tapas are small individual servings, hot or cold, but always highly creative. There are no rules to follow, except sharing. Start with something chilled such as a Spanish-style potato salad in garlic aioli, dusted with snips of parsley. Move on to an Iberian-style cannelloni with a filling of fresh tuna, asparagus and basil for seasoning. A creamy white wine vinaigrette adds some acidic bite to contrast with the other ingredients. Even something as simple as sautéed vegetables in garlic and olive oil can prove to be a perfect introduction to tapas.

I think the hot tapas are more interesting. Try grilled squid with the ever-present garlic and olive oil and you will taste the Spanish version of a food found in most every seaport along the Southern Mediterranean coast from Greece to Gibraltar. Roasted peppers, coaxed down with a chilled sangria or more robust red wine are filled with shrimp and vegetables. Thanks to the New World explorations, the potato found its way into European, and particularly Spanish, cooking. A *galleta*, or potato cake, serves as foundation for a topping of tiny rock shrimp, mushrooms and scallions glazed with lemon butter. Grilled oysters is one of the best of the many choices. Bite into one, and the juices rush out to fill your mouth and wash your taste buds with the sauce of the sea. Sautéed leeks, freshly cracked pepper, sluiced potatoes and a light tomato sauce complete the platter.

As for desserts, there are no mistakes. Four choices are offered: traditional Spanish rice pudding, *flan*, *profiteroles*, pastry puffs filled with ice cream and topped with chocolate sauce, and a Spanish version of the old-fashioned banana split, with pistachios and caramel sauce in lieu of the American rendering.

MIA FRANCESCA
KR 18/20
Decor 4/4 ˙ Hospitality 4/5   Food 9/10   Value 1/1

- **Italian**
- **Chicago/Mid-North**
- **$$**

Clark Street
Chicago
(773) 281-3310
Troubleshooter: Scott Harris
(chef/owner)
Other Locations
Francesca's on Taylor, 1400 West Taylor Street, Chicago; 312-829-2828; Hours: Lunch Mon–Fri 11:30 am–2 pm, Dinner Sun–Tues 5 pm–9 pm, Wed–Thurs 5 pm–10 pm, Fri–Sat 5 pm–11 pm; Credit Cards: Amex, Diners, MC, Visa; Reservations: Taken at all times (on days when Bulls or Blackhawks are at home, reservations suggested at least a week in advance for dining from 5–7 pm and on Sat any time at least 1 to 2 weeks in advance); Bar: Full bar; Smoking and nonsmoking sections: Smoking only in bar area (some dinner seating available in bar); Parking: Valet; Handicapped: Accessible; Party Facilities: Private party room for up to 60 people

Francesca's North 1145 Church Street, Northbrook; 847-559-0260; Hours: Sun 5–9 pm, Mon–Thurs 5–10 pm, Fri–Sat 5–10:30 pm, Lunch Tues–Thurs 11 am–2 pm; Credit Cards: MC, Visa; Reservations: Taken for lunch, but only on limited call-in basis for dinner, i.e. If you want to dine at 7:30 pm on a weekday, call in at 6:30 pm to have your name put on the waiting list, when you arrive at 7:30 pm, your table should be ready. On weekends, same policy, but call 90 minutes in advance; Handicapped: Accessible; Bar: Full service; Smoking and nonsmoking sections: Smoking at bar only; Parking: Free in lot; Party Facilities: Private facilities for up to 110 for luncheon parties only

La Sorella Di Francesca, 18 West Jefferson, Naperville; 630-961-2706; Hours: Sun 4–9 pm, Mon–Tues 5–9 pm, Wed–Thurs 5–10 pm, Fri–Sat 5–11 pm; Credit Cards: Amex, MC, Visa; Reservations: Policy same as at Francesca's North; Handicapped: Accessible; Bar: Full service; Smoking and nonsmoking sections: Smoking at bar only; Parking: Street parking available; Party Facilities:Private party room for up to 60 people

Hours: Sun–Thurs 5–10 pm, Fri–Sat 5–11 pm
Credit Cards: MC, Visa
Reservations: Not accepted
Handicapped: Accessible
Bar: Full service
Smoking and nonsmoking sections: Both available
Parking: Valet
Party Facilities: Private party facilities for luncheons up to 80 people plus "coachhouse" dining for up to 24

Nowhere has the craze for Italian restaurants been more intense than at Mia Francesca. It is not uncommon, with its no reservations policy, for waits to be an hour or two. Gentle reader, I confess my unwillingness to wait so long. By the way, neither should you.

Nevertheless, it is no wonder people flock to this, the Clark Street address, and its siblings in Northbrook, Naperville and on North Taylor Street, in one of Chicago's genuine old Italian neighborhoods.

The menus at all four restaurants are similar and have nightly changes from a repertoire of about 150 of Chef Scott Harris's collection of recipes. Portions are the kind that mean customers usually go home with leftovers. Recently, linguine with mushrooms came out in a very light tomato-based sauce, flavored more with mushrooms and fresh herbs than tomato. In a word, it was delicious. Similar accolades accrue to rigatoni with roasted eggplant. This time, the tomato sauce is a bit more spiced, eased by the addition of creamy mozzarella cheese.

In addition to half a dozen or so pastas, there are meat and fish entrees. Tilapia has been served with a cream of spinach laced with shallots, while roasted salmon is almost classically French, with the inclusion of capers and garlic in a tomato and white wine sauce. An order of roasted chicken yields more than you or I can eat in one sitting. The deliciously seasoned poultry is accompanied by roasted potatoes. The presentation is similar to chicken vesuvio, but with more finesse in the seasonings.

I have not forgotten about appetizers. Risotto has recently been served with grilled calamari. It's a good version, but comes from the kitchen too quickly for me to believe that this risotto is made to order. Mussels bathed in marinara are plump, fresh flavored, without a trace of sand. Several salads and a few other antipasti round out the selections.

Mia Francesca is one of those restaurants where dessert should not be ignored. The *tiramisu* rises above cliché, while a chocolate sorbet tastes almost as if it were really ice cream.

MIMOSA
KR 17/20
Decor 4/4   Hospitality 3.5/5   Food 8.5/10   Value 1/1

- **Mediterranean**
- **Highland Park**
- **$$**

1849 Second Street
Highland Park
(847) 432-9770
Troubleshooter: Kevin
Schwimmer (chef/owner)

Hours: Tues–Thurs 5–9 pm,
Fri–Sat 5–10 pm, Sun 5–8 pm,
closed Mon
Credit Cards: MC, Visa, Amex,
Discover
Reservations: Yes
Handicapped: Accessible
**Smoking and nonsmoking
sections:** Nonsmoking
Parking: No parking

Groupies follow rock stars. Foodies follow chefs. Kevin Schrimmer made his name and following working for the late Leslie Reis, before going on to other stoves and other ventures.

His latest venture, Mimosa, is a handsomely decorated restaurant with a tropical feel that evokes a different time and place than the here and now of Chicago's North Shore. Schrimmer sometimes uses ingredients in a very surprising manner. For instance, he serves a variation of ordinary *gardiniara*, the Italian pickled or marinated vegetables more often seen on the likes of an Italian beef sandwich. But, instead of Italian beef, Schrimmer uses a breaded and boneless chicken breast coated with parmesan cheese and finished in a frying pan. Then, he sets that on a bed of angel hair pasta, and tops everything with a lavish mound of *gardiniara*. Rich? Is it ever! But, delicious and then some.

Though Mimosa is hardly an Italian restaurant, its Mediterranean influenced menu offers some excellent pasta. One is a popular *fruitti de mare*, a selection of shell fish, calamari and what-nots mixed in with linguini bathed in a spicy tomato sauce with just a hint of sweetness.

Usually there will be a *risotto* or two, if not as an entree, then certainly among appetizers. Elsewhere among first course choices, the mushroom *fricassee* is not to be missed by anyone who loves this kind of earthy flavor. The mushrooms are cooked down within an herb and wine sauce that is positively luscious. A mound of creamy polenta sits in the center of the serving bowl like an island, picking up these delicious flavors with every swirl of a fork.

Another winner, with a decidedly different taste and texture, is a vegetable tart, reminiscent of *pissaladiere*, the delectable pastry with vegetable topping popularized in Nice. Roasted red and yellow peppers add some bite to the tomatoes and other ingredients. The pastry crust supporting this small bounty is perfect.

MIRABELL
KR 18.5/20
Decor 3.5/4   Hospitality 5/5   Food 9/10   Value 1/1

- **Austrian/German**
- **Chicago/North**
- **$$**

3454 North Addison
Chicago
(773) 463-1962
Troubleshooters: Werner and
Anita Heil, Jeff Heil (owners)

Hours: Lunch Mon–Sat 11:30
am–2:30 pm, Dinner Mon–Thurs
5–10 pm, Fri–Sat 5–11 pm
Credit Cards: Amex, MC, Visa
Reservations: Suggested
Bar: Two full bars with German
beers on tap, plus large selection
of wines, cordials, call brand
liquors and bottled beers
Parking: Ample street parking or
in nearby lot

Though Austrian specialties are among the choices on the Mirabell menu, the atmosphere of this cozy restaurant strikes more along the lines of a hearty "oom-pah-pah band," rather than the fragile refrains of a Strauss waltz. But, however one might want to make a characterization about decor and ambiance, the hospitality offered here is "*wunderbar!*"

Naturally, the classic *weiner schnitzel* is on the menu, breaded to a golden turn in its rich egg batter; the veal is so tender it really can be sliced with a fork's edge. In fact, one of the distinctive features that marks Mirabell is that all the meats are cut and trimmed to the specifications of Chef/Co-owner Werner Heil.

There are several schnitzels offered, among them Parisian-style with a puffy, almost soufflé-like crust. Diners will also find *zigeuner schnitzel*, made with pork, rather than veal, then topped with a sauté of peppers, mushrooms and onions in a pronounced paprika sauce. True connoisseurs say this is the only legitimate way.

Goulash, heavily seasoned Middle European meat stew, is fine in a small portion of soup, or in the hearty main portion entree size. Yet, another Austrian treat is *weiner roastbraten*, a prime sirloin quickly pan-sautéed in wine and its own juices, served with crisp double-fried onions and mushrooms.

A number of German specialties including traditional *sauerbraten* and assorted sausages round out the menu. And, while this kind of dining does not particularly flatter waistlines, the restaurant has been featuring a variety of fresh seafoods that can be prepared more simply than other entrees might suggest.

MITY NICE GRILL
KR 17.5/20

Decor 4/4   Hospitality 5/5   Food 7.5/10   Value 1/1

* **American**
* **Chicago/Near North**
* **$$**

835 North Michigan Avenue
at Water Tower Place,
Mezzanine level
Chicago
(312) 335-4745
Troubleshooters: Steve LaHaie,
Kevin Brown (managing partners)

Hours: Mon–Sat 11 am–10 pm,
Sun 11 am–9 pm
Credit Cards: All majors
Reservations: Accepted
Handicapped: Accessible
Smoking and nonsmoking sections: No smoking
Parking: Validated discount parking in Water Tower Place garage after 5 pm

Two men walk into a restaurant dressed in denim cutoffs and tee shirts. They are escorted to their table by a maitre d' in full tuxedo. Is something out of place here? Not at Mity Nice Grill. The setting is as far from a shopping mall as one might think possible, located directly behind Food Life (q.v.), the rambling courtyard restaurant that puts a whole new spin on food court mall dining. Mity Nice Grill, on the other hand, has the patina of Chicago dining as it might have been 50 or 60 years ago. But, the food and service are right up to date. It is more than casual dining, but less than formality for its own sake.

The menu seems at first glance like nothing more than comfort food. A closer reading reveals something more, and something less. The less is less oil, less fat, less calories in some recipes. The more involves something like linguine with wild mushrooms and chicken or a grilled filet mignon with a crusting of melted blue cheese. By the way, the linguine, which is one of several pasta choices, is as satisfying and direct as the listing of its ingredients implies. For other, more traditional styles of comfort food, diners will find macaroni with cheese or even turkey with mashed potatoes.

Not everything works. The Enlightened Caesar Salad, as it is called, is made with an oil-free, egg-free, anchovy free-dressing. It may be enlightened; it's also spartan. On the plus side are grilled flatbreads among the appetizers. A flatbread at Mity Nice Grill is like a large cracker that can be embellished with various toppings. Goat cheese, asparagus and roasted garlic brings a wonderful trio of flavors.

Entrees can be as simple as a platter of steamed fresh vegetables or roasted chicken with garlic, peppers and onions. Daily specials recently included excellent grilled salmon with a bed of couscous and balsamic vinaigrette, accompanied by a selection of cooked vegetables. In another version, the salmon is done vesuvio fashion, though without as much olive oil as is usually associated with this kind of cooking.

The menu includes several sandwiches and dinner-sized salads. Dessert is the comeback course for calories. But, there is also the less-is-more approach with an order of frozen vanilla yogurt in a small lake of fat-free chocolate sauce, with a surprisingly rich and satisfying flavor.

mk
KR 19.25/20
Decor 4/4   Hospitality 5/5   Food 9.5/10   Value .75/1

• **American Eclectic** • **Chicago/Near North** • **$$$** 868 North Franklin Street, Chicago (312) 482-9179 **Troubleshooters:** Chef Michael Kornick, Carolyn Bobrowski, David Jones (managing partners)	**Hours:** Dinner Sun–Wed 5:30–10 pm, Thurs–Sat until 11 pm **Credit Cards:** Amex, Diners, MC, Visa **Reservations:** Suggested **Handicapped:** Accessible **Parking:** Valet **Smoking and nonsmoking sections:** No smoking in restaurant

mk is as pristine and understated as its minimalist name. Broad white-washed walls curve along one side of the main dining room, which is built on terraces. The only suggestion that this restaurant is in a building whose genesis is more industrial than culinary are the large front metal framed windows and the overhead skylight, which, in a time long gone, must have poured natural illumination on the anonymous laborers on the production floor three stories below, not in the interests of their comfort, but to save their bosses the cost of electrical lighting.

The mk menu showcases a style of cooking which is elaborate, but not ostentatiously complex. Just as there is an order in the restaurant's minimalist design, there is an order in the culinary architecture. The menu is basically contemporary American, but draws on Continental and occasional Asian touches. Oysters on the half shell, malpeques from Canadian waters, *foie gras* with prunes soaked in armagnac brandy, fettucini shavings of parmesan cheese and with black truffles taken from Italy's Piedmont region and are among starters. Each has its own logic of taste and texture. For instance, sausage is paired with the rather sea-spiced Malpeques while the brandy-infused prunes only add to the sybaritic luxury of the *foie gras*. As for the fettucini and black truffles, what more needs to be said? It is an indulgent, though perfectly natural match.

And, those are only some of the first course choices! Entrees seem prosaic enough as listed on the simple black on white menu. But, read beyond the large type and savor the anticipation of chicken, roasted with a run of herbs, a gratin of salsify and pommery mustard sauce. This is rustic French cookery at its best. Lamb shank is set with a Levantine influence on its bed of couscous, but a reach into southern France brings garlic-infused mayonnaise, or *aioli* to the platter. The lamb soaks up other elemental flavors from its braising in a sturdy *vin rouge*.

Elsewhere among seafood selections, Chef Michael Kornick mates monkfish, often called the poor man's lobster, with the genuine article, chunks of cold water Maine lobster meat in a seasoned lobster–infused stock. Whipped potatoes with saffron bring a delicate spicy taste. I also like what is happening to tuna, seared fashionably rare and plated in a red wine reduction with garlic mashed potatoes. The only improvement would be more of a garlic taste, but I, unlike Mr. Kornick, sometimes forget that less is more.

The dessert menu from Kornick's partner in culinary discovery, Mindy Segal, is imaginative in its own way. Ms. Segal seems to revel more in the excess of display than does Chef Kornick. She plays with ingredients to fashion edible sculptings for several of her recipes. Chances are your server will urge you to try pineapple braised with vanilla and ginger until it is somewhat softened, then layered with pineapple sorbet and a nap of mango and pineapple coulis. It would take several hundred more words to discuss the other selections, even then, justice would not be done.

MON AMI GABI
KR 20/20
Decor 4/4   Hospitality 5/5   Food 10/10   Value 1/1

- **French Bistro**
- **Chicago/Mid-North**
- **$$**

2300 North Lincoln Park West
Chicago
(773) 348-8886
Troubleshooters: Gabino
Sotelino (managing partner),
Claude Gaty (chef), Pamela Parker
(manager)

Hours: Mon–Thurs 5:30–10 pm, Fri–Sat 5:30–11 pm, Sun 5–9 pm
Credit Cards: All majors
Reservations: Recommended
Handicapped: Accessible
Smoking and nonsmoking sections: Smoking section, but no smoking on weekends
Parking: Valet $7

Like Italian restaurants, Chicago has seen a resurgence of French bistros among its most recent and popular dining trends. One of the best has reinvented itself. Mon Ami Gabi, has picked up where its long time predecessor Un Grande Cafe churned out countless topnotch meals.

It could be a busy café in Paris or Lyon with its mosaic tile floor, wall accents, close-together tables and overall bustle. Order a bottle of Parisian-style beer and you almost have it all but the airfare.

Mon Ami Gabi refers to the restaurant's owner, Gabino Sotelino who probably spends more of his time at the sister restaurant Ambria across the hotel lobby. Where Ambria is formal and expensive, Mon Ami Gabi is more the casual restaurant with prices much less dear. Chef de Cuisine Claude Gaty runs the kitchen and there's not a flaw to be found.

Try the classic French onion soup baked in the crock. It may be the very best to be found in Chicago, which I realize is an extravagant assertion. This soup is heady with an intoxicating peppery sweet taste. Be sure to scrape up every bit of cheese, even the crust that rims the crock. Among other first course taste experiences is a lovely presentation of clams steamed in white wine, an herbaceous vegetable terrine and the like. Fresh warm baguettes are excellent as is, or used to sponge any of the several sauces.

For entrees, there are nightly specials as well as those listed on the menu. Lamb shank is somewhat unusual, pounded out into a paillard. So too is codfish, which is then dredged in a light breading and pan-fried. A Franco version of tartar sauce and a heaping portion of curly potato fries round out the platter in a portion that practically dwarfs its serving plate. Steamed halibut is clean tasting as good fish should be. A julienne of vegetables in a mild fish stock makes this another winner. Speaking of seafood, salmon steaks are roasted until savory, sea bass is baked in parchment and whitefish is given a simple steaming, while skate is sautéed, plated with mild garlic mashed potatoes and a caper lemon butter sauce.

Above all else, this is bistro cooking as good as I have found it in Chicago. Service is knowledgeable and accommodating to special needs. And, just as a footnote, the profiterole with chocolate sauce is a slam dunk desert winner.

MOSSANT
KR 18/20
Decor 4/4   Hospitality 5/5   Food 8/10   Value 1/1

- **French Bistro**
- **Chicago**
- **$$**

227 North Wabash Avenue
(Hotel Monaco)
Chicago
(312) 236-9300
Troubleshooter: Will Eudy
(general manager)

Hours: Breakfast Mon–Fri 7–10 am, Brunch Sat–Sun 8 am–2 pm, Lunch Mon–Fri 11:30 am–2:30 pm, Dinner Sun–Thurs 5–10 pm, Fri–Sat 5–11 pm
Credit Cards: All majors
Reservations: Accepted
Handicapped: Accessible
Smoking and nonsmoking sections: Smoking in bar
Parking: Valet $7

Mossant is a spacious French bistro which takes up a good portion of the floor space at the Hotel Monaco. An open kitchen on the far wall showcases a copper accented range hood that stretches its entire length. The cooking is understated. French onion soup is typical. Instead of a blanket of melted cheese that stretches like a rubber band when you try to take some from the bowl, this soup seems made with the theory that less is more. The emphasis is on the broth, a rich onion flavor, not too sweet, certainly not bitter.

The house version of escargots is smoked with garlic coulis, which makes them somewhat more distinctive than typical snails in garlic and butter. Another interesting selection is roasted rouget, a Mediterranean fish not usually seen on American menus. This mullet-like fish is roasted, wrapped in a light phyllo and flavored with olive tapanade and a red wine sauce reduction. As is more evident in French restaurants these days, the old rules about red or white wine and fish no longer apply. Elsewhere on the menu, salmon is roasted and served with a burgundy reduction, just another example of how tradition gives way to change.

Mussels steamed in muscadet wine is classic simplicity itself, served with french fries that come wrapped in a red and white checked paper napkin in an upright silver cup. Grilled lamb chops with a side of pureed turnip and vegetables is more formidable, as might be the pork chop with pommery mustard sauce, or the veal chop, seared with a wild mushroom ragout. Other entrees include a couple styles of roasted chicken, a stylized bouillabaisse, though it is not identified as such on the menu, and steak crusted with crushed peppercorns and a side of Lyonnaise potatoes.

Among desserts, pear helene is gilded with vanilla ice cream and chocolate sauce, while almonds add crunch. Other choices include classic French apple tart, crème brûlée and profiteroles, while white and dark chocolate mousse is paired in a single serving.

MYKHA'S
KR 17/20
Decor 4/4   Hospitality 5/5   Food 7/10   Value 1/1

- **Vietnamese**
- **Glen Ellyn**
- **$$**

476 Forest Avenue
Glen Ellyn
(630) 469-6243
Troubleshooter: Mykha
(chef/owner)

Hours: Lunch Mon–Fri 11:30 am–2:30 pm, Dinner Mon–Sat 5:30–9:30 pm, closed Sun
Credit Cards: All majors except Amex and Diners
Reservations: Recommended, especially on weekends
Handicapped: Accessible
Smoking and nonsmoking sections: No smoking
Parking: On street

If you wonder what Vietnamese and Mexican foods are doing on the same menu, there is an explanation at Mykha's. It has to do with the experiences of Mykha the restaurant's owner, as she explains in a table brochure. That brochure also explains some of the more exotic fare for people who might not be familiar with Vietnamese food, and how certain recipes fit into Mykha's life.

For instance *Grandma Noodles*, a first course selection, is a broad noodle, lightly fried and served with a light oyster sauce. They are crispy and delicious, and according to the informative brochure, learned by MyKha from her grandmother in their small Vietnamese village.

Maybe it is the personal touch which makes Mykha's something different. Servers will guide you through each course, making suggestions when asked, even volunteering some particular detail about a presentation. In addition to the Grandma Noodles, which should not be missed, you might want the Vietnamese egg rolls with their crisp noodle wrap around an array of vegetables or the more delicate spring rolls. These are made with a nearly translucent wrap of rice paper filled with chunks of tofu, herbs and cut-up pieces of rice vermicelli. A light peanut sauce is there for dipping. Other appetizers range from crab rangoon to a couple of Mexican selections, chicken flautas and the house version of guacamole.

Several daily entree specials are offered in addition to the printed menu. Basil chicken is quite flavorful and the lemongrass chicken is almost as good. Each is accented with either of the two flavoring herbs. From several seafood choices, catfish comes as a whole fish with a mix of fruits and vegetables or in another preparation just the fillet is brought with garlic sauce and vegetables. Actually, that fillet is misnamed since the fish is riddled with so many tiny bones that I found it unpleasant to deal with, no matter how good the flavor.

Other entrees range from a hearty portion of Vietnamese pork chop, or a Mexican version, plus several other beef, poultry and seafood choices. Each is handsomely plated with an accompaniment of matchstick cut vegetables or in some cases those delicious Grandma Noodles. Desserts are more American than Asian.

MYKONOS
KR 18/20
Decor 4/4   Hospitality 4.5/5   Food 8.5/10   Value 1/1

• **Greek** • **Niles** • **$$** 8660 Golf Road (one block west of Golf Mill Shopping Center) Niles (847) 296-6777 **Troubleshooter:** Demetrious Merageas (chef/owner)	**Hours:** Sun–Thurs 11 am–11 pm, Fri–Sat 11 am–midnight **Credit Cards:** All majors **Reservations:** Recommended, especially for parties of five or more **Handicapped:** Accessible **Smoking and nonsmoking sections:** Separate smoking and nonsmoking seating **Parking:** Free valet

Mykonos has a history of at least two, maybe three, decades in the same location. Over the years, it has changed physically as improvements have been made to the overall look. Today, it is prettier than it has ever been. And, like so many Greek restaurants, its predominating decor themes are limned out in white with blue accents.

I think the decor has changed more than the menu, which is rife with the likes of *saganaki*, *souvlaki*, roast lamb, leg of lamb, lamb chops, not to mention the casserole dishes, *moussaka* and *pastitsio*.

Begin with the wonderful fish roe spread called *taramasalata*. Here, a creamy mix of pinkish roe combined with olive oil and a touch of lemon juice which helps define the taste, are whipped together with mashed potatoes in some recipes, or with soaked bread as a binder. The faint taste of the sea comes through. The other, more powerful spread is *skordalia*, a heady breeding of garlic and whipped potatoes, smoothed out with olive oil and best when used as a sauce with fish, but delicious on its own, spread on thick slices of crusty country bread.

The best of Greek dining lies with lamb and fresh fish. A whole broiled red snapper, or even tastier to my way of thinking, sea bass, is set out on its platter with a drizzle of lemon juice and a sprinkling of oregano. That's all that is needed, save perhaps a side of roasted potatoes or okra. For those who enjoy codfish, it comes pan-fried in a traditional manner, with plenty of skordalia. Other seafood will also be available in season.

As for the lamb, the meaty chops come sizzling from the heat of the broiler, charred outside, still pink and savory within. The chops are the better choice over braised or roast leg of lamb, which can be too fatty.

The detailed menu offers an array of shishkebabs including chicken, pork tenderloin, beef, shrimp and swordfish. The chicken kebabs I tasted were a bit uneven, some chunks too dry, others moist and flavorful.

For those who simply cannot make up their minds, or have a broad taste, a combination platter is the ready answer. It brings healthy portions of the layered eggplant and potatoes casserole called *moussaka*, its macaroni casserole cousin, *pastitsio*, plus delicate *dolmades*, flavorful slices of gyros, roasted potatoes and vegetables, as well as a heaping mound of rice.

Desserts indulge the sweet tooth in all of us, Greek or barbarian. Of course there is *baklava* and the curious custard called *galaktoboureko*. Or, taste a creamy and light rice pudding, which helps settle the stomach almost as much as a final glass of ouzo.

NACIONAL 27
KR 18.5/20
Decor 4/4   Hospitality 5/5   Food 8.5/10   Value 1/1

• **Latin American**

• **Chicago/Near North**

• **$$**

325 West Huron
Chicago
(312) 664-2727
Troubleshooters: Steve Ottman, Ed Culleeney (managing partners), Randy Zweiban (chef)

Hours: Dining Room Mon–Thurs 5:30–11 pm, Fri–Sat 5:30 pm–midnight, Sun 5:30–10 pm
Bar: Mon–Thurs 5 pm–midnight, Fri–Sat 5 pm–1 am or later, Sun 5:30–10 pm
Credit Cards: All majors
Handicapped: Accessible
Reservations: Suggested
Smoking and nonsmoking sections: Permitted in bar, separate sections in dining room
Parking: Valet

The Nacional 27 menu attempts to encompass the wide range of Latin American cuisine, but with a somewhat modern twist that might stray from strictly authentic. Whatever the goals, results of several selections we tasted from the lengthy menu were mostly successful.

The menu offers an opportunity for tapas dining, though the listings are not actually explained or set up that way. But, by choosing from various categories, it is possible to take from this and that as whim and appetite dictate.

We got off to a solid start with skewered chicken seasoned with cilantro and a complex relish of spices and crushed vegetables. Next, from a listing of seafood cocktails, an order of snapper ceviche was fresh and welcome when contrasted to the spicy introduction of the cilantro chicken skewers. Appearance is all important in how Nacional 27 presents its selections. The ceviche came in a hollowed out avocado shell with a salsa that brought together mild sweet peppers, diced tomatoes and red onions. The lime cured taste of the snapper was deliciously refreshing.

Among other opening courses, an Argentinean-influenced empanada came with a filling of smoked chicken. The crust may have been a little too thick and doughy, but flavors of the chicken and its seasonings were well matched.

Though there are enough choices to make a meal of tapas, some of the full dinner size platings are too tempting to ignore. Grilled tuna comes with a rare center, the fish set in a mild tasting shallot broth with escarole and potatoes on the side. From among other choices, *chimichurri chicken* is served as a paillard, surrounded by roasted peppers and chunky roasted potatoes with a definite bite. The kitchen has been careful to leave the chicken moist, its flavors amplified by a coat of seasonings.

Atmosphere and decor are decidedly club-like, with more than a suggestion of the 1940s and a touch of South American café society as it might have appeared in American film noir of the period. All that's missing are Gilbert Roland and John Garfield sitting at the bar.

NICK & TONY'S
KR 18/20
Decor 4/4   Hospitality 5/5   Food 8/10   Value 1/1

- **Italian/American**
- **Chicago**
- **$$**

1 East Wacker Drive
Chicago
(312) 467-9449
Troubleshooters: Roger Greenfield, Ted Kasemir (owners)

Hours: Mon–Fri 6 am–11 pm, Sat 5–11 pm, Sun 5–10 pm
Credit Cards: All majors
Reservations: Suggested
Handicapped: Accessible
Bar: Full service, good selection of Italian and American wines
Smoking and nonsmoking sections: Both available
Parking: Valet after 5 pm
Party Facilities: Private dining facilities for up to 85 people

Nick & Tony's, the Italian-American art deco, 1940s-style Chicago eatery occupies space that used to be *The Little Corporal*, where I used to eat the best French Toast to be found anywhere. Figuring that French toast was not part of the spread at Nick & Tony's, I asked the man who took our coats what the specialty of the house might be. "Osso buco," came the reply without even a pause. On the way to our table, I asked the host the same question and got the same response. Ditto our waiter.

Suspecting a sure thing when I hear it, we ordered the osso buco for our main course. It was everything as promised, and more. Truth to tell, this is not classic osso buco. There is no *gremolada*, no accompaniment of risotto. Instead, it comes with a side of mashed potatoes.

The osso buco is served on a huge platter, befitting its truly mammoth size. Our waiter compared it to a football helmet. He was not far off the mark. The meat is packed around a central shank bone that towers a good 8 or 9 inches over the platter. The waiter portioned servings for our party of five, and there was plenty to go around. After carving up the meat, he put the shank bone in the center of the table, informing us that the marrow inside is the delicacy.

Osso buco is just one part of a menu which is not necessarily trying to be an authentic Italian restaurant as much as it is trying to be an old-style Chicago Italian restaurant. Its culinary successes are evident, but so are some near hits and misses. Granted, we asked that an order of risotto be prepared with olive oil instead of butter. That does not excuse the intense salted flavor, nor even the fact that the rice was somewhat undercooked, nothing near the creaminess we had expected.

So much for problems. Most everything else we tasted was more than credible. From a selection of appetizers, the calamari gets a light batter coating and is delicious. So, too, is the portobello mushroom, served with a blanket of melted cheese on a bed of spinach.

From among pastas, linguine with seafood is excellent. The tomato sauce has a light peppery bite. Shrimp and scallops predominate. Other pastas include old-fashioned spaghetti and meatballs, the kind served in America, not Italy, as well as lasagna bolognese, baked ziti with ricotta cheese and tomatoes and other selections. The menu goes on for a full three pages of pastas, salads, pizza and specials. The full wine list is bound in a volume as thick as a small telephone book. Service is completely professional. I suggest you share portions, especially the osso buco. The coatcheck guy, host and waiter were all correct.

NICK'S FISHMARKET
KR 20/20
Decor 4/4   Hospitality 5/5   Food 10/10   Value 1/1

- **American**
- **Chicago Loop**
- **$$$**

One First National Plaza (Monroe Street at Clark)
(312) 621-0200
Troubleshooters: Nick Nicholas (owner), Steve Karpf (managing partner)

Other Location

10275 West Higgins Road, at Mannheim, Rosemont; 847-298-8200; Hours: Mon–Thurs 5:30–10 pm, Fri–Sat 5:30–11 pm, Sun 5:30–9 pm; Credit Cards: All majors; Handicapped: Accessible; Smoking and nonsmoking sections: Separate smoking and nonsmoking seating; Parking: Free in building lot or valet

Hours: Lunch Mon–Fri 11:30 am–3 pm, Dinner Mon–Sat 5:30–11:30 pm
Credit Cards: All majors, house accounts
Reservations: Mandatory
Handicapped: Accessible
Bar: Excellent wine list
Smoking and nonsmoking sections: Separate smoking and nonsmoking seating
Parking: Valet after 5 pm, validated garage parking from 11 am
Dress: Casual elegance, jackets preferred for gentlemen

When it comes to power dining, there's nothing like Nick's Fishmarket. Even as the restaurant provides the perfect setting for business entertaining, this is not a restaurant lacking for romance, either. The oversized banquettes and big stuffed chairs are as comfortable as can be. Lighting can be individually adjusted at each table, turned up for you to see the menu and dimmed for a more intimate setting. An in-the-wall aquarium adds a touch of the nautical to what is otherwise a sophisticated, urban setting.

The food remains nearly in a class by itself, as do the prices. But, one is paying for the posh surroundings and the impeccable service. Hardly a detail is missed, whether it comes to something as obvious as lighting a cigarette for a customer, to refolding a napkin, or freshening goblets of water.

In a restaurant where change has been virtually absent since its opening in 1988, there is a new menu. The à la carte vegetables are gone. Now, entrees will include one, and in some cases, two vegetables. And, while seafood remains the substance of the fishmarket concept, diner's will now find some contemporary Italian influences.

Among them is veal chop in barolo wine sauce, a filet mignon *carpaccio* appetizer and pasta bolognese. But, Italian restaurants are everywhere. Nick's Fishmarket shines on its whole finned fish presentations, which range from farm-raised catfish to exotic denizens of the Pacific. Blackened Tuna might be served on a bed of lightly seasoned rice.

Desserts are as lavish as other courses, including several chocolate stylings that are knockouts.

NINE
KR 18.5/20
Decor 4/4   Hospitality 4.5/5   Food 9/10   Value 1/1

- **American**
- **Chicago/Near West**
- **$$$**

440 West Randolph Street
Chicago
(312) 575-9900, 575-9901
Troubleshooter: Myron
Markewycz (general manager)

Hours: Lunch Mon–Fri 11:30 am–2:30 pm, Dinner Mon–Wed 5:30–10 pm, Thurs 5:30–11 pm, Fri–Sat 5:30 pm–midnight, Sun Brunch 10:30 am–2 pm
Credit Cards: Amex, Diners, MC, Visa
Reservations: Recommended for dining, suggested for the caviar bar
Handicapped: Accessible
Smoking and nonsmoking sections: Nonsmoking
Parking: Valet

Nine is a scene, one of the hottest new venues on the Chicago area restaurant map. It is as dramatic and exciting as its name is curious. Two bars are the first eye catchers. The Champagne and caviar bar is a circular affair with a silvered fiber optic–lit glass column around which are wrapped the storage area for bottles and glassware, the granite-surfaced bar itself and its seating. This is separated from the dining room by a circular railing. The second bar is more typical, off to the far side wall, though its back-lit golden lighting makes it more than just another place to hoist a drink or two.

The dining is almost as exciting as the overall style of the restaurant. While the restaurant is billed as a contemporary steakhouse, that's like calling Fort Knox the home of fool's gold. Certainly there are steaks and chops, but there are so many more exciting things to consider.

Try the rock shrimp and you will see how the prosaic is given a boost. The shrimp are fried tempura-style and presented in a Chinese restaurant paper carton. You get not one, but two sauces, spicy cocktail and a stylized tartar. And, yes, you can eat these with supplied chop sticks, stab them with a fork, or even as finger food with your pinkies. If you like the idea of tempura shell-fish, make a bee-line, or a lobster-line, for lobster tempura which also gets two sauces, Japanese *ponzo*, which is nothing more than soy sauce and lemon juice, or a cream-based caviar dressing.

Among other first course crowd pleasers is grilled eggplant, served as a Napoleon with layers of roasted red peppers and goat cheese. Steamed mussels and Manila clams are paired together in a rather typical white wine and garlic bath, while portobello mushrooms are carved *carpaccio* style into parchment-thin slices, set on a bed of arugula and dressed with balsamic vinegar and a top of shaved parmesan cheese.

As for entrees, steak gets lots of attention under the menu heading "1200° F" which is the temperature of the oven where meats get the once-over. Choices read much like any good steakhouse: filet mignon with béarnaise sauce, porterhouse, New York sirloin, the most flavorful of them all . . . rib eye on the bone. I ordered a veal porterhouse which was succulent, juicy and perfectly cooked.

As for those other entree selections, Chilean sea bass is wrapped in pancetta for some added flavor. Black trumpet mushrooms are the garnish, as is white truffle oil. Red snapper is another deep sea selection; the whole fish is roasted and served more or less as it would be in a Greek restaurant with olive oil, lemons and oregano. Ahi tuna is given a seared crust and a rare center. Roasted peppers and a caper relish are the platter companions. Salmon, caught off the coast of Maine, is accompanied by yukon gold mashed potatoes, lightly-flavored caramelized fennel and a green garnish of radicchio and basil.

Desserts follow the American theme of the rest of the menu. The banana tart is served warm on what amounts to more of a cookie dough crust than a tart pastry. Caramel sauce, vanilla ice cream and walnut brittle for crunch make this one a winner.

Noon O Kabab
KR 18/20
Decor 3/4   Hospitality 5/5   Food 9/10   Value 1/1

- **Iranian**
- **Chicago/North**
- **$**

4661 North Kedzie
Chicago
(773) 279-8899
Troubleshooter: Purvi
Mirnaghavi (owner)

Hours: Mon–Sat 11 am–10 pm,
Sun 11 am–3 pm
Credit Cards: No credit cards,
but personal checks are accepted
Reservations: No
Handicapped: Accessibility
limited, probably not possible for
wheelchairs
**Smoking and nonsmoking
sections:** Nonsmoking
Parking: Usually ample on the
street

A guest at a recent dinner party was born in Iran, which prompted my question. "What," I asked, "is the best Iranian or Persian restaurant in the city?" His answer came in the blink of an eye . . . Noon O Kabab.

Noon O Kabab is in a small corner storefront. There are tables with seating for about 30 people. The walls display a small array of Persian carpets and other creations from that complex and often misunderstood land. The sound of Farsi, the native tongue of Persia, is heard in conversation at some tables, mixed in with English and an assortment of accents at others.

We could not have been greeted with more warmth or friendliness. Though she had never seen us before, the hostess did all she could to guide us through the restaurant's menu, with suggestions and explanations. We expressed an interest in eggplant, which our dinner party acquaintance particularly extolled. She urged us to try an eggplant which was not on the menu. It had a deep mustard color, odd we thought. Its flavors were those of mint, lemons that added a bit of sharp bite, some garlic and possibly saffron or even turmeric for the color. It was delicious, especially when spread on the hot warm puffy bread, or *noon*, from which the restaurant takes its name.

The menu lists several appetizers whose names will easily be recognized by diners familiar with Middle Eastern foods, as well as a few not so familiar. But, even before we ordered anything, our hostess brought out a platter with that delicious warm bread, chunks of mild feta cheese, and slices of tomatoes and onions that seemed to have some light seasoning.

The menu has several kebabs, or grilled chicken, lamb and beef in an array of styles. Skewered Norwegian salmon is an unusual addition that is available from time to time. In the face of so many choices, a combination platter brings a bounty of kebabs, resting in their marinades and juices on a bed of the puffy *noon* bread which is much more than a decorative touch. The flavors of the meats and chicken are exceptionally delicious, perfectly cooked, moist and tender.

The restaurant serves no liquor; hot tea is recommended. Desserts include Levantine delights such as a honey sweet *baklava* lavished with ground nuts under a pastry domed crust.

NORTH POND CAFÉ
KR 19.5/20
Decor 4/4   Hospitality 4.5/5   Food 10/10   Value 1/1

- **American**
- **Chicago/Mid-North**
- **$$**

2610 North Cannon Drive in Lincoln Park
Chicago
(773) 477-5845
Troubleshooter: Amy Lewis (general manager)

Hours: (Winter) Dinner Tues–Sat 5–9:30 pm, Sun 5–8:30 pm, Brunch Sun 11–2 pm, closed Mon, (Summer, April 1st–Dec 31st) Lunch 11 am–2 pm, Dinner is the same as winter
Credit Cards: All majors except Discover
Reservations: Recommended
Handicapped: Accessible
Smoking and nonsmoking sections: No smoking
Parking: Street parking very difficult

P arking is such a horrendous problem at North Pond Café, that I had second thoughts about even doing a review. But it is so good that the travails of finding it and getting there are worth the effort. For those who do not live within walking distance, the best access is by taxi, unless you should somehow be lucky enough to find street parking on either Cannon Drive or Lincoln Park West. With that caveat, North Pond Café is one of the more intriguing new restaurants to grace Chicago. It's housed in an old Park District Field house that has been completely remodeled, including its state of the art open kitchen.

For starters, cornmeal-crusted oysters in concert with oyster mushrooms is close in taste and succulence to those found and eaten on Cape Cod. The oysters and mushrooms are served on a bed of arugula and corn kernels, with a light brushing of Tabasco-infused butter. A recent daily special, not on the printed, menu brought incredibly indulgent sweetbreads on a risotto bedding laced with a compliment of flavors.

Other first course selections range from a cream-based pumpkin soup with mushroom and cranberry garnish, a wild mushroom pizza whose topping includes Swiss chard and edible flowers, and roasted quail with a marmalade somehow created from cabbage. The sauce is made of Michigan pears that have been spiced.

From among recent entrees, grilled venison is set on a ragout with a stuffed chili pepper, a rather stylized version of a chili relleno. Other entrees include grilled tenderloin chop plated with sour cream potato terrine, grilled lamb with smoked bacon, soybeans and olives worked down into a stew, and a very indulgent duck breast with Smithfield ham and oyster gumbo. Even good old American turkey gets its due with a crust of berries and a side of saffron potatoes as part of the plating.

For seafood, the choices include grilled halibut. The flavor does not come from the fish, but from a relish of lobster meat, corn and brussels sprouts all set out with lobster sauce stripes painted across the serving platter. In another entree, salmon is roasted and set out on a bed of vegetables with a very light mustard sauce.

Desserts are incredibly tempting, be it peanut and cashew pie, sweet potato pie, cider custard pie or something ravishingly chocolate. You'll hate the parking situation, but love the restaurant.

OCEANIQUE
KR 18.75/20
Decor 3/4   Hospitality 5/5   Food 10/10   Value .75/1

- **French Seafood**
- **Evanston**
- **$$$**

505 Main Street
Evanston
(847) 864-3435
Troubleshooter: Mark Groz
(chef/owner)

Hours: Mon–Thurs 5:30–9:30 pm, Fri–Sat until 10:30 pm
Credit Cards: All majors, no personal checks
Reservations: Recommended
Handicapped: Accessible
Smoking and nonsmoking sections: Smoking permitted only at bar
Parking: On street or in nearby lot, but can be very difficult on weekends

O ceanique is decorated in light earth tones. Walls are a wash of peach, or salmon depending upon the light and your eyes' interpretation of color. The hard tile floor reflects sound without mercy, which leaves the restaurant noisier than I prefer, though swags of drapery hanging from the ceilings add some visual interest, and I suspect some acoustic damping.

The essence of a great kitchen, to my way of thinking, lies in its soups. Consomme, for instance, while hardly thought of as challenging, is in fact one of the more difficult broths to prepare correctly. The goal is clarity, an almost clear broth with a clean, singular flavor. Oceanique's consomme is infused with the flavor of lobster. A *mirepoix* is added to the clear soup for some color and texture. More substantial is the inclusion of small ravioli pillows filled with a forcemeat of dark mushrooms. Together, these are complimentary flavors, and while I don't want to make too much of an issue here, this is a soup which tests the mettle of culinary expertise.

There are several other tempting selections for a first course, ranging from roasted oysters with leeks, truffles and chives to small ravioli stuffed with butternut squash set in a duck stock flavored with brown butter that brings a nutty taste, underscored by parmesan cheese and walnut sauce.

When it comes to the main course listing, the choices only get more difficult. You will make no mistake with the restaurant's version of *bouillabaisse* and its traditional saffron broth.

Chef Marc Groz does wonders with codfish. Traditionally prepared as salt cod, Groz instead roasts the fish, then brings tastes of fresh roasted corn, garlic mashed potatoes and an olive sauce onto the flavor stage. Each ingredient is entitled to take a bow, especially the fish, one of the more identifiably flavored catches.

Skatefish is, like cod, an under appreciated fish. Its pure white meaty flesh is wonderful when sautéed in olive oil and bread crumbs, then paired with asparagus and butternut squash. Tomatoes, tarragon and citrus flavors are brought together for a sauce. While on the subject of sauce, port and beaujolais are reduced into a near syrup to enhance whitefish sauteed with caramelized red onions. Don't ever let anyone get away with telling you that red wine has no place with seafood, at least in this instance.

For those diners whose tastes are landlocked, the choices include roasted rack of venison in a shiraz wine and black currant sauce with cooked red cabbage, spinach and endive. Rack of lamb, roasted sirloin of beef and squab are other selections, each with an appropriate accompaniment of vegetables and saucing.

The dessert plate varies daily with its selection of pastries, plus a choice of ice creams and sorbets. To finish in grand fashion select the platter of cheeses and pears.

OLD ORLEANS
KR 17.5/20
Decor 4/4   Hospitality 4/5   Food 8.5/10   Value 1/1

- **New Orleans/ Cajun/Creole**
- **Evanston**
- **$**

1458 Sherman Avenue
Evanston
(847) 475-4804
Troubleshooters: Charles Murray (chef/owner), Dennis Brown and Mark Fondow (managing partners)

Hours: Lunch Mon–Fri 11 am–2 pm, Dinner Mon–Thurs 5–10 pm, Fri until 10:30 pm, Sat noon–10:30 pm, Sun Brunch 11 am–3 pm, Dinner 5–9 pm
Credit Cards: All majors
Reservations: Suggested
Handicapped: Accessible
Smoking and nonsmoking sections: Smoking is permitted in a small section of the restaurant
Parking: On street or in public garage across the street

Old Orelans looks just about perfect. The only things missing are a cooler out front filled with bottles of Big Orange and RC Cola, a stand holding Moon Pies, and some flies buzzing around a rickety screen door which slams when you close it because it has lost its spring tension. Inside, tables are covered with gingham patterned oil cloth. You probably won't find too many chairs that match.

The menu is kind of a culinary roadmap of bayou country. Old Orleans is the sort of restaurant you want to visit with a few people and order family-style so you can taste some of this and some of that. "Red Beans and Rice" is more than just the name of a good ol' Rhythm 'n Blues tune. It's classic Southern cooking with a sizzle of andouille sausage, which is pretty much the standard issue with its deep smoky flavor. It's also used to spruce up the likes of jambalaya and gumbo as well as a couple of other platters.

Other appetizer selections include cayenne pepper spiced chicken wings, old fashioned Johnny cakes, which are kind of like the Southern version of Italy's polenta, plus other assorted nibbles and salads.

You could order delicious gumbo in an appetizer or dinner portion, which sets the pace for your soup course. The *etoufee*, a crawfish and rice dish smothered with a creamy gravy, is sublime, the ribs virtually fall apart in your hands they are so tender, and the shrimp creole is deliciously seasoned, without being too spicy. You can always add more hot sauce to your taste.

By this time, if you feel guilty about the calories, order a fresh slice of sweet potato pie for dessert . . . but consider it your vegetable course.

ONE SIXTYBLUE
KR 20/20
Decor 4/4   Hospitality 5/5   Food 10/10   Value 1/1

- **Continental**
- **Chicago/Near West**
- **$$$**

160 North Loomis at Randolph
and Ogden
Chicago
(312) 850-0303
Troubleshooter: John Ross
(manager)

Hours: Mon–Thurs 5–10 pm,
Fri–Sat 5 pm–11 pm, closed Sun
Credit Cards: Visa, MC, Diners,
Amex
Reservations: Required
Handicapped: Accessible
Bar: Full service
**Smoking and nonsmoking
sections:** No smoking in dining
room, smoking in bar
Parking: Valet $6 or street

O ne Sixtyblue is called that because it is in a blue building that previously was a pickle factory. The decor, put together at something like $3.5 million is elegant without being flashy, contemporary without being over the top. Most striking may be the floor-to-ceiling wine rack fronted by a glass wall. On the other hand, the open kitchen is a focal point too, though open kitchens are no longer anything special in modern restaurant design.

The food is a formidable execution of a culinary architecture which, like the restaurant's design itself, is startling. As for specifics, a *tian,* or small round baking pot, is used to mold a puree of celery root matched with a course chop of sturgeon gravlox plated with thimble size potato cups, one filled with *creme fraiche* and the other with caviar. Flavors are delicate and in balance. Something sturdier is afoot with a mix of sautéed wild mushrooms set in a broth of their own juices enriched by polenta creamed with creamed mascarpone cheese.

Among other contemplations are crisp sweetbreads with whipped potato and caramelized endive plus bits of lime for bite, while a simple French lentil or bean soup can be had as is, or with the extravagant embellishment of black truffles and chestnuts. The chef's brilliant extrapolations among main course dining choices include seared yellowfin tuna set out with potatoes, green beans and onions, then napped in an oil emulsified with verbena, a tropical herb with a distinctive lemon taste. In another plating, sea scallops are dry roasted, which gives them a bit of a crust, but still tender inside. Porcini mushrooms make up the predominant flavor enhancer, though a touch of curry adds some spice, while thin rounds of roasted cauliflower bring some texture.

Vegetarian platters will be created on request, beautiful arrangements to be sure, while meats include imaginative and stylish renditions of pan-roasted chicken, veal loin, grilled delmonico steaks and duck breast among others.

THE OUTPOST
KR 18/20
Decor 4/4   Hospitality 5/5   Food 8/10   Value 1/1

- **Fusion**
- **Chicago/Mid-North**
- **$$**

3438 North Clark Street
Chicago
(773) 244-1166
Troubleshooter: Kevin
O'Donnell (owner)

Hours: Dinner Sun–Thurs 5:30 pm–midnight, Fri–Sat until 1 am, Sunday Brunch 10 am–2 pm
Credit Cards: All majors
Reservations: Accepted
Smoking and nonsmoking sections: Smoking and nonsmoking seating, smoking permitted at bar
Parking: Lot across the street, street parking tight
Handicapped: Accessibility is difficult

As I wrote a few years ago, without knowing what was going on inside, you would think this just another Wrigleyville bar and grill. Currently, Chef Kevin Shikami brings his style of fusion cooking to a neighborhood where fusion heretofore has been more in the vast array of culinary styles that can be found in a single block or two.

Shikami honed his skills at Jimmy's Place, a truly great restaurant owned by the late Jimmy Rohr. It was there that Shikami became a Chicago pioneer of that cooking technique which melded the French culinary classics with the consummate style of Japan and China. Drawing on two established traditions, he helped make a new one for Chicago diners.

While fusion cooking is no longer the novelty it was, the results can be extraordinary. So it is at The Outpost. Begin with a lovely tuna tartare appetizer. Chunks of tuna are glazed with wasabi vinaigrette; tiny pickled cucumber slices and pink curlicues of ginger establish the Japanese genesis of Shikami's work. On the other hand, seared ostrich is more contemporary, with its use of Balsamic vinegar as basis for a glaze on a meat which I think gets more exposure than it is worth, and is usually more a dining novelty.

A Tasting Plate is a good way to sample delicate spring rolls, each only bite size with a haze of minty flavor. Among other tidbits, wonton noodle wraps contain a mix of fresh corn kernels, with the snap of chili and cilantro, kind of like a corn relish, but with much more panache.

Entrees tend more to the New World than the Old. Still, seared tuna comes plated with a quartet of maki sushi avocado rolls, pickled ginger and a red miso and soy sauce. It's good, though probably not the best that Chef Shikami can do when challenged. His version of duck, primarily the dark meat breast and a spring roll filled with a confit of duck, is far more interesting especially with a sauce based on Chinese Hoison and honey star anise.

The menu turns more mainstream with the likes of a roasted filet mignon in a red wine sauce set with blue cheese flavored risotto, crushed walnuts and portobello mushroom slices. Even pasta is special. Twisted cavatappi noodles get a royal treatment with lots of garlic and basil, plus snips of prosciutto and the bitter underpinnings of rapini, with pecorino and romano cheeses for depth. Desserts can vary from day to day. There is an excellent list of single malt Scotch options as well as wine and other potables.

THE PALM
KR 20/20
Decor 4/4   Hospitality 5/5   Food 10/10   Value 1/1

- **American**
- **Chicago**
- **$$$**

323 East Wacker Drive (at the Swissotel)
Chicago
(312) 616-1000
Troubleshooter: John Blandino (general manager)

Hours: Daily 11:30 am–11 pm
Credit Cards: Amex, Diners MC, Visa
Reservations: Suggested
Handicapped: Accessible
Smoking and nonsmoking sections: Both available
Parking: Valet, street and lot

The Palm is characterized by walls of famous cartoon caricatures of well known celebrities and VIPs, as well as the sawdust-covered floors and overhead ceiling fans reminiscent of Chicago's speakeasy days. But, make no mistake about the fact that the restaurant is part of a vital chain which began in 1926 in New York City and now stretches from the Hamptons to Los Angeles.

The restaurant is famous for its truly gargantuan sized portions, from baked potatoes to whole live Nova Scotia lobsters, plus huge prime New York cut steaks, tender lamb and milk-fed veal. Other seafood in addition to the whole lobsters includes swordfish, shrimp and salmon. All dishes are cooked to order in portions definitely not for finicky appetites. Specials include pepper-seared tuna steak with plum tomato salsa, pecan-crusted soft-shell crabs (in season) with asparagus sauce and fresh crab and wild mushrooms inside a puff pastry shell. For dessert, the specialty of the house is cheesecake, rich, heavy and everything New York–style cheesecake should be.

PAPA MILANO
KR 16/20
Decor 3/4   Hospitality 4/5   Food 8/10   Value 1/1

- **Italian**
- **Chicago/Near North**
- **$$**

951 North State Street
Chicago
(312) 787-3710
Troubleshooter: Rosmarie
(owner)

Hours: Mon–Thurs 11:30 am–
10:30 pm, Fri and Sat noon–
11:30 pm, Sun 1–10:30 pm
Credit Cards: Amex, CB,
Diners, MC, Visa
Reservations: Only for parties
of six or more
Handicapped: Accessible with
difficulty, no space for wheelchairs
Parking: Validated at nearby
garage, tight on street at meters

When it comes to retro Italian dining, Papa Milano sets the mold. It is small, though not cramped. There is nominal separation of smoking and nonsmoking seating, so don't be surprised if you pick up a whiff or two of somebody's cigarette.

But, if you want the old-fashioned kind of spaghetti and meatballs that used to be Italian restaurant cooking, that's what you will find at Papa Milano, along with the celebrity photographs mounted high along the walls. If nothing else, there's character, and plenty of it.

I don't remember the last time I had a *scungilli* salad as good as that at Papa Milano. Scungilli are conch, sliced thin, marinated and plated with sweet peppers, garlic, vinegar and oil. You will also find absolutely delicious roasted peppers as an appetizer along with the likes of baked clams by the half or full dozen. These are buttery sweet, with a sauce that you are going to scoop up with pieces of warm Italian bread and savor to the last, final drop.

Among other appetizers the choices run from a variety of dinner-sized salads, to hearty soups such as minestrone and escarole to fried calamari and a mixed antipasto platter.

Pizzas are popular among regulars, thin crusted and, like the rest of the restaurant, the old-fashioned sort. As for pastas, the portions are prodigious. Linguine in red or white clam sauce is enough to share with two or three people. It's too bad the restaurant serves half orders only to children. On the other hand, chances are there will be something left over to take home. It's that kind of a place.

You'll find the expected list of other pastas including spaghetti and meatballs. These are the kind that bring two or three kinds of ground meat together with a savory mix of herbs and seasonings. The basic red sauce is . . . well, the best description that comes to mind is "old-fashioned," bright colored with fresh tomatoes.

Among other entrees, a classic version of chicken vesuvio comes in a huge portion with deliciously roasted potatoes and chicken that begs to be taken in hand and pulled apart. More than a dozen chicken and veal choices stud the menu. After dinner, each table is rewarded with a platter of Italian cookies and biscotti. The wine list is short, nothing pretentious.

PAPAGUS GREEK TAVERNA
KR 17.5/20
Decor 4/4   Hospitality 5/5   Food 7.5/10   Value 1/1

- **Greek Contemporary**
- **Chicago/Near North**
- **$$**

Embassy Suites,
620 North State Street
Chicago
(312) 642-8450
Troubleshooters: Yorgo Koutsogiorgas and Jimmy Banakis (managing partners)

Other Location

272 Oakbrook Center, Oakbrook; 630-472-9800; Hours: Mon–Thurs 11:30 am–10 pm, Fri–Sat 11:30 am–midnight, Sun noon–9 pm Parking: Free in lot or valet

Hours: Mon–Thurs 11:30 am–10 pm, Fri 11:30 am–midnight, Sat noon–midnight, Sun noon–10 pm (lounge open one hour later every night)
Credit Cards: All majors
Reservations: Accepted
Handicapped: Accessible
Smoking and nonsmoking sections: Both available
Parking: Validated in nearby lot

T he Classical Greek philosophers knew that "less is more," a lesson lost on Papagus. This "restaurant as theatre" seeks to replicate a typical Greek *taberna* and the kind of foods one might be served in a Grecian home.

There is no question that the food served here is exceptionally delicious. But, typical Greek home cooking? The presentations and styles of cookery are simply too elaborate to be anything but stylizations by a very talented chef. So, if you want a real Greek restaurant, go to Halsted Street.

With that said, the brass tacks of Papagus is that it is a fine restaurant, handsomely appointed with cobblestone floors, fieldstone wall accents, an open delicatessen and oven, and some genuinely delicious food, at fairly moderate cost. Soon after being seated, a waiter takes drink orders, then brings over a large wooden tray with seven or eight appetizers, or *mezzes*. These are not show pieces, but freshly prepared menu choices. You can take right from the tray, or go to the menu and make other specific selections. There are some wonderful ideas here, many of them spinoffs of traditional Greek cooking, but with more elaboration and panache. Close to the traditional might be *dolmades*, chilled grape leaves stuffed with a seasoned, even sweetened, rice filling. Or, taste chicken with bulgur wheat, a savory taste and texture experience. Asparagus salad brings thin spears dressed in a balanced oil and herbed vinegar. The choices go on and one including potato spreads, with or without garlic, a blend of peppers, lamb, nuts and raisins, and roasted eggplant puree. From the collection of warm appetizers are Papagus versions of *moussaka*, *saganaki*, Greek sausage and the like.

One can go on and on with the appetizers, without even touching larger portioned entrees. But, should you move on, consider skewered fresh fish. Recently, large cubes of tuna and salmon were served in a slightly sweet herbal sauce that brought together oil, sun-dried tomatoes and other flavorings, to achieve a well-balanced whole. Lamb, the staple of Grecian dining, is served in several fashions. But, sliced from the roasted leg is about as tasty as you can get. The meat comes out with just a hint of its pink center, demonstrating that this is not the kind of stringy lamb that is overcooked to disguise its faults. Roasted fresh vegetables accompany the meat, still crisp and textured. One of the more original selections is chicken gyros, in which the chicken is roasted on the vertical gyros spit, flaked into bite-size strips and served with wedges of pita, dilled yogurt and thinly sliced red onions. Perhaps not authentic, it is demonstrative of the prevalent imagination.

Among desserts, *baklava* stuffed with walnuts is not to be believed, or you might want to try chocolate pita, just as a curiosity.

PAPPADEAUX
KR 17.5/20
Decor 4/4   Hospitality 4/5   Food 8.5/10   Value 1/1

- **American Southern Gulf Coastal**
- **Arlington Heights**
- **$$**

798 West Algonquin Road
(at Golf)
Arlington Heights
(847) 228-9551
Troubleshooter: Jack Gibbons
(general manager)

Hours: Lunch Mon–Fri 11:30 am–2:30 pm, Dinner Mon–Thurs 5–10 pm, Fri 5–11 pm, Sat noon–11 pm, Sun noon–9 pm
Credit Cards: Amex, MC, Visa
Reservations: Not accepted (waits can be long, but large parties of six or more can call ahead)
Handicapped: Accessible
Smoking and nonsmoking sections: Both available
Parking: Ample free lot parking

First time diners will be struck, if not overwhelmed with the restaurant's unusual exterior and its dining areas inside. Pappadeaux looks something like a southern roadhouse, though that description hardly does justice to the subject. It is big, sprawling, a patchwork of shapes and angles. It looks almost futuristic, maybe like a roadhouse from Oz.

This is first and foremost a seafood restaurant. The lobster tank can be populated with crustaceans in the 3- to 4-pound range, as well as more manageable one and two pounders. Whole slabs of cut up fish fillets ice in display cases. The air is filled with a medley of seasonings and spices, evident as a perfume even outside the restaurant.

Begin with oysters Pappadeaux, a variation of oysters rockefeller. Or get down and dirty with boudin, straight out of cajun country. This smooth ground pork sausage is stuffed with dirty rice, a regional specialty in which the rice is mixed with chicken gizzards or livers, leaving a characteristic appearance. The name may not sound nice, but it's delicious.

Pappadeaux takes a bit of a liberty with the classic *beignet* and turns them into deep-fried pieces of fish, plated with spicy french fries. It is possible to get away from the fried appetizers which seem to predominate. Try one of the gumbos, the dark and delicious New Orleans–style seafood soups. The flavors are spicy, but not peppery hot. If you want something milder, crawfish bisque in a cream stock will hit the spot.

Speaking of crawfish brings me to the definitive point I have to make about Pappadeaux. The crawfish etoufee is the very best I have ever tasted. Etoufee has become a benchmark for me, a standard of measurement. A bounty of shelled crawfish have been cooked in butter with onions and garlic and other ingredients until a sauce begins to thicken. It's all scooped out of the pan and served over rice, a smothering portion which lives up to the meaning of the French word *etoufee* as it has been adopted into the language of the cuisine. This is the satisfying, lip-smacking good eating that makes you sorry when you are full because the flavors, textures and all the other pleasurable sensations must finally come to an end.

If you have a taste for frog legs, you will smile with genuine glee at the sizable portion that spills across its serving platter. Blackened seafood, the style of cooking Paul Prudhomme makes so famous, is on the menu, used exclusively for farm-raised catfish fillets.

If seafood is not to your taste, even as good as it gets at Pappadeaux, alternate choices include country-style chicken with garlic mashed potatoes and broccoli and a couple of cuts of beef steak.

Desserts include extra rich sweet potato pecan pie with a scoop of ice cream, bread pudding with bourbon sauce, key lime pie and chocolate praline cheesecake among selections.

PARK AVENUE CAFÉ
KR 19/20
Decor 4/4   Hospitality 4/5   Food 10/10   Value 1/1

- **American**
- **Chicago**
- **$$$**

199 East Walton
Chicago
(312) 944-4414
Troubleshooter: Joan Kim
(office manager)

Hours: Daily 5–11 pm, Brunch
Sun 10:30 am–2 pm
Credit Cards: All majors
Reservations: Recommended
Handicapped: Accessible
**Smoking and nonsmoking
sections:** Both available, no
cigars in main dining room
Parking: Valet available

New York Chef David Burke is the inspiration for the cookery at Park Avenue Café. Diners will find an emphasis on creativity and innovation, but not at the price of contrivance. Salmon, which is usually smoked, is an absolutely fantastic flavor sensation when cured as if it were beef pastrami. The pastrami salmon is plated as part of a trio along with conventional smoked salmon and a portion of salmon tartare. Corn meal blini garnish the platter.

In another sensational appetizer home made cavatelli are portioned with wild mushrooms sautéed in white truffle oil. Among other selections is a whole barbecued squab paired with foie gras worked into the batter of a cornbread cake. Taking the squab and a dab of the rich foie gras mixture together on the palate brings an incredible rush of sensuous texture and flavor.

The creative demiurge comes forward in entrees such as an elaborate presentation of venison. The loin is roasted, then plated with ravioli and butternut squash worked into a spoonbread. The surprise is in the ravioli, maple syrup that spills out when you cut into it, the syrup adding its own essence to the meat.

Park Avenue Café's version of steak brings an aged dry rib eye, while rack of lamb is glazed with rosemary. Seafood abounds on the menu, including the trade marked swordfish chop. Even more astounding than the swordfish chop is grilled lobster steak. In this recipe, whole lobster is removed from its shell, then packed or wrapped into a tight round about the size of a filet mignon. The lobster is grilled just as steak might be, then topped with a huge pile of curry-flavored shoestring potatoes.

Truly, the enthusiastic diner must save an appetite for dessert. They are literally works of art. One brings a selection of candies, cookies and other confections on a model antique cast iron stove. Even more of a fantasy is Opera in the Park. Here, a park bench and lamp post are fashioned out of chocolate.

PARKERS' OCEAN GRILL
KR 18/20
Decor 4/4   Hospitality 5/5   Food 8/10   Value 1/1

- **American Seafood**
- **Downer's Grove**
- **$$**

1000 31st Street
Downer's Grove
(630) 960-5701
Troubleshooter: Manager on
duty

Hours: Lunch Mon–Fri 11:30
am–2:30 pm, Dinner Mon–Thurs
5–10 pm, Fri–Sat until 11 pm,
Sun 4–9 pm
Credit Cards: All majors
Reservations: Suggested
Handicapped: Accessible
**Smoking and nonsmoking
sections:** Smoking only in lounge
Parking: Free in lot or valet $2

There isn't an ocean within a 1000 miles of Parkers' Ocean Grill. That does not prevent this handsome and stylish restaurant from serving some interesting and well-prepared seafood.

The large dining room sits off of a comfortable bar and piano lounge. At one end of the dining room is a warming fire place, and at the other an enclosed porch whose doors can be swung open in warm weather.

Among starters, shrimp speared on sugar cane are tucked yin and yang–style together with sliced avocado, watercress and a mild *wasabi* soy vinaigrette for the greens. The shrimp are roasted in an oven fueled by hardwoods, an oven clearly visible in the restaurant's open kitchen. That wood roasting is also used for some of the main course selections whether it is chicken with rosemary and garlic, or the fresh fish. Atlantic salmon is served in a couple of fashions In one version of the salmon, a bed of mashed potatoes rests beneath the fish which is given a chive butter sauce with fried leeks. The other salmon is coupled with roasted new potatoes and sun-dried tomatoes plus sautéed fresh spinach. Farm-raised sturgeon is set on a cedar plank, and accompanied by a large mound of horseradish mashed potatoes. It's all very tasty. The only flaw with this, and some of the other seafood, is the almost too abundant olive oil or butter sauce, as the case may be, glazed over the fish. As the menu points out, all of the restaurant's featured fish can be prepared in a simpler cooking style.

Parkers' Ocean Grill features its take on *cioppino*, and even a couple of Italian influenced entrees. *Penne* is given a peppery *arrabiatta*-style tomato and light cream sauce and plated with rock shrimp. In another, linguini and manila clams are brought together, with a little cream plus garlic, olive oil and white wine among contributors.

Seafood Risotto Milanese is a delicious creation with a good bit of saffron. The rice has been simmered in a seafood stock with leeks and a collection of soft- and shellfish. The only flaw, as with so many restaurant risottos, is the advance semi-preparation. In this case, the rice should be chewier, but considering how good it all tastes, I hate to be a quibbler.

Desserts include something called an ice cream tower, banana bread pudding with caramel sauce and other rich and heady sweets. Service could not be better. There is valet parking. Expect to spend about $55 a couple for three courses plus add ons.

PARTHENON
KR 16.5/20
Decor 3/4   Hospitality 4/5   Food 8.5/10   Value 1/1

- **Greek**
- **Chicago/Near West**
- **$$**

314 South Halsted
Chicago
(312) 726-2407
Troubleshooters: Chris Liakouras, Peter Liakouras (owners)

Hours: Sun–Thurs 11–1 am, Fri–Sat until 2 am
Credit Cards: All majors and house accounts
Reservations: For parties of six or larger
Handicapped: Accessible
Bar: Full service, wines and beers
Smoking and nonsmoking sections: Separare smoking and nonsmoking seating
Parking: Valet or street
Party Facilities: Private party facilitates for 50–200

Parthenon may not be as old as its namesake on the Acropolis, but this restaurant seems to have been a fixture of Chicago's Greektown just about forever.

Seafood is a natural specialty for Greek restaurants, and Parthenon is no exception. The red snapper is lovely at market price. Sea bass has a milder flavor, and when available, should please most any seafood fancier. Each comes broiled, brushed with olive oil, freshly squeezed lemon juice and oregano proving that golden mean of ancient Hellas which teaches "less is more."

But, when it comes to portion sizes, more is more. Appetizers are large enough to serve two people. Try the traditional rice-stuffed grape leaves called *dolmades* with a creamy lemon sauce, or little cheese pies in phylo dough stuffed to bursting.

And, while the menu presents the tried-and-true Greek specialties found up and down Halsted, there are also some rather unusual choices, such as barbecued whole roast suckling pig for groups of 12. (This requires advance notice). Perhaps most exotic is lamb's head, baked and served with oven-roasted potatoes. For more conventional lamb, try roast loin or leg, or even barbecued on the spit. Most entrees are served with rice or potatoes, some include a side of vegetables.

Combination platters include appetizer mezze priced per person, as well as full dinner combinations rounding up the usual suspects, *moussaka*, *pastitso*, roast lamb, potatoes and vegetables. Desserts are typically sweet, though a homemade yoghurt offers a somewhat different alternative to a meal's conclusion.

PASHA
KR 18.5/20
Decor 3.5/4   Hospitality 4/5   Food 10/10   Value 1/1

- **Eclectic Mediteranean**
- **Chicago/River North**
- **$$$**

642 North Clark Street
Chicago
(312) 397-0100
Troubleshooter: Kenny
Johnson (owner)

Hours: Sun–Fri. 5 pm–3 am,
Sat 5 pm–4 am
Credit Cards: All majors except Transmedia
Reservations: Recommended
Handicapped: Accessible
Smoking and nonsmoking sections: Separate smoking and nonsmoking seating
Parking: Valet $8

Pasha is decidedly hip and very, very cool, a current hot spot for the glitterati of Chicago's nightlife. It has a definite club atmosphere with a great looking copper-topped bar. I have not investigated this myself, but there is also a private bar for women only, where else but in the lady's room? Very cool, indeed!

Yet, if Pasha had none of this it would stand on the merits of its kitchen. Chef Gaetano De Benedetto cooks from a Continental perspective and has created a wonderfully inventive menu. When was the last time you had a dessert with black pepper as an ingredient? You'll find it on the dessert menu, where a signature creation, Black Passion, combines mixed fresh berries in a fruited sauce with a scoop of rich vanilla bean ice cream, a splash of vodka, and a few twists from the pepper mill. An edible chocolate bowl merely gilds the lily.

That's the sort of thing you will want to save room for. But, that might be difficult because selections from the menu are so rigorously tempting. Try a crabcake terrine with a centerpiece of chilled stone crab sandwiched in between slices of salmon, tuna and a layer of bread salad, all flavored with tomato and balsamic vinegar relish.

From among hot appetizers, to say that the mushroom ragout is great is to understate the fact. It may not be as original a concept as some other menu choices, but it is exemplary. So, too, for mussels in saffron flamed with a touch of Armagnac among its index of ingredients.

Among pastas and entrees, the house special named Pappardelle Pasha is a luxuriant preparation with large chunks of lobster and shallots in a rich tomato and cream sauce that coats sheets of home made pappardelle noodles. A splash of Cognac set aflame makes this not only visually hot, but a sensual delight.

Among other entrees, Chef de Benedetto takes white fish, fillets it and layers the fish with wild mushrooms and truffle butter. Then, it's under the broiler for a full glaze set out on a bed of greens and angel hair pasta extruded from potato dough. For something even more elaborate, try a veal chop stuffed with a course chop of stone crab meat, then glazed with a reduction of veal stock, then finished with a topping of baby shrimp. Portions are large enough to be shared, which is probably a good tactic considering how rich much of this cooking can be.

A P P E T I Z E R S

c o l d

Tuna Tartare
Yellow Fin Tuna, capers, cornichons,
parsley, onions, lemon & olive oil $ 10

Beef Carpaccio
Beef Filet, slice black truffle, imported
Parmesan cheese, white truffle oil $ 9

Bruschetta
toast points topped with fresh basil,
chopped tomato & garlic $ 6

Bresaola & Goat Cheese Bundles
aged French goat cheese, imported Bresaola,
baby greens, balsamic vinaigrette $ 9

Seafood Salad
calamari, shrimp, scallops, mussels, octopus,
citronette sauce, kalamata olives, tomato $ 11

Crab Cake Sushimi Terrine
chilled stone crab, fresh salmon, tuna,
tomato balsamic relish $ 11

Pate De Fois Gras
pate, morel mushrooms, truffles, baby
greens, raspberry-vinaigrette $ 9

h o t

Grilled Brie Cheese
baby Brie cheese, grilled, bed of
herb-scented wild mushrooms $ 8

Shrimp & Gorgonzola
gulf shrimp, sauteed with Gorgonzola cheese,
garlic, cream, puff pastry $ 9

Carciofi Alla Loren
artichoke hearts, fresh tomato, touch of
garlic, white wine sauce $ 9

Mushroom Ragout
Portabello, Cremini, Shitake & Oyster
mushrooms,
shaved garlic, parsley, Marsala wine $ 9

Mussels Tomato Fumè
mussels sautéed with garlic, white wine,
basil, parsley and tomato fumè $ 8

Mussels in Saffron
mussels & leeks, tomato concassè, saffron,
sweet cream, basil, armagnac $ 8

Potato Roulade
caramelized onion, mascarpone cheese,
au-gratin with Parmesan cheese $ 6

PATRICK & JAMES
KR 18.5/20

Decor 4/4   Hospitality 4/5   Food 9.5/10   Value 1/1

- **American Eclectic**
- **Glencoe**
- **$$$**

368 Park Avenue
Glencoe
(847) 835-7000
Troubleshooter: Patrick O'Neil
(owner)

Hours: Lunch Mon–Fri 11:30 am–2 pm, Dinner Mon–Thurs 5–9 pm, Fri–Sat 5–10 pm, Sun 5–8:30 pm
Credit Cards: MC, Visa
Reservations: Suggested weeknights, mandatory weekend evenings
Handicapped: Accessible, full wheelchair accessibility (ramp in back of restaurant, call for specifics)
Smoking and nonsmoking sections: Smoking not permitted
Parking: On street, can be difficult

Patrick & James is far and away one of the most ambitiously designed and dramatic restaurants on the North Shore. That design is strikingly eclectic. Massive paired Gothic arabesque chandeliers that came from a South Side synagog are suspended over a huge wood carved sideboard, bar and vast mirror which was taken from one of those riverboats that cruise the Ohio and Mississippi Rivers. Over on a facing wall is a large wall tapestry that looks somewhat like circus sideshow art.

In the main dining room, the focus is the stained glass ceiling which towers overhead as a circular dome, blazing with bold orange and yellow colors. My favorite design touch, however, is a wooden cased clock which looks as if it may have been taken from an old train station where it told the comings and goings of travelers a century ago.

The same care that went into the restaurant's design is reflected in the menu and service. Diners sit at marble-topped tables to await an array of foods whose presentations are as dramatic in appearance as the setting. The quality of preparation is evident in the careful platings.

From a short list of appetizers, selections include deliciously indulgent ravioli with a filling of roasted garlic and artichoke hearts. The flavor is mild enough to be masked by a buttery rich sorrel sauce, perhaps a little more sauce than is needed. A bit of sautéed spinach leaf adds some color and texture.

After enjoying your appetizers, a fresh salad is a welcome transition. Try pears sliced with walnuts, a natural combination if one ever existed. Nauvoo blue cheese, a domestic Illinois veined cheese and a good rival to more widely known maytag blue produced in Iowa, is the perfect third leg for this tripod of flavors, accented with a light vinaigrette. If you go with the standard house issue salad of romaine, onions and tomatoes and honey mustard dressing you won't go wrong, while the house Caesar follows traditional preparation.

Among entrees, filet of beef is a fat hocky puck–sized round of prime meat charred black on the surfaces, garnished with mushroom risotto and set in a pool of garnet colored cabernet wine sauce. Among other meat selections, grilled loin of pork is festive with a cranberry sauce glaze plus a mound of cornbread and mushroom stuffing.

When it comes to seafood, the *cioppino* may not exactly be like that at a fish restaurant on the San Francisco wharf front, but it is still a lavish collection of shell- and soft-fish. Best of the lot may be sea bass, available from time to time. In the past it has been grilled with a crust of trumpet mushrooms and mild garlic mashed potatoes.

One more note . . . be sure to use the bathroom. Don't ask why! Just do it and I promise you'll thank me!

PEGASUS
KR 16.5/20
Decor 4/4   Hospitality 4/5   Food 7.5/10   Value 1/1

- **Greek**
- **Chicago/Near West**
- **$**

130 South Halsted
Chicago
(312) 226-3377
Troubleshooters: John Melidis, James Alexander (owners)

Hours: Daily 11 am–midnight
Credit Cards: All majors and house accounts
Handicapped: Accessible
Bar: Full service, Greek, California and French wines, roof garden café open in warm weather months
Smoking and nonsmoking sections: Separate smoking and nonsmoking seating
Parking: Free valet
Party Facilities: Semi-private facilities for up to 100 people

Pegasus is fairly large, but not cavernous. Its handsome whitewashed walls create the sense of a Mediterranean villa. The restaurant is fronted by French doors, which are opened in warm weather to create a café or *taberna* ambiance.

The menu is typical of Chicago Greek restaurants, the cooking not really any better nor worse than others. I do like the fact that Pegasus uses kaeseri cheese for their *saganaki* and some other dishes, rather than the more salty kefilatori. Pegasus also serves a delicious version of *lokaneko*, a spicy sausage appetizer. Other appetizers include traditional Greek phyllo-wrapped morsels, one style filled with feta cheese, or a more elaborate spinach and cheese version. The appetizer/salad selection lists about two dozen other choices, hot or cold.

Some appetizers can also be ordered in dinner-sized portions, such as spinach pie or gyros. A combination platter brings several slices of gyros, milder sliced leg of lamb, *pastitsio* and *dolmades*, plus rice, roasted potatoes and green beans. Meats are not cooked rare in Greek kitchens, thus the leg of lamb is a little too dry, but free of fat. The *dolmades*, ground meat stuffed in grape leaves, is fairly simple and direct, allowing the light flavor of the filling to contrast with the vegetal flavor of its wrapping. *Pastitsio*, a macaroni and cheese casserole bound together in a cream sauce, is lightly seasoned with cinnamon and other aromatics. The touch suggests moderation, a characteristic I noted in other preparations, too.

I have often said that most of the Greek restaurants up and down Halsted Street serve similar food and are made distinctive by other factors. An experience at Pegasus underscores this observation. Soon after we were seated, a large group of twenty or more people arrived and were shown to an area which they took up almost exclusively. After all had gathered, we noticed everyone stood, bowed their heads in prayer, and began their meal.

A manager explained they all came from, or had parents who came from the same village in Greece; this was one of their periodic gatherings. Such scenes add a unique touch to any restaurant that can only underscore its warmth and hospitality. And, though we by no stretch were any part of that or other groups, there was a warmth, even an intimacy that pervaded the entire dining area, if only for a few moments.

PENANG
KR 18/20
Decor 4/4   Hospitality 4/5   Food 9/10   Value 1/1

- **Malaysian**
- **Chicago/Near South**
- **$**

2201 South Wentworth
Chicago
(312) 326-6888
Troubleshooter: Ken Lim

Hours: Mon–Sun 11–1 am
Credit Cards: MC, Visa
Reservations: Accepted, suggested weekends
Smoking and nonsmoking sections: Both available weekdays, no smoking on weekends
Parking: In nearby lot with validated discount $2

Penang sits right astride the gateway to Chinatown, but it is not a Chinese restaurant. It is Maylasian with a semi-tropical bamboo decor and waiters who wear colorful *batiks* to help create the atmosphere. That atmosphere is also created by the diners who throng here, often large families with children or couples on a date. Clearly this is a restaurant that is accepted enthusiastically by Chicago's thriving Malaysian community.

Start with some finger food appetizers such as grilled *satays*, chicken, beef or even tofu, with a bit of sweet and mildly spiced peanut sauce. Try *roti canai*, a vegetable pancake clearly influenced by Indian cooking, as is another pancake made with oysters, eggs, onions, green chilis, and served with a luscious curried chicken and potato gravy.

Asian soups are some of the best on the planet and Penang has a long listing with or without noodles. What the menu simply calls fish porridge is a delightfully complex broth of herbs, spices and stock.

As is the usual practice with Asian restaurant menus, main course selections are categorized by the type of meat, vegetables or tofu that is the culinary focal point. Mango shrimp is not to be missed. Stir-fried shrimp are set out with slices of sweet fresh mango, bright green banana leaves for color and a somewhat sweet syrup like sauce. Though not on the printed menu, our friends asked for and were served a Malay version of fried rice called *nasi goreng*. This is one of those dishes which will vary with available ingredients and the whim of the chef who is making it. For all the available permutations, what we tasted was mild, satisfying and complex.

For dessert, do not miss the peanut pancake, a perfect example of the restuarant's culinary exotica.

PERIYALI
KR 18/20

Decor 4/4   Hospitality 5/5   Food 8/10   Value 1/1

- **Greek**
- **Glenview**
- **$$**

9860 Milwaukee Avenue
Glenview
(847) 296-2232
Troubleshooter: Dino

Hours: Sun–Thurs 11 am–
11 pm, Fri–Sat until midnight
Credit Cards: All majors
Reservations: Fri and Sat only
for parties of 4 or more
Handicapped: Accessible
**Smoking and nonsmoking
sections:** 75% nonsmoking, 25%
smoking

For most of us, a cruise of the Aegean Islands is out of the question. The next best thing may be a visit to an authentic Greek restaurant, one where the deep blue of the sea and the whitewashed stucco of island village homes and shops is reflected in the decor.

Look no further than Periyali, a Greek restaurant with the look and feel of a taverna, a gathering place for food and drink. A small delicatessen counter is at the front of the restaurant, which expands into a large stone floored dining room. Service is friendly and welcoming.

The menu goes beyond the routine for Hellenic dining. For example, among hot appetizers is a truly succulent roasted quail in a light sauce of olive oil and lemon. Two of the whole birds are served, almost a dinner-sized portion for small appetites. They are meaty and delicious. Of course the usuals are found on the menu, staples such as *saganaki*, the salmon roe spread called *taramasalata* and its garlic-flavored cousin, *scordalia*, both wonderful when spread on thick slices of fresh bread.

From among other tasty nibbles, the grilled octopus is marinated, then cooked over charcoal. Codfish, which requires special treatment for it to show at its best, comes in a version which brings ground fish in deep-fried balls. The Greek pastry pies, such as *spanakopita* with spinach or another with a puree of eggplant and feta cheese are excellent.

While a feast of nothing more than *mezze*, the Greek version of tapas, would be plentiful and satisfying enough, entrees are similarly tempting. Whole fresh sea bass or red snapper are prepared simply with a bit of lemon juice and oregano to underscore the clean flavors of the fish. Skewered boneless swordfish is charcoal grilled. Traditional *souvlaki*, grilled pork tenderloin kebabs, get similar treatment.

The basic thread that seems to run through the cooking is a sense of the natural. Flavors are not forced, not overdone. Wines are sensibly priced; desserts include some favorites, honeyed baklava among them.

PETE MILLER'S
KR 18.5/20
Decor 4/4   Hospitality 4.5/5   Food 9/10   Value 1/1

- **American**
- **Evanston**
- **$$$**

1537 Sherman Avenue
Evanston
(847) 328-0399
Troubleshooter: Bart Steinberg
(general manager)

Hours: Lunch Mon–Fri 11:30 am–2 pm, Dinner Sun 4:30 pm–midnight, Mon–Thurs 5 pm–1 am, Fri–Sat 5 pm–2 am
Credit Cards: All majors except Discover
Reservations: Recommended for all size parties
Handicapped: Accessible
Bar: Two full bars, Billiards room with six eight-foot tables
Smoking and nonsmoking sections: Both available, cigar friendly in separate section
Parking: Valet
Party Facilities: None available

Say what you will about fitness fanatics and dieters, there is no getting around the fact that the great American steak dinner has as huge a following as ever. That's where Pete Miller's, a brawny, no-nonsense steak house fits in. The restaurant suggests an image out of the Jazz Age of the Roaring Twenties. Floors are patterned mosaic tile, there's dark wood trim gleaming with a high polish. A large bar is central, with dining areas adjacent. Down a short hallway there is a billiard room, or in less polite society, a pool hall.

You learn this is serious business with a quick turn of the menu. Shrimp cocktail is described as jumbo, with a price tag to fit. But, that's too simple to test the kitchen's mettle. Taste delicious smoked sturgeon instead, plated with mounds of sour cream, crisp toast rounds, lemon wedges and a sprinkling of capers. One portion provides enough for a party of four. The ubiquitous portobello mushroom shows up, this time in a blanket of melted blue cheese. Other selections include a much milder crabcake, cream-based lobster bisque, and a near entrée sized portion of skewered chicken brochette, plated with a wild rice mix.

But, those are only the beginnings. All entrees include Caesar salad mixed at tableside in a wooden bowl. The dressing is rather lemony; raw egg yolks are left out by deliberate decision.

There's a lucky seven varieties of beef on the menu, headlined by a 22 ounce Kansas City cut, down to the 8-ounce small filet. The house specialty, Pete's Cut, is a large helping of prime rib, still on the bone, of course. The beef is all prime aged stuff; our waiter recommended medium rare with a hot, but still pink center.

If you choose to swim against the current and order something other than beef, a 30-ounce Australian lobster tail, and a smaller companion are offered. Oddly, the restaurant does not serve whole live lobster. Grilled tuna steak is another option, among a handful of other non-meat selections, served with a ginger soy marinade.

You certainly won't need side dishes to satisfy any but the most gargantuan appetite, however the choices include deliciously rich creamed spinach as well as twice-baked potato and large slices of steak fries, absolutely free of oil.

Almost everything on the dessert list includes something with chocolate. The bar stocks a wide inventory of single malt scotch, another sign that this is significant dining.

PIZZA D.O.C.
KR 18.5/20
Decor 3.5/4   Hospitality 4.5/5   Food 9.5/10   Value 1/1

- **Italian**
- **Chicago/North**
- **$$**

2251 West Lawrence Avenue
Chicago
(773) 784-8777
Troubleshooter: Joe

Hours: Daily 5–11 pm, closed Tues
Credit Cards: All majors
Reservations: Only when big party
Handicapped: Accessible
Smoking and nonsmoking sections: Both available
Parking: On street

Just about the only thing I can think of that would make Pizza D.O.C. look more authentic would be a swarm of Vespa scooters parked out front. Oh, and maybe if they took lira instead of dollars.

Short of that, this is as close to a Roman pizzeria and ristorante as we are to find here in Chicago. The restaurant is simply decorated with some wood accents that add an old country touch, as do the photographs of modern day Rome. The heart of Pizza D.O.C. lies with its wood-burning oven. All baking is done on the premises and chances are the bread you will be served was baked within the past four or five hours. The pizzas are thin, crackly sort of crusts that bubble at the edges. Forget Chicago deep-dish pizza. This is entirely different, light and delicate with toppings that do not overwhelm. Even the pizza *quattro formaggi*, or four cheeses, is delicate, and still crisp. It, and others, gets a light flavored tomato sauce, just enough to coat, but not so much as to over burden the crust. If you want, you can go up to the counter and watch your pizza being made from scratch, and that means each dough is rolled out individually. We particularly enjoyed the *pizza porcini* with sliced mushrooms whose flavor exudes taste and a perfume. Classic *pizza margherita* is an example of what this well-known style should be, simple, easy, balanced.

There is more on the menu than pizza. Begin with some fresh roasted vegetables as a mixed antipasto from the sideboard. Try one of the pastas, all of which can be ordered in half portion, including the risotto. Incidentally, the risotto might be the single flaw, not quite creamy enough, and served so quickly that it is evidently not made from scratch.

From a short list of second courses, whole Cornish hen is deliciously roasted in the wood-fired oven, served with roasted potato chunks and wilted greens. Other entrees include *osso buco*, baked ox tail, and a sirloin steak that gets the oven treatment and some other embellishments.

Homemade desserts include as rich and creamy a *panna cotta* as I have ever tasted; cheesecakes, tortes and *tiramusu* are among other selections.

PLAZA TAVERN
KR 18/20
Decor 4/4   Hospitality 5/5   Food 8/10   Value 1/1

- **American**
- **Chicago Loop**
- **$$$**

70 East Monroe
Chicago
(312) 977-1940
Troubleshooter: Karl Runge
(general manager)

Hours: Lunch Mon–Fri 11:30 am–2 pm, Dinner Mon 5–9:30 pm, Tues–Sat 5–11 pm, closed Sun, Oyster Bar has the same hours as Lunch
Credit Cards: All majors except Discover
Reservations: Recommended
Handicapped: Accessible
Smoking and nonsmoking sections: Smoking only in the bar
Parking: Valet $7, complimentary parking 20 South Clark St

We may be in the new millennium, but have you noticed how the 1940s-style clubs and restaurants have come back, big time? One of the spiffiest of the bunch is Plaza Tavern.

Plaza Tavern's Fountain Room has a small bandstand and dance floor, and believe me, both get used. Tables are set back and spaced apart from each other. Interior walls sport handsome deco-style period murals.

Service is contemporary and hip, maybe more so than some of the menu. But, if you are looking to dine on oysters rockefeller, chicken rumaki or the likes of veal oscar and chateaubriand, this is the place.

On the other hand, there are some more up-to-date conceptions. From the list of appetizers, Lobster Martini is a fine starter. Lobster tail is chunked into a salad with a chop of avocado and tomato, set at the bottom of a martini glass. Mango relish brings some sweet tropical flavor, while chili oil adds a contrasting bite. Tuna tartare uses the fresh belly tuna in a grind with the usual accompaniments, though onion sprouts, quail egg chopped fine and sesame oil add a bit of panache.

Panache is what Plaza Tavern is all about, even granted some of its older style offerings. At least one selection blends old with new. Instead of tournedos rossini, Plaza Tavern serves up tuna rossini. A medallion of grilled tuna steak is topped with foie gras and a mushroom ragout over spinach and leeks, all enriched with truffle sauce.

Delicious diver scallops, so called because they are literally hand-picked from sea beds individually, are plump and fresh, the flavor brought out by the intense heat of pan-searing in olive oil or, in this case, probably butter. Corn and leeks are cooked down into a ragout as part of the plating. Among other seafood selections, grilled grouper is crusted with a mild horseradish and served over garlic whipped potatoes plus an array of embellishments. Salmon comes with a side of corn custard and its hints of Fall.

The menu's list of steaks, chops and poultry includes roasted duckling, with lots of good flavored meat over a mound of oyster stuffing plus vegetables and a reduction of the duck's savory juices.

The bottom line is that you will find both older styles and new at Plaza Tavern, a solid addition to Loop dining.

April Lunch

Appetizers

Lobster Martini *Sliced Maine lobster tail, lobster salad, avocado, tomato, mango relish, chili oil and sweet potato chip ... $9.40*

Gulf Shrimp Cocktail *Boiled gulf shrimp served with cocktail sauce and lemon ... $8.40*

Maryland Crabcake *Served with a crisp radicchio slaw and remoulade sauce... $8.40*

Rumaki *Chicken livers and water chestnuts wrapped with Neuske bacon, brushed with honey mustard glaze and bread crumbs. Served with cornichon relish and foie gras butter. $6.40*

Duck Liver Paté *Chef Elder's liver paté served with croustades, cornichon, pickled onions, roasted peppers and Dijon mustard ... $8.40*

Curried Lentil *Lentils tossed in curried-ginger vinaigrette, served with herbed goat cheese stuffed red pepper and baby lettuces ...$7.40*

Soups

Tavern Gumbo *Rich shellfish stock thickened with brown roux, finished with fish, shellfish, andouille sausage, tomato, onion and okra ... $4.40*

Soup du Jour *... $4.40*

Salads

Tavern Salad *Bibb lettuce, radishes, red onion, cucumbers, tomatoes, tossed with herbed-lemon vinaigrette, topped with our signature deviled egg ... $5.40*

Cobb Salad *Mixed field greens tossed with brown derby dressing and topped with avocado, tomato, Neuske bacon, cucumber, blue cheese and garlic croutons.*
Vegetarian...........$8.40
w/Chicken ... $10.40   w/Shrimp ... $11.40

Caesar Salad *Romaine lettuce tossed with house-made Caesar dressing, garlic croutons and shaved parmesan cheese.*
Small ....$5.40   Large ...$8.40
w/Chicken...$9.40   w/Shrimp...$12.40

Green Bean Caesar Salad *Tender green beans tossed with shaved red onions and gumbo shrimp, topped with toasted sunflower seeds......$9.40*

Niçoise Salad with Seared Rare Ahi Tuna *Mixed field greens tossed with lemon-shallot dressing, topped with rare Ahi tuna, green beans, new potatoes, tomatoes, ripe olives, hard boiled egg and garlic croutons ... $13.40*

Sandwiches

Lobster Club with Smoked Salmon *Sliced Maine lobster tail, smoked salmon, avocado, tomato, lettuce and mayonnaise on toasted brioche. Served with slaw and Tavern fries ... $13.40*

Maryland Crabcake Sandwich *Crabcake on toasted brioche with red pepper-mayonnaise, lettuce and tomato. Served with slaw and Tavern fries ... 11.40*

Tenderloin Steak Sandwich *Open-faced on toasted brioche with onion marmalade and horseradish sauce. Served with lettuce, tomato, onion, pickle and Tavern fries ... $12.40*

London Broil *Grilled flank steak served open-faced on butter grilled French bread with horseradish sauce and Tavern fries ... $10.40*

Ahi Tuna Melt *Grilled rare Ahi tuna with roasted onion, tomato, mozzarella cheese and arugula aioli on toasted whole wheat bread. Served with slaw and Tavern fries ... $11.40*

Portobello Sandwich *Grilled portobello mushroom with tomato, onion, roasted red & green peppers, provolone and pesto on a Kaiser roll... $10.40*

Seafood

Grilled Mahi-Mahi *Sesame-soy glazed Mahi over a bed of creamy orzo with spinach and a zesty tomato-ginger sauce ... $14.40*

Cioppino *Clams, mussels, squid, shrimp and seasonal fish. Served in a spicy tomato broth ... $16.40*

Atlantic Salmon *Pan seared on a bed of white rice. Served with wilted baby lettuce topped with brown butter, capers, shiitake mushrooms and a splash of lemon ... $15.40*

Plaza Tavern Signatures

Tuna Rossini *Grilled rare tuna medallion topped with foie gras and bordelaise sauce. Served over spinach with leek and mushroom ragout ... $14.40*

Liver and Onions *Sautéed veal liver with Neuske bacon and onions. Served over roasted garlic mashed potatoes and spinach with lemon rings and liver butter ... $12.40*

Tournedo of Beef *Grilled tenderloin of beef atop croustade with lobster medallion, roasted mushrooms and lobster béarnaise. Served with roasted garlic mashed potato and vegetable ... $14.40*

Chicken Cordon Bleu *Pan seared medallions of chicken breast and prosciutto, topped with a Gruyere Mornay sauce. Served with roasted garlic mashed potatoes and seasonal vegetable. ... $12.40*

Chicken Fettuccine *Black pepper fettuccine, grilled chicken breast, peas, toasted walnuts and button mushrooms in creamy Parmesan sauce ... $14.40*

Black Bean Ravioli *Black bean-stuffed ravioli with roasted tomatoes, spinach and asparagus. Tossed in chipotle-butter sauce...$14.40*

We offer special vegetarian dishes every day

PRIVATE DINING AND MEETING ROOMS ARE AVAILABLE

POT PAN
KR 17/20
Decor 3.5/4   Hospitality 4/5   Food 8.5/10   Value 1/1

• **Thai**	**Hours:** Mon–Thurs 11 am–10 pm, Fri–Sat 11–1 am, Sun noon–10 pm
• **Chicago/Bucktown**	**Credit Cards:** All majors
• **$**	**Reservations:** Taken, rarely needed
1750 West North Avenue	**Handicapped:** Accessible
Chicago	**Smoking and nonsmoking**
(773) 862-6990	**sections:** Separate seating
Troubleshooter: Opars Nimnark	**Parking:** On street, can be tight

Finding a Thai storefront restaurant these days is as easy as shooting fish in a barrel. You can hardly miss. Sometimes, you get really lucky with a find like Pot Pan.

There is no visual standout, not much in the way of what realtors call curbside appeal. But, inside the restaurant is highlighted by open space with handsome woodwork and copper tubing ornamentation in overhead ceiling lamps. There are two seating levels, one of them a raised platform toward the back of the restaurant, reserved for nonsmokers the night we visited.

Like so many small restaurants, no matter what the ethnic derivation, Pot Pan seems to be a family-run operation. So, there might be some children, perhaps the owners', playing in the back. And, service might be a little distracted from time to time. But, it's part of the charm, to my way of thinking.

The food is typical of many Thai restaurants. The spring rolls, wrapped in a soft dough with fresh raw vegetables and bits of scrambled egg, are topped with a light plum sauce. The flavors are, well, spring-like. The egg rolls are more delicate than their Chinese cousins, shrimp dumplings are excellent little bite-sized morsels plumped and juicy. Appropriate sauces are set out for each of these, and other tidbits.

Whatever else you order, do not ignore soup. The *tom yom*, with its lemon grass underpinnings is seasoned with lime juice and cilantro, with a nice, spicy flavor. Tom Kah is similar, though its coconut milk base is clearly evident, adding a tinge of tropical sweetening. Pot pan's version of wonton soup is clearly different from Chinese wonton soup, lighter, more open in flavors, a bit more ephemeral.

Main course choices include salad sized entrees such as *nam sod* that brings chunks of steamed chicken white meat together with hot dried pepper flakes, lime juice, fresh grated ginger and other tastes on a bed of romaine lettuce. More substantial selections include delicious garlic chicken or shrimp with a complexity of tastes in addition to the evident garlic seasoning. Spicy grilled eggplant can be had in a vegetarian version, with or without tofu, or in the standard menu edition with chicken or shrimp. Basil and sweet peppers are combined with more fiery peppers to add to the complexities.

I have not forgotten pad thai, the singular favorite of most Thai diners. It is quite good, maybe a bit gummy and a little sweet. The fairly extensive menu lists other noodle entrees as well as those with or without meats, including a trio of curries.

QUINCY GRILL
KR 18.75/20
Decor 4/4   Hospitality 5/5   Food 9/10   Value .75/1

• **American**	**Hours:** Lunch Mon–Fri 11:30 am–2 pm and pre-opera dining 5–7 pm
• **Chicago**	
• **$$$**	**Credit Cards:** All majors
	Reservations: Suggested
200 South Wacker Drive	**Handicapped:** Accessible
Chicago	**Smoking and nonsmoking**
(312) 627-1800	**sections:** The dining room is
Troubleshooter: Manager on duty	nonsmoking, smoking is permitted in the lounge
	Parking: In nearby lots or valet on opera nights

With so much current dining attention paid to bistros and budget dining, maybe it's time to put the "fine" back into fine dining. That's what's happening at Quincy Grill. To be more formal about it, the full name of the restaurant is Quincy Grill on the River, appropriate enough since one glass wall is open to a river vista and an outdoor patio dining area when weather permits.

Quincy Grill was, at one time, a private dining club, and it still looks somewhat austere and formal with its smart, understated contemporary decor. The menu's prices may appear intimidating, but the serving staff most certainly is not. Neither they nor the menu do not allow diners to forget that this is, after all, a fine dining restaurant. The menu stresses contemporary American cookery and ingredients, with some Continental references. In one case, ravioli appetizers are filled with duck meat and goat cheese, then plated with a seemingly incongruous sauce that brings together oven-dried tomato, jicama and ginger. Another appetizer may be more synergistic, as a delicious mushroom risotto is plated with fennel and hazelnuts. The result is rather elegant.

Recently, tuna has been prepared like a peppercorn steak, with the inside still uncooked, while the surface has been seared at a frying pan heat. Pickled ginger strips, similar to those served in Japanese dining, is part of the presentation.

Like the first course choices, entrees are somewhat selective and limited, but no less inventive. Salmon has been plated with a relish created from pears and black walnut oil, paired with red pepper coulis. The fish is beautifully grilled, moist and flavorful. More interesting, I think, is sturgeon fished from the Columbia River, a fillet roasted with a sharp horseradish rub and set in a fruity, but deep flavored cabernet sauce. Sturgeon is a fish that deserves more attention than it normally gets, especially when prepared as well as it is at the Grill. Other entree choices include grilled chicken breast with a seasonal chestnut and sage stuffing; here the sauce is created with a merlot wine reduction. A classic strip steak is plated with Maytag blue cheese sauce and a compote of roasted shallots. A veal loin chops gets similarly rich treatment, the light meat contrasted to an intense sauce of caramelized pearl onions, apricots and bourbon.

Because of its location, Quincy Grill has been popular as a dining spot before Lyric Opera performances. It is getting and deserves wider attention when the time arises for a fine dining occasion or entertaining.

RAVINIA BISTRO
(MAISON BARUSSEAU)
KR 18/20
Decor 4/4   Hospitality 5/5   Food 8/10   Value 1/1

• **French**

• **Highland Park**

• **$$**

581 Roger Williams Avenue
Highland Park
(847) 432-1033
Troubleshooter: Michel Stillwell
(owner)

Hours: Tues–Thurs 11 am–
8 pm, Fri 11 am–9 pm, Sat–Sun
10 am–9 pm, Brunch Sun
10 am–1:30 pm
Credit Cards: All majors
Reservations: Suggested
Handicapped: Accessible, but
with some difficulty
Bar: Good selection of
moderately priced French wines
and boutique beers
**Smoking and nonsmoking
sections:** No smoking
Parking: Ample on street or in lot

The red, white and blue bunting of The French Tricolor is a color accent against a mostly white interior decor of this restaurant's two dining rooms. Each is small, only a few tables, in keeping with the neighborhood character of Ravinia Bistro.

The menu is typical bistro fare, the accent decidedly French. *Hors d'oeuvres* can be as simple as a wedge of brie cheese with fresh fruit. Simplicity is at the heart of all good cooking, a lesson not lost on this restaurant's kitchen. Flavors and seasonings are direct, without needless complexity. When a diner orders *ratatouille provencal* there is no guessing about what will be coming. This is the traditional vegetable casserole centered around eggplant and zucchini, with tomatoes at the heart of the matter, gently cooked in a fine olive oil, seasoned with a *bouquet garni.* In keeping with custom, it can be had either hot or cold.

Other first course selections follow in turn with a tradition firmly routed in French regional cooking. Onion tart is a specialty in any bistro worth its name. At Ravinia Bistro, the onions are sautéed, matched with sharp Swiss cheese in an egg custard, then baked in a pastry tart shell made from scratch. *Pissaladiere*, a tart like pastry from Nice, is not often found on Chicago restaurant menus. Here, tomatoes and green olives are the central ingredients.

Speaking of traditional, onion soup is so good you might wish you could chew on its intense flavors of sweet onions sweated down into a rich stock, baked with a blanket of gruyere cheese melted over the top and running down the sides of the crock. As is the case with bistros, a light meal could be made consisting of the onion soup and perhaps one of the omelettes, quiches or crepes. Incidentally, the quiches and omelettes can be prepared with egg whites only on request for diners who watch cholesterol.

For the heartier appetites, the Ravinia Bistro holds some fine treasures. Roast duck is glazed with peach sauce, rack of lamb is roasted in a mustard and garlic glaze. Roasted chicken comes in at least two ways. In one preparation, the emphasis appears to be on healthy cooking as much as it is on flavor. A boneless breast is skinned and steamed with tomatoes and fresh herbs, then plated on a bed of spinach. The other chicken is given a typical roast to hold in flavor and juices. The skin is rubbed with fresh herbs. Sautéed potatoes finish the platter and, like all entrees, the chickens are served with a diner's choice of soup or salad.

Seafood includes daily specials as well as menu items. For me, the real test of a French restaurant is *bouillabaisse.* The broth I tasted was fine, though the seafood seemed to suffer from being overcooked.

Desserts include some major temptations ranging from creme brûlee to fruit tarts. Service is adept, rather unhurried by bistro standards. Though Ravinia Bistro has its regulars from the neighborhood, you might just want to leave your neighborhood to visit. It's worth the trip.

RAW BAR & GRILL
KR 16.5/20
Decor 3.5/4   Hospitality 5/5   Food 7/10   Value 1/1

• **Eclectic**	**Hours:** Daily 4 pm–2 am
• **Chicago/Mid-North**	**Credit Cards:** All majors
• **$**	**Handicapped:** Not accessible, doors are narrow
3720 North Clark Street	**Smoking and nonsmoking**
Chicago	**sections:** Smoking in dining
(773) 348-7291	**Parking:** On the street
Troubleshooters: Guilianno and Tony Motomam	

Raw Bar & Grill is a double storefront. Seven or so tables are set about in the bar room side, and unless you did a little exploration, you might not know of the main dining room. It's as eclectic as anything else in the restaurant, sharing space with a pool table and a concert grand centered on a small stage, with several tables for diners in the middle of the room.

With that noted, the cooking is unusual to say the least. If there is a pattern, I have not noticed one. It's almost as if whoever is at the stoves is making it up. And, sometimes it works.

But, sometimes it doesn't. An appetizer called vegetarian eggplant suggested that this might be like Persian *baba ganoush*, especially since another appetizer right above it on the menu brings together hummus and blackened shrimp plated with pita bread. Our waiter indicated that our assumptions were correct. But, what came was a hot, not cold, puree of eggplant chunks, plated with pita. There was an attempt at a complexity of seasonings centered around what I am guessing to be a tomato-based sauce. But, the overwhelming taste was salty.

On the other hand, another appetizer, grilled squid and scallions, was delicious. Here, rolled strips of squid were stuffed with bits of scallion and garlic. Other appetizers range from a selection of clams, oysters, shrimp and even Florida stone crab claws when in season, from the raw bar. There's also crabcake, grilled froglegs or oysters rockefeller, reflecting that eclecticism which marks the menu.

For entrees, the choice includes whole live lobsters, plus dungeness or king crab legs. One interesting entree stacks a wedge of swordfish with tomato and chutney among its ingredients. Grilled scallops get an embellishment of a smoked chili–flavored vinaigrette with saffron-flavored onions wilted down with cabbage on the other side of the platter, in a competition of flavors and textures. It actually works quite well.

Similarly, shrimp sautéed with garlic in olive oil is plated with chunked potatoes and strips of portobello mushrooms. This can also be had with scallops instead of shrimp. Several other selections, meat and seafood, flesh out the menu. Raw Bar & Grill is for the more adventurous casual diner looking for the unusual.

REDFISH
KR 18/20
Decor 4/4   Hospitality 4.5/5   Food 8.5/10   Value 1/1

- **American/New Orleans**
- **Chicago/Near North**
- **$$**

400 North State Street
Chicago
(312) 467-1600
Troubleshooter: Doug Clements (manager)

Hours: Mon–Fri 11 am–11 pm, Sat–Sun 5–11 pm
Credit Cards: Amex, Diners, Discover, MC, Visa
Bar: Full bar and lounge with Southern music, live bands
Reservations: Recommended
Handicapped: Accessible
Smoking and nonsmoking sections: Smoking and nonsmoking seating in dining room
Parking: Valet

Redfish is a real "kick up your heels and have fun" kind of place. And, the food's not too bad, either! The restaurant's menu promises some "Looziana in Chicago," not the first to adopt that theme, and probably not the last. Redfish does it up right. The decor is bright with bright neon beer signs and the volume turned up on a music system churning out C&W mixed with zydeco.

This is not elegant dining, by any means, and if you are squeamish about picking things up with your fingers, such as spicy crawfish or grilled shrimp, you might think about ordering something else. There's plenty on the menu, starting with deliciously tangy gumbos. Gumbo Ya Ya is stoked with smoked chicken and peppery andouille sausage. A little more complex is N'Awlin's Seafood Gumbo with a mess a fixins' that includes oysters, crabmeat, crawfish and whatever soft-fish might be available. Lurking somewhere beneath a subtle layer of pepper seasoning is a little bit of sweetness. You might not notice it, but it's there, and even adding a few drops of Tabasco, or any of the other hot sauces collected on your table will not mask that inherent good taste.

Other appetizers range from crawfish with hush puppies to a sampler of pulled pork, beef brisket, fried chicken and watermelon to fantastically rich redneck rockefellers. Inspired, no doubt by oysters rockefeller, these little suckers are deep-fried, bedded on wilted collard greens, which stands in for spinach in the original oysters rockefeller, and some lemon butter instead of pernod. Crazy me, I add Tabasco to every-thing with this kind of food, and love every drop.

Several salads are served at Redfish including a creole version of Cae-sar and good old-fashioned southern-style fried green tomatoes. As for en-trees, show me an etoufee and I'm pretty well ready to ignore anything else. In this case, the crawfish etoufee is abundant, served with a side of dirty rice, the kind that has a spicy sort of flavor all its own. The etoufee seems to be in a sauce reminiscent of the gumbo, but is outstanding in its own right. Other entrees include interesting pasta jambalaya, with the jambalaya in-gredients served over orzo. A recent nightly special brought penne with cut-up pieces of grilled chicken plus red and yellow peppers in a fairly mild presentation. Elsewhere on the menu, dinners run the gamut from lamb shanks with hominy and a chili barbecue sauce to beef medallions on four bean chili with honey and apple cider aoili. More traditional fare such as fried catfish or blackened redfish also show up.

Desserts are sensational; recently, pecan pie was infused with chocolate.

RED LIGHT
KR 19.5/20
Decor 4/4   Hospitality 5/5   Food 9.5/10   Value 1/1

- **Asian**
- **Chicago/West**
- **$$$**

820 West Randolph Street
Chicago
(312) 733-8880
Troubleshooters: Michael Kornick (co-owner, executive chef), Budi Soehartono (general manager)

Hours: Lunch Mon–Fri 11:30 am–2 pm, Dinner Sun–Wed 5:30–10 pm, Thurs 5:30–11 pm, Fri–Sat 5:30 pm–midnight, closed Sun
Credit Cards: Amex, Diners, MC, Visa
Reservations: Suggested
Handicapped: Accessible
Bar: Full service 78-foot-long granite art nouveau bar, exotic fruit drinks, Asian and domestic beers, extensive wine list, mixed cocktails featured
Smoking and nonsmoking sections: Both available
Parking: Valet and street
Party Facilities: Private party facilities for 80–110, semi-private in Tea or Oval room for 20–60

Driving along Randolph Street through the old produce district, there's no missing Red Light. A large 20-foot tall lamp sits on the top of the former warehouse building that houses this high concept Asian-style restaurant. The restaurant, part of the same group that includes neighboring *Vivo* and *Marché*, is elaborately decorated with bold accents of copper, hardwood floors, high ceilings and windows, and an open kitchen adding to the bustling excitement and well-organized din of cooking. There is almost a sense of the surreal in the free-form shapes of furnishings and ornamentation.

The menu highlights China and several surrounding Asian cuisines, but this is not just another Asian-fusion restaurant. It is more imaginative than that, pushing the culinary envelope to its widest. For all the noise and activity, the food is exceptionally delicious. From among appetizer favorites, eggplant mushroom dumplings are silken, while Vietnamese chicken slaw with spiced peanuts adds a flavor and texture contrast so important to the balance of Asian-style dining. Vegetable spring rolls are mild and delicate. Chicken satay with peanut sauce may be among the least interesting selections on a recent evening. But, tea-smoked squab plated with scallion pancakes makes up for that. The bird is exceptionally flavored. Barbecue ribs, with either Chinese five spice or in a sweet and sticky tomato-based sauce look mouthwatering as they hang from a kitchen rack, along with whole cooked duck, just the way they are seen and prepared in Chinese groceries or restaurants.

Red Light's steamed lobster is a hit. It has a delicate flavor enhanced by black beans and Cantonese-style vegetables. Speaking of seafood, catfish is marvelously pure flavored, deftly boned by a waiter who presents the whole fish first. The fish is lightly glazed with a sweet and sour sauce that is more subtle than bold. Red Light features some unusual clay pot cookery, said to be akin to the sort of street foods one might find in a large Chinese city. Mushrooms and sliced sweet potato are highlighted in a broth redolent of basil, and perhaps lemon grass and mint for a unique combination of flavors.

Desserts are in a class by themselves and include coconut sorbet with hot fudge, caramelized banana, cashew and date cake with cardamon ice cream or a bittersweet chocolate tart embellished with candied kumquats.

RICO'S
KR 19/20

Decor 4/4   Hospitality 5/5   Food 9/10   Value 1/1

* **Italian**
* **Chicago/Near South**
* **$$**

626 South Racine Avenue
Chicago
(312) 421-7262
Troubleshooter: Rico

Hours: Mon–Fri 11:30 am–9:30 pm, Sat 4–9 pm, Sun 4–9 pm
Credit Cards: All majors
Reservations: Recommended
Handicapped: Not accessible
Smoking and nonsmoking sections: No smoking
Parking: Free on street

R ico's has been around since 1987, not as long as some of its neighbors on and near Taylor Street, perhaps, but long enough to establish its own identification and character on the Near South Side Italian dining scene.

White table cloths and contemporary gallery art that hangs on the walls of the spacious, light and airy main dining room helps set the scene. The cooking leans toward the traditional, with roots in Neapolitan recipes.

Begin with something such as a tossed bread salad; Rico's serves casa nostra bread which is arguably the best commercial Italian bakery in the city. Combine the bread salad with an antipasti platter of chilled meats, cheeses and vegetables for some light summertime dining. If you like your vegetables grilled, the zucchini is a knockout, thin slices mildly seasoned. Among other selections, roasted peppers bring a bright red visual accent to the table, and a tangy taste. Other first course choices range from traditional mussels in marinara, baked clams with a bread crumb filling, grilled or fried squid plus several specialty salads.

Moving into the area of pastas and entrees, the printed menu is amplified by evening specials. Recently, swordfish vesuvio was being served. A large and thick swordfish steak is plated with roasted potatoes bringing all the flavor, but less fat and calories than that of the traditional chicken vesuvio. That recipe, by the way, is truly succulent, white and dark meat on the bone that just oozes flavor with every forkful.

The menu is top heavy with veal dishes as one would expect from a Neapolitan Italian restaurant. The choices range from *veal marsala*, *parmigiana*, *piccante*, *limone* and *francese*, to a pair of house specialties: veal chop with peppers and potatoes or *Vitello à la Mario*. This latter brings the meat sautéed in olive oil and a finish of white wine, plated with pieces of eggplant, cheese and a topping of marinara.

As for seafood, in addition to the swordfish vesuvio, *shrimp fra diavolo* or shrimp vesuvio are among signature dishes. In the former, several large shrimp are sautéed in olive oil, and plated atop a mound of linguine in a sauce which is really not as hot and spicy as its name suggests.

That seems to be a key at Rico's; nothing overwhelms, neither flavors and seasonings, nor portion sizes. It is, rather, a restaurant for leisurely, if not thoughtful dining. While still in the "Mom and Pop" tradition of storefront Italian, Rico's is something a bit more distinctive.

RISTORANTE AGOSTINO
KR 19/20

Decor 3.5/4   Hospitality 5/5   Food 9.5/10   Value 1/1

- **Italian**
- **Chicago/West**
- **$$**

2817 North Harlem Avenue
Chicago
(773) 745-6464
Troubleshooters: Agostino and Anna Fiasche (owners)

Hours: Tues–Thurs 4–10 pm, Fri–Sat 4 pm–midnight, Sun 3–9 pm, closed Mon
Credit Cards: All majors
Reservations: Recommended
Handicapped: Accessible
Smoking and nonsmoking sections: Both available
Parking: Lot on the side of the building

Chef and owner Agostino Fiasche and his wife Anna do most of the cooking. Their style reflects Calabria, their home region in Italy. A glance at the map reveals a winding and extensive seacoast, which explains the prevalence of seafood on the menu. The best way to begin might be with the mixed grill and its wide assortment including squid, octopus, succulent shrimp and whatever else might be a fresh delivered catch. Flavors are natural, and a little fresh lemon juice is the best accompaniment.

A couple dozen antipasti are on the menu, most preparations of fish or shellfish. Nearly as many pasta selections are listed for the next course, though with a more even division between land and sea. From a delicious selection of pasta, *penne arrabbiata* is spicy, but not in the way one might expect. Instead of a big wallop, a controlled intensity builds up in the mouth, though not so much as to overwhelm any other flavors. That's to the good considering our companion pasta, fettucini made only hours before in an *amatriciana* sauce of fresh tomatoes, pancetta and onions among its ingredients.

Most of the tomato-based sauces are only barely cooked. They will be warm, of course, but they are delicately seasoned and are as close to fresh tomatoes as a cooked sauce can remain. The menu continues with some classic meat and chicken recipes, which wander all over the Italian culinary map. Selections range from veal or chicken *Saltimbocca* from Rome to Chicago's own contribution, chicken vesuvio. Tender veal *piccata* is lightly floured and sautéed in oil with nothing more than lemon juice and a little white wine, then garnished with plump capers.

Desserts include a homemade *tiramisu* that is 100% mascarpone cheese, flavored with rum and espresso. It restores what has become a menu cliché to worthy respect. The wine list is moderately priced and complimentary to the menu. Service could hardly be better.

DINING ROOM AT THE RITZ-CARLTON
KR 19.5/20
Decor 4/4   Hospitality 5/5   Food 9.5/10   Value 1/1

- **French Contemporary**
- **Chicago**
- **$$$**

160 East Pearson
Chicago
(312) 227-5866
Troubleshooter: Pierre Lasserre
(Maitre 'D)

Hours: Mon–Sat Dinner 6–11 pm, Sun Brunch 10:30 am–1:30 pm, Dinner 6–10 pm
Credit Cards: All majors
Reservations: Required
Handicapped: Accessible
Smoking and nonsmoking sections: Separate seating for smoking and nonsmoking, no cigars or pipes in dining room
Parking: Valet validated for three hours
Dress Code: Jackets required for gentlemen, neckties suggested

The Dining Room at the Ritz-Carlton is old fashioned splendor, rich with elegant wood paneling and crystal chandelier lighting. Tables are spread far enough apart to ensure a degree of privacy for guests. Service is knowledgeable, responsive and unobtrusive.

In contrast to the elegance of the surroundings, Chef Sarah Stegner's cooking style places emphasis on understatement, even minimalism. Her goal appears to be a search for natural flavors, as unadorned as possible, flavorful without ostentatious embellishment.

Food is served on plain white china, often without color or garnish. But, there are exceptions. Among second course salad selections is strudel, the golden layers of pastry dough plumped with small asparagus spears and a course chop of portobello mushrooms, bound with slivers of sweet onion glazed by aged balsamic vinegar. In another salad, bulgur wheat and wild rice are mated with unsweetened pumpkin, all of which is barely moistened by cranberry and walnut oil vinaigrette dressing.

Among entrees, in one recent selection John Dory, a mild-flavored firm fleshed fish, was presented with cuttings of portobello mushroom, braised leeks and crisp, thin cuts of fried potato called "fingerlings." Each component brought its own flavor to the platter, no one thing overpowering another. The fish, as center piece had been cut into sections, much like blocks and laid atop each other in a seemingly random or askew fashion. Another fish entree, halibut, was plated more conventionally. In this case, the halibut was sautéed until flecks of gold colored its otherwise pure white flesh. Whipped potatoes flecked with black truffles, and roasted golden beets filled out the serving. Salmon has been roasted to a bright pink, its inside still glazed, but warm at rest in a dark truffle puree whose heady scent and flavor is so intense that one is almost taken aback, considering the understatement which characterizes so much else on the menu.

The Dining Room has for years been in the forefront of alternative, low calorie dining options. Such selections are clearly marked, but any compromises in preparation are difficult to discern. Venison has been served with pureed chestnut and a julienne of acorn and butternut squash. Venison has a somewhat stronger taste than beef, but is not gamey. For those who avoid beef for reasons of fat and cholesterol, venison is a welcome choice. The meat is napped in a light red wine sauce; slices of poached pear rounds out the platter.

The fairly short menu includes rack of lamb in a honey and thyme glaze. The lamb shares platter space with an artichoke heart filled with goat cheese. In another meat choice, beef tenderloin is paired with braised oxtail, a cut whose tenderness will surprise any who are having it for the first time. The platter is enhanced with porcini mushrooms in a preparation that mimics potatoes dauphinoise.

Desserts can vary from day to day, a course which, unlike the rest of the menu, lends itself to more profound culinary indulgence. The restaurant's wine list runs the gamut from reasonably inexpensive to dauntingly expensive, which means that diners are sure to find something to accompany dinner in keeping with the event or occasion that is the reason for the feast.

RIVA
KR 16.5/20
Decor 4/4   Hospitality 3.5/5   Food 8/10   Value 1/1

- **Italian Seafood**
- **Chicago/Navy Pier**
- **$$$**

700 East Grand Avenue on Navy Pier
Chicago
(312) 644-7482
Troubleshooters: Phil Stefani (owner) or manager on duty

Hours: Mon–Thurs Lunch 11:30 am–3 pm, Dinner 5–11 pm, Fri–Sat Lunch 1:30–3 pm, Dinner 5 pm–midnight
Credit Cards: All majors
Reservations: Strongly suggested
Handicapped: Accessible
Smoking and nonsmoking sections: Both available (see text for details)
Parking: Valet at Navy Pier Entrance 1 or in East Garage

Riva is more elaborate, if not more elegant than the other restaurants in the Phil Stefani chain. Stefani made his reputation with his namesake restaurant on West Fullerton, following it up with a succession of Italian restaurants in the city and suburbs.

On Navy Pier, Riva exploits the nautical, but without ignoring some basic Italian undercurrents. The restaurant has an entire glass wall to showcase the pier, and the gorgeous Chicago skyline in the near distance.

From a selection of several appetizers, tuna tartare takes basic simplicity to extrodinary heights, bringing in green Japanese wasabi horseradish, pickled ginger and caper berries with garlic toast. The tuna has a clean, fresh flavor, while the selection of condiments brings more to the platter.

In another first course, portobella mushrooms are stacked napolean-style with a slice of grilled polenta, spinach and a goat cheese spread acting as mortar. The presentation is set in a pool of roasted shallot sauce. Riva Baked Clams are the sort found in most other Italian restaurants, which puts Riva closer in touch with its roots than do some of the other menu choices.

Among à la carte salads for a following course, one of the best could be dark green spinach leaves with radiccio and frisee lettuce dressed with a light citrus vinaigrette. But, it is the addition of toasted pecans and gorganzola cheese that makes this one a taste sparkler.

As for the entrees, specialties include a 28-ounce serving of baked Dover sole, planked and sauced with a honey and lemon glaze, instead of the traditional almonds and butter sauce. A 16-ounce rack of lamb is more traditional with horseradish mashed potatoes as part of its plating. A quartet of steaks ranging from 10- to 24-ounces establishes an attraction for beef eaters. Alaskan king crab legs come in a prodigious portion while a menu item dubbed "Not Your Ordinary Fish Fry" includes a bounty of shrimp, scallops, oysters and the like, as well as tempura vegetables.

As for other selections, blackened monkfish is intensely flavored with a medly of spices. Horseradish mashed potatoes are on the side, while the large chunk of fish is topped with fried onions. Among other regular whole fish, mahi mahi is crusted in sesame seeds, while swordfish is grilled and perhaps inspired by veal oscar, with fresh asparagus, crabmeat and hollandaise sauce, substituting for bearnaise.

As for pastas, linguine lobster diavolo is generous with the lobster, set in a mildly peppered sauce finished with a bit of cream. On the other hand, farfelle with scampi is a demonstration in simple and direct cookery with little more than olive oil and garlic for basic flavors, though some lemon and a touch of peppers are part of the recipe.

Desserts include a richly chocolate flourless torte topped with equally rich chocolate mousse. Service is good, if not completely attentive to every detail. And, though smoking and nonsmoking sections are designated, people at some nonsmoking tables may pick up the acrid fumes.

RIVERS
KR 19/20
Decor 4/4   Hospitality 5/5   Food 9/10   Value 1/1

- **Euro-American Bistro**
- **Chicago**
- **$$$**

30 South Wacker Drive
Chicago
(312) 559-1515
Troubleshooters: Dan Nemeth (general manager) or Annie Patterson (dining room manager)

Hours: Lunch Mon–Fri 11 am–2:30 pm, Dinner Mon–Thurs 5–10:30 pm, Fri–Sat 5–11 pm, open Sun evenings 4:30–9 pm during lyric opera season
Credit Cards: All majors
Reservations: Suggested
Handicapped: Accessible
Smoking and nonsmoking sections: No smoking except bar
Parking: Free parking in building after 5 pm for two hours (Wacker Street Garage entrance)

Rivers may be the best kept restaurant secret in town. Except when the Lyric Opera is in season, or there is another attraction at the nearby Civic Opera House, you won't find any signs outside the Mercantile Exchange Building indicating the restaurant is even there. And, if it is an evening when there is nothing going on in the neighborhood, it could even be somewhat the challenge to find the correct Monroe Street entrance to just get inside the building's lobby.

From a choice of starters, as the menu calls them, a roasted portobello mushroom is typical, embellished with goat cheese, plus roasted peppers worked down to a coulis or relish and a touch of basil oil. Barbecued shrimp and scallops have been given a southwestern touch with a presentation including jalapeño peppered corn cakes and a corn and mango relish with barbecue sauce.

Other selections have included truly delicious seafood ravioli, a generous portion ideal for tasting by a party of two to four people. Actually, the ravioli is not so much filled as used as a bedding for the likes of shrimp, scallops, salmon, mushrooms, scallions and sun-dried tomatoes set in a sherry sauce with a light infusion of cream. Finally, among recent first course choices, Maryland crabcakes are offered as a traditional touch in either appetizer or entrée-sized portion.

As for entrees, the menu clearly lists a handful of signature selections. Grouper was recently among those choices. The fish was seared in a hot skillet, then topped with a course chop of rock shrimp that the menu describes as "hash"; that's a bit of an understatement for something that contributes to the imaginative preparation. Slices of Florida pink grapefruit bring a touch of acid to the back of the palate, eased by a light beurre blanc. Other signature recipes range from a strip loin steak coated with cracked pepper and served in a madeira au jus, rack of lamb with a glaze of maple syrup and sharp mustard in a rosemary au jus, barbequed pork and sautéed chicken breast rolled around a stuffing of shrimp and spinach. This one should not be dismissed just in passing.

Other menu choices could include halibut grilled with a horseradish and orange glaze that holds in its moisture. Sea bass is exceptional with a spicy tangerine sauce glaze. An Oriental theme is carried out with the inclusion of bok choy and a Korean-style vegetable pancake. Swirls of citrus butter and curry oil complete the platter.

The dessert list is part of an after dinner menu which includes a wide selection of single malt scotches, cognac, armangnac and cordials. As for those desserts, the blueberry sour cream cake with vanilla ice cream cake is as rich as it sounds. Other selections range from traditional *crème brûlée* and *flan* to flourless chocolate cake with fresh raspberry sauce, plus assorted seasonal berries and a dollop of whipped cream.

Because the restaurant draws a pre-theater and opera crowd in season, it is possible to be in an out in about 90 minutes and easily make your curtain.

RL
KR 17/20

Decor 4/4   Hospitality 4.5/5   Food 8/10   Value .5/1

* **Italian**
* **Chicago/Near North**
* **$$$**

115 East Chicago Avenue
Chicago
(312) 475-1100
Troubleshooter: Scott Dahlin
(general manager)

Hours: Mon–Thurs 11:30 am–10 pm, Fri–Sat 11:30 am–11, Sun 1–8 pm
Credit Cards: All majors
Reservations: Recommended
Handicapped: Accessible
Smoking and nonsmoking sections: Smoking at bar only
Parking: Valet $8

RL is a new restaurant that looks like old money. The initials are those of Ralph Lauren of clothing fame, and RL is next to his new store.

The restaurant is all warm, dark woods, polished brass, handsome art, and enough leather to keep a cattle ranch in business for a year. It has the look of a private club and the menu of an Italian restaurant. Lauren wanted to recreate some of his favorite New York dining here in Chicago.

What it all comes down to, of course, is the food. Aside from the stratospheric prices, and the pretentiousness of it all, the fine dining is fine. Begin with an appetizer such as *frito misto*. There's a good selection of deep-fried calimari, baby squid and shrimp in an edible potato basket which is actually tasty enough to nibble. A tangy marinara sauce is there for your dipping pleasure. For something lighter, a mixed green salad with shaved fennel and artichokes is a decent selection, though grilled vegetables in a light white truffle oil is more elegant.

Servers do not suggest that diners might want to share a pasta course, as they probably should, and then move on to an entree. Instead, pastas can be equivalent to the main course. Linguine in white clam sauce is rather ordinary for such dressy surroundings. There was nothing special or memorable, except perhaps for its near bland character. Cheese and spinach ravioli with mushrooms and a bolognese sauce might be more interesting.

As for poultry and meat selections at RL, the highlight may be sirloin from cattle raised at Lauren's Colorado ranch. Other selections include breaded Milanese-style veal chop, grilled loin of veal and a double cut lamb chop. A recent special brought venison fanned out like flower petals on a circular bed of pureed sweet potatoes and spinach, all set in an appropriately fruity wine sauce. Seafood choices will vary from among nightly specials, though sautéed red snapper and pan-seared salmon are on the printed menu every evening.

RODITYS
KR 18/20
Decor 3/4   Hospitality 5/5   Food 9/10   Value 1/1

- **Greek**
- **Chicago/Near West**
- **$$**

222 South Halsted Street
Chicago
(312) 454-0800
Troubleshooter: Mr. Perry
Senopoulos (owner)

Hours: Sun–Thurs 11–1 am,
Fri–Sat 11–2 am
Credit Cards: Visa, MC
Reservations: Recommended
Handicapped: Accessible
Bar: Full
**Smoking and nonsmoking
sections:** Both available
Parking: Free valet
Party Facilities: A room for
200–250 is under construction

Behind the welcoming exteriors of the restaurants that cover a two or three block span along South Halsted Street in the old Greektown neighborhood lies an intense rivalry. Though each has basically similar menus, there are some distinctions and subtleties that come through to separate the best from the others.

One of the best is Roditys. And, though I do not have the opportunity to return to Roditys as often as I would like, each visit has been well rewarded. I still remember the first time; it was almost like a family party. A large part of one of two flanking dining rooms had been taken over by what was evidently a large Greek-American family, complete with infants, grandmothers, and at least one Orthodox priest.

Visiting more recently on a busy Saturday night, I wondered how well Roditys would stack up against such a memory. Though the priest and the infants were not there, the party atmosphere certainly was. And yet, in the midst of intense frolic and large crowds coming in and out through the crowded standing room only bar, came excellent service and food.

To my way of thinking, an order of *saganaki*, the flaming cheese pie, is the ultimate Greek dining cliché. Be that as it may, this was as good as *saganaki* is likely to be, made with a good quality cheese, less salted than most. For balance came some warm *dolmades*, grape leaves filled with plumped grains of rice and ground lamb, covered with a mild bechamel-style sauce. To round out our appetizers and enjoy the thick slices of bread, we took some *taramasalata*, the pinkish salmon roe spread. Sometimes too fishy, this was as mild as a baby's cheek.

There are dozens of selections on the Roditys menu, and while most are standards, there are some more unusual choices. Among them are daily specials. One might be *chicken Napoleon*. Though it stretches the concept of a Napoleon a bit, a phyllo pastry shell wraps a filling of the poultry, course chopped vegetables and pine nuts all bound with melted feta cheese. Just so no one goes hungry, a side of oven-roasted potatoes and rice come as sides.

ROSDED
KR 17.5/20
Decor 3/4   Hospitality 5/5   Food 8.5/10   Value 1/1

• **Thai**

• **Chicago/North**

• **$**

2308 West Leland
Chicago
(773) 334-9055
Troubleshooters: Namyos and Chooski Sudhichitt (owners)

Hours: Tues–Sat 11:30 am–9 pm, Sun noon–8:30 pm
Credit Cards: MC, Visa
Reservations: Not taken on weekends
Handicapped: Accessible
Bar: No bar, diners may bring their own
Smoking and nonsmoking sections: No separate smoking section
Parking: Ample in city lots
Party Facilities: No private party facilities

This is one of Chicago's very first Thai restaurants, and remains much the same as it has always been. My most recent visit was as good an experience as the very first. Rosded is the epitome of the tiny storefront restaurant, not overly decorated, housing just a few tables.

The menu is a simple listing of the 50 or so dishes regularly prepared in the small kitchen behind a service counter. There are certain Thai dishes which serve as benchmark for my taste. Many Thai soups fall into that category, and those at Rosded are exceptional. *Tom ka kai* is a good example. This is a peppery hot clear chicken stock loaded with shrimp scallions, fresh slivers of lemon grass, and burning hot green peppers among its ingredients.

The other benchmark for Thai cookery is *pud thai,* a noodle dish loaded with bits of egg, ground peanuts, onions and bean sprouts in a slightly sweet sauce or gravy. The Rosded version has always been among the best served in the city. In fact, no matter what other choices you make, mild or hot curries, meat or vegetarian, you will be well rewarded. And, be sure to go with enough people so that you can order a wider variety and come away with a richer sampling of what this charming budget restaurant has to offer.

ROSE ANGELIS
KR 18/20

Decor 4/4   Hospitality 5/5   Food 8/10   Value 1/1

- **Italian**
- **Chicago/Mid-North**
- **$$**

1314 Wrightwood
Chicago
(773) 296-0081
Troubleshooters: Larry
Rosenblum (chef/co-owner),
Ralph DeAngelis (co-owner)

Hours: Tues–Thurs, Sun 5–10 pm, Fri–Sat 5–11 pm
Credit Cards: Discover, MC, Visa
Reservations: Accepted for parties of 8 or more
Handicapped: Accessible (two steps up into restaurant)
Parking: Street parking can be tight
Smoking and nonsmoking sections: Both available

Real estate agents talk about curb appeal, the first impression a house makes. When it comes to curb appeal, Rose Angelis has it in spades. A storefront has been dressed up, its front windows decorated with a sea of wine bottle corks on which floats breads and other staples from the Italian larder. The charm continues undiminished inside with high gloss hardwood floors, high ceilings, original paint treatment with *tromp l'oeil* techniques to create muraled vistas, window frames and flower boxes or other artistic tricks.

There's no trickery in the food, or its service. Start with the *bruschetta* appetizer at the very top of the menu. A recent house special begins with a layer of *olivita* spread on thick toast, followed by a layer of gorgonzola cheese and slices of roasted red peppers. A big red wine goes perfectly. Other appetizers are just as exciting, ranging from sliced baby eggplant parmigiana to delicious minestrone soup. The soup has a delicately flavored broth that is enhanced with sliced fresh vegetables.

Salads are à la carte. Our waiter had no problem with a request to split one Caesar salad for the four at our table. Portions were ample, the dressing touched with light anchovy and lemon flavors. The only thing that would have improved its presentation would have been tableside preparation.

Rose Angelis showcases nearly a dozen pastas, and only four second course entrees. Clearly, pastas are substantial enough to serve as main course, even if that breaks with Italian tradition. The fact that each of our four orders had red sauces with distinctly different flavors is impressive. *Linguini al frutti de mare* has the expected mix of shell fish in a sauce touched with a nautical flavor. *Pasta primavera* has a sauce accented with garlic, while *pasta putanesca* has a tomato base but an entirely different taste. Here the complexity includes olives, capers and onions, and in a departure from traditional putanesca, the depth of pine nuts. Pine nuts also show up with *mafaldina*, a long twisting noodle served with strips of grilled chicken and artichoke hearts. The tomato sauce has a natural, freshened flavor.

Some recipes tend to be more elaborate such as ravioli-like *mezzaluna*, stuffed with ricotta cheese and pesto, napped with a browned butter sauce. Others are changed on a daily basis. Some stick closer to traditional roots such as a *linguine al pesto* or fettucini alfredo.

Desserts are elaborate and imaginative. *Tiramisu* is more dense than its mascarpone cheese center suggests it should be. Brown bread pudding with warm caramel sauce comes in a portion large enough to feed a regiment.

SALBUTE
KR 17.5/20
Decor 3.5/4   Hospitality 4/5   Food 9/10   Value 1/1

- **Mexican**
- **Hinsdale**
- **$$**

20 East First Street
Hinsdale
(630) 920-8077,
1-800-SALBUTE
Troubleshooters: Jana Amsler and Edgar Rodriguez (owner-chefs)

Hours: Lunch Mon–Sat 11 am–3 pm, Dinner Mon–Thurs 5–9 pm, Fri–Sat 5–10 pm, closed Sun
Credit Cards: All majors
Reservations: Recommended
Handicapped: Accessible, but there are steps leading to the restaurant
Smoking and nonsmoking sections: Both available
Parking: On street

There is a world of Mexican food that is far more exotic and complex than that found at most taquerías and burrito stands. One top-notch example is Salbute. The model here is the intricate seasonings and recipes of an ancient culture that predates the Spanish conquest by centuries.

Salbute is somewhat small, but charming, with decor that suggests the pre-Columbian cultures of Mexico, without ignoring some common foods with which North Americans might be more familiar. So, there are burritos and enchiladas on the menu, but they are hardly the style commonly thought of as snack or street foods.

For starters, the house version of quesadilla is a good example of how Salbute approaches Mexican food. Instead of a small taco simply folded over and stuffed with melted cheese, these are grilled with a light filling of goat cheese, chicken, basil, jalapeño slices and pine nuts with small buds of mango in a tomatillo and mango fruit sauce. From a small collection of other starters, grilled mushrooms surround wedges of polenta cake with seasonings and spinach in a clear chicken stock. Recently, a soup of the day was yellow tomato, touched with what could have been cumin among its seasonings.

Entrees include the familiar, such as fajitas, though there is no mistaking the care in putting together deliciously grilled steak, for instance, with peppers and onions that can be enjoyed as is, or wrapped in a tortilla covering. Tuna, pan-seared to give it a bit of crust, was a recently featured special. The fish steaks were bedded on flageolet beans with brussels sprouts. Tomatoes and red peppers contributed to the tangy sauce.

You might not think of venison as Mexican, but it is, and excellent when handled as it is at Salbute. Twin racks are plated in a dark molé and as the menu points out, molés are not chocolate sauces. The flavors are subdued, but clearly evident as an accompaniment to the tender venison.

Among poultry choices, duck breast is served with a tropically sweet tamarind sauce, while free range chicken is plated with a Molé whose influence is quite different than that served with venison. There are, of course, several other selections on the printed menu as well as daily specials. Desserts include traditional Mexican flan and a tempting pecan pie which, it is claimed, is made from a 95-year-old recipe.

Salbute has no liquor license because Hinsdale is dry. But, diners may bring their own, a fact which whoever took our reservation failed to tell us. Otherwise, we were hospitably welcomed, though during the course of the evening, service was somewhat poorly timed, if not confused.

SALPICON

KR 17.5/20

Decor 4/4   Hospitality 4/5   Food 8.5/10   Value 1/1

- **Mexican**
- **Chicago/Near North**
- **$**

1252 North Wells
Chicago
(312) 988-7811
Troubleshooter: Vincent Satkoff
(owner)

Hours: Mon, Wed–Thurs, Sun 5–10 pm, Fri–Sat 5–11 pm, Brunch Sun 11 am–2:30 pm
Credit Cards: All majors
Reservations: Accepted
Handicapped: Accessible
Bar: Extensive wine list, specialty margaritas, 35 tequilas
Smoking and nonsmoking sections: Both available
Parking: Valet
Party Facilities: No special private party facility

The bright tropical and festive colors which dominate the walls of Salpicon are almost sure to bring a smile to your face. The restaurant looks joyful! But, if the look doesn't do it, certainly the food will.

Though this is a Mexican restaurant, there is a decidedly interesting twist in its approach to the cuisine. All you need do is taste the house salsa or *"salpicon,"* as it would be called in Mexico's Yucatan region.

Balance prevails when it comes to seasonings, with the sense that just as more is not always better, neither is hot. When chilis are used, as they are in most dishes, they are varied, depending upon the effect intended by the chef. In short, this is not a "one sauce fits all" approach.

Try an order of the codfish *empanadas* for a sense of what is happening. Empanadas are pastry turnovers, usually filled with meat, but in this case, salt cod is used. Actually a rather mild flavored fish despite its name, at least when prepared properly, the cod is combined with green olives, garlic and pickled jalapeño peppers. It is served with a slightly creamed jalapeño sauce.

The Salpicon approach to seafood veracruzana is fairly traditional. Filleted fish is sautéed with capers, olives, those pickled jalapeños, garlic and capers. It sounds excessively salty from the description, but is in truth rather mild, with a balance of seasonings. Among other selections free range chicken is baked in a banana leaf, which sounds good, but does not really add any flavor. The flavor comes from red onions and habanero chile peppers, while achiote brings a pale yellow coloring to the presentation.

Even usually uncomplex enchiladas are given special treatment in a recipe which brings together grilled chicken breast as its center piece plated with shredded cabbage, cooked carrots and potatoes, topped with crumbles of semi-dry white cheese. More familiar menu items include two versions of *ceviche*, the marinated seafood cooked in the juice of lemons or limes, several fashions of pork with sauces ranging from hot and peppery, to the dark intensity of molé.

Desserts include some outstanding highlights such as slices of orange, reduced down with skin into a candy-like consistency, and served in a cinnamon orange syrup. The flan is traditional, with a delicious burnt caramel sauce. Most unusual was a recent evening special, sherbet flavored with serrano peppers and tequila. These flavors sound odd in any dessert context. But, the resulting taste is not only surprising, but deliciously so.

SALVATORE'S
KR 19/20
Decor 4/4   Hospitality 5/5   Food 9/10   Value 1/1

• **Italian**

• **Chicago/Mid-North**

• **$$**

525 West Arlington Place
Chicago
(773) 528-1200
Troubleshooters: Sherife Jusufi (co-owner), Doreen Frenier (party coordinator)

Hours: Daily Dinner 5–10 pm
Credit Cards: All majors
Reservations: Recommended
Handicapped: Accessible (there are a few steps)
Bar: Two full bars (with weekend entertainment)
Smoking and nonsmoking sections: Both available
Parking: Valet

There is a unique quality about Salvatore's, the venerable Italian restaurant, that has to do with more than just the food served. The restaurant is in an older residency building, just a few feet from the bustle and neon of Clark Street. But, it might as well be a world away.

Some years ago, I thought of Salvatore's as representing faded elegance. Now, after what appears to have been some facelifting, the elegance has been restored. Diners walk up three marbled steps into a room flanked with dark wood paneling polished to a subdued gloss. A distant wall is completely mirrored, reflecting back the low lighting. French doors open to an outside patio, now in slumber until warm weather will reawaken it to good use.

Little has changed over the years. One of my all time favorites, pasta with salmon in cream sauce is still there. This is not a restaurant with trendy pizzas, no arugula or raddichio salads, no semblance of *fad du jour* dining. Carpaccio is among appetizers, not because it is fashionable, but because it represents elegant simplicity. Other antipasti selections include simple Prosciutto and melon, fried calamari, stuffed mushrooms and mussels bathed in marinara.

Salvatore's features nearly a dozen pastas that including such traditional recipes as thin angle hair noodles with prosciutto and an egg-based cream sauce à la *carbonara*, pasta with an array of fresh seasonal vegetables and truly indulgent tortellacci stuffed with garlic, bacon, scallions and bits of fresh pear worked down into a creamy rich gorgonzola blue cheese sauce. Among other selections, spinach fettucini is treated to a sauce which brings together olive oil, garlic. spinach, pine nuts, parmesan cheese for texture and red pepper flakes for accent.

One or two pastas are brought over into main course dining, among them an excellent version of *zuppa di mare*, that wonderful presentation of mixed seafoods in a spiced and peppery tomato sauce over linguini. Salvatore's version of Norwegian salmon, not especially Italian, is one of the best around. A variety of chicken, veal and beef entrees completes the entrees.

Tiramisu may be the menu's only tribute to faddish dining, but it happens to be good enough to overlook that. There are other choices, as well as specials of the day. The wine list is quite impressive. Service is proper, but not distant. Salvatore's is one of Chicago's most romantic restaurants.

SANTORINI
KR 17.5/20
Decor 4/4   Hospitality 4.5/5   Food 8/10   Value 1/1

- **Greek**
- **Chicago/Near West**
- **$$**

138 South Halsted Street
Chicago
(312) 829-8820
Troubleshooter: Demetrios Lamar (owner)

Hours: Sun–Thurs 11 am–midnight, Fri–Sat until 1 am
Credit Cards: All majors, house accounts
Reservations: Accepted
Handicapped: Accessible
Bar: Full service, extensive selection of Greek wines plus some American
Parking: Valet
Party Facilities: Private party facilities for up to 100 people

It's my view that there are many more similarities than differences between Chicago's Greek restaurants. But, now and then, one comes along that is seemingly above the crowd. Santorini is such a Greek restaurant. Like others in Greektown, it is noisy and festive. But, although prices are in line with the others, there is the appearance that this is more an upscale, though not necessarily dressy sort of place.

The large bi-level dining room is Mediterranean bright with whitewashed walls, wood accents, a fireplace to one side. There's even a cactus plant, which seems to suggest the American Southwest or Mexico. But, never mind all that; the food is decidedly Grecian.

The food at Santorini is on par with other Greek restaurants, perhaps in some respects a notch or two above. For instance, an occasional special is lamb *exohiko*. In this preparation, chunks of lamb are braised, topped with cubes of feta cheese, sauced with a dark gravy studded with green peas, and wrapped in a phyllo dough for final baking. The portion is enormous, easily enough for two people. The flavors are in perfect balance as the gravy tends to absorb some of the stronger essence of the feta. The crust remains delicately flaked without becoming soggy.

The printed menu offers a number of other lamb, beef and chicken dishes. Almost half the menu, though, is given over to seafood. Whole black bass and whole red snapper are market priced. Other fish run the gamut including Norwegian salmon, orange roughy, grouper and lemon sole as well as various shellfish. Shrimp kebabs, like everything else, come in large portion.

Appetizers include such Greek favorites as *saganaki* and deep-fried Calamari. By some standards the calamari can be a little chewy, but still great to nibble at almost like popcorn. The restaurant serves a delicious sliced eggplant, lightly dredged in flour and given a quick dip in hot oil; the slices are topped with grated cheese and a course tomato sauce. It makes for delicious snacking.

SAVARIN
KR 19/20
Decor 4/4   Hospitality 5/5   Food 9/10   Value 1/1

- **French Bistro**
- **Chicago/River North**
- **$$**

713 North Wells Street
Chicago
(312) 255-9520
Troubleshooter: John Hogan
(chef/owner)

Hours: Mon–Fri 5–10 pm
Credit Cards: All majors
Reservations: Recommended
Handicapped: Accesible
Smoking and nonsmoking sections: Smoking bar
Parking: Valet $8

The mix of diners, the hustle of servers as they make their way from kitchen to tables and the hard tile floor with its late 19th Century geometric patterned look all add up to make this new French bistro a welcome addition to an already crowded community of bistros.

Chef John Hogan takes his restaurant's name and inspiration from early 19th century gastronome and philosopher Jean Anselme Brillat-Savarin, whose defining work about the physiology of taste was a landmark of its time, and still inspires gourmands today.

There are daily specials to expand menu dining selections, and unless one is on a very restricted diet, choosing an evening's meal will be very satisfying work! One could begin with a terrine of smoked sturgeon and crab mousse; the smoky taste of the sturgeon is clearly evident. Among other selections are bistro classics such as snails in garlic butter, an assortment of country patés, traditional French onion soup and an earthy ragout of mushrooms seasoned with smoked bacon and set out on a bed of watercress.

Aside from the nightly specials, main course selections are limited to simple steak and fries, traditional roasted chicken with bacon, pearl onions and mushrooms plated with a side of roasted potatoes, braised rabbit with noodles in a mustard sauce and wonderfully flavored rack of lamb crusted with fine chopped herbs and garlic. There is not a disappointment in the bunch. The steak is seared, topped with melted herbed butter and set out with a huge mound of golden french fries. From among seafood selections, salmon might be simply broiled and plated with steamed vegetables. Another night could bring classic Dover sole and butter sauce. Black sea bass has a taste and texture which suggests that it is poached, then set in a shallow bowl with a light basil broth and a selection of simple vegetables.

Desserts are typically classic, and wonderfully showcased in a restaurant whose brilliance suggests more the likes of fine dining than bistro. Service is perfect. Incidentally, a second floor lounge with upholstered chairs and sofas and long bar provides a perfect setting for a drink or two before or after dinner.

Scoozi!
KR 17.5/20
Decor 4/4   Hospitality 4/5   Food 8.5/10   Value 1/1

- **Italian**
- **Chicago/Near North**
- **$$**

410 West Huron
Chicago
(312) 943-5900
Troubleshooter: Manager on duty

Hours: Lunch Mon–Fri 11:30 am–4 pm, Dinner Mon–Thurs 5–9:30 pm, Fri–Sat 5–10:30 pm, Sun 4–9 pm
Credit Cards: All majors
Reservations: accepted
Handicapped: Accessible (including Braille menus)
Smoking and nonsmoking sections: Separate smoking, nonsmoking seating
Parking: Valet

Scoozi! is where people waiting for tables spend that time watching other people waiting for tables. Scoozi! is also restaurant as theatre to the "ne plus ultra." But, as it turns out, Scoozi! serves some uncommonly, and even surprisingly good food in an atmosphere meant to recreate a large, open Renassiance refectory that might be hosting artists and their students.

The menu is quite detailed without being exhaustive in its exploration of Northern Italian cookery. Specialties from Tuscany, Piedmont, Lombardy, Venice, Naples and other regions are featured among the antipasti, entrees, pastas, salads and pizzas on the menu. A wide range of imported ingredients, including vegetables, cheeses and herbs gives the restaurant's chefs the flexibility to offer a high degree of quality even considering the huge volume and different varieties of dishes that are served.

The best way to begin is by ordering a large pizza. When our waiter brought out two large tomato cans which he said would be a platform for the pizza, I thought this was just an affectation of a trendy restaurant. Then he brought the pizza and I realized it did need a platform. It came out on a large, board, about 18 inches or more long . . . The pizza, instead of the 9 or ten inch circle I expected was gargantuan, a large ellipse of flavor on a thin, but crisp crust. Flavors were absolutely sensational. Scoozi! could earn its reputation just on its pizza.

But, there was much more to be ordered . . . Not only are there some unusual pasta choices, but the kitchen produces fresh risotto every half hour. Properly made, it is a soft blend of rice, light seasonings, especially saffron, butter and cheese. Although *risotto Milanese* may be the most well-known, there are any number of recipes. Each evening may bring a different style.

Among pastas, cavatappi are treated to an unusual roasted tomato and eggplant sauce accented with basil and mozzarella cheese. *Mezzaluna,* half moon shaped ravioli are filled with a fine chop of spinach and ricotta cheese; diners can choose from alfredo, classic tomato or pesto sauces. Meaty entrees to follow pasta include a very special roasted chicken with garlic mashed potatoes and spinach. Fresh fish are featured depending upon season and availability.

SEASONS
KR 20/20
Decor 4/4   Hospitality 5/5   Food 10/10   Value 1/1

- **American**
- **Chicago**
- **$$$**

120 East Delaware Place
(Four Seasons Hotel)
Chicago
(312) 280-8800
Troubleshooters:
Fabian Unterzaucher
(mornings/afternoons),
Jon Garfinkel (evenings)

Hours: Brunch Sun 10:30 am–1:30 pm, Breakfast Mon–Sat 6:30–10:30 am, Sun 6:30 am–10 am, Lunch Mon–Sat 11:30 am–2 pm, Dinner Sun–Sat 6–10 pm
Credit Cards: All majors
Handicapped: Accessible
Reservations: Recommended
Smoking and nonsmoking sections: Both available
Parking: Valet available

Seasons is an exciting experience even before you wend your way into the restaurant. First, there is the treat of going through the lobby of the lovely Four Seasons Hotel, as gracious and welcoming experience as any in Chicago. The ornate public rooms are perfectly decorated, rich, but not too rich, lavish but not overdone, contemporary, but not excessively modern.

A huge floral display greets diners just before they step into the wood-paneled dining room, where tables are set well apart for a sense of privacy in your dinner conversation. Chef Mark Baker compliments these surroundings with a creative American cuisine that makes use of only fresh ingredients, emphasizing local produce and foodstuffs where possible, even to the point of searching out small specialty purveyors.

Daily dinner specials compliment the printed menu, which itself rotates with the seasons and calendar. Past highlights have included roasted cod fillet with smoked cod and scallop hash, roasted free range chicken with tiny pearl barley and sweet corn pilaf, or prime rib eye steak with baked potato stuffed with onion and plated with garlic-mustard and rosemary-flavored grits.

The printed menu always features a vegetarian dinner, each course carefully prepared to compliment the others. But, meat, seafood and poultry lovers are extensively catered to. Many of the restaurant's more unusual recipes are not only delicious, but meet requirements for a low-fat, low-sodium, low-cholesterol diet.

For something truly special, Chef Baker creates an eight course surprise dinner each evening. By the way, Seasons is perhaps the only Chicago restaurant where diners have the rare opportunity to enjoy *essig*, a specialty vinegar from Germany. *Essig* can be enjoyed drunk as an *aperitif* in elegant long stem glasses, or as an enhancement when misted on particular dishes, such as roasted meats. As a *digestif*, at dinner's conclusion, it adds an unusual finish to a night of fine dining at its best.

SEVEN TREASURES
KR 17/20

Decor 3/4   Hospitality 4/5   Food 9/10   Value 1/1

- **Chinese**
- **Chicago/Near South**
- **$**

2312 South Wentworth
Chicago
(312) 225-2668
Troubleshooter: Chung L. Au
(owner)

Hours: Daily 11–2 am
Credit Cards: None
Reservations: Accepted
Handicapped: Accessible
Bar: No alcoholic beverages served
Smoking and nonsmoking sections: Separate smoking and nonsmoking seating
Parking: Street parking can be tight

Think of Chinese food, and chances are you think of rice as the accompaniment. The fact is that noodles are as important to Chinese dining, an Asian version of pasta. If you wonder how common noodles are in the cuisine, have an egg roll–you're eating a noodle. At Seven Treasures, you can still have your noodle, and you won't even have to order an egg roll. In fact, they were doing noodles years before the trendy North Side "Noodle Houses" caught on!

Take a look at their two menus, one with a large list of choices like most conventional Chinese restaurants, and the smaller folder with its selection of soups, dumplings and noodles. Begin with appetizers. The dumplings in oyster sauce brings a large platter of some of the best dumplings I have ever had. These are made with a nearly transparent dough, as thin as a sheet of paper. Wrapped inside are fillings such as chopped mushrooms and meat, whole tiny shrimp. The light oyster sauce clings to each delicious dumpling as you grasp one with chopsticks or fork and enjoy the sensual taste and texture.

Take a platter of braised noodles, with a light topping of fresh ginger and snips of scallions. Braising of noodles gives them a texture not unlike the *al dente* quality found in Italian pastas, yet the flavors and seasonings make them unmistakably Oriental. For a different flavor and texture contrast, try a small side order of duck, with crisp skin and meat that practically falls from the bones.

If you want to eat like the local customers, try one of the soups that range from clear broth to rice soup, to soup and noodles with a wide choice of toppings from which to choose. While largely Cantonese, the menu does list some of the spicier Szechwan dishes that offer more pronounced seasoning. Yet, Cantonese dining still has its own charms. The large portion of stir-fried beef comes in a thick brown gravy, and a topping of Chinese broccoli, leafy spinach and other green vegetables. Seven Treasures is distincitve since a large portion of its kitchen is open to the front window of the restaurant so that you can actually see the preparation of many of the foods. The restaurant is brightly lit, not unlike a cafeteria or coffee shop of the 1950s. But, what really makes Seven Treasures distinctive is that this is where the locals go.

SHAW'S CRAB HOUSE
KR 17.5/20
Decor 4/4   Hospitality 5/5   Food 8/10   Value .5/1

- **American Seafood**
- **Chicago**
- **$$$**

21 East Hubbard
Chicago
(312) 527-2722
Troubleshooters: Kevin Brown, Steve LaHaie (managing partners), Yves Roubaud (executive chef)

Hours: Lunch Mon–Fri 11:30 am–2 pm, Dinner Mon–Thurs 5:30–10 pm, Fri–Sat 5–11 pm, Sun 5–10 pm
Credit Cards: All majors
Reservations: Suggested
Handicapped: Accessible
Bar: Two large bar areas including the immensely popular and likable Blue Crab Lounge serve a variety of wines, beers and cocktails (live jazz and blues Tues and Thurs nights)
Smoking and nonsmoking sections: Both available, pipes and cigars in Blue Crab lounge
Parking: Valet

Shaw's Crab House looked old the first day it opened. I have the feeling it took designers quite a while to find just the right pieces and adornments. The same care and attention that went into the studied decor has gone into preparation of the food. Dinner should begin with appetizer and, if you are lucky, it may be the soft shell crab season. These delectable little critters are quickly sautéed in butter, finished with toasted almonds or garlic as you choose. They come two to the appetizer or four to the dinner portion and are unbeatable.

Since dining is à la carte, and very pricey at that, you may want to move right on to a main course, although skipping something like a clam chowder or seafood gumbo may be hard to do. Perhaps you'll want one of the namesake crabs. The crabcakes are large, meaty, perfectly seasoned and served with a spicy mustard and milder tartar-like sauce. They did not include the word "oysters" in the restaurant's name, but diners can get a veritable crash course in oyster terminology from the menu. The oysters are listed at one side of the menu by geography and name. Thus, you will learn that malpeques, for instance, are fished off Prince Edward Island, Canada, while kumamotos are farm fished off Northern California and Washington State. Then, on the other side of the menu, is a list of current daily offerings, depending upon season and availability.

The entrée selection similarly depends upon season and availability. For example, Alaskan halibut might be plated with asparagus and fennel salad, while grouper could come with a charred mustard glaze and a sautéed melange of seasonal vegetables. Specialties including lake perch and Lake Superior whitefish are regularly available as are lobster and crab dinners.

Desserts are quite good. The key lime pie has all the gusto of the real thing; a chocolate, caramel and nut tart is worth every delicious calorie. Service is friendly and well-informed. Tables are rather close together, so if its quiet intimacy you want, this is not the place. Otherwise, cash in a share or two of IBM and enjoy the authentic decor, and in most cases, unquestionably good food.

SHAW'S SEAFOOD GRILL

KR 18/20

Decor 4/4   Hospitality 4/5   Food 9/10   Value 1/1

- **American Seafood**
- **Deerfield**
- **$$$**

660 West Lake Cook Road
Deerfield
(847) 948-1020
Troubleshooters: Steve LaHaie,
Kevin Brown (managing partners)

Hours: Lunch Mon–Fri 11:30 am–2:30 pm, Dinner Mon–Thurs 5–9:30 pm, Fri–Sat 5–10:30 pm, Sun 4:30–9 pm
Credit Cards: All majors
Reservations: Suggested
Handicapped: Accessible
Smoking and nonsmoking sections: No smoking

Not quite as lavish in decor as its big brother downtown (See Shaw's Crab House), Shaw's Seafood Grill still has plenty to offer in the way of atmosphere and mood. The central bar is a great place for pairing off or group conversation. The large dining areas, like the bar, have an old East Coast oyster house look about things.

Seafood, of course, is what The Grill is all about. Everything is absolutely fresh. Walk over to the raw bar on an early evening and check out some of the availabilities in the area of clams and oysters. I think the Maryland crab cake is just about the best to be found this side of the Chesapeake.

As for those dinners, entrees run a seasonal gamut depending upon freshness and availability. For those who eschew seafood in any form or manner, a sirloin steak is on the menu as are two chicken recipes. Among desserts, the key lime pie tastes as sweet/tart as it would in good old Islamorada.

SHIROI HANA
KR 19/20
Decor 4/4   Hospitality 4/5   Food 10/10   Value 1/1

- **Japanese**
- **Chicago/Mid-North**
- **$**

3242 North Clark Street
Chicago
(773) 477-1652
Troubleshooter: Mr. Somitami
(owner)

Hours: Lunch Mon–Sat
noon–2:30 pm, Dinner
Mon–Thurs 5–10 pm, Fri–Sat
5–10:30 pm, Sun 4:30–9:30 pm
Credit Cards: All majors
Handicapped: Accessible
Reservations: No
**Smoking and nonsmoking
sections:** No smoking in
restaurant
Parking: Street parking can be
tight

I have always felt that it is virtually impossible to find good Japanese sushi and sashimi except at those restaurants that would be considered expensive. But, now I know differently, thanks to some friends who shared their secret with me, and which I am going to share with you. The truth is that Shiroi Hana is hardly a secret. This tiny restaurant, with seating for less than 50 diners, is usually packed. But, turnover is quick, so even if you have to wait for a table, the lingering does not seem to be too long or inconvenient.

The food is excellent, the prices are in the realm of budget dining. The Sushi Deluxe consists of nine pieces of sushi and one maki roll, all laid out with that keen eye for design that characterizes Japanese dining. I suppose that what makes it possible to serve sushi at such a reasonable price is the high turnover. Just like McDonald's, success lies in volume. But, make no mistake about it. Shiroi Hana is not Mickey D's. The dining room has a handsome, but not overdone Japanese character thanks to the tasteful use of blond wood accent trim and light. Tables are small or, if you prefer, cozy. A sushi counter is at the back where there are a few seats for the lucky diners who actually get to watch the preparations.

There is more than sushi and sashimi. The menu is similar to other Japanese restaurants. And, while cost is no measure of value without quality, the quality is maintained, whether it is a simple appetizer such as shrimp-stuffed Japanese eggrolls in crispy thin noodle wraps or an entree of teriyaki chicken, sukiyaki or any of a dozen or so other grilled meat or seafood selections. The menu includes a couple of traditional soba noodle specials, as well as tempura choices, and udon noodle casseroles.

SHRIMP WALK
KR 17.5/20
Decor 3/4   Hospitality 4.5/5   Food 9/10   Value 1/1

- **American/New Orleans Seafood**
- **Highwood**
- **$$**

444 Lakeview Avenue
Highwood
(847) 432-7080
Troubleshooters: Karen and
Bryan Heffernan (owners)

Hours: Sun–Thurs 4:30–9 pm,
Fri–Sat until 10 pm
Credit Cards: All majors
Reservations: Suggested
Handicapped: Accessible
**Smoking and nonsmoking
sections:** Both available
Parking: Ample free parking in
lot or on street

The menu's theme is primarily New Orleans and cajun, a style of cooking which has marked the Shrimp Walk even back in those days before it became TV cooking show trendy à la Emeril. I guess you could say that the Shrimp Walk was doing *bams!!* before anyone else around the North suburbs.

Be that as it may, Shrimp Walk also serves just about the best hamburger you could find, called the Bourbon Street Burger. The ground meat is formed into a thick patty, about half a pound of meat, set out on a bun big enough to hold it and fixin's including your choice of melted cheese as you might prefer it.

But, there are so many more reasons to visit and enjoy its tantalizing Crescent City–style flavors. A friend of ours always swears by the Basin Street Butterflies, a platter full of succulently breaded and fried shrimp. You can use a traditional spicy shrimp cocktail sauce, a tangy tartar sauce or a more *N'Awlins* style remoulade. There's a whole section of menu devoted to a dozen or so styles of shrimp, grilled, steamed in beer, smothered in barbecue sauce, in a tempura-style sauce, old-fashioned 1950s style shrimp de jonghe in garlic butter breading and even *smodded,* which the menu describes as . . . "baked in garlic breading, topped with grated asiago cheese."

I have had the shrimp etoufee on previous visits, though not this most recent. It has been a savory creation. The French word *Etoufee* suggests smothered, the idea being to literally cover shrimp, or more traditionally, crawfish, in a thick brown gravy with lots of onions and green peppers, all set out atop a mound of rice which absorbs this symphony of flavors.

Pastas are more often than not rather elaborate, if not baroque, in their conceptions. Even where a name, such as shrimp or lobster *diavolo* suggest Italian roots, the sauce may be marinara, but the cooking style is more of the Mississippi. Another pasta entree with a mix of seafood is a bit less spiced, its flavors cloaked more or less in a tomato cream sauce over angel hair with sautéed shrimp and lobster meat with scallions and mushrooms.

The fresh seafood selection is embellished by a wealth of cooking styles, blackened, marinated, grilled, broiled and so forth. Grouper is wonderful when prepared simply grilled, while walleye pike is best in a traditional pan sauté with a little lemon butter.

All entrees come with a tasty mix of greens and baby rock shrimp, but if you want a salad as entree, the cobb, seafood or Caesar will do the job just fine. Other first course choices range from a traditional French onion soup baked in the crock, thick and delicious gumbos and chowders, steamed mussels, raw oysters, oysters rockefeller in traditional garb and Louisiana crab cakes, baked or deep-fried, to point out just a few.

Desserts are rich and Southern including a tasty key lime pie, and an ornate and chocolately Mississippi mud pie.

THE SILK MANDARIN & SUSHI RESTAURANT
KR 19.5/20
Decor 4/4   Hospitality 5/5   Food 9.5/10   Value 1/1

- **Chinese (and Japanese sushi bar)**
- **Vernon Hills**
- **$$**

60 Phillips Road
(south of Route 60)
Vernon Hills
(847) 680-1760
Troubleshooter: Andy Tsai
(owner)

Hours: Lunch Mon–Fri 11:30 am–2:30 pm, Dinner Mon–Thurs 2:30–9:45 pm, Fri–Sat until 10:45 pm, Sun 3–9 pm, Chinese Buffet Brunch Sat–Sun 11:30 am–3 pm, sushi bar closed Sun
Credit Cards: All majors
Reservations: suggested, especially weekends
Handicapped: Accessible
Smoking and nonsmoking sections: No smoking
Parking: Free in lot

Silk Mandarin and Sushi Restaurant, to call it correctly by its new name, has been remodeled to allow for the addition of a sushi bar, with a full menu of sushi and sashimi. Add that to the latest from the Chinese side of the Silk Mandarin menu, and it is a superb collection, notable not only for its breadth, but for the unusual presentations and imaginative creations. The kitchen takes a true *gourmet* approach to the cooking. I really do not like to use that word because it suggests something highfalutin, when what it really should convey is a pinnacle of culinary excellence.

The menu reads like a short story of edible delights. The core of American Chinese restaurants is there, but similarities end with name only. Presentations are always something special, with clearly defined flavors, handsome settings and generous portions. *General Tso's chicken* is among house specialties, sort of a Chinese version of chicken or veal marengo, at least as far as the legend of its creation is concerned. The sauce is abundant, somewhat spicy, the cut-up pieces of chicken fried to a crisp, with the meat inside hot and tender. Orange beef is another of the house specials; it is amazing what a bit of tangy orange and its zest can do for a sauce.

The kitchen uses flounder as its primary soft-fish. In one recipe, thin fillets are marinated in white wine, then sautéed and topped with toasted pine nuts. A ring of sautéed spinach frames the platter. In another presentation, flounder fillets are sautéed, then simmered in black bean sauce spiced with chili paste and sliced green onions.

The unusual becomes usual at Silk Mandarin, but never common place. Try an appetizer such as shitake mushrooms in an Oriental five spice wrapped inside tofu formed like a wonton noodle. It is exquisite. Cold noodles in sesame sauce has been a standout every time I have tasted an order. An extensive list of vegetables includes delicious eggplant with a sharp flavored garlic sauce. Bean curd, a form of tofu, gets a trio of presentations, while black mushrooms and bamboo shoots is as delicate as a silken tapestry.

Speaking of silken tapestry, the restaurant is beautifully bedecked with Oriental art. Diners never feel crowded in the high ceilinged and spacious dining rooms. Service is much more than mere order taking. Your server will always suggest when asked, but otherwise, his presence will hardly be noticed except when you need him.

SOJU
KR 18/20

Decor 4/4   Hospitality 5/5   Food 8/10   Value 1/1

- **Korean**
- **Chicago/Bucktown**
- **$$**

1745 West North Avenue
Chicago
(773) 782-9000
Troubleshooter: Michael
Manning (co-owner)

Hours: Dinner Tues–Thurs 6–10 pm, Sat 6–11 pm, Sun 5–10 pm, closed Mon
Credit Cards: All majors
Reservations: Suggested
Handicapped: Accessible
Smoking and nonsmoking sections: Smoking at bar or designated seating
Parking: On street

Soju was the first Korean restaurant in the eclectic Bucktown area. The menu, like the restaurant which seats less than 50 people, is somewhat small, but the basic attractions that draw diners to Korean food are there.

Begin with appetizers such as *mandu*, fried or steamed dumplings folded into half-moon shapes with fillings of meat, tofu or vegetables as you might choose. Take one nimbly with your chopsticks and dip into a peppery sesame and scallion soy sauce, or eat them as they come. Both ways are delicious.

Among other first course nibbles, Japanese-style chicken *yakitori*, or skewered chicken, finds its way to the menu, as do a quartet of sushi and maki rolls. Spicy tuna maki brings small slices of tuna and rice wrapped in green seaweed. A dab of wasabi and a little stack of pickled ginger completes the plate. As for more traditional Korean edibles, the list also includes *kimchi*, or scallion, pancakes. The pancakes can be a bit oily, but they are almost irresistible nibbles. A mild sesame sauce can be used for dipping.

Soju's entrees include choices familiar to anyone who has eaten at a Korean restaurant. This is an Asian cuisine that is easy for first timers because of its ample use of grilled beef. *Kalbi* is not much more exotic than chargrilled beef ribs, except instead of a Texas hot sauce, these have a seasoned Korean glaze that leaves them sweet, if not tangy.

Similarly, *bulgogi*, or strips of flame grilled beef, have been marinated in a seasoned bath that combines flavors of sweet with a light astringency. Other entrees include grilled pork in garlic sauce, pan-seared tofu for vegetarian diners, and a quartet of fish including tuna, salmon, yellowfish and mackerel. Each is charbroiled and accompanied by a different glaze or seasoning.

The first Korean food I ever tasted was *chop chai*, transparent noodles in a thick, somewhat sweet sauce with vegetables. The version at

Soju brings back those memories. It can be ordered with chicken, beef or tofu. Another Korean classic, *bibimbop* is as good to eat as it is odd to say. A large bowl of rice is mixed with spicy Korean pickled and marinated vegetables with a fried egg on top. The idea is to mix things together and make it as spicy, or not as you choose.

Service is friendly. You may bring your own wine or beer, though Soju does have an array of teas that go well with this sort of food.

SOUL KITCHEN
KR 17/20

Decor 4/4   Hospitality 4/5   Food 8/10   Value 1/1

• **American Eclectic** • **Chicago/Northwest** • **$$$** 1576 North Milwaukee Avenue Chicago (773) 342-9742 **Troubleshooter:** Pam Scariano (owner)	**Hours:** Sun–Thurs 5–10:30 pm, Fri–Sat 5–11:30 pm, Brunch Sun 10 am–2 pm **Credit Cards:** MC, Visa **Reservations:** No **Handicapped:** Accessible **Bar:** Full service **Smoking and nonsmoking sections:** Both available, no pipes or cigars **Parking:** Street or nearby lot

Soul Kitchen is characterized by noise and crowds, both of which can be found in fairly abundant supply in the restaurant's large Bucktown dining room. It also happens to be distinguished by some fairly good, sometimes even imaginative American cookery.

The restaurant is handsomely accented by stylized paintings of people with overly emphasized features. Its art might, in that sense, be symbolic of the often heavily spiced food. Certainly the jerk chicken, skewered and served with a cooling culinary emolument of yogurt with cilantro and cucumbers, is almost too sizzling to savor without the sauce.

Less spicy, but certainly tasty, are appetizers such as soul oysters sautéed in olive oil, and seasoned with basil and garlic. You could add some Tabasco sauce, but would you really want to? Other starters range from barbecued frog legs with creole remoulade to sensationally rich hominy cakes with red peppers roasted into the batter, served with eggplant and blue goat cheese, along with the added embellishment of caramelized onions.

The à la carte dining has recently included smoked potato and leek soup in a richly endowed cream and stock base. The restaurant's version of Caesar salad is made unique thanks to a caramelized garlic dressing, which is anything but "ho hum."

From a selection of entrees, peppercorn and garlic chicken might be served, while other entrees can include grilled shrimp with a light curry sauce plus slices of avocado and steamed rice. The plating, by the way, is handsomely done, not some haphazard disarrangement. Jambalaya is a typical collection of ingredients, shrimp, chicken, clams, a bit of sausage. Yellowfin tuna has been glazed in sesame oil, plated with an Oriental bean relish and scallion *aioli*, while grilled beef tenderloin gets treated to a side of smashed garlic potatoes, green peppercorn sauce and tropical fruit chutney.

Other entrees can include catfish fried in pecan crumbs, duck served with a molé sauce and plantains, or traditionally southern pork barbecue with sweet potato and greens. Desserts are as involved as entrees, recently including a mango and lime trifle with rum cream sauce, sweet potato and bourbon pecan tart, topped with whipped cream, and a chocolate walnut brownie with vanilla ice cream and caramel sauce.

SPAGO
KR 19.5/20
Decor 4/4   Hospitality 5/5   Food 9.5/10   Value 1/1

- **California Chinois**
- **Chicago/Near North**
- **$$$**

520 North Dearborn
Chicago
(312) 527-3700
Troubleshooter: Amanda
Larsen Puck (general manager)

Hours: Lunch Mon–Fri 11:30 am–2 pm, Dinner Mon–Thurs 5:30–9 pm, Fri–Sat 5–10:30 pm, closed Sun
Credit Cards: All majors
Reservations: Suggested
Handicapped: Accessible
Smoking and nonsmoking sections: Smoking in bar area only
Parking: Valet

Chicago's restaurant community has a new challenge to match with the arrival of Wolfgang Puck's Spago. The contemporary dining room is a gallery of glass, fabrics, wood and metal free-forms.

The open kitchen, under direction of Chef Francois Kwaku-Dongo, produces Puck's *chinois* style of "East meets West" cookery. While many Chicago chefs have jumped on the fusion cuisine bandwagon, none manage to do it well as Puck and Kwaku-Dongo, his culinary amanuensis in Chicago.

The menu changes regularly. A recent evening's listing included outstanding grilled quail in a large first course portion. The skin was crispy with a tangerine glaze, and an underpinning of Chinese five spice. A garnish of greens and grilled pineapple completed the plate and its flavor contrasts. In another appetizer, Puck bravely uses strong stilton cheese, usually reserved for an after dinner cheese course, in combination with wilted spinach, sliced apples and dots of caramelized pecans in a delicious salad. Other appetizers range from tuna sashimi to smoked sturgeon on a potato galette to a complex fish soup akin to cioppino or bouillabaisse filled with meaty striped sea bass, clams and mussels in a savory stock.

If one word describes the Wolfgang Puck approach to cookery it would be "imaginative." In one dinner entree, salmon is coated with a grind of pine nuts and an herb bouquet, then roasted and plated with cooked celery root. In another, a baked Chinese bun is at the center of a platter circled with pieces of roasted duck, glazed with star anise and napped in a demiglace sauce flavored with pomegranate. The star anise, not so incidentally, is hardly noticeable, more of as an aftertaste that has to be sought after and pursued.

Among other entree selections, seared rack of lamb brings a trio of thick, juicy chops at rest in a pale green mint and cilantro sauce. Proving that perfection is always elusive, the lamb, though delicious, had too much fat to be ideal. At the center of the platter, in a red radicchio leaf bowl, is Puck's version of fried rice; needless to say, it is nothing like that at your local chop suey carryout.

And, that's what makes Spago so special. Though Wolfgang Puck has many imitators, he has achieved his celebrity status because he is one of the American restaurant scene's most inspired innovators.

SPRUCE
KR 18.5/20
Decor 4/4   Hospitality 4.5/5   Food 9/10   Value 1/1

- **American**
- **Chicago/Near North**
- **$$$**

238 East Ontario
Chicago
(312) 642-3757
Troubleshooter: Dan Sachs
(owner)

Hours: Lunch Mon–Fri 11:30 am–2 pm, Dinner Mon–Thurs 5:30–10 pm, Fri–Sat 5:30–11 pm, closed Sun
Credit Cards: All majors
Reservations: Recommended
Handicapped: Not accessible
Smoking and nonsmoking sections: Both available
Parking: Valet

The entrance to this spiffy restaurant is down a short flight of stairs into what amounts to a rather spacious basement. There are wide expanses, large wooden support columns and cross beams, a clean, largely unadorned look except for the wood floor, an occasional splash of art, and the crisp white look of the tablecloths.

The menu and cooking style are as inviting as the restaurant's smart appearance. Begin with salmon rolls, lightly smoked salmon at that, wrapped like Oriental spring rolls with a filling of corn relish with snips of shitake mushroom. Even better is a gazpacho variation that uses a puree of grilled vegetables, with sweet bell peppers as the most pronounced flavor. A trio of large shrimp circle a small mound of avocado sorbet, whose iciness comes as somewhat of a shock if you missed that little bit of information on the menu.

Among other appetizer selections has been a vegetable torte plated with pickled pearl onions, olives and feta cheese which seems to bind things together. Even a field green salad is offered with the embellishment of dried apples and blue goat cheese in a red currant vinaigrette.

Too often fine appetizers give way to only mediocre entrees. That's certainly not the case at Spruce. Where many restaurants serve roasted chicken rubbed with herbs, or some other variety, Chef Luce has been preparing grilled and marinated poussin, a young, but fleshy chicken, somehow leaving it reminiscent of lamb. The cut-up bird rests on a tasty risotto of stewed barley, so creamy rich you might be satisfied if this was all that were on the platter. But, it's not. The presentation is finished with a roasted poblano pepper coulis and stewed whole shallots, with an added surprise of sweet whole figs. It's a wonderful presentation that goes down with some of the best offerings in the city.

Of course there are many other treats on the menu. Salmon, rosy pink in color, is grilled and plated with jasmine-scented rice in a mushroom gravy that delicately informs the other flavors. Roasted lamb loin chops have been served with couscous and a tomato broth the chef calls a fondue that may be more pretension than substantial reality.

Service is youthful, not always as attentive as it could be. The wine list is fine, as are the sumptuous desserts.

STAINED GLASS WINE BAR BISTRO & CELLAR

KR 18.5/20

Decor 3.5/4   Hospitality 5/5   Food 9/10   Value 1/1

- **American**
- **Evanston**
- **$$**

1735 Benson Avenue
Evanston
(847) 864-8600
Troubleshooters: Michael
Weyna, Victoria Fonseca
(proprietors)

Hours: Sun–Mon, Wed–Thurs
5:30–10 pm with full menu, open
until 1 am with limited bar menu,
Fri–Sat 5:30–10:30 pm, open
until 2 am with limited bar menu,
closed Tues
Credit Cards: All majors
Reservations: Suggested
Handicapped: Accessible
**Smoking and nonsmoking
sections:** 100% nonsmoking
Parking: Valet

Despite the restaurant's name, there is no stained glass is in sight. Instead, there are high wood-beamed ceilings with exposed rafters and a large and centrally located wine rack with bins for scores of bottles. The large dining room is functional and, like the rest of the restaurant, completely without any sign of decorative stained glass. Therein lies a mystery.

There is no mystery about pairing food with wines. Wines are offered by the glass and bottle, but also by flights. Once wine choices are made, whether by flight, or individual selection, it is time to get down to the equally serious and pleasurable business of food selection. The menu offers an eclectic choice of global bistro fare, without anything being too exotic. For starters, the house *charcuterie*, a selection of kitchen made *patés*, leads the list and can change nightly. Other appetizer choices range from an unusual crusted shrimp plated with caramelized onions and sweet papaya-infused butter sauce, to richly endowed crepes filled with king crab meat, field mushrooms and a white truffle cream sauce.

Among a selection of entrees, striped sea bass is wrapped in *brioche* along with spinach and shitake mushrooms. The butter sauce is lightly flavored with sweet vermouth. In another selection, large sea scallops, about the thickness of a small stack of silver dollars, are given a pan-roasted glaze and set out with caramelized fennel. This time the sauce is a spiced chipotle pepper and tomato-butter blend.

As for meat, a truly delicious roasted quail glazed with maple syrup is stuffed with apple and chestnut dressing. Braised cabbage is set in a sweet apple cider reduction. This one is good enough to pick up small pieces of the bird and nibble until nothing is left.

If lamb should be your fancy, try the New Zealand rack with a puree of white beans. Pancetta and honey balsamic glaze finish the presentation. Beef eaters will no doubt savor the gorgonzola cheese tart and the brandy-infused meat drippings which garnish a cut of filet mignon. Roasted free range chicken shows up in another entree, with couscous and chunked walnuts. The sauce is a relish connecting roasted bell peppers and black olives in a stylized *tapanade*. In another meaty selection, veal tenderloin is grilled, then napped in a concoction of black mission figs reduced to a thick sauce, with polenta to soak up the flavors and *proscuitto*, just because it works.

On the way out, I told the hostess all I saw was industrial tech, wood-beamed ceiling, open ductwork . . . but no stained glass. She motioned for me to look in the direction to which she pointed as she said, "Here it is." There, sitting on a small café table was a wine glass, with just a touch of claret in the bottom of its bowl. Indeed, it was a stained glass.

STREGA NONA
KR 19/20
Decor 3.5/4   Hospitality 5/5   Food 9.5/10   Value 1/1

- **Italian**
- **Chicago/Mid-North**
- **$$**

3747 North Southport
Chicago
(773) 244-0990
Troubleshooter: Bo Fowler
(general manager)

Hours: Sun Brunch 11 am–2:30 pm, Dinner 4:30–9:30 pm, Mon–Thurs 5:30–10 pm, Fri until 11 pm, Sat 5–11:30 pm
Credit Cards: All majors
Reservations: Not taken, but can call ahead to be put on priority waiting list
Handicapped: Accessible
Smoking and nonsmoking sections: Both available
Parking: Valet

Strega Nona is yet another Italian restaurant with trendy bare brick decor, open kitchen, young, sharp looking waiters and the customers to match. The menu is not huge, but what is offered is exceptional. Various bread preparations as snacks or first course items seem to be the restaurant's signature. In the manner of bruschetti, the breads are grilled and presented with various toppings. The standard issue tomato, mozzarella and basil is there, brushed with olive oil. But, so too are some truly unique and different selections.

One offering brings pieces of roasted chicken atop a Tuscan-style bread with a salad-like setting of mixed greens and tomatoes. Balsamic vinegar flavors barbecued pork in another, while prosciutto and its best culinary friend, cantaloupe, are paired with tomato fig chutney. Seared tuna is outstandingly successful. The yellowtail tuna is rare with a warm center, sliced into sections which are placed on four large slices of black olive–pesto bread. Each piece is topped with an artichoke heart and tomato slice. An olive tapanade adds some presence.

The breads can be enjoyed as simple snack or lunch with a glass or two of wine. Or, they can work as a first course before appetizers. Those appetizers include an excellent variation of Greek *dolmades*, highly stylized and adapted by the Strega Nona kitchen. In this case, grape leaves are stuffed with a mix of goat cheese and pieces of pistachio nuts. A red onion marmalade enhanced with chianti wine brings a little something extra to the recipe.

Maybe it is the idea of flavor enhancers that makes Strega Nona something special. In the case of another appetizer, grilled vegetables with polenta, it's the addition of spicy pepper oil, while in another selection, roasted eggplant is filled with sausage and risotto; and served with a sauce composed of brandied roasted peppers.

Moving to a third course, pastas may be entrees or not as you see fit. Certainly, snail-shaped shells called *lunacone* fit that description with their rich wine-infused porcini mushroom sauce. Just so the mushroom compliment is not lost, the shells are served with slices of porcinis as well as some less expensive button mushrooms. Other selections range from prosaic roasted chicken with garlic and lemon flavored potatoes to the very exotic roasted pork with pasta quills, beans and tomatoes in cilantro salsa. The most difficult part of the evening may be making selections, since everything looks so tempting.

All the restaurant's wines are available by glass or full bottle. Among desserts, chocolate sorbet is almost as luscious as a rich chocolate ice cream.

SUSHI MASA
KR 17.5/20
Decor 4/4   Hospitality 3.5/5   Food 9/10   Value 1/1

- **Japanese**
- **Vernon Hills**
- **$$**

701 North Milwaukee Avenue
(Route 60 at Milwaukee)
Suite 344
Vernon Hills
(847) 549-0101
Troubleshooter: Host or hostess
on duty

Hours: Lunch Mon, Wed–Fri
11:30 am–2 pm, Dinner Mon,
Wed–Fri 5–9:30 pm, Sat 4–10
pm, Sun 4–9 pm, closed Tues
Credit Cards: Amex, Discover,
MC, Visa
**Smoking and nonsmoking
sections:** Unstated, but the
restaurant is small, and the food is
too delicate, so don't do it
Parking: Free in lot

The sushi and sashimi at Sushi Masa is flawless, clean, sweet, varied. Sushi is uncomplicated to eat, if only because the rice makes it easy to pick up by hand, though chopsticks can be used with smaller pieces, if you wish. The restaurant provides the customary pickled ginger, sliced paper thin, as well as almost dangerously hot wasabi. Use too much, and you will feel as if the Great Chicago Fire is raging in your nose and throat.

Sushi Masa serves à la carte pieces, though a combination platter, is the better value. Each combination is described on the menu. The platters are handsomely presented in keeping with the concept that what the eye sees is as important as what the mouth tastes.

While one can make a meal on sushi and sashimi, there are some wonderful appetizers that should not be missed. *Gyoza* are delicious little fried dumplings stuffed with minced meat and vegetables. One of my favorites is *goma-ae*, which is nothing more than steamed spinach that has been chilled and combined with sweet sesame paste. Incidentally, sweet tastes are found in many dishes, including clear miso soup or complex *sukiyaki*.

The *sukiyaki* at Sushi Masa is served in a beautiful lacquer bowl. Perhaps the most widely known of Japanese entrees, it consists of thin slices of boiled beef in a broth with cabbage, mushrooms, tofu, onions and translucent noodles called *shirataki*, all cooked together in a sweetened broth flavored with soy, sugar and rice wine.

Sukiyaki is just one part of the lengthy menu that ranges from several tempuras to excellent broiled salmon, to various teriyaki meats or fish. In Japanese cookery, soups can be meals in themselves, so Sushi Masa features a variety of noodle soup dishes centered around either thick white *udon* noodles or the traditional enriched buckwheat noodles called soba.

One other style of dining is represented on the menu, the bento box. A bento box is compartmentalized, and in each section, the chef places a chosen entree, pieces of sushi and tempura. If a Mondrian painting suggests anything about arranged shapes in Western culture, the bento box achieves the same thing for the Japanese.

Service is responsive, sometimes hurried when it should be more leisurely. I think the key is to let your server know that you are in no hurry, so that you can linger, even savor the beauty of the foods presented at your table. Of course, if you want a little more action, the place to sit is the sushi counter, where you can watch the one or two sushi masters on duty, cut, slice, craft and carefully arrange each order. But, be sure to keep your fingers out of the way.

302 WEST
KR 17.5/20
Decor 4/4   Hospitality 4/5   Food 8.5/10   Value 1/1

- **American**
- **Geneva**
- **$$$**

302 West State Street
Geneva
(708) 232-9302
Troubleshooters: Catherine and Joel Findlay

Hours: Dinner Tues–Thurs 6–9 pm, Fri–Sat until 10 pm
Credit Cards: Amex, Discover, Diners, MC, Visa
Reservations: Recommended
Bar: Full cocktail lounge lofted over dining room, intimate and comfortable, extensive list of Cognacs & Armagnacs, 75 California Wines, some available by the glass
Parking: Street parking easy
Dress: Casual permitted
Party Facilities: Entire restaurant available for private parties Sun and Mon with custom tailored menus for any occasion
Note: Menu changes every four to six weeks

Housed in a former bank building, 302 West takes advantage of the high ceilings and open spaces to create a pleasant and comfortable dining atmosphere. Food leans toward the contemporary American style with imaginative use of ingredients. The menu changes regularly, but you'll always find roasted garlic, which has become somewhat of a house specialty. A full head is roasted until each clove is softened. You can either eat it right from the clove, or dab some with a knife onto the warm bread which is brought out with the garlic. A log of herbed cheese is matched to the garlic along with brine salted nicoise olives for a little added bite.

Among other appetizer selections, could be mild seafood sausage in a buerre blanc sauce. The seafood is slightly coarse, so that there is some texture appeal. Other appetizers include braised duckling "nachos" plated with whipped, herbed goat cheese and crips vegetable chips for nibbling. When they are in season, soft-shell crabs might be sauteéd in an herbed crumb crust coating with a side of herbed mayonaisse. The house salad which follows the appetizer course is a mix of butter lettuce with a crush of gorgonzola cheese and pine nuts in a light tarragon vinaigrette. An à la carte soup course may also be ordered if that is to your taste.

The excellence continues in preparation of entrees. A grilled cut of prime angus beef rib comes with a dark beer steak sauce, while rack of lamb is given a garlicky herbed lamb reduction sauce. Veal chop comes with wild mushrooms in a madeira sauce reduction. Among poultry choices, recent selections have included a hash of pheasant, vegetables and mushrooms in a sauce reduced to its rich essence, plated with haystack potato sticks.

The restaurant seems to excel at seafood. Grilled fillet of sole brings a large piece of yellow sole with a sauté of ground almonds; the richness of the brown butter sauce is broken by a splash or two of lime juice in the finishing. If you have a taste for grilled tuna, the tuna steak is grilled with tomatoes, onions and peppers, a combination as natural as blue skies at morning. Other fish choices, include mahi mahi, grouper and occasional selections depending upon availability. There are almost two dozen fresh dessert selections featured daily.

TAVERN IN THE TOWN
KR 19/20
Decor 4/4   Hospitality 5/5   Food 9.5/10   Value .5/1

- **American**
- **Libertyville**
- **$$$**

519 Milwaukee Avenue,
Libertyville
(847) 367-5755
Troubleshooter: Rick Jansen
(owner)

Hours: Lunch Mon–Sat 11:30 am–2 pm, Dinner Mon–Thurs 6–8:30 pm, Fri–Sat 6–9 pm
Credit Cards: All majors
Reservations: Suggested
Handicapped: Limited accessibility (call for specific information)
Smoking and nonsmoking sections: Both available
Parking: In lot ½ block West of Rt 21 (the lot is actually adjacent to the restaurant's front door which is not on Rt 21)

Despite its name, Tavern in the Town is much more than a tavern. The menu changes regularly and is a match for fine dining tastes. From a short list of appetizers, steamed mussels in a chive *beurre blanc* sauce are a fitting start, perhaps accompanied by a platter of smoked Norwegian salmon with appropriate garnishes. Among other selections, cultivated snails are set in a buttery garlic sauce, and embellished by baby squash and lentils. For something truly special, gray-green beads of *oestra* caviar shining up from a small container would go well with icy Russian vodka, or a beautifully golden champagne.

There are always a couple of pasta selections. Angel hair has been plated with grilled shrimp wrapped into tight little circles of flavor, while littleneck clams and a bouquet of herbs add to the proceedings. For something a bit more substantial, linguini and roasted sweet peppers are paired with sliced pieces of chicken breast and chicken sausage rounds, again with an embellishment of herbs for a bit more zing.

One of the characteristics of the cookery at the Tavern is that flavors are kept in a strict balance. Steamed mussels in *burre blanc* speak to the heart of tradition, though a bit of chive brings a definite flavor of its own. Similarly, roasted Florida red snapper gets a crusting of herbs whose flavors seem to meld into the fish during the roasting process; coriander sauce is an embellishment that might seem to overpower the fish, though it does not.

Other roasted or grilled entrees include hearty cuts of New York Strip Steak with mustard sauce, rack of baby lamb freshened with a merlot reduction, beef tenderloin with wild mushrooms at the heart of its sauce and roasted rack of pork loin with a crusting of cracked peppercorns and an apple calvados brandy sauce. Chicken, hardly the most exciting entree on most restaurant menus is paired with squab plus roasted cloves of garlic and thyme. Bordelaise sauce provides the foundation.

There is an excellent wine list, deep both vertically and horizontally with a hundred or more classified bordeauxs as well as other less intimidating bottles. The beer list is hardly less formidable, perhaps a hundred or so in bottle and on tap, darks, lights, lagers, Pilsners all with a pedigree.

Desserts, the undoing of all but the most determined calorie counters, are appropriately luscious. Each evening's selections are presented on a display platter.

THYME
KR 18.5/20
Decor 4/4   Hospitality 5/5   Food 9/10   Value .5/1

- **American**
- **Chicago/Near West**
- **$$**

464 North Halsted
Chicago
(312) 226-4300
Troubleshooters: John Bubala, Joe Russo (owners)

Hours: Tues–Sun 5:30–11 pm, closed Mon
Credit Cards: Visa, MC, Amex, Diners
Reservations: Recommended
Handicapped: Accessible
Smoking and nonsmoking sections: Both available
Parking: Valet $7

Location, location, location may be the three most important words in real estate, but when it comes to fine dining restaurants, sometimes it doesn't really count. That's why we can find so many posh and trendy restaurants in industrial neighborhoods or in fringe areas. Thyme is located at a fairly busy intersection, yet, the restaurant appears strangely isolated.

Inside, the open ductwork and sometimes stark trim contrast with a handsome bar, open kitchen and the sleek appearance of diners and servers who are right in the thick of fashion, whether it's an evening gown with thigh length split or designer jeans.

Trendy people presumably like trendy cooking, and that's what Chef John Bubala, who honed his craft at Marché offers night after night. Thyme makes no pretense at being anything but a contemporary American restaurant with a menu that speaks of such ingredients as Hudson Valley foie gras, malpeque oysters or spit-roasted pork chops. Still, there is a pan-Continental influence that goes beyond mere geographic borders. So, a vegetarian platter of delicious roasted vegetables is given a

North African kick thanks to lemon-touched couscous, the spicy pepper sauce called *harissa*, offset by a breath of fresh mint.

Among other entrees, spit-roasted chicken brings one half a bird plated with a huge mound of french fries and slivers of grilled onions. It's very basic except for the tangy taste which makes this something more than the usual bistro chicken. The menu features a couple of beef cuts, prime sirloin and grilled tenderloin tails, each with differing vegetable accompaniment. The pork chop is plated with peach chutney and whipped potatoes with leeks. Rabbit is enhanced with smoky bacon and braised leeks, while duck breast is sliced and plated with a wedge of polenta and grilled raddichio in a balsamic vinegar au jus.

A trio of fish offers salmon, halibut and monkfish. The monkfish is chunked and meaty, much like the mock lobster it is often called. Halibut is sautéed, pure white and flaky. Vegetables accompany the seafood selections, which can be ordered with a choice of sauces.

Dining is à la carte. Among appetizer selections, mussels in white wine and garlic are served in a large bowl along with cooked white beans and the fresh tastes of fennel and mint which nicely compliment the garlic. Tuna carpaccio is spiced up with fresh horseradish and milder chive. Our server recommended an order of shrimp with a vanilla sauce and red wine reduction. It's an interesting combination of flavors, but perhaps a bit over the top considering the dessert-like vanilla flavored sauce. The wine list is extensive, but expensive.

TIFFIN
KR 18.5/20
Decor 4/4   Hospitality 4.5/5   Food 9/10   Value 1/1

• **Indian**	**Hours:** Mon–Fri 10:30 am–3:30 pm, Dinner 5:30–10 pm, Sat–Sun Dinner 5:30–10:30 pm
• **Chicago/North**	
• **$$**	**Credit Cards:** All majors
2536 West Devon Avenue	**Reservations:** Suggested
Chicago	**Handicapped:** Accessible
(773) 338-2143	**Smoking and nonsmoking**
Troubleshooter: Sunny Kapoor	**sections:** No smoking in dining room, smoking in bar only

There is nothing I enjoy better as a restaurant critic than returning to a restaurant and discovering how much it has improved since my last visit. A few years ago, I was not recommending Tiffin. But, between then and now, Tiffin has made some vast improvements in service and, more importantly, in the quality of its food.

The restaurant is easily the most beautiful of any in its neighborhood of Indian restaurants. A recessed ceiling is painted with blue sky and clouds. Tables are dark wood and, though somewhat close, the conversational level at Tiffin never becomes so loud as to be intrusive.

Tiffin's menu has many of the conventional choices found at most Indian restaurants. But, the similarity ends with the manner of seasoning. It is more balanced than many other restaurants. While some choices are highly seasoned, there is a restraint which allows taste buds to pick up the entire variety of flavors. This is certainly evident in the curries we tasted, where a chef's selection and the freshness of herbs and spices can make all the difference.

The one shortcoming on selections is with appetizers. Of eight distinct choices, most are deep-fried, leaving little in the way of taste or texture variety. On the other hand, these are typical urban street foods often eaten out of hand. They can be enjoyed as is, with a sweet fruit chutney or spicy green chili chutney.

Indian restaurants are wonderful for vegetarians, and Tiffin is no exception. There is a combination plate that brings several different selections, which to my way of thinking is a good way to go for vegetarians, or even other diners who want a variety of cooked vegetables as side dishes. The gravies, or *masalas*, are marvelously seasoned with a balance that cannot be accidental.

As for meats, the *tandoor* roasts are fine whether lamb, chicken or shrimp. Nothing is overcooked. For other specifics, lamb *pasanda* is bathed in a sauce that brings together yogurt and saffron among other ingredients. Lamb *vindaloo* has a distinct flavor thanks to the use of vinegar in the makeup of its tangy gravy. Shrimp *masala* has seasonings which include a light whiff of garlic, coriander, ginger and saffron.

There is a good choice of desserts; *rasmali*, or sweet cheese balls with cardamom and pistachio nuts is perfect.

TIZI MELLOUL
KR 17.5/20
Decor 4/4   Hospitality 5/5   Food 7.5/10   Value 1/1

- **Moroccan**
- **Chicago/River North**
- **$$**

531 North Wells Street
Chicago
(312) 670-4338
Troubleshooters: Terry
Alexander (owner), Steven Ford

Hours: Lunch Mon–Fri 11:30
am–2 pm, Dinner Sun–Thurs
5:30–10 pm, Fri–Sat 5–11 pm
Credit Cards: All majors
Reservations: Recommended
Handicapped: Accessible
**Smoking and nonsmoking
sections:** Smoking at bar and
lounge only
Parking: Valet $7

Tizi Melloul is a visual garden of sybaritic delight, using bright red mosaic tile, arabesque wood carvings, beaded curtains and exotic lighting fixtures.

The Tizi Melloul menu is a solid introduction to those unfamiliar with Moroccan food. Moroccans prepare a lamb sausage called *merguez*. It is spicy, well endowed with complex seasonings of which cumin, cardamom and pepper may be the most pronounced. Like its European cousins, *merguez* is eaten with a plop or two of whole grain mustard.

For something more exotic, *besteeya* is a pastry pocket of phyllo dough filled with smoked chicken and vegetables. The flavor is indeed smoky, unlike *besteeya* I've tasted elsewhere that had a more pronounced cinnamon and clove tang. Somewhat less than a dozen other appetizer and salad choices round out the opening course choices.

Among entrees are *tagines*, named for their cooking pot, though in the case of Tizi Melloul, that pot is much too decorative to ever have been exposed to high oven heat. From a trio of choices, try a vegetarian *tagine* based on pearl couscous, a grain much like pearl barley. A variety of vegetables are roasted together with the couscous until the flavors marry into something light, but satisfying.

Speaking of light flavors, sturgeon has recently been plated on top of a cracker made of ground chickpeas with a mild, almost indefinably flavored garnish. It allows the taste of the fish to predominate, a virtual guarantee of the seafood's absolute freshness for this preparation to succeed. I mentioned lamb earlier. In one entree, it comes as a Moroccan version of *osso buco*, and in another, as a meaty braised shank coupled with cumin-seasoned fried potato dumplings, sharp tasting oiled greens and the lamb's *au jus*. It's deliciously satisfying, good enough to pick up and gnaw at the bone, though the meat served me had more fat than I would have preferred. Among other entrees, grilled quail is served with an interesting black olive bread pudding to pick the juices from the poultry and a syrupy fig and cippolini onion compote which shares the plating.

For dessert try banana cigars, fried in crushed almonds and literally served in a cigar box. Three dipping sauces, honey yogurt, delicious mocha and fruity pomegranate complete this original concept dessert. Service is excellent, and there is a good wine list. You'll spend about $65 a couple for three courses plus add ons.

TOKYO MARINA
KR 16/20

Decor 4/4   Hospitality 3.5/5   Food 7.5/10   Value 1/1

- **Japanese**
- **Chicago/Far North**
- **$$**

5058 North Clark Street
Chicago
(773) 878-2900
Troubleshooter: Noburu "Jim" Asato (owner)

Hours: Sun–Thurs 11:30 am–10 pm, Fri–Sat 11:30 am–11 pm, closed Christmas and Thanksgiving
Credit Cards: MC, Visa
Reservations: Recommended, especially weekends
Handicapped: Accessible
Smoking and nonsmoking sections: Separate smoking and nonsmoking seating
Parking: Ample street parking

Tokyo Marina offers just about anything you can find at any of Chicago's better Japanese restaurants, but at a near budget cost. Before ordering, you will want to check the handwritten listing of special fish and other seafood, as well as the different kinds of *maki*, the seafood wrapped *sushi* that can contain any number of other ingredients ranging from avacado to omelette. If you choose to order à la carte, you will have more fun when you sit at the sushi bar and tell the chef what you want. More economical, and with nearly as much variety at hand, are combination platters that include *sushi* with mackeral, yellowtail, octopus, tuna or other combinations depending upon what is fresh and available.

The restaurant is perfect for grazing. Try several appetizers. Chicken *yakitori* brings two large skewered sticks of grilled poultry and vegetables in shishkebab fashion, but with distinctly Japanese seasonings. *Tempura* can be too oily, but otherwise the vegetables and shrimp are cooked perfectly. One of the best choices is *scallop butteryaki*. Large sea scallops are stir-fried in butter with sliced button mushrooms. Something like this would be perfectly at home in a more elaborate French or Continental setting.

Tokyo Marina serves a number of noodle dishes and soups as well as casseroles such as *sukiyaki* and a quartet of *nabes*, which are vegetable and meat one pot meals often cooked at tableside. Unless you are seated at the sushi bar, service can be sluggish. But, considering the value at hand, Tokyo Marina should be on your list of regular haunts for Japanese food.

TOMBOY
KR 19/20
Decor 4/4   Hospitality 5/5   Food 9/10   Value 1/1

- **American Eclectic**
- **Chicago/Far North**
- **$$**

5402 North Clark Street
Chicago
(773) 907-0636
Troubleshooter: Manager on duty

Hours: Tues–Thurs 5–10 pm, Fri–Sat 5–11 pm, Sun 5–10 pm
Credit Cards: Amex, Diners MC, Visa
Reservations: Recommended
Handicapped: Accessible
Parking: Street parking can be tight

When it first opened a few years ago, the owners of Tomboy were on to something. It was an eclectic approach that drew an eclectic public to better dining at reasonable cost. Tomboy is even better today, with a menu that is both challenging and Accessible to a broad range of diners, foodies and non-foodies alike. Head Chef Linda Raydl and her Sous Chef Stacey Malow practically revel in the creation of original recipes. The restaurant's list of daily specials is as long or maybe even longer than the regular printed menu, which itself would offer enough choices at most restaurants.

Consider a recent special that began with roasted quail stuffed with spinach, goat cheese and sun-dried tomatoes. If that is not enough, grilled asparagus spears and mashed sweet potatoes are the side dishes, the sweet potatoes topped with homemade peanut brittle glaze.

This sort of complexity is not done for its own sake, but appears when it makes a legitimate contribution. Recently a porterhouse cut of pork chop was plated with an apple and onion confit, flavors that might seem mutually exclusive, but would stand up well to a large cut of meat such as this. A baked potato on the side is topped with a blend of gorgonzola cheese and sour cream.

While this might seem to be lily gilding, consider something that is almost pristine. Yellowtail tuna is grilled and plated with mashed potatoes whipped together with enough wasabi horseradish to give them a little bite. The menu's description of accompanying greens as a gazpacho

TOMBOY

APPETIZERS

PORTA PORTABELLO $8

Topped with balsamic vinaigrette, sun dried tomatoes, calamata olives, basil, goat cheese, served with roasted garlic

PORCUPINE SHRIMP $8

Crispy, phyllo shrimp plated with a savory blueberry sauce and peach melon relish

ESCARGOT $7

Served in a simmering garlic-shallot butter topped with lemon zest crumbs

GRILLED POLENTA $6

Polenta served with sautéed wild mushrooms topped with shaved parmesan cheese

BAKED GOAT CHEESE $7

Warm baked goat cheese encrusted in bread crumbs, served on a bed of tomato sauce with crostinis

SAUSAGE OF THE DAY $8

SALADS

SPINACH $7

Tossed in a warm pancetta dressing with tomatoes, topped with pancetta and goat cheese

BREADED BAKED BRIE $8

Served on a bed of mixed greens tossed in a strawberry balsamic vinaigrette, drizzled with sun dried fruit and walnuts

BETTY O's BALSAMIC $6

Romaine lettuce, tomato, grilled onion, cucumbers, feta cheese and calamata olives in our house dressing

CREAMY CAESAR $6

Romaine lettuce and parmesan cheese tossed in a creamy parmesan dressing topped with crostinis

HEARTS OF PALM $8

Served on a bed of mixed greens in a raspberry vinaigrette with Granny Smith apples, gorgonzola cheese and pecans

FRESH FROM THE MARKET

Ask your server for daily fish specials

VEGGIE LOVER $13

Homemade sourdough bread bowl filled with our hearty vegetable stew

DUCK BREAST $22

Pan seared to medium rare, served with a white & wild rice medley and baby carrots

SEAFOOD STEW $18

A simmering blend of seafood and shellfish in a tomato vegetable stew

GRILLED CHICKEN BREAST $16

With sautéed spinach and roasted garlic mashed potatoes

FILET MIGNON $20

Served medium rare with Anna potatoes and grilled asparagus

PORK TENDERLOIN $18

Served in an Asian Barbecue sauce with vegetable fried rice

NEW ZEALAND LAMB CHOPS $19

Served medium rare, on a bed of sautéed spinach with a port onion-gorgonzola potato

salad merely suggests the inclusion of the cucumbers, onions, tomatoes and seasonings that create the flavors characteristic of gazpacho soup.

The regular menu, and I hesitate in calling it only regular, has its own collection of enchantments. Sausage of the day recently was a smooth grind of game birds, sliced and set out on toast points with some mixed greens. In another choice, what the menu designates as porcupine shrimp are wrapped in delicate phyllo dough while a fruity blueberry and peach melon relish plays its own version of hopscotch on the taste buds. Odd as it sounds, the flavors work.

Among entrees, the seafood stew is a large platter of soft-fish including tuna and salmon with mussels, shrimp and scallops among ingredients in a savory tomato ragout. A few pastas are among other regular entrees. Twisted strands of *gemelli* noodles are tossed with chunks of beef, mushrooms and caramelized onions. A peppery chipotle tomato sauce is the only flaw, too strong and overwhelming.

From the day it opened, Tomboy has had no liquor or wine license and diners are encouraged to bring their own, without so much as a corkage charge. Service is as cordial as the warm welcome from a host or hostess, even on busy nights.

TOPOLOBAMPO
KR 18/20
Decor 4/4　　Hospitality 4/5　　Food 9/10　　Value 1/1

- **Mexican**
- **Chicago/Near North**
- **$$$**

445 North Clark Street
Chicago
(312) 661-1434
Troubleshooters: Rick and Deanne Bayless (chef/owners)

Hours: Lunch Tues–Fri 11:30 am–2:30 pm, Brunch (Almuerzo) Sat 10:30 am–2:30 pm, Dinner Tues–Thurs 5:20–10 pm, Fri–Sat 5:20–11 pm
Credit Cards: All majors
Reservations: Taken for parties of 5–10 people only
Handicapped: Accessible
Bar: Fresh lime juice margaritas, a large choice of Mexican beers, domestic and boutique brewery beers, full wine list selected to match Mexican cooking
Smoking and nonsmoking sections: No smoking in restaurant dining room, small smoking section in bar
Parking: Valet at dinner or space available in lots or street

Topolobampo is literally a restaurant within a restaurant, tucked inside Frontera Grill (q.v). But, while Frontera is noisy and crowded, Topolobampo is shut off by doors and glass. The mood is placid, though the foods can be as exotically seasoned as its larger sibling. The idea with Frontera Grill was to present something more, something different from the usual concept of so-called "border food dining." At Topolobampo that concept is taken elsewhere. The menu, which changes about every two to three weeks is studded with recognizable terms in Mexican cookery, but also with some preparations and ideas that are not so commonly seen in any Chicago-area restaurants, Mexican or otherwise.

For example, a diner might choose an appetizer called *pibipollo*. What is served appears to be a terrine or paté. In fact, the *pibipollo* is a

Yucatan version of a chicken tamale. In this case, chicken flavored with mild but distinctive achiote peppers and a tomato sauce enhanced with chilis and some orange juice, is wrapped in banana leaves and baked. When unwrapped it holds its wedge shape, resting on a bed of the banana leaves, napped with the tomato chili sauce.

Something as common as *sopa Azteca*, the Mexican version of chicken soup, is given unusual treatment. The dark broth is accompanied by a platter of white Mexican cheese, chunked avocado, tortilla strips, sour cream and dried *pasilla* chiles. You add these to the soup according to taste and fondness for these ingredients. The presentation makes something special of what in most restaurants would be a simple soup.

Another treat that pops up on the changing menu might be roasted poblano pepper. The large green pepper is split to form a basket which holds a mixture of chunked roasted potatoes, tomatoes, avocado, chilis and the heart of the matter, smoked marlin. The surprise is the heat generated by the poblano, which in most recipes, such as *chiles relleno*, is almost bland.

Entrees, like appetizers, are handsomely plated on Mexican chinaware with a blue floral pattern. Pork tenderloin may come in half a dozen chunks, arrayed around a center of Mexican pumpkin and bathed in an unconventional *molé* made of the ubiquitous chili peppers plus a bouquet of crushed nuts. Beef eaters can order a tenderloin cross hatched from a wood-fired grill. The beef is framed by *rajas*, strips of garliced and marinated cooked peppers. A small tostada chip holds some black bean sauce.

From the oceans, tuna is grilled with red onions, served with peppers, garlic enhanced rice and peas.

Other entrees include unique fashions of rabbit or pheasant as well as seafood. Desserts go well beyond basic *flan* or *sopapillas* to include fruit tarts, fruit-flavored ice creams and exquisite crepes, lavishly cooked in butter and served with a tangy caramel sauce made from the richness of condensed goat's milk. If all that were not enough, they also serve the best coffee anywhere in Chicago.

TRATTORIA GIACOMO
KR 18.5/20
Decor 2.5/4   Hospitality 5/5   Food 10/10   Value 1/1

- **Italian**
- **Highwood**
- **$$**

810 Sheridan Road
Highwood
(847) 266-8900
Troubleshooter: Giacomo
Ruggirello (owner)

Hours: Tues–Thurs 5–10 pm,
Fri–Sat 5–11 pm
Credit Cards: Discover, MC,
Visa
Reservations: Suggested
Handicapped: Very tight
squeeze through second front
door, probably not
**Smoking and nonsmoking
sections:** No smoking
Parking: In lot

I wish I had a quarter for every time someone asks where I eat out when I'm not reviewing. Like all diners, I have some favorites that I return to again and again when time and circumstance permit. Trattoria Giacomo, a narrow storefront restaurant in a Highwood strip mall is at the top of my comeback list.

Before coming to the Chicago suburbs, Giacomo Ruggirello spent several years in New Orleans restaurateuring to the denizens of the Big Easy. One wall of his Highwood storefront is devoted to decor from that city on the delta, the wall across to his native Italy. While a culinary conjunction is not exactly made in his cooking, Giacomo will quite often prepare something in the way of a jambalaya or a blackened swordfish.

You could start with a simple appetizer of grilled vegetables, so handsomely arranged it could be centerpiece for a still life painting. The vegetables are touched with oil and vinegar, very light at that, with just a touch of mint for sweetness. Wilted spinach serves as bedding for circles of eggplant, strips of roasted zucchini, tangy arugula, tomatoes, carrots and asparagus in a recent collection.

From among other appetizer selections, grilled calamari have the right flavor, but can sometimes be a little chewy. Fresh mussels are excellent in the house marinara, while sautéed escargot are served with a choice of two sauces.

All dinners come with a house salad or thick minestrone soup. As for pasta, favorites include penne with spicy *arrabiata* sauce, *pasta putanesca* and *rigatono à la Giacomo*, the house version of Salmon in vodka sauce. Gnocchi are like little bundles of energy; they're that dense. From among a selection of meats, chops and poultry, chicken marsala is sweet and winy in a sauce fleshed out with thick sliced mushrooms.

Desserts are more Italian than cajun; the cannolis are made in the restaurant, shells and sweet cream filling alike. If Giacomo is busy cooking and not waiting tables himself, you can be sure his two assistants know their jobs well. I don't know how to say *"Laissez les bontemps rouler!"* in Italian, but I'm sure Giacomo would teach me if I asked.

TRATTORIA #10
KR 17/20
Decor 4/4   Hospitality 3.5/5   Food 8.5/10   Value 1/1

- **Italian**
- **Chicago Loop**
- **$$$**

10 North Dearborn Street
Chicago
(312) 984-1718
Troubleshooter: Peggy McAtamney (general manager)

Hours: Lunch Mon–Fri 11:30 am–2 pm, Dinner Mon–Thurs 5–9 pm, Fri–Sat 5:30–10 pm
Credit Cards: All majors
Reservations: Recommended
Handicapped: Accessible via elevator to lower level dining room
Smoking and nonsmoking sections: Separate smoking and nonsmoking seating
Parking: Valet $7

At a time when the restaurant business in Chicago is changing so rapidly it almost seems to be spinning off its axis, there are some enduring locations that keep on going without anything in the way of fundamental alteration. That's the case with Trattoria #10. The restaurant is below street level, and its careful design makes it seem almost like a grotto, thanks to coved ceilings, arches and a dim, romantic light. Trattoria #10 also happens to have one of the handsomest bars in the loop, a stretched marble topped affair that seems perfect.

The years have been kind to this restaurant, whose location makes it popular with the business crowd for lunch, and at dinner with those going to theater, or looking for a comfortable social setting. And, while it is perfect for business dinners, prices are not so daunting as to chase out all but the expense account crowd.

The menu is changed on a daily basis but common threads keep a continuity of style and taste. That continuity includes the same delicious crusted bread, stuffed with sun-dried tomatoes that has been set out for diners from the very beginnings of Trattoria #10. Crisp parmesan cheese crackers, almost like a Middle Eastern lavish, are also part of the bread platter.

Course selection has been simplified on the single page menu into antipasti, first and second courses. Among the antipasti, soups include a house minestrone, though the stock is chicken based, not vegetarian. An alternate soup could be a cream-based seafood chowder flecked with corn and *pancetta*, the distinctive Italian-style bacon, or perhaps a simple peasant-style *pasta e fagiole*. Sautéed soft-shell crabs in a complex plating with asparagus, galette potatoes and mixed greens have been available in season, while a simple mesculin salad with thin slices of parmesan cheese is dressed in a garlic and thyme vinaigrette.

Calamari sautéed in olive oil is plated with white cannellini beans along with chopped plum tomatoes, a little sage, and crostini spread with a light pesto. The calamari are tender and delicious. But, a portobello mushroom–centered terrine layered with spinach and goat cheese was dry to a fault, despite the presence of a chicken demi-glace. And, what the menu described as "pomegranate-molasses" was virtually undetectable.

Usually there are a dozen or so pasta selections each evening, coupled with somewhat fewer second course, or entree selections. The risotto can be an excellent creation. In one version, the grains of rice are chewy and firm, flecked with a selection of fresh vegetables including asparagus, yellow peppers and delicate green beans. Among other pastas, small shell macaroni might come in a delicious caramelized onion reduction with bay scallops, artichokes and asparagus. The scallops have a light brushing of a Moroccan-influenced *harissa*, or pepper sauce, so mild that it leaves only a slight tingle on the tongue.

As for main course entrees, the sophistication is evident in the complexity of menu descriptions. Among them is a plating of roasted veal rib eye and sweetbreads in a garlic au jus. Fettucini bound with caramelized pearl onions completes the plating.

TRATTORIA GIANNI
KR 18/20
Decor 4/4   Hospitality 5/5   Food 8/10   Value 1/1

- **Italian**
- **Chicago/Near North**
- **$$**

1711 North Halsted
Chicago
(312) 266-1976
Troubleshooter: Gianni

Hours: Tues–Thurs 5–10:30 pm, Fri–Sat 5–11:30 pm, Brunch Sun 11:30 am–3:00 pm, Dinner 4–9:30 pm, closed Mon
Credit Cards: All majors
Reservations: Suggested
Handicapped: Accessible
Smoking and nonsmoking sections: Both available
Parking: Valet

Trattoria Gianni was among the first restaurants to serve the adjacent Theatre District. There is variety and sophistication on the printed menu and among nightly specials. Recently, instead of the predictable veal parmigiana, one recipe used richly flavored sharp gorgonzola for the kind of bite only a strong blue cheese gives. A light cream-touched plum tomato sauce supported the ingredients and brought the concept together. Also on a recent list of specials was grouper, seared in a skillet, then glazed with a topping of caramelized scallions, fleshed out with plum tomatoes and a bouquet of herbs.

The regular printed menu, which changes seasonally, presents some intriguing options. Start with a mixed antipasto platter that combines a mild frittata with caponata, the Italian version of ratatouille, roasted red peppers, cheese, slices of chilled marinated zucchini and delicious kalamata olives. Other antipasto choices include shrimp with mushrooms, garlic and white wine, fried calamari, grilled portobello mushroom seasoned with garlic, rosemary and balsamic vinegar, and mussels in traditional marinara sauce.

Pasta portions are large enough to share, but if you care for a half portion, it will be served. Taste penne in a sauce which combines the light acidity of fresh plum tomatoes, sliced portobellos and arugula. It is a delicious combination of contrasting flavors cooked down into a texture which coats the pasta. Or taste *ziti*, small hollow pasta tubes. In this recipe, dry breadcrumbs add a light crunch together with hearts of cauliflower, broccoli stems, plus fresh tomatoes, raisins and pine nuts. The combination is sweet flavored, but not overbearing. Risotto changes daily, while several other pastas complete the listing.

Among meat and seafood selections, slices of grilled duck breast are plated with porcini mushrooms, onions and plum tomatoes prepared in balsamic vinegar and a wedge of polenta on the side.

Desserts include a dense and creamy *panna cotta*, Italian custard made without eggs. Service is accommodating, especially when it comes to making the curtain at one of the nearby theaters.

TRATTORIA PARMA
KR 18.5/20
Decor 3.5/4   Hospitality 5/5   Food 9/10   Value 1/1

- **Italian**
- **Chicago/Near North**
- **$$**

400 North Clark Street
(312) 245-9933

Hours: Lunch Mon–Fri 11:30 am–2 pm, Dinner Mon–Thurs 5:30–10 pm, Fri–Sat 5:30–11 pm, Sun 5–9 pm (Bar opens at 4 pm daily)
Credit Cards: Visa, MC, Amex, Diners
Reservations: Suggested, especially weekends
Handicapped: Accessible
Smoking and nonsmoking sections: Smoking in bar, no smoking in dining room

Trattoria Parma has a *faux* rustic look, with the outward accouterments meant to create a sense of charming decor. The menu emphasizes trattoria style cookery. Diners will find fish specials, and appetizers such as delicious grilled calamari with a breadcrumb and spinach filling, presented as it might be in Leghorn, the seafood capital of Tuscany. A recent soup of the day brought the flavors of fennel and tomato in a clean-tasting stock at its center. And, if you want some embellishments beyond the plain bread basket brought to your table, order a specialty *bruschetta*, whose toppings can change from day to day as selections are rotated.

Osso buco, that Italian version of veal pot roast, is about as comfortable as comfort food can get. The veal shanks are typically tender set on a bed of creamed polenta perfumed with saffron, all of which is in a savory gravy. This is one of those dishes best left unanalyzed and simply enjoyed for its innate good tastes.

Other entrees range from a traditional roasted chicken with rosemary herbed potatoes, to roasted pork loin with wilted spinach or grilled vegetables for diners who avoid meats. Among pastas, bow tie noodles, called *farfalle*, are sauced with a rich garlic gravy, dolloped with snow white goat cheese and chunky fresh roasted vegetables. This one is not to be missed. Several other pastas include a tempting linguini with a variety of shell-fish and calamari. Those pillars of the Italian kitchen, garlic, virgin olive oil, tomatoes, basil and white wine make up the sauce.

Chef Paul Loduca is competing in an overcrowded field brought about by America's love affair with Italian cooking. Rather than offering a world of recipes, he has chosen a few to showcase his talents, without compromising a sense of authenticity. Among dessert choices, the simplicity of strawberries in balsamic vinegar exemplifies perfectly the appeal of contrasting flavors.

TRIO
KR 17.75/20
Decor 2.5/4   Hospitality 5/5   Food 9.5/10   Value .75/1

- **French/Asian Fusion**
- **Evanston**
- **$$$**

1625 Hinman Avenue
Evanston
(847) 733-8746
Troubleshooter: Henry Adinaya
(owner)

Hours: Tues–Thurs 5:30–9:30 pm, Fri 5:30–10:30 pm, Sat 5–10:30 pm, Sun 5–9 pm, closed Mon
Credit Cards: All majors
Reservations: Required
Handicapped: Accessible, dining room is easily accessible, restrooms require three steps (assistance is available)
Smoking and nonsmoking sections: No smoking permitted
Parking: Valet
Dress: Jackets required for gentlemen, neckties preferred is stated, but sadly not enforced

Something wrong is occurring at better restaurants. Though restaurateurs may give lip service to a dress code for diners, the bar has been lowered. The look of the restaurant suffers, and clearly we as diners who expect the best similarly suffer.

Frankly, I think that when one dresses well for dinner, the evening seems just that much more special. Khakis and a polo shirt are fine in many restaurants, but when "fine dining" is the occasion, clothing should reflect the event.

Thus, I was somewhat abashed on a visit to Trio to see several men in short sleeved sport or polo shirts. One man was actually wearing walking shorts and deck shoes, without socks. I don't know whether his polo shirt was Ralph Lauren, but does it really matter?

Trio is a restaurant which asks for jackets, with neckties preferred for men. Women presumably know how to dress for the occasion without any prodding. The restaurant is hardly stuffy, but, there is a greeter who sits outside in the lobby of the residence hotel. That suggests a certain propriety which evidently no longer extends inside the dining rooms.

Chef Shawn McClain has been at the kitchen stoves ever since he was sous chef for the late Leslie Reis at Café Provencal. His work continues to meet a higher level of dining, though presentations are not nearly as elaborate, nor are plate designs anywhere near as artistic or imaginative as they were only a few years ago. Clearly this is a management decision, much like the one which looks the other way at sloppily dressed customers.

Well dressed or not, diners may opt for the multi-course tasting degustation, or choose from the à la carte menu. Either route will be a pleasant culinary trip. Begin with an appetizer portion of sashimi day boat hamachi, a Japanese fish much like red snapper. Chef McClain is a pioneer on the Chicago dining scene with his Asian-fusion creations. If he was not the first to cook this way here, he was among the early starters. McClain creates presentations with an eye for artistry and taste, even if he no longer has available the designer china and other table accessories to showcase them that way. The sashimi still is a fairly handsome affair, with citrus flavors, tarragon and a touch of sesame oil. This is a dish to savor not just for flavor, but texture, a near melt-in-the-mouth sensation.

Similarly exciting is the porcini mushroom *fricassee*. This one clearly has its roots in Europe with shavings of fresh truffles perfuming the reduced sauce which glazes the porcini slices. Other first course selections include lobster filled wontons, risotto with tomato confit and under-pinnings of smoked yellow tuna, or a lusciously rich domestic *foie gras* in a terrine with crushed hazelnuts and vanilla rhubarb preserves adding texture and flavors that practically cry out for a wine with heady sweet fruit accompaniment.

The chef's entrees include the handful on the printed menu, plus rotating nightly specials in his evening degustation. Recently, halibut has been set in a lightly flavored corn chowder with truffle oil essence. Napa cabbage, fava beans and manila clams were the garnish, with a light flavoring of smoked bacon. Halibut is such a versatile fish, and in the hands of someone with McClain's talents the results are extraordinary.

In addition to ala carte desserts, a chef's *amuse* is offered guests at the beginning of dinner, while a platter of sweet candies and other morsels is presented at the end, in addition to any of the desserts which might be chosen. Service is polite and proper, the wine list apropos of dining. Trio would be a finer fine dining experience if its stated dress code were actually enforced.

TRU
KR 20/20
Decor 4/4   Hospitality 5/5   Food 10/10   Value 1/1

- **American/Continental**
- **Chicago**
- **$$$**

676 St. Clair Street
Chicago
(312) 202-0001
Troubleshooters: Scott Barton
(general manager), Patricia
Mowen-Ziegler, (dining room
manager), Gale Gand and Rick
Tramanto (chef/owners)

Hours: Lunch Mon–Fri noon–
2 pm (two or three course prix
fixe lunches are served), Dinner
Mon–Thurs 5:30–10 pm, Fri–Sat
5–11 pm, closed Sun
Credit Cards: All majors
Reservations: Mandatory
Handicapped: Accessible
**Smoking and nonsmoking
sections:** Smoking not permitted
anywhere in the restaurant
Parking: Valet $8
Dress Code: Jackets are required

Tru is clearly out of the ordinary. There are attentive details such as the valet who takes your car, checking your name with his reservation list. Inside, there is a handsome bar area with a glass wall that reaches almost to the high ceiling. A striking blue female nude torso, by the late French neo-realist Yves Klein and suggestive of classical Greek sculpture grabs the eye. It is only one of several pieces of museum quality art that accent the restaurant.

The main dining room is swathed in walls of diaphanous white drapery whose folds reach from ceiling to floor, covering the frosted windows. Carpeting softens the tread and helps to diminish the bustle of dining. Thankfully, Tru is a quiet restaurant, its tables spaced far enough apart for comfort and quiet. The thoughtfulness of customer comfort extends to small upholstered ottomans where women can set their purses for the evening, secure, Accessible and always in sight.

Once seated and welcomed, diners have the opportunity to order a 3 course prix fixe dinner, or any of several collections, as they are designated on the menu. They range from a 6 course vegetable, seafood or seasonal market collection to the ten or more courses of The Chef's Grand Collection. When everyone at the table orders the Grand Collection, each diner is likely to receive something different from the others.

As much as I enjoy writing about food, no words will really convey the exquisite subtleties or detail that is at the core of dining at Tru. At best, this will be an impressionistic rendering of a particular dining experience.

For true spectacle nothing will compare to the caviar presentation. A green glass staircase is set at the center of the table, pieces of glass forming the inclining steps. Each piece is indented. Four pieces hold mounds of caviar, while the four lower steps hold mounds of chopped egg white, yolk, capers and a fine dice of red onion. At the highest level is beluga, its oil shimmering against the glass. One step below is pink salmon roe, next flying fish roe made green by the infusion of wasabi horseradish. Finally, the quartet of roes is concluded with smoked white fish, golden colored. The caviar is scooped out with a small mother of pearl spoon, to be spread with or without the condiments on toasted brioche. Take a sip or two of wine or champagne, a small taste of the caviars and another course becomes memory.

Perhaps you have sensed by reading this far, that a burden of attention is placed on diners, if Tru is to be appreciated to the fullest. There is a transcendence at work which virtually demands that small talk be put aside, so that consideration can be given to the food. Tru is worthy of the same sort of attention given other art forms.

Try to picture a seafood course set in a frosted bowl of ice supporting a whole oyster in its shell, bedded with fennel. When a server saw that I had eaten the oyster, she removed the ice dome and revealed a second oyster underneath. This one, also in its shell was beneath a light blanket of lime flavored creme fraiche, topped with a large truffle slice.

For meat, the selection could be venison medallions with a huckleberry swirl and red wine reduction. A touch of chocolate contributes to the sauce, much the way Mexican cooks use it to create a molé. In this case, the chocolate is blended with the natural juices of the roasted venison. Truth to tell, the taste is virtually imperceptible; I think its effect is to enrich rather than add to the venison au jus.

As for desserts, selections can be highlighted by an apricot tart, the fruit sharp and sweet in its aftertaste, set on a flaky puff pastry with a side of red bean ice cream perhaps to suggest the Chinese origin of the apricot fruit.

Dining at Tru is a special experience in the way that all art is to be experienced and absorbed. The wine list is a volume of choices in heavy leather binding. Service is that kind that is anticipatory, nothing is overlooked, nothing taken for granted. At the same time, it is neither stuffy nor pretentious.

TSUKASA
KR 17.5/20

Decor 4/4   Hospitality 4.5/5   Food 8/10   Value 1/1

- **Japanese Teppan House & Sushi Bar**
- **Vernon Hills**
- **$$**

700 North Milwaukee Avenue (SW corner of Milwaukee and Route 60)
Vernon Hills
(847) 816-8770
Troubleshooter: Manager on duty

Hours: Lunch Tues–Fri 11:30 am–2 pm, Dinner Tues–Thurs 5–9:30 pm, Fri 5–10:30 pm, Sat 5–10:30 pm, Sun 4–9 pm
Credit Cards: All majors
Handicapped: Accessible
Smoking and nonsmoking sections: Both available

There are basically two kinds of Japanese restaurants. While sushi and sashimi bars may seem the more authentic, and the *teppanyaki* houses mere affectations catering to American tastes, the fact is that both are readily accepted in Japan. It is true, the teppan restaurants, in which diners sit around a large flat griddle table where foods are cooked by a dexterous chef, were first introduced to Japan after World War II as an attraction for Western visitors.

But, in more recent years, the teppan restaurants have become popular among the Japanese themselves, whose appetite for grilled meats has grown prodigious. The concept is simple. A single chef works a table seating as many as eight or ten people, not all of whom may be part of the same group. The cooking is done in front of the diners; it's part of a show that can be highly entertaining when the cook working the griddle has the talent.

Despite their similarities, not all teppan restaurants are alike. One of the best is Tsukasa. Each teppan table sits under a huge range hood to draw off the smoke and odors. A waitress takes drink and food orders. Then, in a short while, a chef comes to the table, introduces himself and begins working. There is a certain architecture to the structure of a teppan meal. First, after the griddle is good and hot, oil and butter are spread out, the proper shortening used for either fish, chicken or beef, as appropriate. Vegetables are sliced in an instant, deftly spread onto the hot surface. They sizzle and are turned.

Meanwhile, the chef works the meats and seafood, careful to keep them separate, so flavors do not intrude upon one another. Finally, with the skill of a culinary surgeon, he will flip his wrist, while his spatula or large spoon catches the grilled foods, which are set out on warmed platters ready to be eaten. The Tsukasa menu is one of the more extensive for this type of dining. More recently, a sushi bar has also been added.

Portions are large, and prices reasonable. Some dishes fair better than others. Teriyaki steak has more flavor than does the simple teppan-grilled filet mignon. The seafood combination is more interesting than either shrimp or golden shrimp alone. In the latter, the grilled prawns are topped with a creamy egg yolk sauce that adds some color, but not much flavor. As for the combination, scallops, squid and shrimp are all worked together. The squid looks like a fillet of white fish, and is nearly as tender. Mild mustard and sweet ginger sauces are set out for dipping.

The tempura choices are well prepared and can be ordered as appetizers or full dinners. Dinners include a consomme-based soup, tossed salad with ginger dressing and rice. Expect to spend about $40 a couple with tax, plus drinks and tip.

TUFANO'S
KR 19/20
Decor 3/4   Hospitality 5/5   Food 10/10   Value 1/1

- **Italian**
- **Chicago/South**
- **$$**

1073 West Vernon Park
Chicago
(312) 733-3393
Troubleshooter: Joseph
DiBuono (owner)

Hours: Tues–Fri 11 am–10 pm, Sat 4–11 pm, Sun 3–9 pm
Credit Cards: None, house accounts
Reservations: No
Handicapped: Accessible
Parking: Valet

Though substantially remodeled and enlarged in recent years, Tufano's (also known as The Vernon Park Tap) continues to serve the same delicious home-style Italian red sauce cooking that people have been eating here for decades. And, though the restaurant looks different, the service and welcome is as honest and genuine as it has ever been, whether the customer is a regular or a newcomer.

Tufano's serves several kinds of salads; the house special family-style is a large bowl brimming with lettuce, artichoke hearts, roasted peppers, hot peppers, slices of salami, cubes of provolone cheese, strips of mozzarella and some choice red ripe tomatoes. Picking a dressing is easy; there's only one . . . a delicious Italian herbed oil and vinegar.

Moving on, the blackboard menu is an exercise in indecision because of so many great selections. The lemon chicken is a platter of cut-up pieces steaming hot from the sauté pan, perhaps finished under the broiler, plated with whole lemons also broiled, and a brush of oregano and oil. Rigatoni and mushrooms with the house marinara brings some color and contrasting flavor to the table, while another platter of shells with broccoli, shrimp and oil offers its own sweet pleasure.

Other entrees range from traditional sausage with peppers, to grilled pork chop and peppers as well as the usual lineup of veal parmigiana or marsala. Other restaurants may serve their own delicious versions of good Italian food, but, Tufano's is one of those Chicago restaurants where it all began. If you have trouble finding it, just ask someone in the neighborhood. Everyone knows Tufano's!

TUSCANY
KR 18/20

Decor 4/4   Hospitality 5/5   Food 8/10   Value 1/1

• **Italian**	**Hours:** Lunch Mon–Fri 11 am–3 pm, Dinner Mon–Thurs 5–11 pm, Fri–Sat. 5 pm–midnight, Sun 2–9:30 pm
• **Chicago/South**	
• **$$**	
1014 West Taylor Street	**Credit Cards:** Amex, Diners, MC, Visa
Chicago	
(312) 829-1990	**Reservations:** Suggested
Troubleshooter: Phil Stefani	**Handicapped:** Accessible
(owner)	**Smoking and nonsmoking sections:** Both available
	Parking: Valet in protected lot

Fashionable crowds are as much a part of the decor at Tuscany, as are the open kitchen, the French café doors that open up the front of the restaurant in warm weather, and the bare brick and hardwood. Tuscany is not the typical "mom and pop" restaurant which made Taylor Street's Little Italy a dining mecca for so many years.

It is, however, typical of what is happening today in Italian dining. The restaurant is crowded and noisy. The cooking eschews overcooked spaghetti, spicy meatballs, and red checkered tablecloths. Instead, diners are finding herbed olive oil, designer pizzas, more unusual pastas with untraditional saucing.

From the list of pizzas, all on thin crusts, one is piled high with fresh chopped tomato, basil, slices of grilled eggplant and onion, and a liberal amount of melted goat cheese. The crust is crisp without being burned, the toppings identifiably flavorful. A simple *bruschetta*, topped with chopped tomatoes and basil, is another choice, short of a full antipasto spread. Tuscany offers a house version of *carpaccio* as well as typical appetizers such as fried calamari and baked clams.

Each evening brings some house specials. Recently, risotto with rabbit was being served, as were grilled salmon and several other entree selections. If you choose the risotto, let your waiter know right away because its preparation takes 35 minutes.

Back on the printed menu, any of several pastas ranging from *mezzaluna* stuffed with chicken and vegetables in a prosciutto-laced cream sauce to *gnocchi* with a quartet of cheeses, to simple tomato and bolognese sauces, are regularly served. Though pasta is a separate course in true Italian dining, an order of linguine with shrimp in a spicy *diavolo* sauce is a meal in itself. A variation might be to forgo the marinara and have a lighter oil and garlic combination with the expected bite of hot peppers. The shrimp are firm and fresh, the pasta *al dente*.

On the far back wall of the main dining room at Tuscany there is a large wood-fired rotisserie in which whole chickens are slowly roasted. One version brings the chicken split with an accompaniment of deliciously seasoned roasted potatoes. Even with the skin of the chicken stripped away in the interest of calorie saving, the meat has a woodsy fresh flavor. Other meats on the menu include several fashions of grilled steaks and chops, as well as some traditional sautéed veal preparations. Desserts are typical, *tiramisu*, *cannoli* and the like, but we think it more fun after dinner to walk a couple of blocks west on Taylor and get an Italian ice at Mario's.

VA PENSIERO
KR 20/20
Decor 4/4   Hospitality 5/5   Food 10/10   Value 1/1

- **Italian**
- **Evanston**
- **$$$**

1566 Oak Avenue
(inside The Margarita Inn)
Evanston
(847) 475-7779
Troubleshooter: Brett Callis
(manager)

Hours: Lunch Mon–Fri 11:30 am–2 pm, Dinner Mon–Thurs 5:30–9 pm, Fri–Sat 5:30–10 pm (Outdoor Garden Terrace open during warm weather months from Lunch through Dinner)
Credit Cards: All majors
Reservations: Suggested
Handicapped: Accessible (call for details)
Smoking and nonsmoking sections: No smoking
Parking: Valet

Some years ago, on my first visit to Va Pensiero, I was struck by its gracious charm, a sense of faded elegance, almost one of wistful remembrance. Not, bad for a restaurant that was brand new at the time! It suggested a dining room in a hotel perhaps on one of Italy's Northern Lakes, probably in the late 1920s or early '30s when the world was between conflicts.

Today, the restaurant still has a look of elegance, if not faded, then well-mannered. Pale salmon is the predominant color, while dark wood trim provides accent. It is the sort of place that almost demands a necktie for gentlemen, one where the few men without jackets look out of place. Attention to detail shows up in such minutiae as a wedge of butter, sliced along its horizontal axis so that a layer of fresh basil can be sandwiched inside. It shows up in the crisp linen and napery, in the beautifully arranged plating of each course.

This is a restaurant for unhurried dining from first aperitif to final sip of coffee. Lingering over the menu is an anticipatory pleasure. From among *antipasti* choices char-grilled calamari is set on a bed of wispy thin cucumber slices arranged like a doily of sorts. Flashes of basil and mint are among flavorings, while tomato adds a garnish of color. *Carpaccio*, thin, almost translucent slices of raw sirloin, is garnished with grilled radicchio, and topped with a trio of sauces. Among other antipasti is duck breast fritters plated ornately with oyster mushrooms, greens and white truffle oil.

The restaurant will also serve smaller, first course portions of pasta, often rather complex presentations that beg to be sampled and tasted. Consider *tagliatelle*, a noodle sauced with several kinds of field mushrooms cut up into small pieces, reduced with onions, red wine and veal stock, then finished with a glaze of mascarpone cheese.

Entrees include a salad of greens dressed with Balsamic vinegar and fresh extra virgin olive oil. Sautéed sea bass, when served with spinach and a flavorful sauce that brings together capers and yellow tomatoes, is almost as rich as lobster. Other entrees include veal tenderloin medallions with artichokes and fontina cheese polenta, as well as a variety of other choices on the printed menu and from among nightly specials.

The evening can be capped by a luscious dessert. The wine list is one of the best collections of Italian white, red and sparklings in the Chicago area. Service is flawless, correct, but not stuffy.

ANTIPASTI

Sformatino di Carciofi $ 6
warm artichoke soufflé, lemon-sage brown butter, crispy artichoke chips

Funghi alla Griglia $ 7
grilled rosemary scented portobello mushroom, roasted garlic flan, tomato vinaigrette

Gamberi con Salsa di Pistacchi $ 7
sautéed gulf shrimp, crispy onion-risotto cake, pistachio pesto

Calamari alla Griglia $ 7
grilled calamari, roasted red onion, grilled pineapple, basil-mustard dressing

Crostata Val d'Aosta $ 8
caramelized leek tart, pancetta, fontina cheese, grilled asparagus, white truffle cream

ZUPPE

Le Zuppe sono Secondo Stagione   seasonal
soups according to the season

INSALATA

Insalata Cesare $ 5
romaine lettuce, crisp croutons, roasted peppers, anchovy vinaigrette

Insalata del Giorno   seasonal
special salads reflecting the season

PASTA

Ravioli di Gorgonzola $ 16
gorgonzola cheese filled ravioli, roasted pears, greens, toasted hazelnuts, brown butter

Spaghettini con Cape Sante $ 18
housemade spaghet'ini, grilled sea scallops, spicy garlic lobster broth, tomato caper pesto

Pasta di Prezzemolo con Pollo e Carciofi $ 17
sheets of parsley pasta enveloping roasted chicken,
artichoke hearts, roasted plum tomatoes, lemon rosemary cream

Garganelli con Anitra Arrosto $ 15
quill shaped pasta, roasted duck, baby spinach, Valencia oranges, port wine glaze

PIETANZE

Funghi Piccata con Rotolo di Spinaci $ 17
pan-browned portobello mushroom steaks, rolled spinach artichoke soufflé, goat cheese, sautéed cherry tomatoes

Agnello al Forno $ 26
pan-roasted rack of lamb, pecorino braised greens, white wine-lamb ragu

Arrosta di Salmone Senape $ 19
roasted Atlantic salmon, mustard mascarpone glaze, sautéed greens, saffron potatoes

Pollo Marinato alla Griglia $ 17
one half grilled chicken marinated with garlic, rosemary and lemon, butternut squash-parmesan mashed potatoes

Lombo di Vitello $ 23
porcini crusted veal loin, polenta cheese pancakes, asparagus and Belgian endive sauté

Filetto di Manzo $ 25
grilled tenderloin of beef, prosciutto-potato rotolo, roasted shallot and grappa sauce

VIA EMILIA
KR 19.5/20
Decor 4/4   Hospitality 4.5/5   Food 10/10   Value 1/1

- **Italian**
- **Chicago/Mid-North**
- **$$**

2119 North Clark Street
Chicago
(773) 248-6283
Troubleshooter: Leonardo
Balessio (owner)

Hours: Mon–Sat 5–11 pm, Sun 5–9:30 pm
Credit Cards: All majors
Reservations: Accepted
Handicapped: Accessible
Smoking and nonsmoking sections: Smoking at bar only
Parking: Valet every evening $6

It seems to me a good sign that when you visit an Italian restaurant, the staff speaks Italian to each other. That's how it is at Via Emilia. White-washed walls and ceiling, a bare bleached wood floor are striking in simplicity. The style strikes me as neo-classical with suggestions of an Italian villa. The food is similarly direct with minimal embellishment.

Via Emilia exploits the larder and cooking style of the Emilia-Romagna. You won't find much in the way of red sauces, though the stock-in-trade bolognese uses tomatoes to draw together its component meats and herb seasonings.

But, before getting to a pasta course, enjoy the antipasti. Grilled calamari is as simple as cooking can be, the cut-up squid flavored with nothing more than olive oil, garlic and fresh lemon juice. *Vitello tonnato* is more ambitious, maybe a touch too much. Thin slices of pink veal are chilled and covered with a mayonnaise-like sauce flavored by bits of fresh tuna and capers. Unfortunately, the portion we were served came smothered in the sauce, making the search for delicacy all the more difficult. In this case, more is less is better. Other antipasti return to the more direct approach.

If one takes the time to dine in true Italian style, a pasta course comes next. Portions are ample for sharing among two to four people. A risotto of the day was perfumed with saffron, studded with the likes of scallops, given a bit of color by flecks of vegetables. The rice was chewy, giving, but not gummy. Pairing the risotto with another pasta proved difficult because of so many tempting selections. *Gnocchi* is, sturdy in contrast to the risotto, made even more so when served with a deliciously spicy *arrabiatta* sauce. Other pasta choices range from delicate *pappardelle* with mushrooms, *tagliatelle* with the classic bolognese, as well as a couple of *tortellini* and other choices.

Second courses in Italy are our entrees, usually meat, poultry or seafood. Grilled shrimp were presented as a seafood of the day, the flavors of the grill gathered with a bit of lemon juice. We asked if the chef would prepare chicken marsala. Though not on the menu, it came out without complaint or delay. This is not a starchy marsala, but rather a light coating with slices of mushrooms amidst the pieces of chicken breast. Roasted potatoes and vegetables accompany all of the second course platters.

A trio of desserts is offered which can be combined into a combination as a fourth platter. And what do you know? There is no sign of *tiramisu!* Service is very good, though perhaps more time could be allowed between courses.

VINCI
KR 18.5/20
Decor 4/4   Hospitality 5/5   Food 8.5/10   Value 1/1

- **Italian**
- **Chicago/Near North**
- **$$**

1732 North Halsted Street
Chicago
(312) 266-1199
Troubleshooters: Paul and Kathy LoDuca (owners)

Hours: Tues–Thurs 5:30–10:30 pm, Fri–Sat 5:30–11:30 pm, Sun Brunch 11:30 am–3 pm, Dinner 3:30–9:30 pm
Credit Cards: All majors except Discover
Reservations: Suggested
Parking: Valet
Smoking and nonsmoking sections: Both available
Handicapped: Difficult entry, but otherwise accessible

Vinci is a favorite with the pre- and after-theatre crowd, but stands up well as a destination restaurant on its own. Chef/Owner Paul LoDuca has decorated his restaurant with large wall frescoes based on the drawings of Leonardo da Vinci. Earth tones give the three dining rooms a warm, comfortable feel.

Among dining favorites on the regularly evolving menu, polenta with mushrooms is a truly Italian version of comfort food. The polenta is grilled, giving it a bit of a crust, which contrasts with the soft, almost sensual textures of portobello and crimini mushrooms in a reduced sauce. Other appetizer choices include excellent grilled baby octopus plated with cannellini beans and roasted peppers, steamed mussels with saffron and tomatoes in a fine chop simmered in white wine and smoked trout, indulged with *giardinara*.

Among pastas, "Grandma's Linguine," or *Linguine della Nonna*, is a constant favorite. The pasta is tossed with breadcrumbs which adds an unusual texture not usually associated with noodle dishes. Roasted zucchini, tomatoes and plenty of garlic add to the fresh flavors. Among other tempting pasta selections is spaghetti with pancetta and reduced caramelized onions as the basis of a sauce enhanced by fresh basil and grated parmesan cheese. Thick and chewy bucatini noodles are at the heart of another treat, prepared with an array of shrimp, clams, mussels and calamari in a white wine broth with the presence of basil and tomato for color and flavor.

Though many diners enjoy pasta as a main course, Vinci's main course choices, listed on its menu as "Secundi," are too good to pass up. Among favorites is marinated Cornish hen that has been grilled under a hot brick to diffuse the heat, plated with roasted potatoes coated with chopped garlic and grated parmesan cheese. Other selections include grilled duck in balsamic vinegar sauce with roasted onions and polenta. Grilled veal chop is served in its own natural juices with wilted spinach and a plum tomato garnish. For dessert, the selections include several cakes and tortes, *tiramisu*, simple baked biscotti, homemade ices and gelatos, as well as fresh fruit and *zabaione*, a sweet sauce of egg yolks, sugar and marsala wine.

VIVO
KR 19/20
Decor 4/4   Hospitality 5/5   Food 9/10   Value 1/1

• **Italian**	**Hours:** Lunch Mon–Fri 11:30 am–2:30 pm, Dinner Mon–Thurs 5 pm–midnight, Fri–Sat until 1 am, Sun 4:30–11 pm
• **Chicago/Near West**	
• **$$$**	
838 West Randolph Street	**Credit Cards:** Amex, CB, Diners, MC, Visa
Chicago	**Reservations:** Mandatory
(312) 733-3379	**Handicapped:** Accessible
Troubleshooters: Jerry Kleiner,	**Parking:** Valet
Dan Krasny, Howard Davis	**Dress:** "Urban Chic"
(owners)	

It's almost a toss-up as to whether the food or the people-watching is the better attraction at Vivo. Both are so very fascinating. Vivo, in the heart of Chicago's old West Side produce industry, is on the cutting edge of fashion and dining.

The restaurant is noticeably post-modern with high ceilings, pin-point spot lighting, dark woods and handsome granite accents. The food is Italian, but with the kind of neo embellishments that push it into the near twilight zone of contemporary dining. While many dishes are firmly rooted in tradition, the style of service and presentation, not to mention the overall ambiance of decor and diners, make Vivo noticeably different.

For starters, the mixed antipasto selection brought from the sideboard near the restaurant's entranceway is without fault. The platter is loaded with grilled and roasted fresh vegetables, including slices of eggplant, zucchini and whatever else is seasonally fresh, plus delicious sautéed peppers and snatches of olives and mushrooms. Other antipasti includes *carpaccio alla arugola*, thinly sliced beef, almost translucent with arugula, capers and lemon. Polenta, or corn meal by its more ordinary designation, is grilled, and plated with imported gorganzola cheese and a mushroom broth. À la carte salads include a classic Caesar, as well as an imaginative fantasy of blue cheese, toasted walnuts and pears on watercress.

Vivo features several pasta selections, ranging from the simple spaghetti with garlic, basil and fresh tomatoes to fettucini with an imaginative lamb ragout. The restaurant also features a daily risotto. Spaghetti with a mix of seafood is substantial enough to serve as either pasta course or entree. Fresh mussels and clams still in their shells bring a platter that includes shrimp and scallops, in a marinara-style sauce with enough bite to be interesting. For something a bit more earthy, rigatoni with spicy Italian sausage would also satisfy as a main course.

Many items are prepared on a wood- and charcoal-burning grill in the restaurant's open kitchen. Grilled red snapper or sautéed salmon might be among seafood choices. Grilled chicken with fresh herbs and garlic comes in white wine sauce. Other grilled meats include medallions of veal with asparagus or lamb chops roasted with white beans. A veal chop might be roasted with prosciutto, picking up its flavors as well as those from a layer of fontina cheese and sautéed mushrooms. Sliced sirloin is roasted, then paired with arugula and shaved parmesan cheese, at rest in the meat's au jus. Side dishes not to be missed include a roasted sweet potato stuffed with parmesan cheese, or the very simple but delicious roasted potato wedges with rosemary.

VONG
KR 20/20
Decor 4/4   Hospitality 5/5   Food 10/10   Value 1/1

- **Asian Fusion**
- **Chicago/Near North**
- **$$$**

6 West Hubbard Street
Chicago
(312) 644-VONG (8664)
Troubleshooter: Michael Waugh
(general manager)

Hours: Lunch Mon–Fri 11:30 am–2 pm, Dinner Mon–Thurs 5:30–10 pm, Fri–Sat 5–11 pm, Sun 5–10 pm
Credit Cards: All majors
Reservations: Required
Handicapped: Accessible
Smoking and nonsmoking sections: Nonsmoking in restaurant
Parking: Valet

To say that Vong is just another Asian-fusion restaurant is to say that Alfred Hitchcock was just another director, Charles Dickens was just another novelist, Albert Einstein was just another scientist. It is Asian-fusion but much more. It is a personal way of cooking, a statement by New York restaurateur Jean-Georges Vongerichten.

Right there, you know why the restaurant is named Vong. But, if you think this is some Big Apple ploy intended to impress us flatlander hicks, think again. The welcomes are profuse; they have the genuine ring of sincerity.

Service is similarly solicitous. The menu offers only a bare bones description of each listing. A waiter amplifies with elaborate detail. There is not a restaurant in the city or suburbs which could not learn something from the sincere welcome given first-time and repeat diners alike.

The cooking certainly draws on Asia for most of its influence, but things are tempered the way a French painter might look at a bowl of apples and come up with an impressionist work of art. For an appetizer one might choose what the menu describes simply as "crab spring roll–tamarind dipping sauce." That is only the beginning for a recipe which is every bit as good as any spring roll you have had in your favorite Vietnamese or Chinese restaurant, and then becomes somehow better by way of presentation, appearance, and, of course, taste and texture. The same could be said of any of the dozen or so first course selections. Warm Duck Roll, as it is called, may be the tastiest way to prepare and serve duck that I have ever tasted.

There is similar excitement at work among entrees. Black sea bass has been roasted, dusted with a complex spicy crust, much like Chinese five spice, and set in a light vegetable broth, or vinaigrette as the menu calls it. Vongerichten knows the importance of a broth as not just a flavor enhancer, but a flavor diffuser. He uses a clear stock seasoned with cardamom and a few other spices as a setting for bright red king salmon. Morels and turnips finish the plating, bringing East and West together one more time.

There are other seafood incarnations, of course, but poultry and meat are hardly ignored. Veal loin harkens back to Oriental seasonings that are more a rub than marinade. Kumquats are at the base of a chutney served with the meat that has been roasted only to a light pink. Rack of lamb gets taro root croquettes for accompaniment. If taro makes you think of tapioca, the similarity is in name only. Even simple roast chicken gets some assistance lifting it above the mundane. It is flavored with the essence of lemon grass, plated with a mound of sweetened rice and set in a banana leaf just so it will look as pretty as a picture and taste as good.

As elaborate as it sounds, this is understated cooking, in perfect balance with the understated decor whose simplicity and muted range of color, or absence of it, shuts the city outside for a relaxing dining experience inside.

WASHINGTON GARDENS
KR 17.5/20
Decor 3.5/4   Hospitality 5/5   Food 8/10   Value 1/1

- **Italian**
- **Highwood**
- **$$**

256 Green Bay Road
Highwood
(847) 432-0309
Troubleshooters: Alex Scornavacco, Bill Bernstein (co-owners)

Hours: Sun 5–9 pm, Mon–Thurs 5–9:30 pm, Fri–Sat 5–10:30 pm
Credit Cards: Visa, MC, Discover, Amex
Reservations: Preferred seating for parties of 5 or more
Handicapped: Accessible
Smoking and nonsmoking sections: Both available
Parking: Complimentary valet

Walk into Washington Gardens and you might see a silver-haired man sweeping up with an electric broom or carrying a large tray of food to a table. He is not a busboy; he is co-owner Alex Scornavacco, a man who knows his business inside out and from the bottom up.

Anyone familiar with Highwood's restaurant history recognizes the name Scornavacco. Washington Gardens has a history that goes back half a century. To be perfectly candid, I have always believed that the best Italian dining lies elsewhere in the Chicago area, even though Highwood's dining reputation was built on its gathering of Italian restaurants.

There's nothing fancy about it. A bar is the first thing you see when you walk inside. The small dining room is behind, in the back, though certainly not an afterthought. Nor is there anything special about the decor, though cloth table coverings, not paper, suggest a standard.

What is there to say about most Italian restaurant menus except that they are usually similar? So, that at Washington Gardens presents the usual collection including such appetizers as shrimp cocktail, fried calamari, baked ravioli or roasted peppers. But, there is also shrimp de jonghe, a throwback to another dining era when butter was king and fat and calories did not count.

Monthly specials speak more about contemporary styles of dining. For instance, mushrooms might be sautéed in olive oil, and served with goat cheese, while scallops are sautéed in wine and butter, coupled with shallots, dates and a blush of cream to suggest more about North African than Italian cookery. Of course, the heel of Italy's boot is just a step away from the shore of Africa, and Mediterranean cultures have had a way of mingling amidst the cross currents over the mellennia.

Not surprisingly, the menu ranges all over the culinary map, to Rome for tortellini alfredo and its rich cream sauce, to calabria for chicken baked in lemon butter sauce, or north to Livorno and the Ligurian coast for large sea scallops bathed in spicy marinara sauce over black pasta.

Washington Gardens is the kind of Italian restaurant where pasta courses can be shared as a prelude to a main course. But, more often than not, they are served American-style as the entree. Baked ravioli has all the dining contentment of comfort food, Italian style. Lasagna can be ordered in its traditional recipe, or in a lighter version with chicken and low fat ricotta cheese.

As might be expected of a small restaurant that caters largely to a neighborhood crowd, service is exemplary, warm and welcoming.

WATUSI
KR 19.5/20
Decor 4/4   Hospitality 5/5   Food 9/10   Value 1/1

- **New World Cuisine**
- **Chicago/Bucktown**
- **$$**

1540 West North Avenue
Chicago
(773) 862-1540
Troubleshooter: Steven Harris

Hours: Sun–Thurs 5:30–10 pm,
Fri–Sat 5:30–11 pm
Credit Cards: All majors
Reservations: Recommended
Handicapped: Accessible
**Smoking and nonsmoking
sections:** Smoking at bar only
Parking: Valet $5

Watusi is housed in a sleek, narrow room with contemporary design, using bold squares of mahogany woods, mohair seating and spiffy light fixtures. The name suggests something African, something exotic. Chef de Cuisine David Weeks calls his cooking "New World Cuisine," blending influences of the Caribbean, Latin America and the West Indies.

The result is worth the effort. Try lobster and conch fritters with a tangy mango and pepper hot sauce. The taste and texture combo works just right. Contrast that with an order of quail with brush strokes of tamarind sauce glazed over the top, while a swirl of sweet potato grits circles the plate. Though the menu says the quail has been smoked, I could not detect that distinctive flavor accent. Among other first course choices on the menu, diners will find grilled octopus, pork dumplings with barbecue sauce, a couple of leafy salads and cod cakes with *chipotle* tartar sauce.

Moving down to the list of entrees, the menu promises the house specialty, roast suckling pig fresh from the spit, with the admonition that . . . "when it's gone — it's gone." For more of a sure thing, check out delicious sea bass plated with a curry-like salsa of sweet corn and red pepper julienne strips all cooked down into a flavorful sauce whose individual components are not lost in the preparation. Even better might be a fricassee of shrimp and scallops. In this one, the sautéed seafood is served with cut-up cooked-down tomatoes, and *achiote*, which offers some coloring, but also an ephemeral taste experience which is sensed almost as an aspiration than an actual defined flavor. The point is that this and other seasonings are worked together for one of the most interesting presentations I have seen recently on any restaurant menu.

Other entrees include more unusual seafood preparations, including red snapper given further snap by the scotch bonnet which shows up with mangos and raisins on a bed of steamed chayote, a squash-like vegetable.

Service has somewhat the sassy and friendly style that seems to fit well with Watusi. There is a good, reasonably priced wine list. Desserts are as imaginative as the rest of the menu.

THE WEBER GRILL
KR 18/20
Decor 4/4   Hospitality 5/5   Food 8/10   Value 1/1

- **American**
- **Wheeling**
- **$$**

920 North Milwaukee Avenue
Wheeling
(847) 215-0996
Troubleshooter: Jeff Bauer
(manager)

Hours: Lunch Mon–Fri 11:30 am–2:30 pm, Sat noon–2:30 pm, Dinner Mon–Thurs 4:30–10 pm, Fri–Sat 4:30–11 pm, Sun 3–9 pm
Credit Cards: All majors
Reservations: Suggested
Handicapped: Accessible
Smoking and nonsmoking sections: Both available
Parking: Free in lot

Almost everybody loves the flavor of charcoal grilled foods in the back yard. But, except for weekends, you might not feel like lugging out the charcoal after a hard day's labor, firing up the grill, and then standing out in the yard to do all the work yourself. That's where The Weber Grill comes in.

The idea is simple. The kitchen has a bank of huge, professional-sized Weber cauldrons all manned by professionals. The menu features most of those meats and fish you would associate with grilling: steaks, ribs, chicken, chops.

There are views into the kitchen from two windows, so you can watch how things are done. Dinners include a soup of the day or salad. Salad dressings are excellent. Among à la carte appetizers a platter of onion curls brings a huge mound of crisp fried onions that are great for finger snacking. Selections from the grill in appetizer or entree portion include grilled scallops with bacon in a ginger and lime marinade, chicken kebabs and beef kebabs. In the case of the beef, here is grilling from the masters of the craft.

Similarly, among dinners, barbecued ribs in full- or half-slab portion will be a rib picker's delight. The ribs are given a good smoking, which makes the meat look oddly red, and then they are finished over the charcoal. You can have a sweet and sour or spicy red sauce. Either way, the meat is tender, and almost falls from the bones. Among seafood choices, a mixed grill could bring scallops, tuna and monk fish. Each variety holds its own flavor and texture. Grilled tuna is a particular treat.

Desserts include cheesecakes, ice creams, custards and other yummies.

WILD FIRE
KR 16/20
Decor 4/4   Hospitality 3/5   Food 8/10   Value 1/1

- **American**
- **Chicago/Near North and Suburbs**
- **$$**

159 East Erie Street
Chicago
(312) 787-9000
Troubleshooters: Russell Bry
(chief proprietor), Luis Garcia
(general manager)
Other Locations
232 Oakbrook Center, Oakbrook;
630-586-9000
235 Parkway Drive, Linconshire;
847-279-7900

Hours: Mon–Thurs 11:30 am–10 pm, Fri 11:30 am–11 pm, Sat noon–11 pm, Sun noon–10 pm
Credit Cards: All majors
Reservations: Accepted
Handicapped: Accessible
Smoking and nonsmoking sections: Smoking permitted only in bar, no pipes or cigars
Parking: Valet

Everything about Wild Fire says "big." The restaurant is big, the seating is big, the portions are big. This is not a ladies' tea room, but rather a masculine sort of place, with lots of open spaces and three huge ovens which make up the heart of Wild Fire's open kitchen.

The specialty is grilling and roasting, or in the case of pizzas and meatloaf, baking. The ovens are the focus, one with a carousel-like device for moving wood up and around, while a rotisserie slowly turns chickens or other meats, exposing them to heat that reaches 600 degrees.

Wild Fire hardly seems like a goat cheese sort of place, but as an appetizer, baked goat cheese is delicious with a peppery tomato sauce and garlic croutons. The restaurant's version of mussels is quite different from other eateries. Here, they are roasted at a heat so intense that the shells literally crumble when you touch them after they have cooled down enough. Inside, the mussels remain moist, succulent, fresh tasting. Other appetizers range from pizza, with a recipe that varies each day, a tomato cheese bread loaf which can be ignored in favor of the regular baked bread which comes free with dinner, to a selection of salads, some entree sized themselves. The Caesar salad is given a peppery dressing, instead of the conventional one, that sets taste buds tingling.

Among entrees, those who eat no meat, fish or fowl will still find roasted vegetables, baked pasta baked with broccoli, tomatoes and a melted cheese topping, or somewhat more conventional angel hair pasta with roasted vegetables. It's rather bland, which comes as no surprise since Wild Fire is really a meat eater's restaurant.

Try pork from the rotisserie, a huge a double chop doused with maple syrup, whiskey and seasonings. Just so you won't feel too hungry, mashed potatoes and apple cabbage slaw rounds out the platter. Several steaks and chops make up the bulk of the hardwood grilled portion of the menu, joined by a daily seafood selection. Salmon was prepared the night we visited, not my favorite fish, but those who enjoy it will be tantalized by this version.

Naturally, rotisserie chicken is served, taking full advantage of the kitchen's talents that are also lent to the kind of prime rib that is covered in rock salt and black pepper as its simple seasonings, slowly roasting within. Among other chicken choices, barbecue-style is served as a combo with ribs, though each can be taken as a full order. The sauce has an underlying peppered taste, but its really more complicated than that alone.

YIANNIS OPA!
KR 18/20
Decor 4/4   Hospitality 4.5/5   Food 8.5/9   Value 1/1

• **Greek**	**Hours:** Mon–Fri 11 am–11 pm, Sat 4–11 pm, Sun noon–10 pm
• **Highwood**	**Credit Cards:** All majors
• **$$**	**Reservations:** Suggested, especially weekends
440 Green Bay Road	**Handicapped:** Accessible
Highwood	**Smoking and nonsmoking**
(847) 266-1700	**sections:** Both available
Troubleshooter: Peter Sakoufakis	**Parking:** Ample free parking

Yiannis Opa! has the familiar look of a Greek taverna with whitewashed walls, Aegean-blue color accents and a handsome multi-colored tile floor. The menu is similarly familiar to anyone who enjoys what Greek-American restaurants have to offer. Among deep sea treasures is grilled octopus. In this case, the seafood has been chopped and plated with lemons and scallions on shredded lettuce. It is a version of grilled octopus that stands as testament to the concept that simple cooking is often the best.

Among other appetizer selections, a combination platter offers a wide variety of delicious spreads, garlic flavored *scordalia*, the earthy flavor of pureed eggplant, the ocean taste of *taramasalata*. The salmon roe spread is decidedly mild, which I think is a positive attribute. The combo platter is finished with a healthy portion of cucumber and yogurt sauce. Incidentally, the sesame bread brought to our table was warm, a hospitable touch if ever there was one.

Like the appetizers, most entrees are straightforward versions of good Greek-American dining. The *gyros* may have been a bit drier than I would prefer, but a dab or two of yogurt takes care of that problem. Shrimp with feta cheese is a rather large portion, five or six big prawns bathed in a tomato and onion sauce with softened chunks of feta that can be swirled about to add more flavor. Greek roasted potatoes or rice and green beans in a light tomato sauce are fine accompaniments.

Among other selections, chicken can be ordered in simple shishke-bab fashion, moist and juicy with a tangy chargrilled flavor. Also, chicken breasts are rolled with spinach in a rather uncomplex manner with tomato sauce that allows the natural flavors to come through. Lamb chops are, of course, part of the menu as are several other cuts of meat. Seafood includes whole red snapper or sea bass.

YOSHI'S CAFE
KR 18.5/20
Decor 4/4   Hospitality 4.5/5   Food 9/10   Value 1/1

- **French-Japanese Fusion**
- **Chicago/Mid-North**
- **$$**

3257 North Halsted
Chicago
(773) 248-6160
Troubleshooters: Yoshi and Nobuko Katsumura (owners)

Hours: Tues–Thurs 5–10:30 pm, Fri–Sat 5–11 pm, Sun 5–9:30 pm
Credit Cards: All majors except Discover
Bar: Full service
Reservations: Suggested, but not necessary
Handicapped: Accessible (narrow entry way with step or wheelchair ramp through kitchen)
Smoking and nonsmoking sections: Both available
Party Facilities: Private party facilities available on inquiry

There is a television set tuned to a sports channel at Yoshi's Cafe. And, that's not the only thing new at one of Chicago's more established restaurants. Gone is the formal setting and in its place is an open bistro with tile floors, peach trim and blond wood, giving a sense of space and light.

Chef/Owner Yoshi Katsamura has completely remodeled his restaurant. And, while his menu has changed along with the times and the tastes, he has not ignored the basics which in the past made his work so unique, so admirable.

Yoshi's Café was one of the first in Chicago to offer fusion cuisine between East and West. He continues in that direction, utilizing Japanese cooking techniques along with French. For example, a recent daily listing that supplements the printed menu offered fried oysters with Japanese Worsctershire sauce. That same listing presented tempura sushi, one of the most unusual and delicious choices available. Starting with the concept of a California maki, Yoshi stuffs the round of sticky rice wrapped in seaweed with tempura-fried shrimp. The flavor combinations are exquisite.

Looking toward Europe, the menu might also present cassoulet for cold winter evenings, or cream of cabbage baked with brie for the soup course. Herb ravioli brings two large circles plumped with creamed California goat cheese. A bit of pesto sauce and tomato concasse add some accent. The menu includes several salads and gourmet pizzas, even portobello mushrooms will show up in a gesture to popular taste.

Other choices are more challenging. A daily style of risotto will vary. Usually served as a side dish, the mushroom studded risotto we tasted was rich and expansive in taste and texture.

A large rotisserie is prominent in the open kitchen, suggesting its products are house specials, perhaps. In any event, chicken is rubbed with herbs and seasonings, coated with a honey glaze. It's basic cooking taken a little bit further.

Among desserts, an apple tart is delicious, a flaky crust rich with fruit. Service is knowledgeable and accommodating, though attention to small details such as side tasting platters could be improved. But, the change wrought should please those who knew the restaurant before, and those who are discovering it for the first time.

ZEALOUS
KR 19.25/20
Decor 4/4   Hospitality 5/5   Food 9.5/10   Value .75/1

- **Fusion Eclectic**
- **Chicago/River North**
- **$$$**

219 West Superior
Chicago
(312) 475-9112
Troubleshooters: Michael Taus
(chef/owner), Amy Cairns
(general manager)

Hours: Dinner Mon–Sat 5:30–10 pm
Credit Cards: Amex, MC, Visa
Reservations: Required
Handicapped: Accessible
Smoking and nonsmoking sections: Zealous is entirely smoke-free
Parking: Valet

That Chef Michael Taus zealously pursues culinary innovation and excellence is a given among those who know his work. Now that he has moved his restaurant, Zealous, from West suburban Elmhurst to Chicago's River North neighborhood, even more demanding diners are likely to learn firsthand of his achievements.

Taus is a disciple of Charlie Trotter among others. To be sure, there is reason to compare his work with Trotter, as well as Rick Tramanto at Tru. All three chefs are concerned with the cutting edge of creative and artistic cookery.

The menu at Zealous is a complicated selection of delights whose realization can be visually startling. Consider a salad of hearts of palm around a center of French beans and caramelized fennel. The beans are stacked like the log framework of a house, while the fennel fences it in. A Middle Eastern yogurt and *tahini* sauce coats the beans, giving them a fresh aromatic taste that contrasts with the mild licorice of the fennel. The hearts of palm bring a sense of tactile substance.

In another opening course, mache and watercress are the greens that garnish tiny Indian samosas dressed with a blend of pomegranate and ever so light cumin. Sea scallops are roasted, coming to the table with a brown glaze set on a duxelle-style chop of green and orange sweet melon.

Entrees are often based upon Chef Taus' fusion conceptions. *Japanese tai*, a fancy way of describing red snapper, sits atop warmed rice noodles in a fermented black bean sauce. The Asian connection is unmistakable, the flavors light and perfect. In another conception, sea bass is grilled and set with a flan that brings together cauliflower and turnips for a vegetal sweet flavor. The fish is grilled, and set with roasted elephant garlic in an anchovy and oil emulsion.

As for meats, roast loin of lamb has been sliced and spread out on a platter with roasted spaghetti squash rolled into pierogis; red cabbage is the flavor accent. The medium rare I asked for came out more to the medium side. Another good main course selection plates roasted Guinea hen with a fruited stuffing of apricots and prunes. The au jus is touched with juniper berries, while a setting of sweet potatoes is layered lasagna-style.

These and other entrees are formidable challenges, generally well executed by Taus and his kitchen support team. Desserts similarly stress the fusion concept found in the previous courses. The restaurant itself is large, quiet by most dining standards today, and elegant in a restrained fashion. A smaller dining room features a floor-to-ceiling wine rack. That list, by the way, is like the menu, on the higher priced side. But, Zealous is certainly a destination restaurant likely to make its mark once more people learn of its existence. In addition to the à la carte menu, there are several degustation options.

ZIA'S TRATTORIA
KR 18/20
Decor 3.5/4   Hospitality 5/5   Food 8.5/10   Value 1/1

- **Italian**
- **Chicago/Far Northwest (Edison Park)**
- **$$**

6699 North Northwest Highway
Chicago
(773) 775-0808
Troubleshooters: Joseph
Calabrese (chef/owner), Tom
Penkala, Jr. (general
manager/owner)

Hours: Lunch Tues–Fri 11:30 am–2 pm, Dinner Mon–Thurs 4:30–9:30 pm, Fri–Sat 5–11 pm, Sun 4–9 pm
Credit Cards: All majors
Reservations: Taken only for parties of 6 or more (waits on weekends can be lengthy)
Handicapped: Tables rather close, could be difficult for wheelchairs
Smoking and nonsmoking sections: Smoking only in small bar, no pipes or cigars
Parking: Free valet (tips accepted)

The restaurant, as its name suggests, is Italian. The dining room is very loud on busy nights. You can peek into the semi-open kitchen and get a glimpse of what's going to be heading your way once you order. The choices include some tried-and-true Italian restaurant favorites such as fried calamari, *carpaccio* and *bruschetta.* Among other antipasti, ravioli filled with shredded duck is not to be missed. A touch of sage is the major seasoning, but the natural roasted duck *au jus* makes this one a real winner.

The menu rambles on with a collection of pastas and entrees, amplified by nightly specials. Grilled octopus is marinated in balsamic vinegar, plated with arugula. Lemon olive oil is the flavor bonus on this one. Roasted tilapia is served with a blanket of tiny rock shrimp, capers and citrus butter sauce. Grilled shitakes, asparagus and a small potato frittata complete the plating. For my taste, there is too much going on here for a fairly delicate fish such as tilapia, and the butter sauce turns a simple dish into something much too rich. In this case, less is definitely more.

But, there is nothing wrong with *rigatoni bolognese*, a tasty meat and tomato ragout. Similarly, *linguine alla pescatore* is a delicious collection of pan-sautéed seafood including shrimp, mussels, clams and calamari in a delicately seasoned tomato sauce over perfectly *al dente* linguini. Among other selections, *rigatoni piedmontese* brings pieces of roasted chicken breast and peas in a white wine and garlic sauce with a little sage as the foundation for its seasoning. This is a dish that can be appreciated for its texture as much as taste.

A collection of grilled meats, including steak, pork tenderloin, veal and chicken recipes round out the printed menu. Rack of lamb has the makings of a true crowning glory. The rack is plated with a little polenta and asparagus, while the lamb has been roasted with shallots, oregano, white wine, and of course, some garlic.

The desserts run a familiar track of Italian *dolci*. The wine list is reasonably priced, and service is excellent. There is even free valet parking. Expect to spend about $55 a couple for three courses, plus add ons.

ZINFANDEL
KR 18.5/20
Decor 4/4   Hospitality 5/5   Food 8.5/10   Value 1/1

- **American**
- **Chicago/Near North**
- **$$**

59 West Grand, Chicago
(312) 527-1818
Troubleshooters: Drew and Susan Goss (co-owners)

Hours: Lunch Tues–Fri 11:30 am–2:30 pm, Brunch Sat 10:30 am–2:30 pm, Dinner Tues–Thurs 5:30–10 pm, Fri–Sat 5:30–11 pm, closed Sun–Mon
Credit Cards: All majors
Reservations: Taken
Handicapped: Accessible
Bar: Full service bar features American drinks and spirits only
Smoking and nonsmoking sections: Both available
Parking: Valet in evening
Party Facilities: Semi-private party facilities for 20–40

There's lots more than wine at Zinfandel. What Rick and Deanne Bayless have done to the perceptions of Mexican food at their well established Frontera Grill and Topolobampo (see listings), is being done for Mom, Chevrolet and apple pie at Zinfandel.

This is probably the most original American contemporary restaurant in the city. Its menu changes monthly. There is no attempt to put any sort of regional, or even traditional spin on what is coming forth from the kitchen. Consider a version of scrapple, which by all accounts owes its origin to Pennsylvania Dutch country. In its original form, scrapple was made from scraps, usually pork, whatever else might be handy, plus apples and brown sugar. The Zinfandel version is meatless, made with hazelnuts, dried cherries and a maple syrup glaze, then paired with a slightly tart mushroom relish. Similar imagination comes with green chili soup. For one thing, green chilis are hardly ever at the centerpiece of soup, but in this case, you would think someone had been making it for years. The broth is studded with chopped potatoes, laced with cilantro for flavor balance. And, while the soup is spicy as the menu suggests, it is comfortably so.

Among other starters could be Seafood Pie, suggestive of New England comfort food. In this case a pastry crust nests a hearty mix of shrimp, clams and hunks of monkfish, bound with some familiar root vegetables and a dash of sage. The top crust is cornmeal, which adds more texture than flavor.

From among entrees, one of the more unusual has been Spaghetti Squash matched with chunks of eggplant and sliced field mushrooms, all of which is worked together into a stew or ragout. Its sauce leaves a mild bite, almost a wine flavor on the tongue. In another creation, shrimp has been enriched with garlic, blanketed beneath a collection of peppers and tomatoes, as well as rice studded with bits of pecan. It is suggestive of an *etoufee*, though not as complex or buttery as that traditional Cajun smothered shell-fish might be.

Among other entrees, venison stew is about as satisfying as can be. Served in a bowl, chunks of venison are cooked up with cranberries, chanterelles and a vegetable bouquet, plus a dash of horseradish for bite.

Desserts are the kind that are difficult to turn down, no matter how restrictive a diet. The wine list is 100% American, reasonably priced, and, as might be expected, heavy on Zins. Service is well-informed, the restaurant comfortably decorated with a mix of contemporary and folk art.

SHERMAN'S DREAM LIST

(When time, calories, dollars or location don't matter,
or just when the whim strikes!)

Arun's, 8-9
Atwood Café, 13-14
Brasserie Jo, 47-48
Caliterra, 64-65
Carlos', 68-69
Catch 35, 74-75
Charlie Trotter's, 77-78
Club Lucky, 84-85
Everest, 118-19
Fahrenheit, 119-20
Gennaro's, 133
Giannotti Steak House, 135-36
Gibson's, 136-38
Gioco, 139-40
Hudson Club, 154-55
La Paillote, 180-81
Le Francais, 185-86
Le Titi de Paris, 188-89

Les Nomades, 191-92
Lou Mitchell's, 193-94
Marché, 201-2
Marco!, 202-3
Mon Ami Gabi, 215-16
Nick's Fish Market, 223-24
Nine, 224-25
One Sixtyblue, 231
Periyali, 247
Pizza D.O.C., 249-50
Seasons, 280-81
Shiro Hana, 285
Spago, 291-92
Trattoria Giacomo, 310-11
Tufano's, 320-21
Va Pensiero, 322-24
Vong, 329-30

$$$ = $40-??? a person